Economic Liberalism and the Developmental State

"Bryan Cheang challenges two competing explanations for the phenomenal success of the Singaporean economy since the 1960s—economic freedom and developmental state. The former points to the top ranking of Singapore in the Economic Freedom Index; the latter to the testimonies of Lee Kwan Yew, the founding father of independent Singapore. Against the economic freedom school, Cheang provides detailed information to show that Singapore's high ranking is a misleading result of ignoring dominant government-linked corporations and sovereign funds that have been powerful instruments of government controls and industrial policies. Against the developmental state school, Cheang points to the comparable economic performance of pre-1997 Hong Kong and its greater development of "creative industries". With survey results on social attitudes towards innovation, Cheang also highlights shortcomings of the Singaporean developmental state model. Cheang has made important contributions to the field of economic development."

—Young Back Choi, *Professor of Economics, St John University, USA*

"*Developmental State and Economic Liberalism* stakes out a bold new position that challenges established views on both sides of the debate surrounding the merits and demerits of state development planning. Cheang shows how macro economic statistics have misled advocates of development planning into overstating successes. Meanwhile, he challenges claims of liberal economists that successful East Asian economies were beacons of free markets. Future debate surrounding the developmental state will have to grapple with the ideas in this book."

—Benjamin Powell, Director, *Free Market Institute, Texas Tech University, USA*

"Cheang's book provides an empirically rich account of the economic development of Hong Kong and Singapore, and it sets out to rethink and challenge conventional wisdom in several important respects. This is a very welcome addition to the literature and will be essential reading to anyone interested in the developmental state, the economic history of Hong Kong and Singapore or economic growth and development more generally."

—Magnus Feldman, *Senior Lecturer in Politics, Bristol University, UK*

"Using holistic data analysis and thick description, this book overwhelmingly challenges whether the on-going developmental state model of Singapore is sustainably viable. Looking beyond the traditional measurements of economic performance, Dr. Bryan Cheang brilliantly focuses instead on factor markets and examines the discrete components of productivity, innovation, and entrepreneurship, all of which are relevant for the knowledge-based economy. This timely book sheds a bright light for countries seeking to forge ahead toward innovation-driven growth. For those who believe that the 21st century is of Asia, how to thrive in the market for ideas will be imperative and this pioneering book is a must-read."

—Ho-Don Yan, *Professor of Economics, Feng Chia University, Taiwa*

"The author revisits the respective contributions of the state and market to economic development in Hong Kong and Singapore when both cities took off in the final forty years of the twentieth century to achieve spectacular success. Singapore's state approach and Hong Kong's market approach both succeeded as judged from hard data like national income. Bryan Cheang's analysis is more subtle in identifying the shortfalls of the state approach, its sacrifice of productivity, innovation and entrepreneurship that crowded out small and medium enterprises to the detriment of sustainable economic vitality. While Hong Kong is beginning to pursue an innovation and technology driven path to reindustrialization after experiencing state-society upheavals, Singapore is exhibiting diminishing returns over time from its state-driven industrial policy. Bryan Cheang's book is a timely reminder that sustaining economic development is more than a binary choice between the state and the market."

—Richard Wong, Provost and Deputy Vice-Chancellor, *Professor of Economics and Philip Wong Kennedy Wong Professor in Political Economy, Hong Kong University, Hong Kong*

"For many years, East Asia has drawn attention from development economists who search for applicable lessons for developing countries. Hong Kong is often taken as an exceptional case of market-led growth and Singapore, also a former British colony, is often compared as the "tale of the two cities". In this regard, Cheang's book adds value to this debate. Challenging the "developmental state model", Cheang highlights how some scholars treat East Asia as homogenous, ignoring significant differences among them. His reviews on the growth experiences and strategies are illuminating, reminding us that the "development state" should be used with care. This book pays close attention to differences in culture, institutions and entrepreneurship and is an essential reader for scholars, policymakers and students in economic development, comparative public policy and Asian studies. It is also a great reference for practitioners interested in global development."

—Tony Yu, Professor of Economics, *Hong Kong Shue Yan University, Hong Kong*

"If the Singapore establishment is smart, it will treat this book as a serious and sophisticated critique of its model of economic development and social management, and engage fully with its arguments and detailed analysis. If it is not so smart, it will dismiss it as an attempt to tear down its legacy of achievements. In fact the achievements are acknowledged, but placed in historical, theoretical and comparative perspectives that go beyond the headline big-picture claims on which the 'Third World to First' mythology is built. Bryan Cheang combines micro-statistical analysis of economic data with cultural evidence gleaned from anything from contemporary censorship practices to pre-independence newspaper advertisements to demonstrate the severe limitations of independent Singapore's version of the developmental state. Notionally the book is using the contrast between the development patterns of independent Singapore and pre-Carrie Lam Hong Kong to elicit lessons about the functioning and limitations of East Asian developmental states. It does do this, but the lessons about Singapore are worthy of study in their own right."

— Michael Barr, *Associate Professor in International Relations, Flinders University, Australia*

"This book is essential reading for anyone interested in the developmental state and the economic performance of East Asia. Bryan Cheang decisively moves the debate on from what has at times become sterile, dichotomised 'neoliberal' vs 'state-led' caricatures, through an approach rooted in deep empirical engagement with the political economy of the region. He overturns conventional wisdom concerning the economic performance of Singapore and Hong Kong and meticulously deconstructs the statistics used to support conventional wisdom. Along the way, Cheang makes a powerful case for integrating cultural elements into economic analysis. This is an outstanding book that deserves to be widely read."

—James Scott, *Senior Lecturer in International Politics, King's College London, UK*

Bryan Cheang

Economic Liberalism and the Developmental State

Hong Kong and Singapore's Post-war Development

palgrave
macmillan

Bryan Cheang
Department of Political Economy
King's College London
London, UK

ISBN 978-3-031-08099-9 ISBN 978-3-031-08100-2 (eBook)
https://doi.org/10.1007/978-3-031-08100-2

This Palgrave Macmillan imprint is published by the registered company Springer Nature Switzerland AG.
The registered company address is: Gewerbestrasse 11, 6330 Cham, Switzerland

Preface

This study is a product of my academic background and practical work experience. For a long time, I have been interested in the importance of market institutions and economic freedom in generating human progress that liberal scholars have written about. Understandably, I wanted to explore the role of the state in the development of East Asia, which experienced rapid growth in the late twentieth century. According to the liberal viewpoint, East Asian success, and modern prosperity more broadly, is a result of freedom.

However, my practical work experience as a civil servant in Singapore suggested that economic freedom was very much overstated by classical liberals, Western organisations, and foreign observers. Almost no one I know in the administrative service and in the local academic scene agree with the foreign characterisation of Singapore as a "free-market success story". East Asian scholars saw Singapore, Korea, Taiwan, and Japan as part of a larger class of "developmental states", where governments strategically intervene in markets through industrial policy to catalyse growth.

I participated first-hand in the Singapore developmental state's industrial policy initiatives, and wondered how it was possible for a nation that practises authoritarianism, interventionist economic policies, establishes numerous government-linked corporations be both seen by liberals as a market exemplar and others as a developmental state archetype? This conundrum formed the initial inspiration behind this book, in which I argue that Singapore's economic freedom is overstated, especially when put beside Hong Kong. I however also object to developmental state theorists who believe in the normative value of this model; I show that pre-1997 liberal Hong Kong is more attractive than Singapore. This puts me in between two camps, liberals and their critics.

What I have observed about capitalism in Singapore and Hong Kong is the dichotomy between the formal institutions and the economic culture they are embedded within. Even though both are generally capitalist in orientation, the way residents and businesses thought about the role of government in society could not be more different. Hong Kong citizens have a healthy distrust of state power—which is understandable given their increasing anxiety over China—while Singaporean citizens, for lack of a better expression, are more compliant. Singaporean firms expect and support government subsidies, while Hong Kong firms do not see much value in them. Such cultural differences necessitated an exploration of political development in both countries, where Singapore's authoritarianism stands in stark contrast to the decades of liberal freedom Hong Kong enjoyed under the British.

Some may object to my negative portrayal of Singapore, as the following pages will show. Given Hong Kong's many domestic challenges in recent years (social upheavals, COVID mismanagement, etc.), much of it linked to concern over its place in China's sphere of influence, why wouldn't the Singapore model be more attractive? In response, I will say that those concerned about the problem of China in Hong Kong affairs should realise that China's leaders have long admired (and sought to emulate) Singapore's governance.[1] Given Singapore's seeming ability to repress political opposition but maintain economic growth, it is easy to see why. This book is a cautionary tale on the ill effects of state repression, suggesting that efforts to control citizens but yet achieve positive outcomes are more difficult than assumed.

Some might question the larger value of this study. Isn't the debate over East Asia over? What is the larger relevance to political economy and public policy? Singapore, Hong Kong, and East Asia experienced vast transformations in the past decades, and the lessons drawn from their experience are instructive for others. China's increasing prominence on the world stage also makes this study valuable, given the way it has emulated Singapore's authoritarianism but emasculated Hong Kong's liberalism.

[1] Ortmann, S., & Thompson, M. R. (2018). Introduction: The "Singapore model" and China's Neo-Authoritarian Dream. *The China Quarterly*, *236*, 930–945.

Such a body of work is not possible without having received constructive feedback. For this I must thank Mark Pennington first and foremost, as well as Samuel DeCanio and James Scott from the Department of Political Economy at King's College London, my academic home for the past few years. I also wish to extend appreciation to the Institute for Humane Studies and the Adam Smith Fellowship programme at the Mercatus Center, for the various opportunities provided to present my work and network with other scholars.

I am also grateful to Chandran Kukathas, Razeen Sally, and Christine Henderson, for their support, both academic and personal. The sound advice offered by Tom Palmer, Nigel Ashford, and Farhan Firdaus in various areas have also kept me on target. Feedback from various reviewers on earlier drafts is also greatly appreciated.

I would like to show my appreciation also to Jennifer Dodgson from Vox Dei, for her expert advice on survey methodology, and her recommendation to use Pollfish to collect survey responses. This saved tremendous amounts of time and effort. Most significantly, I am grateful to Hanniel Lim, Julian Lim, and Eugene Chia for their vital assistance with editing, proofreading, and data collection.

London, UK Bryan Cheang

Contents

Abbreviations and Acronyms

ASEAN	Association of Southeast Asian Nations
BCA	Building and Construction Authority (Singapore)
CAAS	Civil Aviation Authority of Singapore (Singapore)
CCCS	Competition and Consumer Commission of Singapore (Singapore)
CIC	Christian Industrial Committee (Hong Kong)
CPF	Central Provident Fund (Singapore)
EDB	Economic Development Board (Singapore)
ESG	Enterprise Singapore (Singapore)
EMA	Energy Market Authority (Singapore)
EFW	Economic Freedom of the World Report
EIC	East India Company
EIU	Economist Intelligence Unit
GCR	Global Competitiveness Report
GIC	Government Investment Corporation (Singapore)
GLC	Government-Linked Corporation (Singapore)
GLE	Government-Linked Entity (GLCs + GLREITs) (Singapore)
GLREIT	Government-Linked Real Estate Investment Trust (Singapore)
GOVTECH	Government Technology Agency (Singapore)
HDB	Housing Development Board (Singapore)
HKEX	Hong Kong Stock Exchange
HKIA	Hong Kong International Airport
HKMA	Hong Kong Monetary Authority
HKPU	The Hong Kong Polytechnic University
HKSAR	Hong Kong Special Administrative Region

HKU	The University of Hong Kong
HKUST	The Hong Kong University of Science and Technology
HSA	Health Science Authority (Singapore)
IDA	Infocomm Development Authority (Singapore)
IE	International Enterprise (Singapore)
IMDA	Information Media Development Authority (Singapore)
IMF	International Monetary Fund
IRAS	Inland Revenue Authority of Singapore (Singapore)
ITE	Institute for Technical Education (Singapore)
ITF	Innovation and Technology Fund (Hong Kong)
JTC	Jurong Town Corporation (Singapore)
LGBTQ	Lesbian, Gay, Bisexual, Transgender, Queer
LKY	Lee Kuan Yew
LTA	Land Transport Authority (Singapore)
MAS	Monetary Authority of Singapore (Singapore)
MCCY	Ministry of Culture, Community and Youth (Singapore)
MCI	Ministry of Communications and Information (Singapore)
MDA	Media Development Authority (Singapore)
MEWR	Ministry of the Environment and Water Resources (Singapore)
MFA	Ministry of Foreign Affairs (Singapore)
MHA	Ministry of Home Affairs (Singapore)
MINDEF	Ministry of Defence (Singapore)
MinLaw	Ministry of Law (Singapore)
MITI	Ministry of International Trade and Industry (Japan)
MND	Ministry of National Development (Singapore)
MOE	Ministry of Education (Singapore)
MOF	Ministry of Finance (Singapore)
MOH	Ministry of Health (Singapore)
MOM	Ministry of Manpower (Singapore)
MOT	Ministry of Transport (Singapore)
MP	Member of Parliament (Singapore)
MPA	Marine Port Authority (Singapore)
MSF	Ministry of Social and Family Development (Singapore)
MTI	Ministry of Trade and Industry (Singapore)
MTRC	Mass Transit Railway Corporation (Hong Kong)
NAC	National Arts Council (Singapore)
NCB	National Computer Board (Singapore)
NEA	National Environment Agency (Singapore)
NLB	National Library Board (Singapore)
NP	Ngee Ann Polytechnic (Singapore)
NRF	National Research Foundation (Singapore)

NSTB	National Transportation Safety Board (Singapore)
NTU	Nanyang Technological University (Singapore)
NTUC	National Trade Union Congress (Singapore)
NUS	National University of Singapore (Singapore)
NWC	National Wages Council (Singapore)
NYP	Nanyang Polytechnic (Singapore)
OB	Out-of-Bounds
OECD	Organisation for Economic Co-operation and Development
PAP	People's Action Party (Singapore)
PIE Improvements	Improvements in a Nation's Productivity, Innovation and Entrepreneurship
PMO	Prime Minister's Office
POFMA	Protection from Online Falsehoods and Manipulation Act (Singapore)
PPP	Purchasing Power Parity
PSA	Port of Singapore Authority (Singapore)
PSC	Public Service Commission (Singapore)
PUB	Public Utilities Board (Singapore)
RIE	Research Innovation Enterprise (Singapore)
RIEC	Research Innovation Enterprise Council (Singapore)
RP	Republic Polytechnic (Singapore)
RTTP	Reindustrialisation and Technology Training Program (Hong Kong)
SBA	Singapore Broadcasting Association (Singapore)
SDC	Sentosa Development Corporation (Singapore)
SGX	Singapore Exchange Limited
SME	Small-Medium Enterprise
SMRT	Singapore Mass Rapid Transit (Singapore)
SMU	Singapore Management University (Singapore)
SOE	State-Owned Enterprise
SP	Singapore Polytechnic (Singapore)
SPRING	Standards Productivity and Innovation Board (Singapore)
STEM	Science, Technology, Engineering and Mathematics
SWF	Sovereign Wealth Fund
TAS	Telecomms Authority of Singapore (Singapore)
TFP	Total Factor Productivity
TP	Temasek Polytechnic (Singapore)
UNCTAD	United Nations Conference on Trade and Development
UNESCO	United Nations Educational, Scientific and Cultural Organization
URA	Urban Redevelopment Authority (Singapore)

USPTO	United States Patent and Trademark Office
WEF	World Economic Forum
WIPO	World Intellectual Property Organization

List of Figures

List of Tables

CHAPTER 1

Developmental State and Economic Liberalism

The role of the state is highly contested in the study of the political economy of development. After World War II (WWII), development theory envisioned an activist role for the state, whether in terms of injecting capital investment into the economy, pursuing import substitution industrialisation, or facilitating the economy's move towards "higher stages of growth". Key to such approaches is the belief that central planning was desirable or even necessary to realise economic growth. This did not necessarily imply full-scale central planning as in the Soviet Union, but a variety of developmental planning approaches persisted until the 1980s (Perkins et al., 2012, pp. 130–137).

National economic planning soon gave way to more market-oriented approaches to economic management. This was in part due to the collapse of the Soviet model of central planning, which had previously been perceived as a model worth emulating. The end of the Cold War saw a transition of numerous socialist economies towards the market system. These developments were also encouraged by an intellectual undercurrent led by influential figures like Milton Friedman and Friedrich Hayek, who separately also inspired market-oriented policies like deregulation, privatisation, and liberalisation in numerous countries.

In the larger context of this paradigm shift, a specific dispute arose over the contribution of the state to the rapid economic growth of East Asian countries. Hong Kong, Singapore, Taiwan, South Korea, and Japan had all experienced successful industrialisation and a concomitant rise of living

B. Cheang, *Economic Liberalism and the Developmental State*,
https://doi.org/10.1007/978-3-031-08100-2_1

standards in the space of a few decades, a phenomenon that is commonly referred to as the "East Asian Miracle" (see World Bank, 1993).

While the economic successes of these countries are obvious, the relative contributions of the state and market in East Asian development remain disputed. This debate is fuelled by the fact that the East Asian model of development does not fit neatly into the standard state-centric and market-centric theories of development that had previously been advanced, allowing both sides to claim East Asia's success as their own. While the East Asian economies were fundamentally market-based capitalist ones that respected private property, their respective governments had played a highly active role that went beyond the standard prescriptions proffered by development experts in international organisations.

Consequently, the East Asian experience catalysed the emergence of a new school of thought, namely, the "developmental state" theory, which envisions a strong state conducting industrial policy interventions, supported by a pro-growth economic culture in the bureaucracy and society at large. This approach was motivated primarily by a rejection of the standard neoclassical explanation of East Asia's development success. Best encapsulated in the seminal World Bank Report (1993), this neoclassical explanation—also called the Washington Consensus perspective—portrays East Asia's success as a product of "getting the fundamentals" right, that is, maintaining a stable macroeconomic environment and undistorted price signals in product and factor markets, thus providing positive market incentives for savings and investments. The development state theorists criticised such an approach as nothing short of ideological "narcissism", seeing the West's own neoliberal image in the economic history of East Asia (Amsden, 1994).

More than two decades later, the East Asian model seems to be on the rise again. With problems such as financial crises, fractured state-society relations, economic populism seen in the Western world, scholars are looking to East Asia for its unique blend of managed capitalism and semi-authoritarian democracy, with the technocracies of China and Singapore being the centre of attention.[1] What should we make of the developmental state model?

[1] Khanna, P. (2017, January 20). *To beat populism, blend democracy and technocracy, S'pore style*. The Straits Times. https://www.straitstimes.com/opinion/to-beat-populism-blend-democracy-and-technocracy-spore-style / Ortmann, S., & Thompson, M.R. (Eds.). (2020). China's 'Singapore Model' and Authoritarian Learning (1st ed.). Routledge. https://doi.org/10.4324/9780429425554 / Horesh, N., & Lim, K.F. (2017). An East Asian Challenge to Western Neoliberalism: Critical Perspectives on the "China Model" (1st ed.). Routledge. https://doi.org/10.4324/9781315683041

Challenging the Developmental State

This book challenges the developmental state model of policymaking. I argue that its economic achievements have been overstated. While the developmental state is effective in generating rapid growth in national incomes, it has struggled in achieving higher-order aspects of economic development.

I make this argument with reference to a comparative case study of Singapore and Hong Kong, two successful East Asian economies that are uniquely suited to revealing the dynamics of state-market arrangements. The developmental state model, by virtue of its ability to shape social relations and mobilise economic actors, was able to generate higher and more rapid rates of economic growth in Singapore than in Hong Kong in the late twentieth century, evident through national income statistics. However, this has come at the expense of higher-order aspects of economic growth characterised by productivity, innovation, and entrepreneurship. In the absence of generous industrial subsidies and government-linked corporations, the Hong Kong economy exhibited higher performance in these aspects.

Not only are its economic achievements overstated, the use of this model has also brought about some negative consequences. With reference to the case study of the book, the interventionist policies of the developmental state hampered domestic entrepreneurship, indigenous innovation capacity and the creative industries which poses a problem for overall economic competitiveness. Its practice of authoritarianism has also stalled political development. This is not to say that Hong Kong has no problems; rather it faces a different concern in particular: the uncertainty over its constitutional future is at present deterring foreign investment and generating poor business confidence.

Significantly, my argument is not a rehash of the "neoliberal consensus" that prevailed in the 1980s, which developmental state theorists opposed in the first place. My argument concedes that developmental state theorists were spot on in their understanding of the unique institutional configurations in East Asia and the way they diverged from the laissez-faire model. Market liberals, to the extent that they have naively viewed East Asian nations like Singapore and Hong Kong as paragons of economic freedom, have failed to account for the peculiar arrangements of the developmental state model and its extensive interventions. East Asia did not adopt the neoliberal path.

However, while correct in their depiction of East Asia's state-market arrangements, developmental state advocates have also been too sanguine about the effectiveness of their policies to achieve good economic performance. Using Singapore and Hong Kong as reference points, I show that the activist state in Singapore, despite generous support for businesses, fared poorly when it comes to cutting-edge economic growth, characterised by productivity, innovation, and entrepreneurial activities. The specific industrial successes achieved by the developmental state in Singapore come with costs that other nations would be wise to avoid.

So What?

My critique of the developmental state is especially timely, given its rise to prominence in contemporary debates over economic policy.

Though the developmental state model emerged in the context of East Asia's economic development, its advocates have since applied this paradigm to explain the growth of many other countries. Beyond East Asia, some consider if India has followed the developmental state model (Mukherji, 2016), while others place China within the same tradition (Baek, 2005; So, 2016; Zhao, 2017). Theorists have also looked beyond Asia, with some interested in the extent to which Latin America (Smith, 2018) and even Africa (Mkandawire, 2001; Edigheji, 2010; Routley, 2014) have resorted to developmental state policies. Some even insist that there exists a "hidden" developmental state in the United States, given its efforts to promote new technologies (Block, 2008).

A radical perspective insists that most, if not all Western developed nations, have conformed to the theory in some way. Ha-Joon Chang (1999) insisted that the writings of early development economists like Gunnar Myrdal, Simon Kuznets, and Paul Rosenstein-Rodan were essentially developmental state positions, in that they posited how states could play a positive role in economic development. In a similar vein, he also argued that prosperous nations such as the United States have always practised developmental state policies like tariffs and infant industry protection, even as they hypocritically advocate for neoliberal policies elsewhere (Chang, 2002). Chang's reasoning suggests that "development" is inherently a state-driven phenomenon, since there is "no such thing" as a free market (Chang, 2012, ch. 1).

Moreover, the developmental state is today recommended as a strategy (Evans & Heller, 2015; Centano et al., 2017). Specifically, some adapt the model to the challenges of the twenty-first-century economic landscape, hence the concept of the "developmental network state", coined by Sean O'Riain (2004). This new variant will help to develop research and innovation capabilities in society by facilitating collaborations between different companies and research organisations. Closely associated is the "entrepreneurial state" model popularised by Mariana Mazzucato (2015). The basic premise behind these recent arguments is that in the new economic landscape characterised by disruptive technology, the proliferation of transnational actors and global supply chains, government interventions to promote economic development are essential.

Consequently, this book offers useful policy implications. It acts as a cautionary tale against the use of state-centric mechanisms to manufacture wealth, which is a common proposal today in development circles. My book is a challenge to the popularity of the developmental state model championed by scholars like Dani Rodrik, Mariana Mazzucato, Ha-Joon Chang, and Joseph Stiglitz.

In so doing, I recall the important arguments put forth by the economists William Baumol et al. (2007) who distinguished between four different conceptions of capitalism: state-guided, oligarchic, big-firm, and entrepreneurial. The authors argue that in the context of achieving sustained economic development, the "best form" of capitalism would be a mixture of "entrepreneurial" and "big-firm" elements. Such arrangements ensure that growth can proceed at the technological frontier and that private entrepreneurs can innovate, pushing the economy towards a higher level of productive capacity. This contrasts with oligarchic capitalism, which is characterised by patronage and thus resource misallocation and perverse incentives that do not encourage private enterprise. This is also distinct from state-guided capitalism, where the state plays a key role in centrally planning the economy or influencing resource allocation.

According to Baumol, Litan, and Schramm, state capitalism is inferior since the top-down nature of development it employs, despite achieving effective mobilisation of resources, prevents development from proceeding towards the cutting-edge, innovation frontier. With this framework, I argue that Hong Kong and Singapore differ in that the former has a stronger degree of productivity and innovation than the latter. The top-down, state-centric nature of Singapore's political economy has crowded out small-medium enterprises and diminished the culture of entrepreneurial innovation that is a mark of a dynamic economy.

What Is the Developmental State in the First Place?

It is now important to understand what the developmental state is in the first place. Not only is conceptual clarification always useful, it will also become clear in the subsequent section why a different methodological approach is necessary, one that is atypical in mainstream economics. Importantly, the developmental state incorporates not only a set of policies but also a larger set of accompanying institutions, both hard and soft (see Chu, 2016, ch. 1; Thurbon & Weiss, 2016). The complex interplay of industrial policy and the developmental state's institutional hardware and software is at the heart of this model.

The lowest common denominator that unites all developmental states is the extensive use of industrial policy, whereby the government strategically invests in private industries and firms using fiscal incentives, state financing, and subsidies to create nationally competitive industries and upgrade the industrial mix to higher-value-added activities (Johnson, 1982; Wade, 1990; Low, 2001). Policy tools are aplenty and include providing subsidies, tax breaks, favourable infrastructural provisions and loans, private-public partnerships, joint ventures, etc.

But the developmental state is not just a bag of policies but a larger institutional configuration. A key institution within the developmental state is the pilot agency, a government ministry charged with spearheading strategic industrial policies. In the East Asian context, they include Japan's MITI, S. Korea's Economic Planning Board, Taiwan's Council for Economic Planning and Development, and Singapore's Ministry of Trade and Industry and its subordinate statutory boards (Gold, 1986; Amsden, 1989; Haggard, 1990; Wade, 1990; Castells, 1992; Low, 2001). Importantly, these agencies are structured to ensure that they possess the knowledge and incentive to carry out their plans successfully. On a human resource level, this agency, and the entire bureaucracy as well, is staffed by the best talent, who may be specialists in their field or trained at top business schools. This is to ensure that state bureaucrats are amongst the most trained and educated elites in society (Johnson, 1982, pp. 314–320; Woo-Cummings, 1999, p. 14). Not only is knowledge important, but bureaucrats must also be insulated from short-term pressures and special interests that may divert their attention away from "mission-critical" national objectives. This is achieved either by fostering a strong public sector culture that imbues civil servants with national solidarity, or rules that heavily sanction corruption.

The pilot agency is in turn part of a general institutional framework that is characterised by "state capacity". The developmental state is one that has the capacity to achieve its national development plans with minimal interference from external pressures. On the one level, this involves the state suppression of democratic forces and rival interests which could lead to factions capturing the state apparatus and the displacement of national development aims. Scholars have explored how strong East Asian states managed to supersede traditional class interests and impose their will (Gold, 1986; Cumings, 1987; Cheng, 1990; Johnson, 1995). Stephan Haggard (1990) goes as far as to say that each policy transition in East Asia was accompanied by an expansion of authoritarianism.[2]

Crucially, there is also an important layer of "institutional software", or what the institutional economist Douglass North famously labelled as "informal institutions". In developmental states, political elites, and citizens more generally, share a *culture* that is geared towards national development (see Chu, 2016; Thurbon & Weiss, 2016). Such a cultural orientation is important in discouraging state predation. When state agents are imbued with a "developmental mindset" (Thurbon E., 2016), they are often willing to experience personal sacrifices on behalf of national objectives rather than seek rents to enrich themselves. Crucially, these goals are closely aligned to the political legitimacy of state actors: "a state is developmental when it establishes as its legitimacy its ability to promote and sustain development, understanding by development the combination of steady rates of economic growth and structural change in the production system..." (Castells, 1992, p. 56).

This ideational foundation is important because it suggests that not all governments that pursue strategic industrial policy can be classified as developmental states, no matter how effective they are in this regard. While industrial policy has been popular throughout the years, seldom has there been a common developmental aim that unites a nation's elites. This is explained by Michael Loriaux (1999) who reasoned that while the French state did implement industrial policies in the same fashion as East

[2] The relationship between democracy and the developmental state is complex, considering that Taiwan, S. Korea, and Japan have since matured into liberal democracies (see Robinson & White, 1998, for more on this relationship).

Asian governments, the country lacked a "solidaristic vision" and "moral ambition" that are central to developmental states.[3]

With this clarification, the developmental state clearly encompasses a complex institutional configuration that is not easily accounted for in mainstream economics. How can the standard toolkit of economists be sufficient to analyse concepts such as "moral ambition", "solidaristic vision", and "developmental mindset"? This book fills this gap by approaching the developmental state from an interdisciplinary political economy angle, one that avoids the preoccupation with aggregate economic statistics.

Transcending Economic Statistics

Much has been written about the developmental state over the years, with the latest incarnation being the famous "entrepreneurial state" depiction by Mariana Mazzucato, whose TED Talk on the topic attracted more than a million views since.[4]

Not only does this book provide a contrarian perspective to developmental state advocates like her, it approaches this topic from a unique approach that blends various disciplines and methodologies. Significantly, I avoid the preoccupation with economic statistics and quantitative modelling that is all too common in economic development studies. While there is nothing wrong with the use of such methods per se, I am of the persuasion that the facts of the social sciences include what people think and believe, and such phenomena must entail an eclectic approach to understanding the social world.

Development economists have previously made serious errors in their preoccupation with quantitative statistics. The classic example is the Soviet Union, whose performance was severely overstated. The preoccupation with aggregate figures led to a positive interpretation of the USSR's growth record, but simultaneously obscured the micro-level composition of its economic structure (Boettke, 1993). Deeper analyses reveal that the USSR's seemingly impressive record belies massive resource misallocation,

[3]These terms are generally similar to the "developmental mindset" as used by Thurbon (2016) and refer to the institutional software that underpin developmental states.

[4]*Mariana Mazzucato: Government—investor, risk-taker, innovator*. (2013, October 28). YouTube. https://www.youtube.com/watch?v=3r1IPsldbBg

a failure to meet consumer demands, and economic imbalances (Hewett, 1988, pp. 31–93; Roberts, 1990).

The point made here is not merely about the limits of national income accounting, or the lack of accurate data. The argument runs deeper. For greater social scientific understanding, one must transcend the positivist paradigm and embrace an interpretivist approach too, since "aggregate macroeconomic data is not the only data we can analyse" (Boettke et al., 2005, p. 295). Qualitative data is crucial for illuminating contextual, micro-level factors in operation, and thus provides richer understanding of state-market relations and the resulting economic effects.

This methodological conviction is why I manage to show in the first part of the book that mainstream economic statistics have misrepresented the nature of Singapore and Hong Kong as "beacons of economic freedom". By diving deep into the local context of my two cases and examining the unique ways in which states and markets actually operate on the ground, the reality is far more complex than neoliberal, neoclassical economists have portrayed.

It is also why I arrive at a different evaluation of the developmental state's record in the second part of the book. The conventional wisdom inferred from very visible macro statistics of Singapore's economic performance and concluded that the developmental state policies adopted were successful. I debunk this perspective by disaggregating these macro-level statistics and by diving into non-economistic factors such as culture, the mindset, and behaviour of entrepreneurs and the health of the arts and culture in both countries. It is with an expansive notion of what counts as "data" do I arrive at my conclusions.

One commonly neglected type of data in mainstream economics is culture, which I actively investigate in this book. While pro-growth institutions are necessary for economic development, they need to be embedded within a supportive culture (Pejovich, 2003; Boettke et al., 2008). Additionally, there are certain values, norms, and informal institutions that block growth and trap societies in poverty or economic underperformance (Harrison, 2002). Accordingly, this book argues that the developmental state in Singapore had shaped culture in ways that diverge from that in Hong Kong. The authoritarian regime in Singapore has managed to exercise cultural hegemony in society in a way that is not possible in Hong Kong. This reflects the developmental state's overarching control over society that it uses to mobilise resources for its national economic plans. On another level, culture is also explored as an ingredient in economic competitiveness, which traditionally looks at measurable, technical factors rather than culture. It is argued that the prevailing economic and political culture in Hong Kong positions it to enjoy more innovative economic development than in Singapore.

Knowing More About Less

Some social scientists of a positivist persuasion may balk at the use of case study methods. After all, what can two cases prove? Would not regression analyses involving a large number of cases reveal more powerful truths? To this, I respond: at times, it is better to know more about less, rather than less about more. Aggregate statistics have their place but can omit unique contextual factors on the ground that only an up-close analysis will reveal. The case study expert John Gerring (2009) defended the use of case studies in that they offer "holistic analysis and thick description", a feature that is particularly amenable to this book's purpose of transcending aggregate statistics.

Why Singapore and Hong Kong specifically? The developmental state literature has tended to treat East Asia as homogenous, obscuring the significant differences within it (see Chiu et al., 1997; Hundt & Uttam, 2017, ch. 1–2). A stark example is Joseph Stiglitz's (1996) critique of the World Bank position, which wrote that "most of the eight economies that are part of the 'East Asian miracle'—Hong Kong, Indonesia, Japan, Korea, Malaysia, Singapore, Taiwan, and Thailand—government undertook major responsibility for the promotion of economic growth". The rest of his article referred to East Asian economies as a largely undifferentiated entity, implying more commonality than the reality suggests.

Moreover, past studies have largely chosen to focus on the Northeast Asian countries of Japan, S. Korea, and Taiwan (see Walter & Zhang, 2012; Chu Y.-W., 2016).[5] Being more open to trade and capital, both Singapore and Hong Kong constitute interesting counterpoints to the

[5] Tellingly, it was the Japanese development experience that first gave rise to the developmental state concept in the work by Chalmers Johnson (1982). He had argued that Japan's economic miracle was a product of the actions of Japanese MITI bureaucrats who picked industrial winners and channelled resources into favoured sectors. Johnson (1985) then further extended this reasoning to argue that S. Korea and Taiwan adopted the Japanese model. Other classic works in this tradition include Robert Wade's (1990) *Governing the Market* and Alice Amsden's (1989) *Asia's Next Giant: South Korea and Late Industrialization*, both of which focused on the three Northeast Asian countries.

experiences of their northeastern counterparts. Yet, Singapore differed from Hong Kong and resembled S. Korea, Taiwan, and Japan in its active use of industrial policy. Significantly, Singapore also differed from all the other East Asian countries in its heavy reliance on multinational companies, imports of foreign labour and talent, and tight control over land and the domestic labour market (Lim, 1983).

Significantly, both Singapore and Hong Kong, being colonial territories, enjoy very similar histories, geographical conditions, and demographic composition, setting the stage for a suitable comparison. The critical divergence in this case is the nature and scope of government intervention in their respective economies, which led to very different economic outcomes. I argue that the adoption of the developmental state model in Singapore, despite its higher GDP growth rates, has negatively affected economic performance in a way absent in Hong Kong, which operated a comparatively freer system.

Empirical Richness and the Use of Facts

The use of a case study should not imply that it is unreliable. In fact, it presents an opportunity to provide intensive understanding of the topic. For one, the present author has had first-hand experience of East Asia's development policies, being a civil servant in the developmental state's industrial policy apparatus. Of course, personal experience is "inadmissible" in the "court of social science", which is why this book is extremely dense in its incorporation of data.

The data gathered in this book is based on analyses of more than 1000 official government documents, records and historical archives, an international survey with cross-national responses, two focus groups, and statistical analyses, all of which cross-referred one with another. I also interviewed more than a hundred subjects, ranging from top civil servants to undergraduates to business leaders. Additionally, I even construct a new dataset on government consumption in Singapore based on a review of hundreds of government financial reports from the 1990s, an exercise that is warranted given the systemic under-reporting of state activities in official budgets (Asher et al., 2016).

This strategy adopted is akin to that by Chinese political scientist Huang Yasheng (2008) who criticised Western economists for simply inferring from visible statistics of China's high growth that "there must have been some good policies driving them". Opting for a "direct observation" approach, he amassed extensive empirical documentation on China's "microeconomic processes—referring to policies, institutions and the nature, behaviour and conditions of economic agents" (Huang, 2008, p. 24). With this, he arrived at a revisionist view: China's rapid GDP growth did not translate into welfare gains, and that the "technocratic industrial policy blueprint" introduced in the 1990s undermined the previous gains brought about by "directionally liberal" policies (Huang, 2008, p. xv). He also examined how productivity, indigenous innovation, and entrepreneurship has lagged in China (Huang, 2008, ch. 4), which suggests that its previous performance may not be sustainable in the future.

My argument is similar. The extensive amount of empirical facts gathered lend weight to my reassessment of economic performance in both nations: while Singapore's GDP performance has clearly eclipsed that of Hong Kong, a deeper examination reveals that its actual performance is far from stellar. Just as in China, productivity performance, indigenous innovation, and entrepreneurship in Singapore have fallen below the developmental state's expectations and are poorer than in Hong Kong despite enjoying greater state support.

Thus, the unique feature of this book is that it employs a wide range of data to understand the impact of state-market relations on economic performance—including hitherto undiscovered sources and unconventional data such as interviews and surveys typically not found in conventional development studies—and does so in an intensive, focused manner. The weight of the evidence gathered in turn provokes us to revise and reconsider the popular acceptance of the developmental state model in contemporary policymaking, much of which originated from a particular understanding of East Asia's experience.

Structure of the Book

Part 1: Getting the Facts Right

The first part of the book takes aim at the popular characterisation that Singapore and Hong Kong are paragons of economic freedom. This view is held not only by neoliberal and conservative think tanks but also by some market-oriented professional economists. For example, Johns Hopkins University's Steve Hanke has commended the Singapore model for its economic freedom and recommended it to countries from Bulgaria to Zimbabwe.[6] Guilty of what Huang pointed out in his study, Western economists typically infer from visible economic freedom statistics that these East Asian nations followed a market-led path to economic success.

Through a deep examination of the facts on the ground, I show that this view is inaccurate. In fact, I show that the divergence in state-market arrangements between Hong Kong and Singapore is greater than is commonly believed. Developmental state theorists are indeed right that the political-economic reality on the ground in East Asia are unlike what neoliberal perspectives typically portray.

The Neoliberal Portrayal

Many popular portrayals make Hong Kong and Singapore seem like largely similar cases of "free-market success stories". The development economist Deepak Lal (1997) had depicted East Asia's experience has one of market liberalism erasing mass poverty. The Nobel Laureate Milton Friedman also praised Singapore as "having done development right", due to its economic freedom (Friedman, 1980). Organisations such as the Heritage Foundation, Fraser, and Cato Institute have written and continue to write articles praising the low-tax, pro-business orientation of the Singapore economy and promote it as an exemplar for Western politicians to emulate. The portrayal of Hong Kong as a free-market economy is even more extensive both in academic circles and popular culture (Hampton, 2015).

This perception is largely reinforced by the high rankings of both city-states on the Index of Economic Freedom and the Freedom of the World Report. Being consistently ranked 1st and 2nd, respectively, it seems straightforward to accept that both Hong Kong and Singapore share little differences in terms of their state-market relations, and that both are indeed paragons of economic freedom.

Most studies on Hong Kong have focused on its political history under British rule rather than specific aspects of economic development. Such research focuses on the challenges of public administration under various British governors and the scope of Hong Kong's autonomy which comes

[6]Hanke, S. H. (2019, July 6). *The Singapore Strategy for Zimbabwe | Steve H. Hanke*. African Liberty. https://www.africanliberty.org/2019/04/20/the-singapore-strategy-for-zimbabwe/ / Hanke, S. (2013, July 15). *Steve Hanke: Bulgaria Should Learn from Singapore—Novinite.com—Sofia News Agency*. Novinvite. https://www.novinite.com/articles/152026/Steve+Hanke%3A+Bulgaria+Should+Learn+from+Singapore

into question since the handover in 1997. Despite the research not having a central focus on Hong Kong's economic development, most scholars generally acknowledge the economic philosophy of "positive non-intervention" used by the colonial government and the positive effects this has had on growth (Endacott, 1973). This is similar to the abovementioned portrayal of Singapore as a "free-market success story", so much so that the laissez-faire nature of the Hong Kong state is even less disputed.

To a lesser extent, there are also scholars who view both Hong Kong and Singapore as essentially similar in their use of government interventions. While the abovementioned group sees both as paragons of economic freedom, this smaller minority lump both together as interventionist developmental states. For example, Hundt and Uttam (2017, pp. 119, 146), while accepting that both were entrepôt economies, concluded that both governments pursued a "top-down capitalist development" strategy and "played a dominant role". More recently, Woo Jun Jie (2018) argued that both city-states are amongst the more successful East Asian states that have undergone positive economic transformations over the last two decades, driven by developmental state policies. In addition, it insists that both were able to overcome global economic challenges and transform themselves into "smart developmental states" (Woo, 2018).

The Institutional Divergence

In response, I insist that the divergence in political-economic arrangements is greater than commonly believed. My account begins with Chap. 2, which criticises the use of economic freedom statistics used to justify the narrative of both places as "free-market success stories". This chapter is meant to "get the facts" right concerning the extent and scope of government intervention in both countries and will show that the true size of the public sector in Singapore is significantly under-reported. Transcending the use of economic statistics, I undertake an institutional analysis and show that in both city-states, while product markets are generally liberalised, factor markets like land, labour, and capital are state-dominated.

The book will then delve deeper into one aspect of the market economy, namely, the presence of competition. Chapter 3 shows that market competition is hampered in both city-states, albeit for different reasons. In Singapore, the generous subsidies and industrial activities of the developmental state has crowded out SMEs, which has also caused them to develop a dependency mindset. A product of state policy, local, private entrepreneurship in

Singapore is highly constrained relative to Hong Kong. The Singaporean developmental state has maintained a heavy presence of government-linked corporations and multinational corporations, which has pushed local, small-medium enterprises out of the economic space. In 2019, Singaporean SMEs comprise a mere 44% of the industry value-added, much lower than the OECD average of 60% (OECD, 2017).

My argument is further developed in Chap. 4, which compares political culture, a variable that is commonly neglected in economistic studies. I establish a vast divergence in political culture across both countries. The interests of the incumbent People's Action Party (PAP), which is the longest-running ruling party in modern times, translate into the entrenchment of the developmental state system, spearheaded by government-linked corporations and sovereign wealth funds, and other public institutions that dominate the economy. This contrasts with the Hong Kong case, where the colonial government faced no pressures to change its course in the twentieth century. What we witness is that the divergence in state capacity has led to a sharp contrast in the state of political culture: there exists a deep penetration of the hegemonic PAP state into various aspects of society, and the product is a depoliticised citizenry, pliant political culture, and a disciplined mindset, which is in sharp contrast to Hong Kong's contested state-society relations.

The relative under-development of Singapore's political society stands in sharp contrast to the vibrant civic culture in Hong Kong, a contrast that forces us to reconsider the economistic way we often define developmental success. Even though the developmental state in Singapore has achieved higher national incomes than in Hong Kong, the lack of liberal democratic progress is the price that has been paid. After all, to be developed is not just having wealth but to be free (Sen, 1999).

Part 2: Evaluating Economic Performance

The second part of the book argues that the divergence in state-market arrangements as established in the first part has had a big impact on relative economic performance in both countries. While developmental state advocates were essentially right in identifying the existence of extensive government policies in East Asia, they have been too sanguine about its effectiveness. I question the popular notion that Singapore has economically outpaced Hong Kong due to its deliberate decision to adopt a developmental state model.

This section therefore takes aim at a range of views which have attributed the economic success of Singapore to the developmental state's strategic interventions. Some have described Singapore's economic success as "government made" (Low, 1998), the product of "intrusive economic interventionism" (Huff, 1995), and a result of intelligent engineering (Ghesquiere, 2007). The apparent success of Singapore, coupled with its heavy use of developmental state policies, may seem to some that its model is worthy of emulation. A leading advocate of the developmental state model today, Ha-Joon Chang et al. (2013, p. 33), has said that out of all the cases of industrial policy use, Singapore's case was "in many ways the most successful", since becoming "the most industrialised country in the world" in 2010.

Here, I begin in Chap. 5 with the colonial history of both city-states and show that the modern economic success of Hong Kong and Singapore owes much to the positive legacies of British colonialism. Through a process of (positive) unintended consequences, British colonial rule set in motion an economic system of entrepreneurial capitalism in both colonies, which developed rapidly through free trade and the influx of foreign immigrants.

This chapter is especially significant because it acts as a corrective to the popular position of developmental state theorists that Singapore's modern success stems from the establishment of the developmental state. Contrary to most accounts, I show that the colonial era in Singapore had seen the formation of a vibrant entrepreneurial class, comprising mainly of Chinese businesses. Rather than acting as an "entrepreneurial agent", the developmental state had in fact crowded out these local indigenous businesses, a trend that persists to the present day and which explains why, historically, Singapore has had a weak indigenous private sector. The "miraculous" growth record of Singapore's developmental state must therefore be tempered, since this view neglects the high base from which Singapore had started, and the economic progress that had already been achieved before independence.

My argument then shifts to an examination of recent economic performance in Chap. 6, which compares the achievements of both growth models. While Singapore has achieved higher growth rates and national incomes than Hong Kong in the past few decades, it has fared relatively poorly in terms of higher-quality aspects of development, namely, entrepreneurial culture, productivity growth, and innovation. Singapore's growth is not high-quality economic development. I point out that aggregate statistics have painted a misleading picture, once its *composition* is taken account. Much innovation activity in Singapore, while quantitatively outstripping that in Hong Kong, is largely driven by foreign multinationals, which is a poor representation of the city's indigenous innovation capacity. Due to the crowding out effect, local SMEs have had a historically poor record, despite having received generous state support to improve their competitiveness, innovation, and productivity. This foreign-local imbalance in turn means that a large share of national income in Singapore is not retained by local citizens but rather sent abroad.

Chapter 7 deepens the analysis of the preceding chapter by zeroing in on the arts and cultural sectors as a microcosm of a nation's "creative class". The political authoritarianism in Singapore, coupled with the "permission-based" economic and political culture resulting from developmental state policies, has meant that Singapore fares poorly in terms of innovation culture and creative outputs. Arguably, the constrained political arena, with the pliant and disciplined society, has translated into the under-development of certain sectors of the economy, namely, the arts and media. Entrepreneurship exists in Singapore, but it is not as "free-wheeling" as it is in democratic Hong Kong. The creative industries in Hong Kong have performed much better than those in Singapore, and have done so not because of state support, but despite its absence. The disparity in performance in the creative industries reflects the inability of the developmental state to engineer high-quality economic performance characterised by innovation and entrepreneurial creativity. Interesting, it also supports Amartya Sen's famous observation that freedom is both a means for successful development and an end in itself.

Collectively, Chaps. 6 and 7 draws from and builds on an established academic literature on the role of the state in Singapore's economic development.[7] It shows that through a deconstruction of available statistics, cross-referred with qualitative data gathered and secondary sources, Singapore's developmental achievements are not as impressive as its supporters have claimed, especially considering the way Hong Kong attained its development without the same degree of state investment.

[7] This literature is extensive. Leading (but by no means the only) works include those by Linda Low (1998) and Linda Lim (2016, 2018).

The Paradox of Success

Developmental state advocates may take issue with my negative characterisation of the Singapore developmental state's economic performance. How does my critique square with the very obvious successes of the Singapore economy, a contrast which becomes starker when considering the slowdown of Hong Kong since the turn of the twenty-first century?

Everything turns on the word "success", and what we mean by it. How do we evaluate "economic success"?

My position readily concedes that industrial policy has had its "successes", but it should be pointed out that these refer to the successful establishment of specific industries, be it shipping, airfreight, and aviation, as well as the higher level of R&D activity, all of which are real and undeniable. It is indeed true that there is a dearth of technology-oriented industries in Hong Kong. Yet, to conflate industrial successes with economic development more generally is to be guilty of the conflation between "technical" and "economic" problems pointed out by the British economist Lionel Robbins (1932).

Economics, and economic development more generally, requires the successful allocation of resources across competing ends (the economic problem) and is not about the maximisation of a single end (technical problem) (Skarbek & Leeson, 2009; Coyne, 2013; Martin & Petersen, 2019). Martin and Petersen (2019, p. 206) explain that "a technological problem involves achieving some particular goal—such as increasing the quantity of medicine provided—with the most effective means. The economic problem, by contrast, involves determining how to balance a multiplicity of ends in a world of scarcity." Industrial policy, by virtue if it enjoying state support, can easily achieve particular goals, be it the construction of new infrastructure or support of the aviation industry. Yet, development more generally requires that scarce means be properly allocated across competing demands, balanced in a way that enhances individual welfare. This is why the Soviet economy may be said to have been "successful" in sending a man into space (the achievement of a single end) and even generating high GDP, while simultaneously failing in economic development more generally. Of course, this is not to say that Singapore is equivalent to the Soviet basket case (though Paul Krugman had famously insinuated as such[8]), but it is to acknowledge that there are limitations in the developmental state growth model, especially in the achievement of higher-order indicators such as productivity, innovation, and entrepreneurship.

Moreover, the industrial successes achieved by the Singapore developmental state come with strings attached. Every "success" comes with costs, such as the historically weak domestic entrepreneurship scene in Singapore and weak creative sectors. More seriously, the extensive use of industrial policy in Singapore were implemented through an authoritarian, almost intrusive state. The industrial successes it enjoys are made possible by disciplining of civil society, the private sector, and individuals more generally, which in turn does not represent a conducive environment for the kind of free-wheeling Schumpeterian innovation being desired today. This is the paradox of developmental state "success" that its supporters should be cautious of emulating elsewhere.

References

Amsden, A. (1989). Asia's next giant—How Korea competes in the World-economy. *Technology Review, 92*(4), 46–53.

Amsden, A. (1994). Why isn't the whole world experimenting with the East Asian model to develop?: Review of the East Asian miracle. *World Development, 22*(4), 627–633.

Asher, M., Bali, A. S., & Chang, Y. K. (2016). Public financial management in Singapore: Key characteristics and prospects. In L. Lim (Ed.), *Singapore's economic development: Retrospection and reflections* (pp. 113–133). World Scientific.

Baek, S.-w. (2005). Does China follow 'the East Asian Development Model'? *Journal of Contemporary Asia, 35*(4), 485–498.

Baumol, W., Litan, R., & Schramm, C. (2007). *Good capitalism, bad capitalism, and the economics of growth and prosperity.* Yale University Press.

Block, F. (2008). Swimming against the current: The rise of a hidden developmental state in the United States. *Politics & Society, 36*(2), 169–206.

Boettke, P. J. (1993). *Why Perestroika failed.* Routledge.

Boettke, P. J., Coyne, C. J., & Leeson, P. T. (2008). Institutional stickiness and the new development economics. *American Journal of Economics and Sociology, 67*(2), 331–358.

[8] Krugman, P. (1994). The Myth of Asia's Miracle. *Foreign Affairs, 73*(6), 62–78. https://doi.org/10.2307/20046929

Boettke, P. J., Coyne, C. J., & T., P., & Sautet, F. (2005). The new comparative political economy. *The Review of Austrian Economics, 18*(3–4), 295.
Castells, M. (1992). Four Asian tigers with a dragon head. In I. R. P. Applebaum & J. Henderson (Eds.), *States and development in the Asian Pacific Rim*. Sage.
Centano, M., Kohli, A., & Yashar, D. (2017). *States in the developing world*. Cambridge University Press.
Chang, H.-J. (1999). The economic theory of the developmental state. In *The developmental state* (pp. 182–199). Cornell University Press.
Chang, H.-J. (2002). *Kicking away the ladder: Development strategy in historical perspective*. Anthem Press.
Chang, H.-J. (2012). *23 things they don't tell you about capitalism*. Bloomsbury Publishing.
Chang, H.-J., Andreoni, A., & Kuan, M. L. (2013). *International industrial policy experiences and the lessons for the UK*. Government Office for Science.
Cheng, T.-j. (1990). Political regimes and development strategies: South Korea and Taiwan. In G. Gereffi & D. Wyman (Eds.), *Manufacturing miracles: Patterns of development in Latin America and East Asia*. Princeton.
Chiu, S., Ho, K. C., & Lui, T.-l. (1997). *City states in the global economy: Industrial restructuring in Hong Kong and Singapore*. Westview Press.
Chu, Y.-W. (2016). *The Asian developmental state*. Palgrave Macmillan.
Coyne, C. J. (2013). *Doing bad by doing good: Why humanitarian action fails*. Stanford Economics and Finance.
Cumings, B. (1987). The origins and development of the northeast Asian political economy. In F. Deyo (Ed.), *The political economy of the new Asian industrialism* (pp. 44–83). Cornell University Press.
Edigheji, O. (2010). *Constructing a democratic developmental state in South Africa*. HSRC Press.
Endacott, G. (1973). *A history of Hong Kong*. Oxford University Press.
Evans, P., & Heller, P. (2015). Human development, state transformation, and the politics of the developmental state. In S. Leibfried, E. Huber, M. Lange, J. Levy, & J. Stephens (Eds.), *The Oxford handbook of transformations of the state*. Oxford University Press.
Friedman, M. (1980). Free To Choose: The Original 1980 TV Series. Free to Choose Network. Available at: https://www.freetochoosenetwork.org/programs/free_to_choose/index_80.php.
Gerring, J. (2009). The case study—What it is an what it does. In C. Boix & S. Stokes (Eds.), *The Oxford handbook of comparative politics*. Oxford University Press.
Ghesquiere, H. (2007). *Singapore's success: Engineering economic growth*. Thomson Learning.
Gold, T. (1986). *State and society in the Taiwan miracle*. M. E. Sharpe.

Haggard, S. (1990). *Pathways from the periphery: The politics of growth in the newly industrializing countries.* Cornell University Press.

Hampton, M. (2015). *Hong Kong and British culture: Postwar contexts.* Manchester University Press.

Harrison, L. (2002). *Culture matters: How values shape human progress.* Basic Books.

Hewett, E. (1988). *Reforming the soviet economy.* Brookings Institution.

Huang, Y. (2008). *Capitalism with Chinese characteristics—Entrepreneurship and the state.* Cambridge University Press.

Huff, W. (1995). The developmental state, government, and Singapore's economic development since 1960. *World Development, 23*(8), 1421–1438.

Hundt, D., & Uttam, J. (2017). *Varieties of capitalism in Asia: Beyond the developmental state.* Palgrave Macmillan.

Johnson, C. (1982). *MITI and the Japanese miracle: The growth of industrial policy: 1925–1975.* Stanford University Press.

Johnson, C. (1995). *Japan, who governs?: The rise of the developmental state.* WW Norton & Company.

Lal, D. (1997). *The poverty of 'development economics'.* Institute for Economic Affairs.

Lim, L. (1983). Singapore's success: The myth of the market. *Asian Survey, 18*, 73–94.

Lim, L. (2016). *Singapore's economic development: Retrospection and reflections.* World Scientific.

Lim, L. (2018). *Business, government and labor.* World Scientific.

Loriaux, M. (1999). *The French developmental state as myth and moral ambition.* Cornell University Press.

Low, L. (1998). *The political economy of a city-state: Government-made Singapore.* Oxford University Press.

Low, L. (2001). The Singapore developmental state in the new economy and polity. *The Pacific Review, 14*(3), 411–441.

Martin, A., & Petersen, M. (2019). Poverty alleviation as an economic problem. *Cambridge Journal of Economics, 43*(1), 205–221.

Mazzucato, M. (2015). *The entrepreneurial state: Debunking public vs. private sector myths.* Anthem Press.

Mkandawire, T. (2001). Thinking about developmental states in Africa. *Cambridge Journal of Economics, 25*(3), 289–313.

Mukherji, R. (2016). Is India a developmental state? In *The Asian developmental state* (pp. 217–236). Palgrave Macmillan.

O'Riain, S. (2004). *The politics of high tech growth: Developmental network states in the global economy.* Cambridge University Press.

OECD. (2017). *Entrepreneurship at a glance. OECD.*

Pejovich, S. S. (2003). Understanding the transaction costs of transition: It's the culture, stupid. *The Review of Austrian economics, 16*(4), 347–361.

Perkins, D., Radelet, S., & Block, S. (2012). *Economics of development.* W. W. Norton & Company.

Robbins, L. (1932). *An essay on the nature and significance of economic science.* Macmillan.

Roberts, P. C. (1990). *Meltdown: Inside the soviet economy.* Cato Institute.

Robinson, M., & White, G. (1998). *The democratic developmental state: Political and institutional design.* Oxford University Press.

Routley, L. (2014). Developmental states in Africa: A review of on-going debates and buzzwords. *Development Policy Review, 32*(2), 159–177.

Sen, A. (1999). *Development as freedom.* Alfred A. Knopf.

Skarbek, D., & Leeson, P. (2009). What can aid do? *Cato Journal, 29*, 391–397.

Smith, P. H. (2018). The rise and fall of the developmental state in Latin America. In *The changing role of the state in Latin America* (pp. 51–73). Routledge.

So, A. Y. (2016). The post-socialist path of the developmental state in China. In *The Asian developmental state* (pp. 175–196). Palgrave Macmillan.

Stiglitz, J. (1996). Some lessons from the East Asian miracle. *The world Bank research observer, 11*(2), 151–177.

Thurbon, E. (2016). *Developmental mindset: Revival of financial activism in South Korea.* Cornell University Press.

Thurbon, E., & Weiss, L. (2016). The developmental state in the twentieth century. In E. S. Reinert, J. Ghosh, & R. Kattel (Eds.), *Handbook of alternative theories of economic development* (pp. 637–650). Edward Elgar Publishing.

Wade, R. (1990). *Governing the market: Economic Theory and the role of government in east Asian industrialization.* Princeton University Press.

Walter, A., & Zhang, X. (2012). *East Asian capitalism: Diversity, continuity and change.* Oxford University Press.

Woo, J. J. (2018). *The evolution of the Asian developmental state: Hong Kong and Singapore.* Routledge.

Woo-Cummings, M. (1999). *The developmental state.* Cornell University Press.

World Bank. (1993). *The east Asian miracle: Economic growth and public policy.* Oxford University Press.

Zhao, S. (2017). Whither the China model: Revisiting the debate. *Journal of Contemporary China, 26*(103), 1–17.

CHAPTER 2

Economic Freedom, Institutional Arrangements, and Local Context

Economic Liberalism

Inspired by Adam Smith, liberal political economists have long emphasised the importance of economic freedom for national prosperity. A free-market system in this case comprises not only policies such as low taxes, minimal regulation, and privatisation, but is also one embedded within a set of legal institutions that uphold private property rights, the rule of law, and efficient contract enforcement. Market exchanges do not take place in a vacuum and are grounded on these fundamental institutional pillars.

Importantly, scholars have sought to ground this insight on objective empirical grounds, using various tools to measure nations' degree of economic freedom, rank them, and compare their relative performance. The key factors that make up economic freedom, such as the size of government, economic openness, the extent of property rights protection, and the degree of interventionist regulations, are quantified into measurable variables in order to compare nations in an aggregate manner. The two leading efforts in this regard are the "Index of Economic Freedom" by the Heritage Foundation and the *Wall Street Journal* and the "Economic Freedom of the World" report (EFW) by the Fraser Institute (Hanke & Walters, 1997).

These studies on economic freedom have expanded our understanding of the contributing factors of human welfare. Research has found that higher economic freedom is associated with not only higher rates of

B. Cheang, *Economic Liberalism and the Developmental State*,
https://doi.org/10.1007/978-3-031-08100-2_2

economic growth (Gwartney et al., 1999) but also non-material aspects of well-being such as international peace and cooperation, gender equality, and environmental quality (Gartze, 2005; Wood & Herzog, 2014; Russell et al. 2020). These results strongly support the classical liberal belief that individual freedom contributes to human flourishing in a holistic manner.

Naturally, liberal political economists and organisations have held up some countries that rank highly on these indices as exemplars. Significantly, the two city-states of Singapore and Hong Kong have been frequently singled out as beacons of economic freedom. Consistently ranked in the top few positions for long stretches of time, economists, journalists, think tanks, and public intellectuals have heaped praise for their economic performance and the high degree of openness, freedom, and competitiveness that supposedly enabled it.

This book argues that this conventional portrayal of Hong Kong and Singapore as beacons of economic freedom is mistaken. There are significant aspects of government intervention in both economies that have been systematically underestimated by these aggregate indices. While East Asian economies generally enjoy relatively free product markets, their factor markets are comparatively state dominated. Additionally, the case of Singapore is especially complicated, due to the complex state-market arrangements that exist due to its nature as a "developmental state capitalist" regime type, which diverges from the laissez-faire model in Hong Kong. A closer look at both political economies, especially in Singapore, will reveal more extensive state interventions into the private sphere than commonly believed.

The problem of ascertaining economic freedom in Singapore and Hong Kong is not merely an isolated issue limited to both cases but speaks to a larger problem confronting scholars who construct aggregate indices. Due to the aggregate nature of such research, the complex ways in which market institutions and policies are socially embedded are necessarily omitted. If the hundreds of countries in the world are to be ranked in a single metric, then what is gained in breadth must be lost in depth. The complex interactions of state-market institutions and government policies in each local context must be abstracted away. Additionally, economic freedom may not always be so easily quantified objectively, due to its important but often neglected subjective component. Economic freedom also comprises the extent to which people actually *imagine and believe* themselves to be free from state coercion.

What Economic Freedom Indices Say

Economic freedom indices consistently rank Hong Kong and Singapore as the freest economies in the world. The Fraser Institute's Economic Freedom of the World reports clearly rank both as the freest.[1] Not only is this true for specific years, but they are also ranked consistently in the top few spots since the rankings' inception. Since 2002, both have occupied the top three positions (Fig. 2.1).

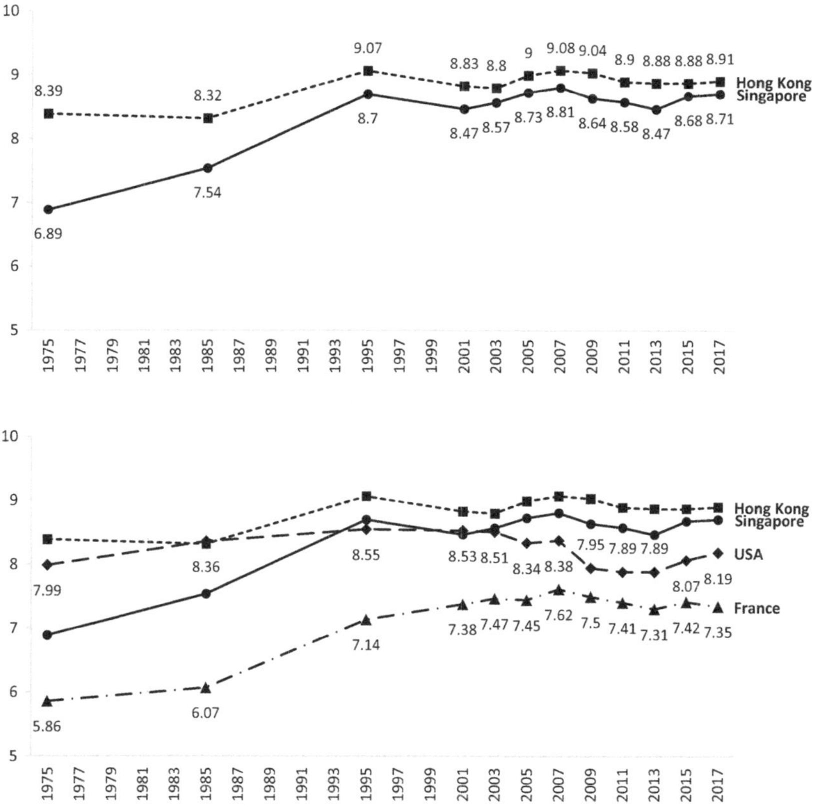

Fig. 2.1 Comparison of Hong Kong and Singapore's (with the United States and France) EFW performance by overall score from 1970 to 2016. (Source: Fraser Institute (2020))

[1] Due to the bigger number of data sources used and *The Wall Street Journal*'s differing period of analysis stretching to 1970 instead of 1995, this study shall subsequently focus on the indices used by the Fraser approach.

The high rankings of Singapore and Hong Kong, coupled with their dramatic economic growth in the twentieth century, have attracted much praise from liberal economists. The Nobel Laureate Milton Friedman (1991, pp. 5–6) featured Hong Kong as an exemplar: "Hong Kong has been one of the freest, if not the freest, of countries in the world in every aspect but one. Hong Kong has had an extraordinary degree of economic freedom, no tariffs and no import or export quotas…Taxes have been very low. There are few regulations on business, no price controls, no wage controls". Friedman similarly cited Singapore as a beacon of economic freedom (Friedman, 1980). Conservative and libertarian organisations, some of whom sponsor and produce these indices, have also jumped on this bandwagon. Daniel Mitchell (2017) has written consistently about the "free-market" recipe for Singapore's prosperity, pointing to its low taxes, limited government spending, and regulations. Marian Tupy has also pointed to both countries as examples for the rest of the world to follow: Singapore as reflecting the "power of economic freedom" (Tupy, 2015) and Hong Kong similarly as one of the "greatest success stories of all time" owing to free markets (Tupy, 2017).

Public figures with a political agenda have also cited them as models to emulate, such as free-market Brexiteers calling for the United Kingdom to pursue a "Singapore-on-Thames" model of free trade and deregulation. For example, Daniel Hannan (2017) has written on how Singapore's economic model is a growth strategy for post-Brexit Britain, praising the way "lower tariffs, lower taxes and lower regulations...have turned Singapore from a steamy island with no resources into a gleaming metropolis".

Such sentiments are not merely concentrated in political and think-tank circles but are also echoed by academic scholars. Johns Hopkins University's Steve Hanke is a fervent supporter of Hong Kong and also the "Singapore Strategy" (2016), one where productivity was "unleashed" when "government gets out of the way" (2019a). He has actively recommended this "Singapore Strategy"', that is, free-market capitalism to other countries—from Zimbabwe (Hanke, 2019b) to Paraguay (Hanke, 2020a) to Albania (Hanke, 2020b). Development economists also echo this line of reasoning. Arvind Panagariya, in his influential work on the importance of free trade, considers both city-states as "uncontroversial" examples where free trade generates prosperity (Panagariya, 2019, ch. 9). Significantly, the classical liberal William Easterly dismisses the statist interpretation of Singapore's growth story. To him, accounts that explain Singapore's success as a product of technocracy are simply the "psychological biases" of humans when they view great leaders as causal agents for positive outcomes (Easterly, 2013, p. 323).

What East Asian Scholars Tell Us

What is interesting is that local area experts, especially those working on East Asian political economy, do not share this sentiment. It is this sharp divergence of views that this book wishes to explain.

While Hong Kong's status as a free-market economy is largely undisputed, Singapore on the other hand has been largely characterised by comparative political scientists and East Asian scholars[2] as resembling a technocratic, developmental state-capitalist system (Amsden, 1994; Wade, 2005; Ortmann & Thompson, 2020; Low, 2001). Linda Lim (1983), a leading Singaporean economist, expressed that "what has made Singapore successful is not the Invisible Hand of the free-market, but rather the very visible hand, indeed the Long Arm, of the state". Singapore is also part of the group of East Asian Tiger Economies, who are also largely characterised as "developmental states", a peculiar regime type that emerged in the late twentieth century and which features proactive industrial policies, social engineering, state capacity, and a national culture centred around rapid growth and performance legitimacy (Haggard, 2018). The leading advocate of this model, Chang Ha-Joon et al. (2013, p. 33), considers Singapore to be a paradigmatic example of a developmental state, having been the "most successful" at the use of interventionist industrial policy.

I argue in the first half of this book these East Asian scholars are generally right in their characterisation. Economic freedom indices have failed to account for the peculiar state-market arrangements that are uncovered when in-depth studies are undertaken. This is particularly true for Singapore, which due to its unique developmental state model blends state and market elements in ways that are hard to capture in aggregate indices. Rather than large-N aggregate statistics, I employ an in-depth comparative case study, an approach which sheds light on contextual institutional details that are difficult to ascertain at a distance. I show that economic freedom, especially in Singapore, is greatly overstated, and thus the gap between Hong Kong and Singapore—which indices rank as the top two freest—are much greater than previously understood.

[2] These scholars are not necessarily East Asian in nationality or ethnicity, but display in-depth knowledge of the region through their works, akin to area studies experts.

Culture of Economic Freedom

Economic freedom may not always be so easily measured in an objective fashion, since there could be unseen, subtle, but nonetheless real factors constraining it. This is especially so when the notion of culture is accounted for. The degree to which an individual is free to exchange goods and services, trade with others, use property, etc. is not just a function of the external regulations imposed on them by the state, but also related to the values and attitudes that individuals have towards the state and others in society. This is of course difficult to quantify and thus cannot reasonably be expected to feature in economic freedom calculations. Yet, they are important.

The aspect of culture raises the issue of the state's informal control over its citizens. State power is not merely a function of its monopoly on the use of violence and its ability to exact force on people but also includes the way it shapes the values, mindsets, and ideology of its people (Foucault, 2000; Gramsci, 1971; Lukes, 1974). Logically, ideological hegemony has been identified as a crucial aspect of state power. This is important in Singapore. Scholars have identified how the Singapore state has intrusively shaped the very values and ideas imbibed by people from the education system to other levels of society. Beyond "social engineering", this has been called "ideological indoctrination" in some quarters, where the PAP government has achieved a conflation of party values with national values (Bellows, 1970; Tremewan, 1994). The clear separation of state and society in Hong Kong for most of its history precludes this. In fact, only in the post-1997 period of Hong Kong history was there concerns of Chinese intrusion into domestic Hong Kong affairs, and even so this has elicited pushback from civil society which is comparatively tame in Singapore.

The Singapore state's "informal intervention" in society and the economy will be demonstrated in Chap. 4. I will show that aside from formal control over strategic aspects of society, the Singaporean developmental state has been able to project informal control over people in a way not mustered in Hong Kong.

Complexity and Institutional Details on the Ground

The key source of difference between Hong Kong and Singapore is the fact that Hong Kong's continued on its colonial laissez-faire model until the 1997 handover, while Singapore's independence in the critical juncture of the 1960s saw it adopt a wholly new set of institutions. The establishment of Singapore's developmental state has led to a storied history of intrusive social engineering of private lives, authoritarianism, disciplining of civil society, and large presence in state-owned enterprises, and industrial policy—points that have never been used to describe the colonial Hong Kong state (Chua, 2017). This critical break has institutional implications that have not been, and cannot easily be, captured by aggregate indices.

One important difference is that the Singapore system has been authoritarian, while civil liberties are better protected in Hong Kong. How this affects the economic performance of both city-states is a question that has been largely unaccounted for in existing studies. In fact, the abovementioned economic freedom statistics assume away the importance of democracy and political institutions and focus only on economic institutions. In Chap. 7, I will show how political authoritarianism in Singapore has stifled the creative class's development in a way not seen in Hong Kong, thus undermining the innovative potential of its economy.

Besides the possibility that Singapore experiences a higher degree of state intervention relative to Hong Kong than is suggested, there are also doubts as to whether economic freedom in these two city-states is as high as most reports suggest. Both Singapore and Hong Kong have intervened in key areas not seen in other economies. For instance, land in both countries is completely owned and monopolised by the state, giving the state tremendous influence over both residential and commercial property (Haila, 2000). One should also take note that both city-states have constantly been singled out for their high rental prices, cost of living, and housing prices which are arguably linked to land policy. This begs the following question: How do these concerns square with the conventional wisdom of both nations as beacons of economic freedom?

Additionally, an important component of economic freedom is competition, which is why the "market" component of capitalism is important. A healthy capitalist economy features a high degree of competition between many economic agents rather than economic concentration amongst elites. Yet, there are concerns today both in Singapore and Hong Kong over the presence of elites in society that control the levers of political and economic power. The closed political system in Singapore has led to concerns that there exists a government business elite that benefits itself at the public's expense (Rodan, 2016). Similarly, scholars have extensively written about how capitalists have been co-opted by both colonial and mainland officials in Hong Kong, excluding the wider public from participation (Goodstadt, 2005). If true, one may challenge the rosy picture of economic freedom in conventional wisdom. Indeed, in Chap. 3, it will be shown that market competition in both city-states has been stifled, though to a larger extent in Singapore due to its developmental state model.

Such institutional details are difficult to aggregate in large-N studies, because they require an up-close analysis of the way institutions and policies interact and are configured, which vary from one country to another. Aggregate figures on a cross-national basis do not account for how specific institutions in each society are arranged, the way they consequently interact with one another, and their variation across countries. These details are necessarily abstracted away to derive variables that can be compared across many cases.

Purely using economic freedom statistics to compare the size of government may lead one to simplistic conclusions. The ex-Head of Singapore Civil Service, who was interviewed by this author, remarked that Singapore only spends 17% of its GDP on government, while in Hong Kong the figures go up to 25%. According to the interviewee, this implies that Singapore has "more of a free-market" than Hong Kong. Yet, simply extrapolating from such figures is problematic. Insightfully, the development economist Peter Bauer (1969, p. 84) warned:

> These political results or corollaries of state control of economic life depend largely on the closeness and the types of state control of economic life, matters which cannot be inferred simply from conventional statistics of the size of the public sector. For instance, government expenditure may be comparatively small, and yet government control over the economy...if there are many state trading monopolies, or if there is extensive licensing of economic activity. (Conversely, even if government expenditure, as a proportion of the national income, is substantial, this need not imply close control over the economy, if the expenditure is on the performance of the familiar traditional functions of government.) Thus, in assessing the political implications of state control of economic life, the character of the control is of major relevance, and this character often cannot be inferred from readily accessible statistics.

Aggregate statistics can mislead, and thus, it is important to supplement them with experience, personal judgement, and contextual evidence. Jerry Muller, in his influential *Tyranny of Metrics*, documents not only how metrics have been misused in various aspects of society, but how they often rest on an overconfidence in rationalist quantification. Metrics, while useful, should also be supplemented with accumulated wisdom and local knowledge (Muller, 2018).

Therefore, Western economists who cite economic freedom indices and countries' rankings on them may not have the full picture.[3] It is, for example, curious that William Easterly, in his influential critique of the "tyranny of experts" (2013), dedicated only half a page to the Singapore case, despite it being widely acknowledged by many local area experts as typifying the success of a technocratic approach to development. Such a position fails to account for the significance of the wider developmental state tradition in the academic literature, and Singapore's unique context more specifically, which hence requires a deeper case study approach. Similarly, Arvind Panagariya's characterisation of Hong Kong and Singapore as free trade successes (2019) is also problematic. Developmental state theorists admit that while free trade may contribute positively, such market-oriented policies may co-exist and in fact be complemented with extensive government coordination of markets through industrial policy and the leadership of SOEs, which if used may generate additional returns not seen otherwise. This point is why some scholars lament the lack of industrial policy in Hong Kong and blame it for their supposed backward status vis-à-vis Singapore (Fuller, 2010; Leung G. L., 2018). By lumping both Hong Kong and Singapore as undifferentiated entities, Panagariya overwhelmingly focuses on a single point of convergence which is their similar free trade policy, neglecting weighty institutional differences within their respective state-market arrangements.

Factor Markets

The comparative study of this book begins with an examination of factor markets, which have strategic importance in any economy. They differ from product markets, which is where goods and services are sold. Factor markets are where production inputs are exchanged and include land, labour, and capital. They constitute three strategic resources, which if controlled, gives the economic agent tremendous power over the economy. The importance of factor markets ties in with the larger literature on

[3] The divergence in opinion between foreign observers and the institutional context may be due to various reasons, ranging from an ideological agenda to a lack of reliable information. Refer to Linda Lim (2018, pp. 97–99) for an interesting discussion of how both conservatives and liberals (such as Prof. Joseph Stiglitz) in the United States have misunderstood Singapore.

natural resources, how they influence political economic arrangements, and how they developed in a society (Auty, 1997; Ross, 1999).

The control over a strategic pillar means that even a small government can wield outsized influence over the private sector. Even if government spends very little, runs only a few departments, and employs a small number of civil servants relative to other countries, it does not necessarily imply that it does not exert an active effect in the private sector. A simple thought experiment illustrates this: State A may only have 50 civil servants governing a huge population. However, State A controls a strategic resource within the economy: the harbour through which all foreign goods must enter. The control over this singular factor of production is sufficient for the state to wield enormous influence over economic activity, regardless of the level of general taxation or business regulation in the macro-economy. This suggests that government size may be a misleading indicator that obscures the specific *scope* of state policy which may further reveal the exertion of state power.

The following diagram is adapted from the Keynesian concept of the circular flow of income (Fig. 2.2). In this reconstruction, factor markets are one half of the economy, with product markets the remainder. State control over the bottom half affords it indirect control of firms and households in the wider economy. Land as a factor of production is monopolised in both city-states. Labour and capital markets are also heavily shaped in Singapore by the developmental state.

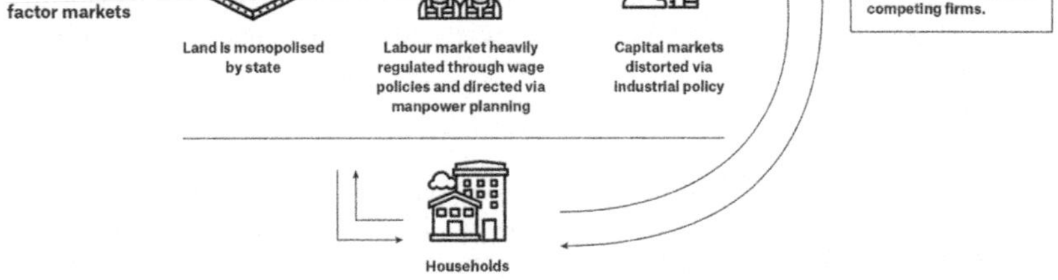

Fig. 2.2 State-controlled factor markets vs. liberalised product markets

Many Asian countries have liberalised their economies, moving from closed to open economies in the late twentieth century (Sally, 2013). However, this process remains incomplete because unlike their product markets, factor markets as in land, labour, capital, and energy resources remain unfree (Huang & Tao, 2010; Sally, 2015). On this note, there is a point of similarity in both countries: land is monopolised, though land is tied to industrial policy more closely in Singapore than in Hong Kong. This poses a significant challenge to the conventional wisdom of both city-states being economically free since factor markets represent half of market exchanges; indeed, entrepreneurs must combine factors of production to serve the consumer-product market.

However, once factor markets are analysed as strategic pillars of the economy, we realise that both Hong Kong and Singapore, typically viewed as economically free, exhibit far greater levels of state intervention. This is mainly due to the state monopoly of land in both countries. The control over factor markets is more extensive in Singapore, however, mainly since labour and capital are more heavily controlled than in Hong Kong. As part of the developmental state's missions, Singapore's government has over the years deliberately shaped the allocation of labour and talent and private capital towards industries deemed strategic to the nation's growth.

State Monopolisation of Land

Land is a very important factor of production within the economy. Until entrepreneurs can innovate solutions to fully escape the physical limits of land, it remains a constraint on market exchange. Considering that all buildings must be built on some parcel of land and that firms must either own land or rent it for their enterprises, any control over this resource by the state provides it tremendous influence over the economy. Land cost also feeds into the larger cost of production that firms face, affecting wages as well. Land is monopolised by the state in both Singapore and Hong Kong, with the added caveat that land-use planning in Singapore is more systematic due to the developmental state apparatus.

Singapore

The Singaporean developmental state, since its birth in the 1960s, has increased its ownership of land, from about one-quarter of Singapore's land area in 1968 to more than 90% today (Kim & Phang, 2013). The state has achieved this through a variety of legal approaches. Chief among these is the legal power the state has reserved for itself to seize private property in land, through the Land Acquisition Act of 1966, which allows the state to acquire land not just for public use, but "for any residential, commercial or industrial purposes" (Yeung, 1973, p. 38). Between 1959 and 1984, the state acquired a total of about 44,000 acres of land which was about one-third of the total land area of Singapore then, the bulk of which was acquired through the Act. By 1985, the government became the biggest landowner (Aleshire, 1986; Wong & Yeh, 1985, pp. 44–45). It should be noted that these acquisitions involved forced relocations and displacement of families. According to Koninck (1992), up to over 1200 sites were expropriated and nearly 270,000 families were displaced. Another legal instrument was the Foreshores (Amendment) Ordinance in 1964 that prevents private landowners affected by foreshore reclamation to seek compensation for the loss of sea frontage. This was significant in enabling the state to pursue extensive land reclamation.

Not only is the government the country's largest owner of land, it also closely regulates the private use of land according to its national development plans. Through the Government Land Sales (GLS) programme, it enables the state to release state land for sale to the private sector, but only according to predefined plans. Additionally, state land is not actually sold to the private sector but leased for 99 years for public housing and 30 years for industrial use This means that land and property owners do not acquire actual property titles to their assets and that the state has the option to recover land approaching the end of its lease and reallocate it for further development needs. In sum, the state receives land through forced acquisitions, the expiry of private leases, and the two-way exchanges between the government and its subsidiary statutory boards.

State control over land in Singapore is part of larger urban planning exercises. This distinguishes it from Hong Kong and most other countries. While Hong Kong's land policy may have been co-opted by special interests due to policy loopholes, Singapore's land policy is calibrated to fit into larger analyses done by government bodies as to society's future needs, that is, how land should be allocated for various purposes. This is reflected in the government's Concept Plan, implemented in 1971, which strictly determines how land is distributed across different uses. Testament to the effort to coordinate policy areas, the developmental state in Singapore would also involve organising various officials into committees to systematically plan land allocation needs. This was confirmed in an interview with a former government official, who has also called the approach "integrated and long term in perspective", with a "whole of government approach" that helps "facilitate the realization of Singapore's plans".[4]

This clearly contrasts with the situation in Hong Kong, which never had a systematic blueprint for the allocation of land amongst competing uses on such a macro level. In fact, urban planners had recommended the formulation of such a plan, but it was either resisted or not continued. It was only in the 1990s that a semblance of macro-level urban planning was conducted.

Hong Kong

Land as a factor of production is also monopolised by the state in Hong Kong based on a system beginning in the colonial era. Specifically, land policy is based on a leasehold system where land is owned by the state and subsequently leased on fixed terms (Yeh, 1993). The 1997 handover has not fundamentally changed this practice, with Article 7 of the Basic Law clearly stating that "the land and natural resources within the Hong Kong Special Administrative Region shall be State Property", with "the revenues derived therefrom shall be exclusively at the disposal of the government of the Region".

The government monopoly on land is closely tied to its housing policy which has generated much controversy considering Hong Kong's high housing prices and increases in cost of living. Historically, beginning in the post-war period, land was resumed and cleared for massive public housing projects to be established. Clearly, in addition to land, housing is a state-dominated area, with a majority of Hongkongers living in government-provided social housing, where dwellers do not possess the property rights to resell or sublet the unit. The number of people living in private accommodation as a percentage of the total has only begun changing slightly after 2006 (Table 2.1).

The large role of the Hong Kong government in providing housing requires a closer examination of its housing policy, which is surprising for a high level of state control in a supposedly laissez-faire economy. Hong Kong's repeated extensions of rent control, for example, is worth examining.

[4] Interview with Professor Heng Chye Kiang from National University of Singapore, who has served on boards of urban planning agencies in Singapore including URA, HDB, JTC, CLC, and BCA.

Table 2.1 Percentage of Hong Kong population living across different forms of housing

	1991	*1996*	*2001*	*2006*	*2011*	*2016*
Social housing						
Public rental housing	40.5	38.5	31.9	31.0	29.6	29.1
Government-subsidised home ownership housing	7.5	11.4	16.9	17.8	17.0	15.8
Non-domestic housing	1.4	1.1	1.2	1.2	1.2	1.2
Temporary housing	3.6	2.0	1.1	0.7	0.7	0.7
Private home ownership						
Private permanent housing	47	46.9	49.0	49.3	51.5	53.2

Source: Various years of the Population Census conducted by the Hong Kong government (HKSAR, 1991–2016)

Rent control, a type of price ceiling, has been widely criticised by economists for its inefficiency and adverse impacts, including the degradation of housing quality. A proper understanding of Hong Kong's control over the factor market of land should also incorporate the role of rent control in the management of housing. Despite Hong Kong's free-market credentials, housing has been subject to much intervention; rent control was implemented in 1947 and persisted all the way till 1998.

One predicted effect of rent control is that landlords have no incentive to maintain the quality of rental apartments. This was reported to be the case in post-war Hong Kong, in the early 1950s, when it was reported that many housing estates and apartments were rife with war damage and remained unrepaired for a long time, especially since rent control was implemented in 1947 through the Landlord and Tenant Ordinance (HKSAR, 1947). This was explored briefly by Steven Cheung (1979) who found that the ordinance prevented housing reconstruction since it made it almost impossible for landlords to evict tenants which is necessary for rebuilding. Landlords were prevented from evicting tenants, so as to enforce rent control.[5] Not only has this "severely complicated the achievement of urban renewal", the interventions in the housing sector represent "a series of severe and sometimes blundering governmental regulations" which has affected "the city's most valuable housing sector" (Cheung, 1979, pp. 28–29, 52).

[5] See Sects. 18–20 of the Landlord and Tenant Ordinance.

The rent control legislation did not stand alone but interacted with other contemporaneous policies. Landlords were further prevented from reconstructing their property and expanding private offerings due to various legislation. These included the 1935 Building Ordinance, which had restrictive height guidelines, required all development proposals to be approved after long consultations, lease conditions that dictated what and how developers could build, and the state's monopoly over land (HKSAR, 1935). This is most clearly reflected in the debates in the Legislative Council in 1947 where Unofficial Members had petitioned for the relaxation of rules but were outnumbered by Official Members (Hong Kong Legislative Council, 1947). According to Alan Smart (1992, pp. 38–39), "for a combination of technical reasons, bureaucratic interests, distrust of private developers as speculators, concern for government revenues, a commitment to town planning and building standards...the government resisted these pressures", that is, pressures from Unofficials.

There is long-term significance of these early legislation on Hong Kong's government's control over land. A path dependent effect was created because these early circumstances pushed the government to further intervene in the housing sector. First, this is seen by rent control lasting till 1998 which effectively meant that throughout the post-war colonial period, it persisted. The rent control legislation was amended multiple times before it was finally phased out on 31 December 1998.[6]

Second and more significantly, the birth of Hong Kong's modern public housing programme can be traced to rent control and development controls. Due to these controls' restriction on the supply of new housing, coupled with the increasing population at the time, squatter settlements arose to cope with overcrowding. Due to the unsanitary conditions in squatters and public pressure, the government launched massive public housing programmes from 1962 onwards which present-day programmes can be traced to. Richard Wong (1998, p. 33) articulated this best: "by choosing to impose rent control in 1945, the government set in motion a sequence of events whose consequences have continued to plague Hong Kong's people".

A common perspective pushed today is that high property prices which lead to higher housing prices and commercial rental are a result of the real estate developers' hoarding and speculation on land. This was most

[6] For example, the Landlord and Tenant (Consolidation) Amendment Bill of 1992 proposed to eliminate rent control by 1994, but the phasing out process was then extended.

pointedly observed in the Consumer Council reports in the 1990s showing a severe lack of competition in various markets, including property, which has high levels of concentration amongst big real estate developers (Consumer Council, 1996a, 1996b).

The dominance of large firms in the real estate market in Hong Kong has been blamed on the lack of market regulation by the government. This has supposedly allowed firms to artificially raise prices to the detriment of commercial renters and subsequently Hong Kong residents who face exorbitant housing costs. Numerous studies and popular commentaries have pointed to the economic and political influence of property-based conglomerates owned by powerful Hong Kong families: the Cheung Kong/Hutchinson group, Sun Hung Kai Properties, Henderson Group, New World Development Group, Wheelock Group, and CLP Holdings Group.

Except for Lai's studies (1998, 2000), what has not greatly featured in the analysis is the role of zoning regulations and development control. Zoning regulations have elsewhere been shown to have stifled the supply of new housing units and slowed the private development of land, leading to high property and residential prices. This was anecdotally suggested by Richard Wong (2015, p. 153), who asserted that "what prevents the land (in Hong Kong) from being developed is regulatory prohibition, a very formidable barrier to development", though this was left unsubstantiated.

Impact on Cost

A direct and negative consequence of the land system in both countries is high land prices, translating into a loss of economic competitiveness. This happens on several levels, because the high land prices mean high rental costs for businesses who must compete with either the large property developers in Hong Kong or the government-linked property developers in Singapore. Additionally, high land prices lead to high housing prices which could deter foreigners and push citizens abroad.

Repeated business surveys in both Hong Kong and Singapore have revealed a high-cost environment. An annual survey conducted by DP Information Group which focuses on Singaporean small-medium enterprises (SMEs) constantly cites high rental amongst the top five business problems business owners say they face. This can be analysed in a more industry-specific manner, since not all firms are equally affected by costs. Considering the various industries, the retail and lifestyle sector has been particularly affected, as it is an industry where rents comprise almost one-third of the costs. Additionally, many of these retailers must rent spaces in shopping malls and major landmarks which are owned by the government-linked REITS. A grants manager at the Singapore Retailers Association recounted many SMEs facing high rental costs with frequent rent increases amounting up to 50%, leaving them with slim profit margins.[7]

No analysis of the rental rates by government-linked REITs has previously been done. The author gathered the annual reports of the three largest GLREITs and tracked the rental rates charged by them to their tenants over the years. The significance of these three GLREITs lie in the fact that they cumulatively house numerous shopping and industrial facilities in Singapore. Thus, rent increases by these organisations have a large ripple effect on business costs (Table 2.2).

CapitaLand Mall Trust is a GLREIT substantially owned by Temasek Holdings which holds 40% of its shares as of 31 March 2019. It is the largest shopping mall owner in Singapore and its portfolio includes 15 shopping malls such as Bugis Junction, Plaza Singapura, Westgate, and the newly refurbished Funan Shopping Mall. With a market capitalisation of S$6.6 billion, it is currently the largest retail REIT in Singapore. The average rental cost has increased by 25.72% from 2010 to 2019 (Fig. 2.3).

Mapletree Commercial Trust is a GLREIT, which is 100% owned by Temasek Holdings as of 31 March 2019. Its portfolio includes Vivocity, the largest shopping mall in Singapore, Mapletree Business City, and the

Table 2.2 Announced rent increases by GLREITs in Singapore

Major GLREITs by market capitalisation	*Affiliation with government*	*Total % increase in rental from 2010 to 2019*
CapitaLand Mall Trust	Government-owned company	25.72%
Mapletree Commercial Trust	Subsidiary of Temasek Holdings	175.94%
Keppel REIT	Subsidiary of Keppel Corporation, which is a subsidiary of Temasek Holdings	96.11%

Source: Respective annual reports and authors' calculations

[7] Interview with Grants Manager at Singapore Retailers Association (SRA), Oct 2018.

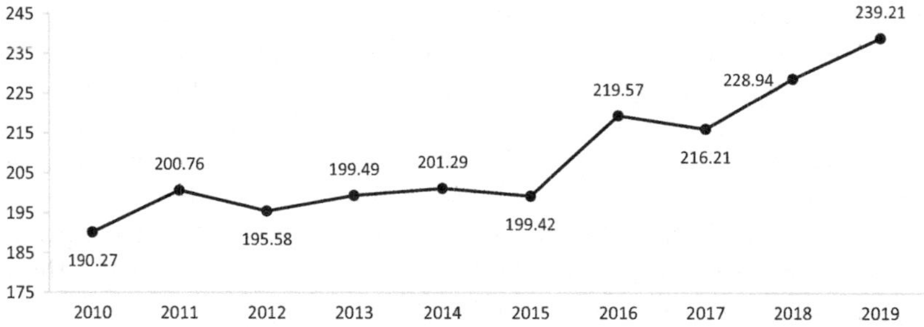

Fig. 2.3 Average rental cost per tenant (S$ thousand) for CapitaLand Mall Trust. (Source: Annual Reports of CapitaLand Mall Trust (2010–2019))

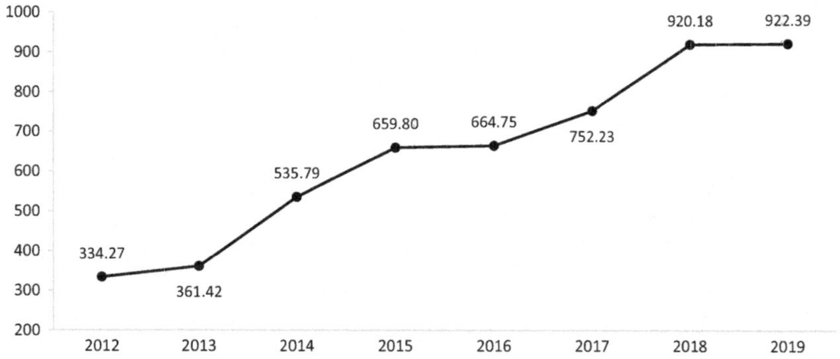

Fig. 2.4 Average rental cost per tenant (S$ thousand) for Mapletree Commercial Trust. (Source: Annual Reports of Mapletree Commercial Trust (2011/2012–2018/2019))

PSA Building. With a market capitalisation of S$6.3 billion, it is currently the second largest retail REIT and the largest commercial REIT in Singapore. The average rental cost increased by 175.94% from 2012 to 2019 (Fig. 2.4).

Keppel REIT is a GLREIT owned by Temasek Holdings which holds 20% of its shares as of 31 March 2019. Its portfolio in Singapore includes Ocean Financial Centre, Marina Bay Financial Centre, and One Raffles Quay. With a market capitalisation of S$3.6 billion, it is currently the fourth largest commercial REIT in Singapore. The average rental cost has increased by 96.11% from 2010 to 2019 (Fig. 2.5).

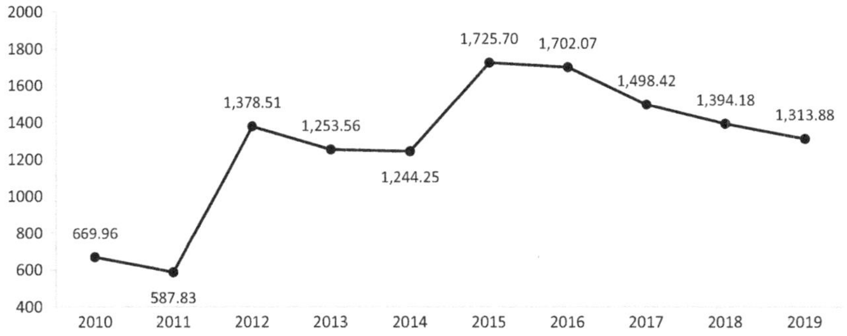

Fig. 2.5 Average rental cost per tenant (S$ thousand) for Keppel REIT. (Source: Annual Reports of Keppel REIT (2010–2019))

Reports have also indicated how retailers have had to accept unfavourable terms by the REITs. For example, it was reported by Mr. Victor Tay, the CEO of Singapore Business Federation in 2014, that "tenants may be required to renovate their units every time they renew their leases, which is typically once every three years", which raises business costs (Tan M., 2014). Additionally, he also added that "the landlord may also take a portion of the tenant's sales on top of the base rent even when sales are poor or may prevent the tenant from opening another outlet at a competing mall nearby" (Tan M., 2014).

A similar story emerges in Hong Kong. An investment article declared in 2002 that "property is an artificial market made so by the fact that many of the companies listed on the stock exchange are property firms that pull in even more investment capital. One result: exorbitant rents, which have made Hong Kong one of the most expensive places in the world to do business" (Fortune, 2002).

Manpower and Capital

The monopolisation of land by the Singapore and Hong Kong states provides them enormous influence over the economy and society, to the extent that they have been called "property states" (Haila, 2015). In the Singaporean developmental state, control over land is its chief lever to pursue national development plans.

When one examines the other factors of production however, that is, manpower and capital, the similarities start to fade away. Owing to the fact that Singapore is a developmental state, it has always sought to direct the flow of capital and labour resources across different industries, developing state-market linkages that are otherwise not present elsewhere.

Capital

Capital markets are critical to the proper functioning of a market economy. Firms participate in the capital market by borrowing funds to expand their business; thus access to financing affects the economy's prospects. Banks are thus an important intermediary between households and firms in a market economy. This is an important pillar in factor markets, which have far-reaching impacts if subject to government control, whether beneficial or adverse.

Since its independence, Singapore's government, as part of its developmental state objectives, has intervened in the capital market to direct capital investment into industries and areas it deems important. This has been done in many ways, by acquiring significant stakes in the major local banks, banking regulation, and the direct provision of credit to influence entrepreneurs to invest in specific sectors.

The government's intervention in capital markets has been quite direct. Most obviously, it has directly managed the Development Bank of Singapore (DBS), and at one point had a shareholding as high as 48%, though this has since declined to less than 30%. A major function of DBS was to complement the Economic Development Board from 1968 onwards to serve as a development bank. This meant that it would provide financing to companies wanting to grow and DBS would hold shares in the firms that it supported (DBS Bank, 2018, p. 10). The provision of industrial financing by this bank was in fact recommended by the Dutch economic advisor Albert Winsemius, who was responsible for instigating Singapore's state-led industrialisation plans (Economic Development Board, 1968). The close inter-linkage of DBS bank with government industrial policy is seen by the fact that the first chairman of EDB and DBS was the same person: Hon Sui Sen.

Aside from its banking services, DBS is also a group of companies, which once comprised 26 subsidiaries. These companies had enjoyed lines of credit from the government, which in 1988 formed 81.3% of its total borrowings as DBS bank and 83.5% as DBS group. Additionally, the government provided guarantees for its loans from foreign sources and waived underwriting fees and stockbrokers commission for DBS (Pillai, 1983).

The government sector's involvement in the capital markets has an industrial policy bent. The developmental state has partnered with leading financial institutions in Singapore to provide loans at favourable rates to spur business growth (Enterprise Singapore, 2018). While some are industry-neutral, other are reserved for "innovative" and "high-growth" enterprises in fields such as technology and biomedicine, like the SME Venture Loan. The government, through the statutory board Enterprise Singapore, would accept 50% of the loan default risks.

An important distinction between the role of government in both cities' financial sectors is that Hong Kong's purpose of intervention is not sectoral but regulatory. The Hong Kong state, contrary to popular opinion, has intervened in the financial sector, though not to spearhead industrial development like Singapore. In the 1960s, during what some have called the era of "wildcat banking", Hong Kong's government implemented banking ordinances that effectively led to the industry's cartelisation. This has been called the interest rate cartel based on the "Interest Rate Rules" (IRRs). Under this arrangement, banks were classified into several categories, so that the largest international banks offered the lowest rates, while the smallest local banks offered the highest rates on time deposits. The rate on savings deposits was uniform for all banks, while that on demand deposits was identically zero (Jao, 1974). Meant to prevent excessive competition, interest rates were set by the Association of Bank's Interest Rate Committee, which was a cartel of banks maintained by state privilege (Schiffer, 1991).

The Hong Kong state's role in the financial industry is significant as it challenges conventional accounts that criticise the economy's supposed laissez-faire orientation for leading to business cartelisation. A leading critic is (Leo Goodstadt, 2005, p. 4) who argued that the Hong Kong state's non-interventionism has led to the people being exploited by "business cartels and other anti-competitive practices". Indeed, many accounts have criticised Hong Kong's pro-capitalist orientation for the excessive market concentration in a range of sectors.

However, market concentration theory should be supplemented with a distinction between political and natural barriers to entry. Arguably, most monopolies and cases of market power stem from state-created barriers such as occupational licencing, rather than the natural barriers of market competition. This distinction means that market concentration alone need not necessarily imply an undesirable situation. I argue that this insight is relevant for analysing the situation in Hong Kong. In this case, banking ordinances were at the root of the cartelisation in the banking sector, which has been rightly criticised for exploiting depositors and extracting abnormal profits for the banks (Consumer Council, 1994).

The Hong Kong Association of Banks (1-1KAE) was pressured by rising public anger to partially deregulate interest rates on time deposits of more than seven days from 1994 to 1995. Further deregulation was postponed in early 1995 due to the Mexican crisis and the impending change of sovereignty. Since then, however, the HKMA decided to remove the remaining IRRs, which were phased out within two years from 1 July 1999.

Overall, Singapore still intervenes more heavily than Hong Kong in the aspect of capital. A critical aspect of the Singapore state's control over capital that has not been discussed yet is its forced savings policy through the Central Provident Fund, which diverts away large proportion of household incomes (see Chia, 2016). Not only does it direct disproportionate amounts of savings to housing and state assets, it also makes possible Singapore's consistent budget surpluses and large foreign reserves (Lim, 2018, pp. 101–102; Lim & Pang, 2016, p. 137; Asher et al., 2016). In other words, Singapore's seemingly "low tax and low spending" reputation belies its centralised direction of capital flows, a cornerstone of its political economy. Hong Kong by contrast has never exhibited either the willingness or capacity to do likewise. Aside from the abovementioned banking regulations, which are relatively minimal, there have been little capital controls in Hong Kong's colonial history. As Alvin Rabushka (1979, ch. 2) shown in his excellent account, Hong Kong has been a "genuine financial haven", attracting large amounts of voluntary savings that financed industrial development. Just like Singapore, Hong Kong has also had persistent budget surpluses, yet, the crucial difference is that this was achieved through genuine fiscal discipline and not via Singapore's complex social engineering.

Manpower

Another contrast between Hong Kong and Singapore concerns the management of labour. In Hong Kong, organisation of labour along class lines has been relatively weak, as seen by low levels of trade union membership and ideological fragmentation. The colonial state had also never treated labour as a resource subjected to sectoral interventions across various industries the way Singapore's government did.

Various indicators clearly demonstrate that labour as a social class has always been insignificant in Hong Kong (Ng & Sit, 1989; Turner, 1980;

Table 2.3 Proportion of Hong Kong workers in trade unions[a]

	2014	*2015*	*2016*	*2017*	*2018*
Number of employee unions	819	821	828	836	846
Declared membership of employee unions	826,729	869,528	888,466	904,210	911,593
Trade union participation rate	23.24%	24.30%	24.91%	25.02%	25.06%

Source: Annual Statistical Report of Trade Unions in Hong Kong (HKSAR, 2018)

[a]The following formula is used: Trade Union Participation Rate = [(Declared Membership of Employee Unions) / (number of salaried employees and wage earners)] × 100%

Chao & Lai, 1997). Importantly, the union membership of workers relative to employment is very low. The following statistics show relatively low levels of workers in different industries joining unions (Table 2.3).

The result is that "Hong Kong does not depend on formalised collective bargaining as a pivotal institution for regulating pay and other labour-management relationships issues" (Ng & Sit, 1989, p. 88). The individualistic character of Hong Kong society is also expressed in employment relationships between employer and worker since most workers and even union leaders strongly prefer to negotiate individually rather than collectively. Arguably, labour relations have also been relatively peaceful in Hong Kong's colonial past, with minimal work disruptions.

The Hong Kong state's attitude towards labour as a class has been one of arms-length benign neglect. Not only are trade unions free to mobilise organically, labour legislation has been slow to come by. A most revealing incident concerns the Butters Report of 1939 which recommended legislation to improve working conditions, but which was rejected multiple times and never implemented. The dearth of labour legislation was only realised in 1968 when the comprehensive Employment Ordinance was enacted following the Star Ferry riots. A degree of labour legislation exists in many economies, as is the case in Hong Kong, but what has crucially been pointed out is that these ordinances during its colonial history reflected pre-existing employment realities rather than being arbitrarily imposed (Rabushka, 1979, pp. 74–77).

The key point stressed here is that the Hong Kong state's treatment of labour is unlike the Singaporean developmental state's, which not only implements labour legislation but has consistently exercised social control over the labour class and directed the flow of labour through industrial policy. The basic rationale for this stems from the Singapore state's deliberate choice of an export-oriented development strategy in the 1960s which necessitated low wages and labour discipline to attract foreign multinationals. Singapore's reliance on foreign multinationals also meant that foreign labour was privileged through various incentives, which have at times even included the wages of foreign workers being subsidised by the state (Lim, 2018, p. 95).

The socio-political control over trade unionism is well known in Singapore. The government has passed extensive legislation to depoliticise the labour movement and establish control over unions. In fact, there are no independent labour unions in Singapore, and all unions are subsumed in a tripartite body known as the National Trades Union Congress (NTUC).

Political control over labour is instrumental because it allowed the government to push its wage policy onto firms without the reprisals that would be guaranteed in other countries. In fact, the most direct intervention into the labour market was the establishment of the National Wages Council (NWC) in 1972 which can set wage guidelines and recommend wage adjustments for private firms. Far from simply being an advisory body, it was instrumental in allowing the government to force low wages onto the economy from 1972 to 1978 which was key to maintaining labour-intensive manufacturing and attracting foreign firms (Toh & Low, 1990, p. 264). Testament to its power over the private economy, from 1979 to 1981, it reversed course and pursued a "wage-correction" policy to reverse the low wages of the previous decade. However, as some scholars have shown, the higher wages that were artificially set unintentionally contributed to Singapore's first recession in 1985 (Rigg, 1988; Hwang-Wong, 1990; Oun, 2018, ch. 14).

Labour is a strategic economic asset not only due to its physical features but also due to its latent human capital. Understandably, the Singaporean developmental state has sought control over the allocation of human capital across the industrial structure since 1965. In fact, the Singapore state has engaged in very intrusive social engineering to shape demographic patterns (Wilkinson, 1988). It is well known, for instance, the infamous attempt by the state to encourage the sterilisation of mothers who were not university educated (Today Online, 2015). Yet, some of these initiatives are usually not considered in economic analyses of Singapore since they are considered the domain of other policy areas.

In contrast, this study understands that different policy areas are interconnected. The social engineering of Singapore's government reflects the developmental state's desire to shape socio-economic development to fit its larger plans. This can be understood in several ways. First, the state has engaged in deliberate manpower planning to funnel talent into industries deemed important for future growth. This has also allowed it to siphon talent from the private sector. Second, the state has also consciously and repeatedly disciplined the labour force to achieve its post-war development goals.

Manpower Planning

One significant aspect of the state's control over labour as a factor market is manpower planning. This begins at an early age through education policy. On the one level, it sets the curriculum and education framework for all levels, including the tertiary level. This is not distinct from common practice elsewhere since almost all governments today set national education policies. However, what distinguishes the Singapore approach is its careful calibration of the education pathways available to students, mainly in the post-secondary and tertiary levels to meet what it deems as the economy's future manpower needs. This constitutes part of industrial policy more generally where the state influences the type of workers created through the education system to produce human resources to fit its desired economic structure.

The Singaporean developmental state conducts extensive manpower planning for economic purposes. This was overseen previously by the National Manpower Council, now replaced with the Ministry of Manpower's Manpower Planning and Policy Division. These parties are responsible for regular projections of future manpower needs and whether educational institutions can provide them. They then decide on the allocation of places in tertiary institutions and the distribution of disciplines available to students.

The difficulties of projecting future needs and anticipating changes in the economic structure are substantial. Singapore's government had to reverse course multiple times. In fact, in the late 1980s the government wanted to cut medical school intake and reduced the number from 200 to 150 a year for the purpose of preventing "supply-induced demand" (Tan et al., 2009, p. 162). However, in the subsequent decade, an unanticipated population growth necessitated more doctors. Additionally, the growth of biomedical technology as a field became clear. Thus, in 1998, the government increased medical school intake back to 200 and gradually even higher. In the late 2000s, the government established a new graduate medical school and increased the list of approved foreign medical schools from 28 to 140.

This manpower planning does not end with education policy but is carried forth through the government's national manpower policy which affects private employers. Based on the developmental state's identification of the economy's strategic sectors, it anticipates the manpower and skills needs throughout the economy, including the kinds of investments that firms need to restructure. Executed on repeated occasions, the most recent is the Sectoral Manpower Plan, which includes various industries, ideal progression pathways for workers, and the skills they need to have (Tay, 2015). Based on these plans the government funds a slew of training programmes backed by incentives. The large-scale nature of this exercise means that private firms are influenced by the provision of these incentives to act in ways they otherwise would not. This in turn directs labour resources into areas that are pre-identified by the government.

In contrast, such manpower planning and deliberate allocation of labour into specific industries has simply not occurred in Hong Kong.

Government Scholarships

The government's manpower policy is also connected with another powerful lever of control—the scholarship system. Far more than any other country including Hong Kong, Singapore's government provides generous scholarships to university students annually whose tertiary education is sponsored in return for employment in ministries and statutory boards. Discussion on this topic is extensive and this chapter will not revisit it in depth. The constant concern has been about whether the public sector has crowded out the private sector due to its ability to cream off the best talent (see Lim, 2017, p. 115).

I conducted an interview with two high ranking officials in the Public Service Division.[8] The interviewees opined that the top scholarships given out by the Public Service Commission (PSC) yearly only amount to just a handful and so cannot possibly account for the supposed crowding out. This is true, since PSC scholarships are given only to elite students and number less than ten each year. The Public Service Division also does not administrate all the other scholarships given out each year.

[8] The two individuals are from the executive management of the Public Service Division, Prime Minister's Office. Interviewee 1 is from the PSC Secretariat and Interviewee 2 is from the Leadership Development Department. Interview conducted in June 2018.

However, a counterpoint to the abovementioned is that beyond the elite scholarships given, all the other prevailing scholarships are predominantly government based. The logic here is as follows. According to existing research data, aspirations amongst students to acquire university education is high, with most of them—79% in the largest survey done on this—opting for scholarships as the preferred option to finance further education (Brightsparks, 2018). This, however, is associated with the fact that almost all available scholarships in Singapore are provided by government ministries and associated statutory boards.

Not only are an overwhelming majority of scholarships linked to government ministries, the best-scoring students themselves flock towards these government scholarships. Table 2.4 shows that out of the ten most preferred scholarship providers, eight are directly linked to government. It should be noted that the typical government scholarship carries a bond period of a minimum of four years, providing a direct pipeline of top talents for the public sector. This is further reinforced by the other data point in the survey that among the top scoring performers in pre-university level as well as the general pre-university population, government administration is consistently ranked as one of the top three preferred industries to work in (Brightsparks, 2018, p. 15).

Table 2.4 Most preferred scholarships by the top-performing "A"-level and IB diploma students and graduates for 2018

2018 rank	*Scholarship provider*	*Link to government?*
1	National University of Singapore	Indirect
2	Nanyang Technological University	Indirect
3	Changi Airport Group	Yes
4	Agency for Science, Technology and Research	Yes
5	Defence Science and Technology Agency	Yes
6	MOH Holdings	Yes
7	Civil Aviation Authority of Singapore	Yes
8	Singapore Industry Scholarship	Yes
9	Public Service Commission	Yes
10	Singapore Management University	Indirect

Source: 2018 Brightsparks Scholarship and Higher Education Survey Report

I also conducted further data collection on this matter to triangulate my findings. Based on several interviews with students from the top-performing junior colleges and a focus group discussion, I am of the opinion that the developmental state indeed enjoys an overwhelming advantage over the choice of talents. A student from Raffles Institution, Class of 2018, shared in an interview with me that almost 70% of his classmates had successfully been accepted for government scholarships which funded overseas studies at top universities.[9]

Aligning with the deeper point of this book, the state's influence does not just stem from the number of scholarships it administers and thus the number of students that eventually work for it but also the way it shapes their perceptions and attitudes. The economic control the developmental state enjoys over manpower and education has buttressed its political dominance. Specifically, the state has crafted a set of values and ideas that are disseminated through national education. Education policy has been a tool for the developmental state to justify its legitimacy and perpetuate itself. In the context of Singapore, the state has manipulated cultural values such as Confucianism and other Asian values and changes in the national education syllabus to perpetuate the ideal image of the "good citizen" which disciplines the populace to imbibe the developmental state's narrative about its policies (Chia, 2015).

Comparative Analysis of Public Sector Institutions

Conceptual taxonomies also help illuminate differences in state-market relations. The state sector's specific role within the larger economy can be understood with reference to different types of state entities on a public-private continuum. This is especially important because the public-private dichotomy is not black and white but very complex (Perry & Rainey, 1988). Additionally, typical of developmental states, public-private entities are highly enmeshed with one another; thus a closer examination of specific differences is necessary.

Based on the taxonomy in Table 2.5, there are key institutional differences obscured by economic freedom statistics. It should be conceded first that both city-states are relatively similar in the fourth and eighth categories of regulated enterprises and private enterprises, respectively. Since both countries prize the ease of doing business very highly, government

[9] Interview with graduating student from Raffles Institution, Class of 2018.

Table 2.5 Taxonomy of public-private divide in both city-states

	Ownership[a]	*Funding*	*Mode of social control*	*Hong Kong*	*Singapore*
Government department	Public	Public	Polyarchy	Education Bureau Environment Bureau	Ministry of Defence Ministry of Education Various statutory boards
Government corporation	Public	Private	Polyarchy	NA	HDB (since it relies on housing sales)
Government-sponsored enterprise	Private	Public	Polyarchy	Comparatively fewer due to the less generous industrial subsidies offered; most funding schemes started after 1997	Industrial subsidies abundant in Singapore, especially to SMEs, which may translate into many SMEs being GSEs
Regulated enterprise	Private	Private	Polyarchy	Minimal since business regulations are either avoided or not numerous, owing to the desire to maintain ease of doing business	
Government enterprise	Public	Public	Market	Null set	
State-owned enterprise	Public	Private	Market	Mass Transit Railway Corporation (MTRC) is a common example	Minimal on a *de jure* basis, but numerous on a *de facto* basis Includes GLCs owned directly or indirectly by Temasek Holdings, the national government holding company, and subsidiary companies under various government ministries and statutory boards
Government contractor	Private	Public	Market	Numerous, since both public sectors practise outsourcing to external contractors	
Private enterprise	Private	Private	Market	Numerous, since both are market economies	

Source: Conceptual taxonomy provided by Perry and Rainey (1988)

[a]Includes enterprises that are substantially owned by state entities (usually min. 30% shareholding as benchmark), and not just 100% ownership

regulations on businesses are minimal. Private enterprises are understandably abundant since both are primarily market-based economies.

However, some institutional peculiarities of Singapore are revealed. First, due to the generous provision of industrial subsidies in Singapore, there is a high number of government-sponsored enterprises. As the subsequent chapter will show, some recipients of subsidies have become overly dependent, to the detriment of their firm's autonomy. Second, from a superficial reading, state-owned enterprises are few and far between in both places. However, the *de facto* reality in Singapore does not comport with the *de jure* appearance. While there are technically only a few state-owned companies in Singapore, there are numerous government-linked companies. These are essentially SOEs in a different garb, since they are not owned by government departments but mainly by Temasek Holdings which is a government holding company. Such institutional particularities matter greatly in understanding the state's presence and size which are obscured by macro-level statistics.

Peculiar Institutional Arrangement of Singapore's Developmental State

In the context of this study, Singaporean society is governed by a developmental state which possesses certain features not found in other countries, including Hong Kong, which was run on a colonial basis until 1997. Unpacking this difference allows a vast gulf in economic freedom to be detected. Specifically, the economic freedom indices severely under-report the true size of government in the Singapore context because they draw from international data comparing the government's official size but omit the larger public sector.

How the size of government is calculated is critically important. There are several peculiar features of the Singaporean developmental state not found in Hong Kong, particularly the entities known as statutory boards which are omitted in official calculations. Statutory boards are semi-autonomous bodies in Singapore which execute the government ministries' official plans but are omitted from the official budget. This section will attempt to estimate the impact of including this sector. Secondly, Singapore also operates significant sovereign wealth funds that exercise indirect but significant influence over economic activities, a feature that cannot be adequately captured within statistics. This will be explored in Chap. 3.

Table 2.6 maps the core government entities in both city-states. Core government entities are defined as those established by law and are either fully funded by the state or receive a substantial proportion of state funding. If established by law, they are subject to legal review and accountable to public scrutiny. In the context of both city-states, they comprise major organs of state and government ministries in Singapore. Policy bureaus are the Hong Kong equivalent.

Omission of Statutory Boards

What is significant from the table is that both city-states, in line with the theory of New Public Management, operate with a degree of decentralisation whereby the functions of each department are delegated to lower-level entities. The salient point that should be noted here is that in the Singapore context, statutory boards are not included in the official government budget, whereas Hong Kong government departments are, by virtue of their close connection to respective policy bureaus.

Statutory boards are semi-autonomous bodies distinct from the civil service; hence their budgets are excluded from official calculations and do not enjoy the legal privileges and immunities of higher-level government ministries. The purpose for such a division was to create greater autonomy for these bodies to pursue their functions, rather than be subject to a bureaucratic centre. These bodies are responsible for their own lawsuits, agreements, and contracts and acquire and dispose of property in their own names. Their purpose has been to introduce flexibility and private-sector managerial techniques into a system that would otherwise be constricted by bureaucracy (Quah, 2010, ch. 4).

However, these characteristics aside, statutory boards do not substantially differ from core government entities. In the end, they were still "set up by special legislation to perform specific functions" (Tan C.H., 1976, p. 102). Each of them was established "by an Act of Parliament" making them subject to public scrutiny and thus influenced by the political process. As with higher-level ministries in Singapore and typical government bodies elsewhere, statutory boards are still subject to financial control since they are audited by the Auditor-General and are subject to political control since their annual budgets and financial statements are still presented to parliament and approved by a minister (Ow, 1976, p. 173).

Thus, official statistics undercalculate the true size of the government sector. These statutory boards' revenues, expenditures, and balance sheets are not included in the budget. This is confirmed by numerous experts on

Table 2.6 List of core government entities in both city-states

	Type of entity	*Legal foundation*	*Funding source(s)*	*Examples*	*Revenues and expenditures included in official budget?*
Core government entities					
Singapore	Organs of state	Established by law	Fully funded by government	Attorney-General's Chambers Auditor-general's Office Industrial Arbitration Court Istana Parliament of Singapore Public Service Commission The Cabinet Government courts, including the Supreme Court, State Courts, Family Justice Courts	Yes
Hong Kong				Hong Kong Monetary Authority Executive Council Legislative Council District Councils Government courts: Court of Final Appeal, the High Court (which includes the Court of Appeal and the Court of First Instance), the Competition Tribunal, the District Court (which includes the Family Court), the Lands Tribunal, the Magistrates' Courts (which include the Juvenile Court), the Coroner's Court, the Labour Tribunal, the Small Claims Tribunal, and the Obscene Articles Tribunal	Yes

Singapore	Ministries	Established by law, specifically, the Constitution of Singapore	Fully funded by government	MCI MCCY MINDEF MOE MOF MFA MOH MHA MinLaw MOM MND MSF MEWR MTI MOT PMO	Yes
Hong Kong	Policy Bureau	Recognised under Basic Law but established by an executive order or decision		Civil Service Bureau Constitutional and Mainland Affairs Bureau Education Bureau Environment Bureau Food and Health Bureau Home Affairs Bureau Labour and Welfare Bureau Security Bureau Transport and Housing Bureau Commerce and Economic Development Bureau Development Bureau Financial Services and the Treasury Bureau Innovation and Technology Bureau	Yes

(*continued*)

Table 2.6 (continued)

	Type of entity	*Legal foundation*	*Funding source(s)*	*Examples*	*Revenues and expenditures included in official budget?*
Singapore	Statutory Boards	Semi-autonomous bodies and do not enjoy legal privileges and immunities of government ministries. But was created by an Act of Parliament, execute policies of Ministries and subject to financial audit by Auditor-General	Mostly fully funded by government. Some engage in commercial transactions and thus generate revenue	HDB JTC ESG HPB CAAS HSA EMA CCCS	No
Hong Kong	Government Department	Recognised under Basic Law but established by an executive order or decision	Mostly fully funded by government. Some departments providing commercial services may operate as Trading Funds	Civil Aviation Department Home Affairs Department Environmental Protection Department Innovation and Technology Commission Marine Department The Post Office operates as a Trading Fund	Yes

Source: Government directory of both countries, with the conceptual framework enhanced based on work by Scott (2010)

government finance in Singapore (see Low, 1991, p. 48; Toh & Low, 1990, ch. 4; Asher et al., 2016). Despite the importance of these statutory boards and sovereign wealth funds (funded mostly through past fiscal surpluses), they are considered part of the "public sector" rather than the core "government sector" which means their activities are excluded from the budget. The scholars Mukul Asher et al. (2016, p. 116) express in their analysis of Singapore's fiscal management that "the role of the broader public sector in Singapore's economic management is much larger than what is reflected in the government budget and accompanying documents". This translates into an under-reported government size in the IMF finance statistics which are used by the EFW rankings.

I correct this by examining the financial statements of statutory boards in Singapore since 1995 till the present day, including these omitted numbers for a more complete analysis of the public sector's true scope. This builds on the previous effort by the local Singapore economist Linda Low who has to date produced the most comprehensive study of the size of Singapore's government. She found that in the year 1990 alone, the operating surplus of 10 major statutory boards was $2.7 billion, which together with 3.2% of the government sector, accounted for 9.4% of the country's GDP, measured by government budget surplus. A total of 65,100 people was employed in statutory boards in 1990 alone, more than the 63,000 in the public service, making the true employment of government more than double (Low, 1991). It was also noted that "the less tangible measurements of government intervention in markets such as for non-priced or subsidised social goods and services produced by statutory boards, the labour market and financial market are not captured in the above measures" (Low, 1991, p. 49).

Our approach, building on previous work, has involved collecting 449 financial statements from 25 statutory boards over 25 years from the financial years 1994 to 2018. As of 2020, there are 65 statutory boards in operation, and compiling the statements of all these entities over a 25-year period would require looking at 1625 documents, which is logistically unfeasible. The author has instead focused on major entities which have been subject to a previous study done by Linda Low, which stopped in the year 1993.

Correcting the Omission

To understand the impact of statutory boards, we may compare public finance statistics before and after statutory boards are included. Current IMF government finance statistics tabulate the size of government in both countries as follows. It appears that Singapore's government spends a smaller portion of its GDP than Hong Kong. From Table 2.7, Singapore's government expenditure (1) is a smaller proportion of GDP (2) as compared to Hong Kong over a similar period since 2002.

However, these statistics are misleading since statutory boards, a vital component of the Singaporean developmental state, are omitted. This author has collated revenue and expenditure data of major statutory boards in Singapore since 1995 to fill the gap, yielding column 3. The new results show a much higher government expenditure as a percentage of GDP in Singapore once statutory boards are included. The gap [compare (3) and (2) in Table 2.7] has closed drastically.

Table 2.7 Summary comparison of government expenditure as % of GDP

Year	*Singapore government expenditure as % of GDP (1)*	*Hong Kong government expenditure as % of GDP (2)*	*New Singapore government expenditure as % of GDP, once statutory boards are included (3)*
1994			
1995	11.93		22.2
1996	16.16		23.8
1997	13.63		27.6
1998	15.72		25.7
1999	14.77		25.1
2000	15.72		20
2001	18.17		23.4
2002	16.15	20.97	23
2003	15.94	21.24	20.2
2004	14.39	19.26	18.4
2005	12.59	19.65	17.8
2006	13.06	16.25	15.5
2007	12.15	15.94	15.6
2008	14.5	18.52	15.5
2009	14.3	18.81	17.1
2010	12.41	19.09	15.9
2011	12.77	19.09	15.9
2012	12.38	19.15	17
2013	12.38	19.92	17.1
2014	13.15	18.32	16.8
2015	15.93	19.1	17
2016	14.49	19.04	19.8
2017	14.51	18.38	17.7
2018	15.2	19.0	17.2

Source: IMF Government Finance Statistics (2020), and author's own calculation for column 3

Another way to compare the size of government is to compare government expenditure per capita. Once this is considered, we realise that Singapore's government spends more per citizen than Hong Kong's. This was already true from 2003 as shown in column 3 in Table 2.8, a difference which has increased over time. Once the expenditures of statutory boards are considered (based on the new dataset generated), it becomes clear that in recent years, Singapore's government spends about twice as much per citizen than Hong Kong's, for example, 217% in 2017 (Table 2.8).

Significance of the Omission

There were other significant findings made from this exercise of including statutory boards. Overall, it was found that over the 24-year period, an average of SGD 14,167 million in expenditure and SGD 8555 million in revenue per year are unaccounted for, equivalent to approximately 43.01% and 17.43% of the annual budget, respectively, and approximately 6.16% and 3.70% of annual GDP, respectively (see columns 9 and 10 in Appendix 4).

The omission of statutory boards is not insignificant. Rather than simply nit-picking, I believe that once they are included in official calculations, the IMF Government Finance statistics above would be rendered highly inaccurate. This is largely because most policymaking in Singapore is done within these statutory boards and specific statutory boards wield a large influence over economic activity. This sharply contrasts with the more traditional structure of Hong Kong civil service.

As of February 2019, there were 64 listed statutory boards in Singapore reporting to the respective 16 ministries that oversee them. This can be illustrated by mapping the organisational hierarchy of just one government ministry, the Ministry of National Development, which oversees six statutory boards (Fig. 2.6).

This peculiar structure of the executive branch of Singapore's government contrasts with that of Hong Kong. As of March 2019, there were 13 policy bureaus, which are equivalent to the ministries in Singapore and 56 departments and agencies distributed under each bureau. The key distinction here is that the staff strength and annual budgets of the 56 departments are included in the official service and are not omitted from the budget the way Singapore statutory boards are (Fig. 2.7).

Table 2.8 Comparison of government expenditure per capita in Hong Kong and Singapore

	Hong Kong	*Singapore*			
	Government expenditure per capita (in ID) (1)	*Government expenditure per capita (excl. adjustments for stat boards) (in ID) (2)*	*Percentage of Hong Kong's government expenditure per capita (in ID)* *(3) = (2) / (1) × 100%*	*Government expenditure per capita (incl. adjustments for stat boards) (in ID)* *(4)*	*Percentage of Hong Kong's government expenditure per capita (in ID)* *(5) = (4) / (1) × 100%*
1995		3980.21		7736.53	
1996		5672.44		9625.21	
1997		5094.00		9473.64	
1998		5620.43		10380.05	
1999		5614.39		9929.69	
2000		6547.88		10090.93	
2001		7451.77		10395.88	
2002	7406.155883	6925.81	93.51%	9916.62	133.90%
2003	7353.979027	7386.30	100.44%	9821.54	133.55%
2004	6892.14314	7428.52	107.78%	9430.03	136.82%
2005	7411.318736	7024.48	94.78%	9298.76	125.47%
2006	6458.756582	7934.73	122.85%	10,487.87	162.38%
2007	6909.22809	7924.74	114.70%	10,255.53	148.43%
2008	7990.551387	9320.55	116.64%	12,064.64	150.99%
2009	7601.252797	8987.98	118.24%	11,063.94	145.55%
2010	7010.769828	8882.63	126.70%	10,728.72	153.03%
2011	7663.827989	9716.29	126.78%	12,905.32	168.39%

2012	7633.088695	9780.68	128.14%	13,066.90	171.19%
2013	7968.317295	10,257.93	128.73%	14,097.59	176.92%
2014	7274.882239	11,391.42	156.59%	15,735.41	216.30%
2015	7551.220467	14,166.87	187.61%	18,235.93	241.50%
2016	7754.725441	13,233.00	170.64%	17,302.77	223.13%
2017	8279.95553	13,984.79	168.90%	18,015.91	217.58%
2018		15,418.51		19,487.83	

Source: Author's calculations based on new dataset generated

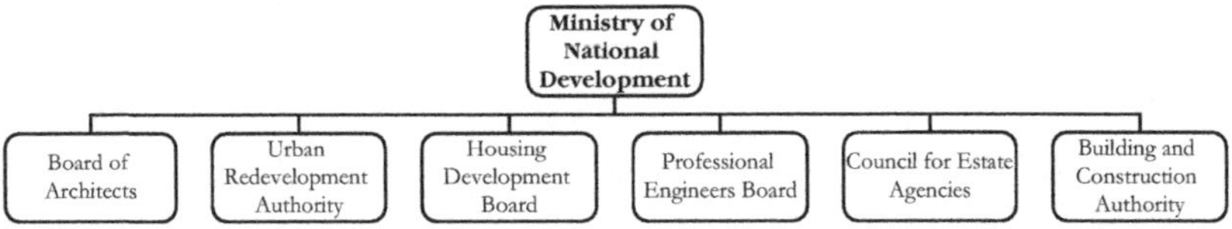

Fig. 2.6 Organisational Chart of Statutory Boards under the Ministry of National Development of Singapore, 2019. (Source: Singapore Government Directory)

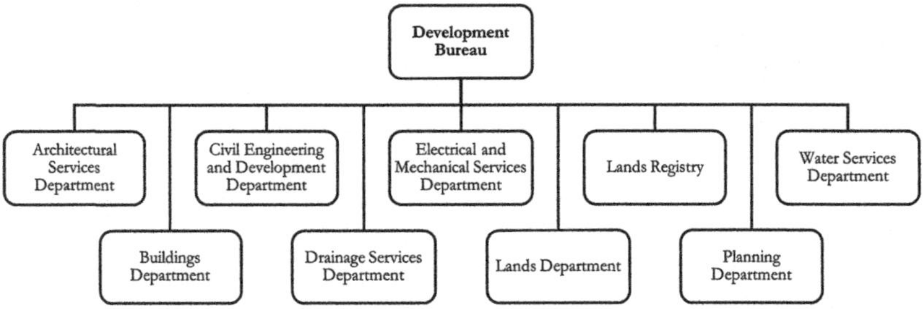

Fig. 2.7 Organisational Chart of Departments under the Development Bureau of Hong Kong, 2019. (Source: Hong Kong Government Directory)

In the year 2019 alone, the total combined budget of the six statutory boards and staff strength eclipsed that of the parent ministry. The numbers are shown in Table 2.9.

This omission is replicated throughout all the other 15 ministries, each of which oversees statutory boards. Clearly, the true size of Singapore's government is severely underestimated because one-half is omitted simply due to institutional peculiarities. Not only is the size of government underestimated, but it should also be noted that specific statutory boards have an outsized influence over the economy which cannot be fully quantified. The Housing Development Board (HDB) is especially important, because it manages the construction, financing, and operations of government housing, which houses nearly 80% of Singaporeans (Phang, 2001). Additionally, land as a factor of production in Singapore is approximately 95% owned by the state and is managed by the Urban Redevelopment Authority (URA). This agency alone, regardless of its size and annual operating revenue, wields an outsized influence over the economy.

Table 2.9 Operating revenues of Statutory Boards under the Ministry of National Development (MND) compared with MND for FY2018

Name of organisation	*Annual budget*		*Staff*
	Revenue (SGD)	*Expenditure (SGD)*	
Ministry of National Development	NA	4149 million	404
Urban Redevelopment Authority	254 million	210 million	883
Housing Development Board	2632 million	10,314 million	5618
Council for Estate Agencies	10 million	10 million	92
Professional Engineers Board	1 million	1 million	16
Building and Construction Authority	210 million	196 million	1037
Agri-Food and Veterinary Authority	187 million	188 million	899
National Parks Board	24 million	307 million	1009

Source: Various departments' annual reports and financial statements (Ministry of Finance, Singapore, 2019)

For URA, staff strength is an estimate obtained from the 2007 Annual Report since these numbers are not annually available. For PEB, it is the size of the board. Annual reports obtained from Ministry of National Development, URA, AVA, and NParks

Once statutory boards are included, a better picture of the Singapore state's actual size can be gleaned. Including statutory boards shows that the number of public sector employees as a percentage of total employment is much higher than conventional statistics show and that government revenue, expenditure, and consumption as a percentage of GDP is also higher than what has been previously reported. Consequently, this means that there is severe under-reporting of the gap in size of both countries' state sectors.

Conclusion

As clarification, I do not claim that both cities are akin to Soviet-style central planning. Indeed, market forces exist and are used heavily in policy-making in capitalist Hong Kong and Singapore. Nevertheless, state-market arrangements vary greatly within the umbrella of capitalism, a fact long recognised by the Varieties of Capitalism literature in comparative politics (see Feldmann, 2019). The in-depth analysis of contextual factors in this chapter reveals that considerable interventions exist in Hong Kong and Singapore, especially when the distinction between factor and product markets is recognised. Once the peculiar features of the Singapore developmental state are considered, the differences in state-market relations between both nations become stark.

References

Aleshire, I. (1986, October 18). Land Acquisition Act to be amended, says ministry. *The Straits Times.*

Amsden, A. (1994). Why isn't the whole world experimenting with the East Asian Model? *World Development, 22*(4), 627–633.

Asher, M., Bali, A. S., & Chang, Y. K. (2016). Public financial management in Singapore: Key characteristics and prospects. In L. Lim (Ed.), *Singapore's economic development: retrospection and reflections* (pp. 113–133). World Scientific.

Auty, R. (1997). Natural resource endowment, the state and development strategy. *Journal of International Development, 9*(4), 651–663.

Bauer, P. (1969). Dissent on development. *Scottish Journal of Political Economy, 16*(3), 75–94.

Bellows, T. J. (1970). *The people's action party of Singapore: Emergence of a dominant party system.* Yale University Press.

Brightsparks. (2018). *BrightSparks Scholarship and Higher Education Survey.* Retrieved from Brightsparks Portal: https://brightsparks.com.sg/files/BSPExtractreport2018.pdf

Capitaland Mall Trust. (2010–2019). *Annual Report.* Retrieved from Capitaland Mall Trust: https://cmt.listedcompany.com/ar.html

Chang, H.-J., Andreoni, A., & Kuan, M. L. (2013). *International industrial policy experiences and the lessons for the UK.* Government Office for Science.

Chao, K., & Lai, B. (1997). *Labour relations and law: Theories, cases and labour-management issues in Hong Kong.* Open Learning Institute Press.

Cheung, S. (1979). Rent control and housing reconstruction: The postwar experience of prewar premises in Hong Kong. *The Journal of Law and Economics, 22*(1), 27–53.

Chia, N.-C. (2016). *Singapore Chronicles—Central Provident Fund (CPF).* Straits Times Press.

Chia, Y.-T. (2015). *Education, culture and the Singapore developmental state.* Palgrave Macmillan.

Chua, B. H. (2017). *Liberalism disavowed: Communitarianism and state capitalism in Singapore.* Cornell University Press.

Consumer Council. (1994). *An evaluaion of the banking policies and practices in Hong Kong–Focusing on their impacts on consumers.* Government Printer. Consumer Council.

Consumer Council. (1996a). *Competition policy: The key to Hong Kong's future success.* Hong Kong Consumer Council.

Consumer Council. (1996b). *How competitive is the private residential property market?* Hong Kong Consumer Council.

DBS Bank. (2018). *The 50 Years.* Retrieved March 30, 2019, from https://www.dbs.com/livemore/uploads/DBS-The-50-years.pdf

Easterly, W. (2013). *The Tyranny of Experts.* Basic Books.

Economic Development Board, Singapore. (1968). *Annual report 1967.* Economic Development Board, Singapore.

Enterprise Singapore. (2018, August 17). *Loans & Insurance.* Retrieved March 30, 2019, from Enterprise Singapore: https://www.enterprisesg.gov.sg/financial-assistance/loans-and-insurance#loans%2D%2Dinsurance

Feldmann, M. (2019). Global varieties of capitalism. *World politics, 71*(1), 162–196.

Fortune. (2002). *Who needs Hong Kong?* Fortune Magazine.

Foucault, M. (2000). *Power. Essential works of Foucault, 1954–1984.* New Press.

Fraser Institute. (2020). *Economic Freedom of the World Report.* Retrieved from Fraser Institute: https://www.fraserinstitute.org/studies/economic-freedom

Friedman, M. (1980). Free To Choose: The Original 1980 TV Series. *Free to Choose Network.* Available at: https://www.freetochoosenetwork.org/programs/free_to_choose/index_80.php

Friedman, M. (1991). *Economic freedom, human freedom, political freedom.* Smith Center for Private Enteprise Studies.

Fuller, D. (2010). *Innovation policy and the limits of laissez-faire: Hong Kong's policy in comparative perspective.* Springer.

Gartze, E. (2005). *Chapter 2: Economic freedom and peace.* Retrieved from Economic Freedom of the World: 2005 Annual Report: http://www.columbia.akadns.net/itc/journalism/stille/Politics%20Fall%202007/readings%20weeks%206-7/Economic%20Freedom%20and%20Peace%20%2D%2D%20Garzke.pdf

Goodstadt, L. (2005). *Uneasy partners: The conflict between public interest and private profit in Hong Kong.* Hong Kong University Press.

Gramsci, A. (1971). *Selections from the prison notebooks.* International Publishers.

Gwartney, J., Holcombe, R., & Lawson, R. (1999). Economic freedom and the environment for economic growth. *Journal of Institutional and Theoretical Economics, 155*(4), 1–21.

Haggard, S. (2018). *Developmental states.* Cambridge University Press.

Haila, A. (2000). Real estate in global cities: Singapore and Hong Kong as property states. *Urban Studies, 37*(12), 2241–2256.

Haila, A. (2015). *Urban land rent: Singapore as a property state.* John Wiley & Sons.

Hanke, S. (2016). *Doing business: Singapore style.* Retrieved from Institute for Economic Affairs: https://iea.org.uk/wp-content/uploads/2016/08/EA-Spring-2014-perspective-SMALL_0.pdf

Hanke, S. (2019a, November 29). *Steve Hanke's Twitter.* Retrieved from Twitter: https://twitter.com/steve_hanke/status/1200460194272202759?lang=en

Hanke, S. (2019b, April 20). *The Singapore strategy for Zimbabwe.* Retrieved from African Liberty: https://www.africanliberty.org/2019/04/20/the-singapore-strategy-for-zimbabwe/

Hanke, S. (2020a, January 24). *Paraguay should adopt Singapore strategy*. Retrieved from Eurasia Review: https://www.eurasiareview.com/24012020-prof-steve-hanke-paraguay-should-adopt-singapore-strategy-interview/
Hanke, S. (2020b, March 16). *An Interview on Albania with Prof. Steve H. Hanke*. Retrieved from Institute of World Politics: https://www.iwp.edu/articles/2020/03/16/an-interview-on-albania-with-prof-dr-steve-h-hanke/
Hanke, S., & Walters, S. (1997). Economic freedom, prosperity and equality. *CATO Journal, 17*(2), 117–146.
Hannan, D. (2017, February 26). *Daniel Hannan: A Singapore-style economy isn't a threat, it's a growth strategy*. Retrieved from Conservative Home: https://www.conservativehome.com/thecolumnists/2017/02/daniel-hannan-a-singapore-style-economy-isnt-a-threat-its-a-growth-strategy.html
HKSAR. (1935). *Buildings ordinance*. Retrieved from Historical Laws of Hong Kong Online: https://oelawhk.lib.hku.hk/items/show/1877
HKSAR. (1947). *Landlord and tenant (consolidation) ordinance*. Retrieved from Hong Kong e-Legislation: https://www.elegislation.gov.hk/hk/cap7
HKSAR. (1991–2016). *Population censuses*. Retrieved from Census and Statistics Department, HKSAR: https://www.censtatd.gov.hk/hkstat/sub/so20.jsp
HKSAR. (2018). *Annual statistical report of trade unions in Hong Kong*. Retrieved from Labour Department of HKSAR: https://www.labour.gov.hk/eng/public//content2_4a.htm
Huang, Y., & Tao, K. (2010). Factor market distortion and the current account surplus in China. *Asian Economic Papers, 9*(3), 1–36.
Hwang-Wong, J. (1990). *The Lee Hsien Loong report and the Singapore economy*. Murdoch University.
International Monetary Fund. (2020). *Government finance statistics*. Retrieved from International Monetary Fund: https://data.imf.org/?sk=a0867067-d23c-4ebc-ad23-d3b015045405
Jao, Y. C. (1974). *Banking and currency in Hong Kong*. Macmillan.
Keppel REIT. (2010–2019). *Annual report*. Retrieved from Keppel REIT: https://www.keppelreit.com/investor-relations/publications/
Kim, K., & Phang, S. (2013). *Singapore's housing policies: 1960–2013* (pp. 123–153). *Frontiers in Development Policy*.
Koninck, R. (1992). *Singapore: An atlas of the revolution of territory*. Groupement.
Lai, L. (1998). *Zoning and property rights: A Hong Kong case study*. Hong Kong University Press.
Lai, L. (2000). *Town planning practice: Context, procedures and statistics for Hong Kong*. Hong Kong University Press.
Leung, G. L. (2018). *Innovative and creative industries in Hong Kong*. Routledge.
Lim, L. (1983a). Singapore's success: The myth of the market. *Asian Survey, 18*, 73–94.

Lim, L. (2017). Beyond the 'Global City' paradigm. In L. Lim (Ed.), *Business, government and labor: Essays on economic development in Singapore and Southeast Asia* (pp. 105–136). World Scientific.
Lim, L. (2018). Singapore's success: After the miracle. In L. Lim (Ed.), *Business, government and labor: Essays on economic development in Singapore and Southeast Asia* (pp. 69–104). World Scientific.
Lim, L., & Pang, E. F. (2016). Labor, productivity and Singapore's development model. In L. Lim (Ed.), *Singapore's economic development: Retrospection and reflections* (pp. 135–168). Singapore.
Low, L. (1991). *The political economy of privatisation in Singapore.* McGraw-Hill Publishers.
Low, L. (2001). The Singapore developmental state in the new economy and polity. *Pacific Review, 14*(3), 411–441.
Lukes, S. (1974). *Power: A radical view.* Macmillan.
Mapletree Commercial Trust. (2012–2019). *Annual Report.* Retrieved from Publications: https://www.mapletreecommercialtrust.com/Investor-Relations/Publications/Annual-Reports.aspx
Ministry of Finance, Singapore. (2019). *Ministry of National Development Annual Budget.* Retrieved from Singapore Budget 2019: https://www.singaporebudget.gov.sg/docs/default-source/budget_2019/download/pdf/45-MND-2019.pdf
Mitchell, D. (2017, July 17). *The recipe for Singapore's prosperity.* Retrieved from Cato Institute: The Recipe for Singapore's Prosperity
Muller, J. (2018). *The Tyranny of Metrics.* Princeton University Press.
Ng, S.-H., & Sit, V.F.-S. (1989). *Labour relations and labour conditions in Hong Kong.* Basingstoke, England: Macmillan.
Ortmann, S., & Thompson, M. (2020). *China's 'Singapore Model' and authoritarian learning.* Routledge.
Oun, H. L. (2018). *Industrial relations in Singapore.* World Scientific.
Ow, C. H. (1976). Statutory boards. In N. Truong (Ed.), *The role of public enterprise in national development in southeast Asia: Problems and prospects* (pp. 153–256). Regional Institute of Higher Education and Development.
Panagariya, A. (2019). *Free trade and prosperity: How openness helps the developing countries grow richer and combat poverty.* Oxford University Press.
Perry, J. L., & Rainey, H. G. (1988). The public-private distinction in organization theory: A critique and research strategy. *Academy of Management Review, 13*(2), 182–201.
Phang, S. (2001). Housing policy, wealth formation and the Singapore economy. *Housing Studies, 16*(14), 443–459.
Pillai, P. (1983). *State enterprises in Singapore: Legal importation and development.* Singapore University Press.

Quah, J. (2010). *Public administration Singapore-style*. Emerald Group Publishing Limited.

Rabushka, A. (1979). *Hong Kong: A study in economic freedom*. The University of Chicago.

Rigg, J. (1988). Singapore and the recession of 1985. *Asian Survey, 28*(3), 340–352.

Rodan, G. (2016). *The political economy of Singapore's industrialization: National state and international capital*. Springer.

Ross, M. (1999). The political economy of the resource curse. *World Politics, 51*(2), 297–322.

Russell, H. M., Tervo, W., Ariail, D. L., & Smith, L. M. (2020). Relationship of economic freedom to economic performance, gender equality, and social progress. *World Economics, 21*(4), 171–190.

Sally, R. (2013). Asia's story of growing economic freedom. *Cato Policy Analysis, 725*, 1–12.

Sally, R. (2015). The halting progress of capitalism in Asia. *Quadrant Magazine*, pp. 31–38.

Schiffer, J. (1991). State policy and economic growth: A note on the Hong Kong Model. *International Journal of Urban and Regional Research, 15*(2), 180–196.

Scott, I. (2010). *The public sector in Hong Kong*. Hong Kong University Press.

Smart, A. (1992). *Making room: Squatter clearance in Hong Kong*. Centre of Asian Studies.

Tan, C. H. (1976). *Measures to improve the transport system in Singapore*. Focus on Transportation.

Tan, M. (2014, June 3). *Retailers' woes go beyond Reits*. Retrieved March 30, 2019, from Straits Times: https://www.straitstimes.com/opinion/retailers-woes-go-beyond-reits

Tan, S. T., Leong, F. L., Chan, B. A., Tan, C. M., & Tan, D. H. (2009). *Economics in public policies—The Singapore story*. Marshall Cavendish.

Tay, K. (2015, April 20). *Game-changing plan to create new specialities, jobs*. Retrieved from Business Times: https://www.businesstimes.com.sg/government-economy/skillsfuture/game-changing-plan-to-create-new-specialities-jobs

Today Online. (2015, March 23). *Policies for the bedroom and beyond*. Retrieved from Today Online: https://www.todayonline.com/rememberinglky/policies-bedroom-and-beyond

Toh, M. H., & Low, L. (1990). *An economic framework of Singapore: Principles and issues*. McGraw-Hill.

Tremewan, C. (1994). *The political economy of social control in Singapore*. Martin's Press.

Tupy, M. (2015, November 24). *Singapore: The power of economic freedom*. Retrieved from Cato Institute: https://www.cato.org/blog/singapore-power-economic-freedom

Tupy, M. (2017, June 30). *What the rest of the world can learn from Hong Kong*. Retrieved from Human Progress: https://www.humanprogress.org/what-the-rest-of-the-world-can-learn-from-hong-kong/

Turner, H. (1980). *The last colony, but whose?: A study of the labour movement, labour market and labour relations in Hong Kong*. Cambridge University Press.

Wade, R. (2005). Bringing the state back in: Lessons from East Asia's development experience. *Internationale Politik und Gesellschaft, 8*(2), 98–115.

Wilkinson, B. (1988). Social engineering in Singapore. *Journal of Contemporary Asia, 18*(2), 165–188.

Wong, A., & Yeh, S. (1985). *Housing a nation: 25 years of public housing in Singapore*. Maruzen Asia.

Wong, R. Y. (1998). *On privatising public housing*. Hong Kong University Press.

Wong, R. Y. (2015). *Hong Kong land for Hong Kong people—Fixing the failures of our housing policy*. Hong Kong University Press.

Wood, J., & Herzog, I. (2014). *Economic freedom and air quality*. Fraser Institute.

Yeh, A. (1993). *Urban planning under a leasehold system*. Center of Urban Planning and Environmental Management, University of Hong Kong.

Yeung, Y.-m. (1973). *National development policy and urban transformation in Singapore: A study of public housing and the marketing system*. University of Chicago Press.

CHAPTER 3

State Capitalism vs. Entrepreneurial Capitalism

Competition in Market Economies

Competition is an important pillar of any market economy. Market economies run not just on private property ownership but require substantial competition between economic agents. An economy based on private property but suffering from stifled competition is nonetheless rife with private monopoly power, precluding market gains such as increased quality, variety, and reduced prices. Of course, competition does not necessarily imply the presence of numerous buyers and sellers as per the notion of perfect competition outlined in the neoclassical model of economics. However, it does mean that entrepreneurs generally have the freedom to compete in the absence of special privileges or policies that favour one group at the expense of another.

Consequently, the role that entrepreneurs play within the competitive market process is especially important (Kirzner 1973; Schumpeter 2009). A healthy market economy is one where a large degree of freedom is given to them, as opposed to one where their operations are hampered. The importance of entrepreneurs is in turn connected to the dynamics between firms. If large corporations or government enterprises dominate the economy, this could crowd out entrepreneurial activity, especially that carried out by small firms. It is with this understanding that the political

B. Cheang, *Economic Liberalism and the Developmental State*, https://doi.org/10.1007/978-3-031-08100-2_3

economists Baumol et al. (2007) classified economies as whether they resemble entrepreneurial capitalism, big-firm capitalism, oligarchic or state-guided capitalism.

This chapter specifically analyses the dynamics of competition in the two city-states of Hong Kong and Singapore, showing that there are significant barriers in both economies—more so in Singapore—that stifle market competition. Specifically, Hong Kong's economy can be largely described as an entrepreneurial form of capitalism, while, in Singapore, the hybrid big-firm/state-guided form of capitalism has dominated the economy at the expense of smaller indigenous firms. This distinction is one that has not been adequately captured in aggregate economic freedom indices and which therefore merits a closer investigation of the economic facts on the ground.

Economists have looked at the dynamics of competition in the context of Hong Kong and Singapore before. On one hand, some have pointed out the severity of market concentration in Hong Kong due to the presence of large property developers and "tycoons" in the real estate market (Williams, 2009). In the Singapore case, it has also been shown that there are state entities that dominate the market, such as sovereign wealth funds and GLCs. I build on these existing studies in two ways. First, I show that the reason why competition may have been hampered in both countries is not due to any inherent feature of the market process but rather due to problems of the state. This is applied specifically to the Hong Kong context, to show that the problem of large real estate developers dominating the market can be traced to institutional factors within the Hong Kong state which has afforded these entities outsized power. Second, I also show that *on balance*, despite the presence of market concentration in the real estate sector in Hong Kong, SMEs still play a larger role *in the wider economy* than in Singapore and contribute more to the total value-added. SMEs in Singapore have been crowded out due to the presence of GLCs and foreign MNCs (see Lim, 2016, 2017, ch. 4). Despite SMEs being afforded proactive help by the Singaporean developmental state, they have not managed to significantly contribute much to the total economy as compared to larger companies.

Taken together, this chapter provides further evidence to doubt the conventional wisdom that both countries are beacons of economic freedom. While aggregate indices have managed to show that on net, economic freedom contributes to various aspects of human welfare, it may comparatively be unable to shed light on the microeconomic properties of specific markets. The case study conducted here advances understanding by disaggregating the Hong Kong and Singapore economies and examining the *structural composition* of their markets.

Path Dependence and the Pattern of Market Competition

The dynamics of market competition in Hong Kong and Singapore can be traced to several key historical developments. While both city-states experienced a rather similar economic trajectory during the colonial era, a major divergence occurred in the immediate post-WWII period, which saw Singapore achieve sovereignty and Hong Kong remaining under colonial rule. Developments during this period established a precedent for large foreign MNCs and GLCs to dominate the local market in Singapore, which crowded out SMEs and micro-enterprises. In fact, a previous study on SMEs in Singapore declares that "the role and development of SMEs in Singapore cannot be fully understood without referral to the pervasive influence of government in the country and the crucial role it plays in setting directions, marshalling resources, and coordinating the overall strategy of the different players in the economy" (Lee & Tan 2002).

This sharply contrasts with the case of Hong Kong which never had a deliberate strategy during the colonial era of favouring firms of certain sizes or industries. Admittedly, Hong Kong's government has also intervened in the economy through industrial grants. However, it has never occurred on the same scale as in Singapore, which pursued industrial planning in a concerted rather than ad hoc manner. This difference in policy choice has led to clear differences in market competition dynamics in both city-states.

Policy Choices Made in the 1960s Had a Path-Dependent Effect

The pattern of market competition seen today can be traced to deliberate policy choices adopted in the post-WWII 1960s during which both city-states pursued economic growth. The main contrast was that the Singaporean developmental state, due to its very nature of utilising industrial planning and state investments, penetrated the local economy to execute its centrally designed plans, while the Hong Kong government allowed entrepreneurship to evolve organically. This is best seen in the sudden influx of Chinese immigrants to Hong Kong which changed the industrial structure of the economy, in contrast to the deliberate clamp-down on SMEs in Singapore.

Singapore

In Singapore during the 1960s, the Singapore government decided to pursue its state-led industrialisation policy which involved attracting foreign MNCs. These firms were deemed necessary to jumpstart industrialisation owing to the lack of local capital and industrial capacity. This not only involved favourable conditions granted to multinational corporations, but a deliberate government attempt to undermine the local business community in Singapore, then dominated by SMEs led by Chinese entrepreneurs.

This is substantiated by the fact that the traditional Chinese elites from the Singapore Chinese Chamber of Commerce were marginalised in the early 1960s, at the same time as the developmental state was being established. These elites represented leading businesses of the time within the laissez-faire, colonial entrepôt economy, which was precisely what the new developmental state had wished to abolish. The choice of industrialisation meant that the commercial sector had to be deprioritised. This is clearly seen in the way the Chinese Chamber heavily engaged in lobbying to petition the government to not entirely side-line commerce in favour of industry (The Straits Times, 1960).

This deprioritisation was not just a matter of economic policy but was also political. The developmental state elites were mainly educated in Western universities and saw themselves as a technocratic elite who would transform Singaporean society. This confidence in their own ability to conduct central economic planning stemmed from their "high level of formal education with more specifically, extensive training in economics" (Huff, 1994, p. 359). Alternative power bases were an impediment to be removed. Thus, the traditional Chinese elites, the leading power base then, were a political rival. Unsurprisingly, the government aimed to abolish Chinese clan societies, called *huiguan* (*The Straits Times*, 1959).

Numerous clashes occurred from 1959 to 1966 between the new developmental state elites and traditional Chinese elites which cumulatively saw the Chinese power base "disciplined" and "marginalised politically, socially, culturally and economically" (Visscher, 2002, p. 140). One such instance was the attempted passing of an Income Tax (Amendment) Bill to raise revenue which was indignantly opposed by the Chamber who claimed that these new powers were excessive. Key Chinese leaders were also politically targeted over disputes involving education and language policy, workers' rights, and the merger with Malaysia (see Thum, 2012). For example, the Chamber President Ko Teck Kin, who pleaded with the government to retain focus on trade and commerce rather than on just industry, was publicly humiliated for his stance to defend Chinese as the medium of education in schools. Other prominent Chinese leaders like Soon Peng Yam and Kheng Chin Hock were also chastised for their call for Mandarin to become the national language.

The most revealing incident, however, was the stripping of citizenship of Tan Lark Sye, who was not only a key Chinese community leader but also then one of the wealthiest rubber industrialists. The economic and political logic of the developmental state are intertwined. There was a strong fear amongst the new state elites that the traditional wealth and status of leaders like Tan Lark Sye would become a challenge to their power and would be co-opted by communist insurgents. At the same time, the state elites had perceived the local Chinese businesses as a stubborn obstacle preventing the much-needed industrial restructuring of Singapore. Significantly, the opposition to traditional Chinese business was a conscious personal preference of Lee Kuan Yew himself.[1]

A core feature of the developmental state is its deep penetration into society and the economy. The above actions can be interpreted considering this feature. On the economic level, the SMEs and trade associations dominated by the Chinese elites were marginalised in favour of big GLCs and MNCs. The loss of economic power also meant political marginalisation of these elites. As the developmental state started to establish its own grassroots social organisations in Singaporean society, it also started to marginalise the traditional roles played by Chinese welfare organisations, such as the *bang* and *huiguan* (Bellows, 1993).

Hong Kong

This situation in Singapore contrasts with that in Hong Kong in the same period. In the post-war period, there was a massive influx of immigrants who fled Mainland China who sought to escape Chinese communism, famines, and political upheaval. A significant share of these immigrants

[1] Lee had stated that "the old family business is one of the problems of Singapore. It is not so with European or foreign enterprise", referring to the traditional structures of local Chinese businesses (Josey, 1980).

was from Shanghai who had a track record of industrial experience (Wong S. L., 1988). They brought with them their industrial knowledge, connections, and capital into Hong Kong.

It should be acknowledged that the influx of immigrants was not unprecedented, but there were several key distinguishing factors of the immediate post-war immigration to Hong Kong. Many of these immigrants were upper-class Chinese capitalists with considerable business pedigree as opposed to the poor immigrants as seen more typically throughout Hong Kong's history. Also, the Shanghainese immigrants were a "new type of Chinese people who could speak and write English fluently and were familiar with Western culture" which made them attractive partners of colonial administrators and businesses in Hong Kong (Goodstadt, 2005, p. 10). Additionally, Wong Siu-Lun's extensive interviews (1984) with Shanghai industrialists detected a self-selection effect, such that the most resourceful and resilient of them were the ones who eventually settled in Hong Kong, further contributing to their dominance in local business life.

Coupled with the considerable industrial capital brought in, these new immigrants were responsible for contributing to Hong Kong's post-war economic take-off. What is significant is that this period of industrialisation which saw the rise of manufacturing, textiles, and consumer electronics industries in Hong Kong was achieved not through state initiatives as in Singapore but through the unexpected shifts in demographics caused by immigration.

Hence, in the post-war critical juncture, there was a policy precedent in both city-states. In Singapore, the patterns of local entrepreneurship were distorted by deliberate government policy which favoured large foreign multinationals and the establishment of GLCs. In contrast, the patterns of local entrepreneurship in Hong Kong experienced dynamic shifts independent of government policymaking. This contrast is further evinced by the vastly different governing philosophy of key policymakers then. Since both had rather elitist governing structures, examining the statements of key political actors would be reflective of the general policy orientation of the times.

Policy Orientation of State Elites in Hong Kong and Singapore in the Post-WWII Period

In Singapore, the developmental state elite believed in the power of technocracy and Western education to centrally direct the economy. By hiring the most intelligent individuals, the elite believed that they could engineer a "socialism that works" (Nair, 1976).

This sharply contrasts with the then colonial governing elite in Hong Kong which saw a highly non-interventionist role for the state. This policy orientation was deeply shaped by the office of the Financial Secretary who was the key person in charge of economic policy. For two decades, 1961 to 1981, there were only two financial secretaries, each serving 10 years: Sir John Cowperthwaite (1961–1971) and Sir Phillip Haddon-Cove (1971–1981).

Since there were only two individuals occupying this position and colonial policymaking was highly elitist and insulated from popular pressure, the personal philosophies of these two individuals cast a long shadow over Hong Kong's subsequent development. The libertarian instincts of Cowperthwaite were so entrenched that he refused to even collect national income statistics, believing they would be used for interventionist purposes (Monnery, 2017). That historical GDP figures have been sorely lacking stems from Cowperthwaite's personal imperatives.

The policy orientation established in the post-war period of the 1960s set the tone for the subsequent development trajectory of both city-states. There are two significant impacts. First, one witnesses the dominance of GLEs in Singapore, contrasting with the dominance of private corporations in the Hong Kong context. Second, the Singaporean developmental state initiated a precedent of engaging in an activist industrial policy which was absent for most of Hong Kong's colonial era. This has led to the state domination of the Singapore economy which has had adverse impacts on the SME sector.

Big Firms in Hong Kong vs. Big State Entities in Singapore

When corporate behemoths dominate the market, smaller players, whether individual entrepreneurs or small-medium enterprises, are crowded out. Such entities dominate both the Singapore and Hong Kong economy. It is said that Hong Kong suffers from a concentration of big property tycoons in the real estate sector, while sovereign wealth funds and GLCs pervade Singapore. I provide evidence here to make two claims. First, the true extent of these state entities in the Singapore economy have been underestimated. This is once again because of the unique structure of Singapore's developmental state framework and the complex ways in which it owns assets through multiple layers of the private economy. Second, I also show that market concentration in Hong Kong have its roots in the structure of the state.

Extensive State Presence in the Singaporean Private Sector

Sovereign Wealth Funds in Singapore

Sovereign wealth funds (SWFs) are characteristic of state capitalism in various countries and are not unique to Singapore (Musacchio & Lazzarini, 2014). There are two main SWFs in Singapore: Temasek Holdings and Government Investment Corporation (GIC). In Singapore, these sovereign wealth funds are largely financed from accumulated budgetary surpluses. They act as venture capitalists and investors, extending the government's reach into the domestic market and even the foreign economies it invests in.

The Government Investment Corporation (GIC) stands out through its lack of official information of its activities. GIC has never disclosed the amount of funds it manages as well as annual profit-loss statements. It has been argued that such revelations would expose the true amount of Singapore's reserves, making speculative attacks on the local currency by overseas parties easier:

> GIC manages the Government's assets. We have publicly stated that it manages well over US$100 billion of assets. However, revealing the exact amount would, taken together with the published assets of MAS and Temasek, expose the full size of Singapore's financial reserves. This is against our national interest. It would make it easier for speculators to attack the Singapore dollar during periods of vulnerability. Further, our reserves are a strategic asset, especially for a small country with no natural resources or other assets. It would be unwise to reveal the exact amount at our disposal for defending our currency, or for use in an emergency. (Ministry of Finance, Singapore, 2019)

Despite this secrecy, some estimates have been made. These estimates number the range of assets managed by GIC as anywhere from US$100 billion to US$390 billion. According to the Sovereign Wealth Fund Institute (2018), this makes GIC amongst the largest SWFs in the world. Combined with Temasek Holdings, the total value of assets managed by both Singaporean SWFs (USD 390 + 375bn) rank as one of the top few in the world.

It may be argued that as a sovereign wealth fund that primarily invests in overseas markets, GIC does not constitute an intervention into the domestic political economy. Superficially, that is true. However, the state remains the central fund manager and dividends are directed towards the public purse, financing education, research, healthcare, the upgrading of infrastructure, etc. The mechanism making this possible is the Net Investment Returns Contribution (NIRC), which was worth S$14.1 billion in the 2017 financial year (FY); the government generally plans to receive 50% of the NIRC at the start of each FY (Ministry of Finance, Singapore, 2019). Collectively, this means that the Singapore state enjoys a substantial source of revenue not collected via taxation. This allows the state to spend at a level far higher than what it can collect in tax revenues. These aspects reiterate the point made in the previous chapter that conventional statistics underestimate the true size of the government budget.

The combined portfolio value of both SWFs in Singapore has grown tremendously since the 1985 privatisation exercise and has since 2004 been larger than the entire size of Singapore's GDP (Table 3.1).

The growth success of Temasek over the years adds further spending power to the public sector. Just like GIC, Temasek's dividends contribute to the government budget. Of note is that Temasek's latest recorded net portfolio value in 2018 was S$308 billion, its highest ever (Temasek Holdings, 2001–2019). This translates into large injections into the state's budget to fund its programmes. In fact, contributions from Temasek's net investment income and net investment returns are "now the largest source for Singapore government spending, at 18% of the 2018 government budget" (Temasek Holdings, 2018, p. 13).

Table 3.1 Size of Temasek Holdings and GIC as compared to Singapore's GDP

	Temasek Holding's portfolio value (S$ in respective years)	*GIC's estimated portfolio value based on SWFI (S$ in respective years)*	*Total portfolio value of both entities*	*Size of portfolio value as percentage of GDP (2019's GDP)*
2004	$90 billion	$507 billion	$597 billion	126%
2010	$186 billion	$507 billion	$693 billion	146%
2017	$275 billion	$507 billion	$782 billion	165%

Source: Annual reports from Temasek Holdings, estimates by the Sovereign Wealth Fund Institute, GDP figures from the International Monetary Fund

GLCs and GLREITs in Singapore

Aside from GIC, Temasek Holdings is a highly influential entity in Singapore, incorporated in 1974 to take over several enterprises the government were already managing. Temasek is not just a SWF, meaning its activities go beyond mere investments. Its investments are mainly in equities, making it either a full or partial owner of many companies and assets. The focus of Temasek is not just global and regional but also domestic. This means that Temasek Holdings is also a holding company through which many Singaporean firms are owned by the state. These firms are called government-linked corporations (GLCs),[2] which have played an important role in Singapore's economic development.

Much has been written about state enterprises and GLCs in Singapore (Ramirez & Ling, 2004; Low, 2002). However, this chapter focuses on the continued prevalence of these entities in the domestic economy *despite* the privatisation exercise of the government in 1985. A recession then prompted the government to review its economic policies, which included a realisation that the domestic private sector had to be given more space to drive development. The then Minister for Trade and Industry, Tony Tan, had declared that "in the 1980s, the engine of development should be the private sector and not the Government" (Tan T., 1985).

The privatisation exercise embarked from 1985 to 1990 led to the divestment of 36 companies. In the only comprehensive review of this exercise thus far, the economist Linda Low concluded that "what has been achieved so far with privatisation appears rather superficial and cosmetic. The government's coffers have been topped up, enabling it to re-arrange its portfolio of companies somewhat at least to meet up with one of its aims of pulling out of industries which the private sector can handle and re-investing in new ones" (Low, 1991). This insight is significant because it suggests that even though privatisation was executed by the Singaporean developmental state, it did not genuinely reduce the size of the state sector and may have in fact allowed it to further consolidate its presence in the domestic political economy.

This section extends Linda Low's analysis by showing that since 1990, there remains an extensive amount of GLCs within the Singapore economy, with the role of Temasek Holdings growing since then, rather than

[2] This is defined as company whereby the government, whether directly or indirectly through its holding company, is the controlling shareholder, which means at least 15% of the voting shares are held, according to the definition by Singapore Exchange.

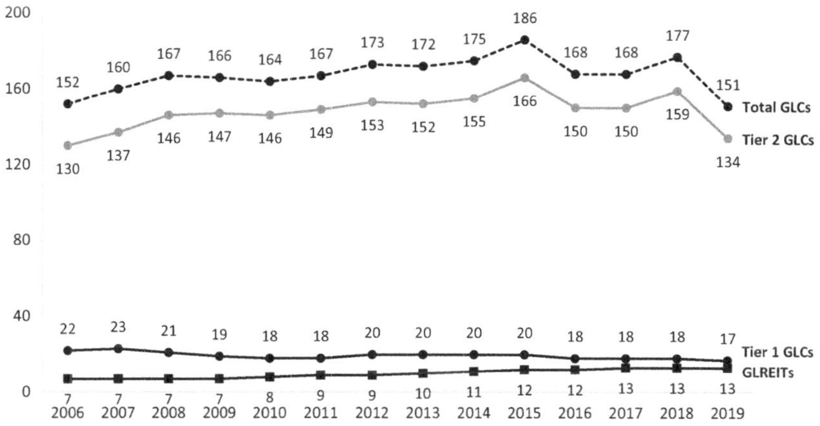

Fig. 3.1 Number of Tier 1 and 2 GLCs and GLREITs over time since 2006. (Source: Temasek Review, 2006–2019 and Annual reports of Tier 1 GLCs)

diminishing. In fact, it has been shown by some scholars that since the 1990s, new GLCs were formed, including some spun off from restructured statutory boards such as the Media Corporation of Singapore, Singapore Petroleum, and Singapore Post (Shome, 2006; Lyons, 2007). Government-Linked Real Estate Investment Trusts (GLREITs) also dominate the real estate sector in Singapore.

Based on this author's own investigations, the number of GLCs and GLREITs have remained constant since the early 2000s, with no significant decrease in this sector. These numbers are derived by analysing the annual reports and public statements of 290 Tier 1 and 2 GLCs and dozens of GLREITs over the period 2006 to 2019, with the full list and notes in Appendices 5 and 6 (Fig. 3.1).

What makes the analysis here even more complicated is that the ownership of firms by Temasek, and thus the government, operates on multiple levels. A Tier 1 GLC is a local company with at least 15% of its shares owned by Temasek Holdings, as stated in the various editions of the Temasek Review. The reality is that these Tier 1 firms may themselves own, whether fully or partially, other firms which are considered Tier 2, 3, 4, etc., depending on the degree of separation from the parent company. For example, DBS Group Holdings Ltd is a Tier 1 GLC, as 29% of its shares is owned by Temasek Holdings. DBS Bank Ltd is a Tier 2 GLC as it is a subsidiary wholly owned by DBS Group Holdings Ltd which is a Tier 1 company (Fig. 3.2). Thus, not only does Temasek Holdings control the major firms as shown in Fig. 3.2, it also indirectly does so through many layers of ownership.

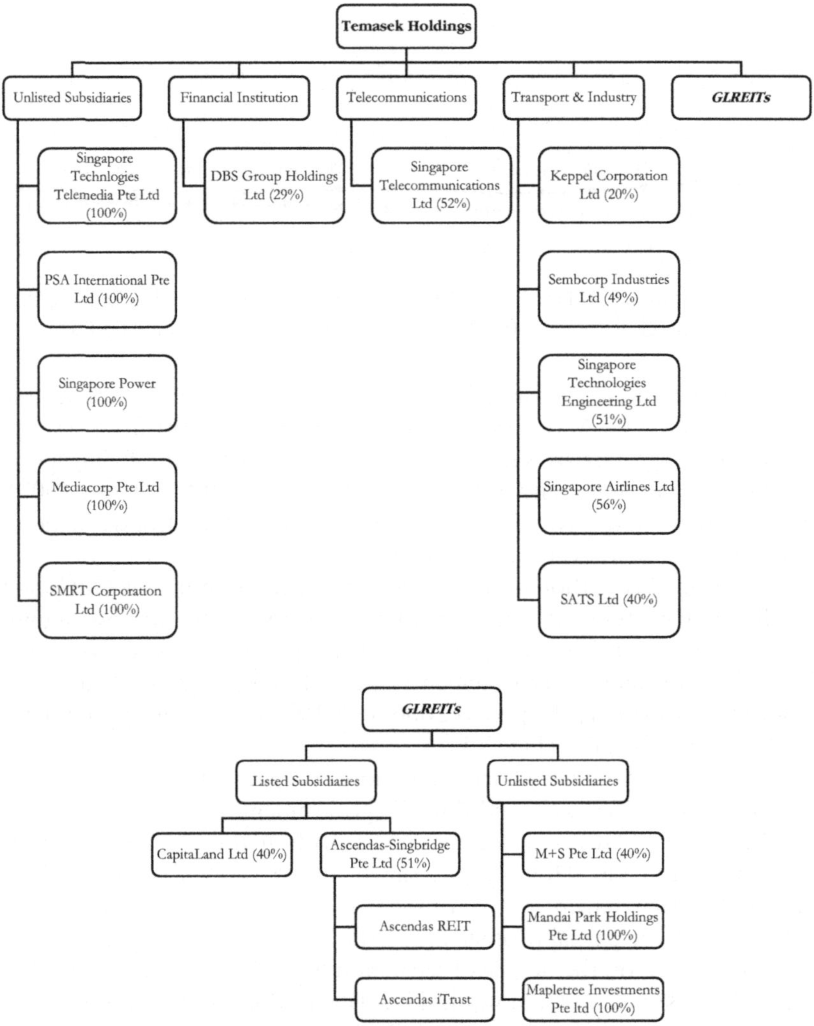

Fig. 3.2 Temasek's multi-layer ownership structure of SGX-Listed GLCs and GLREITs with Ownership Share (FY2018)

Given the impracticality of investigating every single tier of ownership, only Tier 1 and 2 GLCs have been tracked, the analysis from which suggests that the true extent of government ownership in Singapore's economy remains understated.

Another way to measure the dominance of the state sector in Singapore is to look at the percentage share of GLCs and GLREITs as part of the overall stock market capitalisation. In 2006, GLCs initially accounted for 42.23% of the total stock market value excluding the REITs market, with this number slightly decreasing over time to 38.78% in 2019 (Fig. 3.3).

The dominance of the state sector is however made evident when looking at the stock market capitalisation of GLREITs. From 2006 to 2019, GLREITs usually comprise more than 60% of the total stock market capitalisation (REITs market only) (Fig. 3.4).

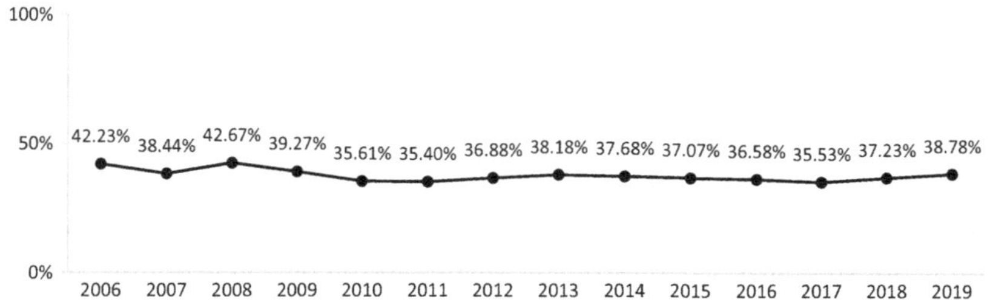

Fig. 3.3 Percentage of Stock Market Value (Stock Market Capitalisation) of SGX-Listed GLCs, excluding REITs. (Source: Bloomberg Stock Market Capitalisation Data)

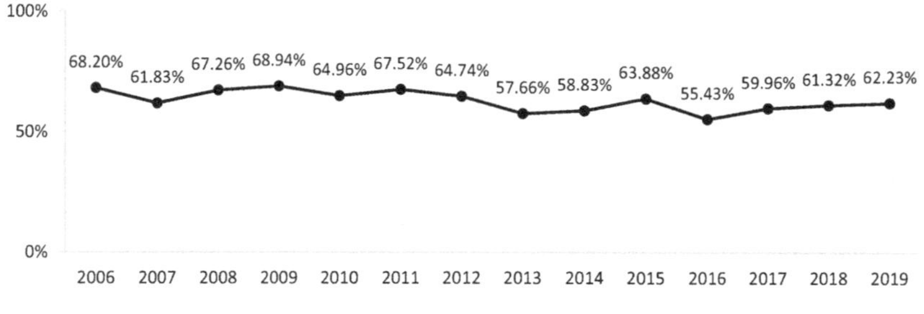

Fig. 3.4 Percentage of Stock Market Value (Stock Market Capitalisation) of SGX-Listed GLREITs. (Source: Bloomberg Stock Market Capitalisation Data)

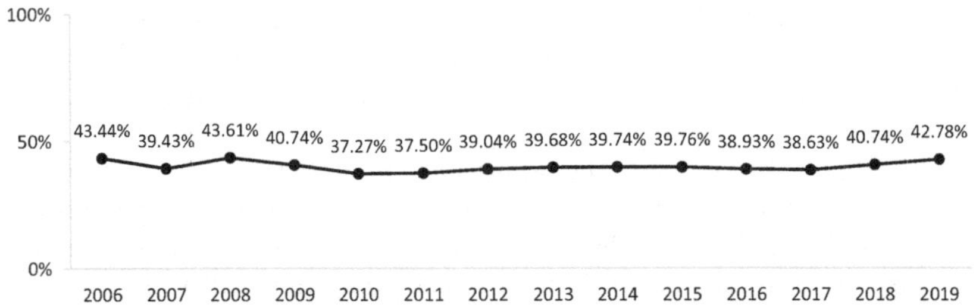

Fig. 3.5 Percentage of Stock Market Value (Stock Market Capitalisation) of All SGX-Listed GLEs (GLCs + GLREITs). (Source: Bloomberg Stock Market Capitalisation Data and author's calculations)

A fuller understanding can be gleaned when adding up the stock market capitalisation of both GLCs and GLREITs. Government-Linked Entities (GLEs), which refer to both GLCs and GLREITs, initially made up 43.44% of the total stock market value in 2006. Since then, this number has remained relatively constant. In 2019, GLEs make up 42.78% of the total stock market value (Fig. 3.5).

Strategic Position of GLCs and GLREITs in Singapore

Not only are government-linked entities extensive in the Singapore economy, but they also occupy strategic sectors in the overall economy, which further multiplies their power and influence.

The first piece of evidence for this claim can be found by examining the list of the top 30 public companies on the Straits Times Index (STI) where all the local companies are government linked (Table 3.2).

It is not only the size of the state that matters but also the exact form of control that it wields. Ownership of the ten largest comic book stands is qualitatively different from that of the ten largest infrastructure firms in the country since the latter is a strategic resource in the economy. Analysis of three annual reports (the first publicly available one is 2004) shows that Temasek Holdings continues to be involved in a wide spread of industries and has retained control over strategic sectors, such as infrastructure, real estate and property development, telecommunications, and transportation (Table 3.3).

Table 3.2 Top 30 public companies on Singapore's Straits Times Index in 2019

Industry	*Company name*	*Singaporean company defined as having at least 30% local shareholding by Singaporean individuals or companies*	*Government linked?*
Real estate	Ascendas	Yes	Yes, by Temasek
	CapitaLand	Yes	Yes, by Temasek
	CapitaLand Commercial Trust	Yes	Yes, by Temasek
	CapitaLand Mall Trust	Yes	Yes, by Temasek
	City Developments Ltd	No	NA
	Genting Singapore PLC	No	NA
	Global Logistics Properties Ltd	No	NA
	Hong Kong Land Holdings Ltd	No	NA
	UOL Group Ltd	No	NA
Finance	DBS Group Holdings Ltd	Yes	Yes, by Temasek
	Oversea-Chinese Banking Corporation Limited	No	NA
	Singapore Exchange Limited	No	NA
	United Overseas Bank Limited	No	NA
Transportation, logistics and infrastructure	ComfortDelGro Corp Ltd	Yes	Yes, by Temasek
	Hutchison Port Holdings	Yes	Yes, by Temasek
	Jardine Cycle and Carriage Limited	No	NA
	SATS Ltd	Yes	Yes, by Temasek
	Singapore Airlines Limited	Yes	Yes, by Temasek
	Yangzijiang Shipbuilding Holdings Ltd	No	NA
	Sembcorp Industries Ltd	Yes	Yes, by Temasek
Agribusiness	Golden Agri-Resources Ltd	No	NA
	Wilmar International Ltd	No	NA
F&B	Thai Beverage PLC	No	NA

(*continued*)

Table 3.2 (continued)

Industry	*Company name*	*Singaporean company defined as having at least 30% local shareholding by Singaporean individuals or companies*	*Government linked?*
Holding Companies	Jardine Matheson Holdings Ltd	No	NA
	Jardine Strategic Holdings Ltd	No	NA
Telecommunications and media	Singapore Press Holdings Ltd	Yes	Yes, by Temasek
	Singapore Telecommunications Limited	Yes	Yes, by Temasek
	Starhub Ltd	No	NA
Engineering Services	Singapore Technologies Engineering Ltd	Yes	Yes, by Temasek
	Keppel Corporation Ltd	Yes	Yes, by Temasek

Source: ASEAN Up Straits Times Index List (2019) and related annual reports

Table 3.3 Companies in which Temasek is a significant shareholder since 2004 (holds at least 20% of shares)

Industry	*Name of company*	*% of shares owned by Temasek in 2004*	*% of shares owned by Temasek in 2010*	*% of shares owned by Temasek in 2017*
Telecommunications and media	Singtel	65	54	52
	ST Telemedia	100	100	100
	Mediacorp	100	100	100
	Shin Corporation Public Company Limited	0	42	0
	STATS ChipPAC Ltd	0	84	0
	Intouch Holdings Public Company Limited	0	0	20
Financial services	DBS	28	28	29
	Bank Danamon	53	68	67
	Bank International Indonesia	26	0	0
	Fullerton Fund Management	100	0	0
	NIB Bank Limited	0	74	0
Property, real estate, consumer and life Sciences	CapitaLand	61	39	40
	Raffles Holdings	36	0	0
	Ascott Group	42	0	*Merged and part of CapitaLand
	Mapletree Investments	100	100	100
	Olam International	0	14	52
	Surbana Jurong Private Limited	0	0	100
	Mandai Park Holdings	0	0	100
	Ascendas-Singbridge Pte Ltd	0	0	51
	A.S. Watson Holdings Limited	0	0	25
	M+S Pte Ltd	0	0	40
	Pulau Indah Ventures Malaysia	0	0	50

(*continued*)

Table 3.3 (continued)

Industry	*Name of company*	*% of shares owned by Temasek in 2004*	*% of shares owned by Temasek in 2010*	*% of shares owned by Temasek in 2017*
Transportation and logistics	Singapore Airlines	57	54	56
	PSA International	100	100	100
	Neptune Orient Lines	29	66	0
	SMRT Corporation	62	54	100
	SembCorp Logistics	31	49	0
	Singapore Airport Terminal Services	0	44	40
	Wildlife Reserves Singapore Pte Ltd	0	88	0
Energy resources	Singapore Power	100	100	100
	Tuas Power	100	0	0
	Senoko Power	100	0	0
	Power Seraya	100	0	0
	Sembcorp Utilities	51	0	0
	Pavilion Energy Pte Ltd	0	0	100
Infrastructure, engineering, and technology	Singapore Technologies	100	0	100
	ST Engineering	55	50	51
	Keppel Corporation	32	21	20
	SembCorp Industries	51	49	49
	Keppel Offshore and Marine	32	0	0
	SembCorp Marine	32	0	0
	Chartered Semiconductor Manufacturing	60	0	0
	ST Assembly Test Services	66	0	0

Source: Annual reports of selected years from Temasek Holdings

Table 3.4 Current list of all Hong Kong state-owned entities

Name of entity	*Description*
Kowloon-Canton Railway Corporation	Firm operates significant portions of railways and is fully owned by the HKSAR government, with senior officials making up chairman and members of the managing board
Hong Kong Link	Operates significant portions of railways, toll tunnels, and is fully owned by the HKSAR government
MTR Corporation Limited	MTR Corporation operates significant portions of railways and was established in 1975 with the government as the only shareholder. It remains government owned, though ownership today has dwindled down to 77%. It is a major property developer and landlord, thus having indirect control over private property owners
Link REIT	It was the first government-linked real estate investment trust (GLREIT) founded in 2004 in Hong Kong by the Housing Authority
Radio Television Hong Kong (RTHK)	Founded in 1928, it is Hong Kong's public broadcasting service, and today remains state-funded
Hong Kong Observatory	Formed in 1883 by the Hong Kong government, it is responsible for weather forecasts and warnings on climate hazards
Hong Kong International Airport (HKIA)	The HKIA is the main airport of Hong Kong and is owned by the Airport Authority, a component of the HKSAR government

Source: Author's review of government annual reports

State-Owned Companies in Hong Kong

In contrast to the dominance of GLCs in Singapore, there are fewer state-owned companies in Hong Kong. Based on available government documents, I have compiled a list showing the entities associated with the Hong Kong government (Table 3.4).

A critical juncture in Hong Kong's political economic development came in 1997 when China took over. Over time, this has led to not only fears over Hong Kong's constitutional future but also to concerns of Hong Kong losing its free-market statue due to Chinese intervention. It is too early, and not within the feasibility of this study, to assess so wide a claim.

There is some tentative evidence of increasing Chinese encroachment. Figure 3.6 charts the number of state-owned Chinese firms—measured in

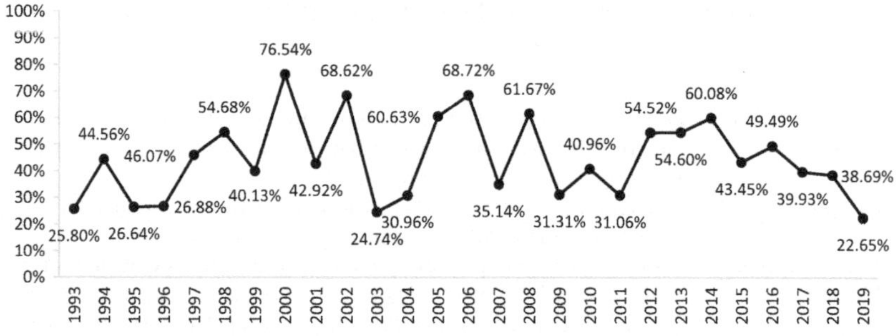

Fig. 3.6 % of total funds raised in the Hong Kong Exchange by Red Chips and H-Share firms (1993–2019). (Source: HKEX Fact Book, Hong Kong Exchange (1993–2019))

terms of H-Share and Red Chip type firms[3]—listed on the Hong Kong Exchange from 1993 to 2019. Over the entire period, there is no clear evidence of an increase in the presence of foreign Chinese state-owned enterprises entering the Hong Kong economy, with the trend line exhibiting a negligible upward trajectory (Fig. 3.6).

Market Concentration in HK Real Estate

One distinctive feature of the Hong Kong economy is the dominant presence, not so much of state-owned companies, but of large, private corporations in the property and real estate sector. These are typically family-owned conglomerates that have control not just in real estate but in the larger domestic non-traded services sector. Many have commented on the presence of such sizeable oligopolies and the consequent dearth of competition. The government's Consumer Council Reports highlighted the presence of anticompetitive behaviour and the cartelisation of consumer, banking, finance, and real estate industries (Consumer Council, 1996a, 1996b).

[3] Red Chip firms are the largest Chinese state-owned enterprises that entered Hong Kong to become incorporated and which went public in the Hong Kong Stock Exchange (HKEX). They come from a range of fields such as finance, energy, and utilities. H-share companies are those which are incorporated within China but came to be listed in the HKEX since 1993 when Chinese firms became accepted on HKEX.

Significantly, the biggest companies listed on the Hong Kong stock exchange are real estate firms. They made up 45% of total stock market capitalisation in 1996. Their dominance has persisted, and in 2005, more than 12% of total stock market capitalisation was occupied by 100 real estate related firms with 6 of the top 20 listed firms being real estate giants themselves (Newell, 2007). Additionally, the richest individuals in Hong Kong earned significant portions of their wealth from property (Table 3.5).

Hong Kong's socio-economic problems, such as income inequality, have been blamed on the dominance of these property magnates. Critics of Hong Kong's economic model see this as a problem of unconstrained "laissez-faireism" since the government has allegedly failed to rein in these corporations through adequate regulation and an overarching competition law (Chen & Lin, 2002). Demonstrations in Hong Kong have also had a socio-economic element; protestors and commentators trace public dissatisfaction of the high costs of living and home prices to the dominance of these cartels (Tan H., 2019).

Government Land Policy as a Root Cause

The mainstream academic consensus sees the market concentration in the HK real estate sector as stemming inherently from within the private sector rather than the public sector itself. Competition scholar Mark Williams (2009, p. 549), in his comparative analysis of competition policy in Hong

Table 3.5 List of the richest individuals in Hong Kong

Richest individuals in Hong Kong	*Source of wealth and business activities*
Lee Shau Kee (first)	Co-founder of the property development conglomerate Sun Hung Kai (considered the second most valuable real estate firm in world) and founder of Henderson Land Development
Henry Cheng and family (third)	Chairman of New World Development, a large property developer in HK, which also owns the Rosewell Hotel Group
Lui Che Woo and family (fifth)	Chairman of K. Wah International Holdings, a large property developer in HK
Kwong Siu Hing (seventh)	Biggest shareholder of Sun Hung Kai with a 26% stake
Peter Woo (eighth)	Chairman of the property developer Wheelock & Co, which has a stake in telecom, retail, and shipping industries

Source: Article by Chung and Karmali (2020) and the author's investigations of each person

Kong and Singapore, states that "most competition problems (in Hong Kong) are not public sector issues, as they are in Singapore, but private sector issues". This creates a dichotomy which Mark Williams (2009, p. 533) describes as follows: "in Singapore, the state is in control, in Hong Kong, the private sector is in control".

This perspective is incomplete because it omits the responsibility of the public sector in granting market power to these large corporations in Hong Kong. Government monopolisation of land—explored in the previous chapter—which fosters rent-seeking and regulatory capture by real estate developers is a big part of the problem.

Government Fiscal Dependence on Land Sales

The market concentration can also be further understood in relation to the artificially restricted land supply due to deliberate government policy which allows large developers to capture a larger-than-usual share of the real estate market. The HK government has and continues to maintain a monopoly over all land, on Hong Kong Island and Kowloon as the "main leaseholder" of all land in New Kowloon and the New Territories. After the 1997 handover to China, the government remained the owner and the Sino-British Joint Declaration of 1984 renewed the state's assets in the New Territories until 2047 (Hong Kong Legislative Council, 2016).

Additionally, the high property prices are largely due to the artificial restriction of the supply of property. This can be understood by examining the political incentives faced by state actors. The bulk of the Hong Kong government's revenue has historically come from the sale of land, creating a vested interest in perpetuating land scarcity and hence high land prices. In fact, about a third of government revenues typically stem from land sales and premiums, property-related taxes, and stamp duties. The following Table 3.6 shows the significant proportion of land premiums and stamp duties specifically as part of government revenue for a ten-year period.

Ten years ago, 17.4% of all government revenue were from the sales of land. Once property-related taxes are included, one can conclude that up to 69% (17.4% + 51.6%) of total government revenues stem from land-related activities. This has been a sustained trend. The latest available figures collected by the author show that in 2019, 72.8% (20% land premium + 52.8% property-related taxes) of total government revenue stems from property-related activities. Clearly, the ownership of land by the colonial government since the 1800s allows it to capitalise on rising property prices

Table 3.6 Contribution of land premium and stamp duties to HK government revenue[a]

	Land premium (HKD$ billion)[b]	*Stamp duties (HKD$ billion)*[c]	*Property-related tax (HKD$ billion)*
2010–2011	65.5 (17.4%)	51.0 (13.5%)	194.4 (51.6%)
2011–2012	84.6 (19.3%)	44.3 (10.1%)	221.4 (50.6%)
2012–2013	69.6 (15.7%)	42.9 (9.7%)	225.6 (51.0%)
2013–2014	84.2 (18.5%)	41.5 (9.1%)	225.6 (49.6%)
2014–2015	77.8 (16.3%)	74.8 (15.6%)	281.2 (58.7%)
2015–2016	60.9 (13.5%)	62.7 (13.9%)	270.0 (60.0%)
2016–2017	128.0 (22.3%)	61.9 (10.8%)	269.2 (47%)
2017–2018	163.6 (26.7%)	92.7 (15.1%)	304.4 (49.1%)
2018–2019	121.0 (20%)	100.0 (16.5%)	316.8 (52.8%)

Source: Major sources of government revenue, Legislative Council Secretariat Research Office (2018) and Hong Kong Annual Digest of Statistics, HKSAR (2011–2015)

[a]Stamp duties are a subset of property-related taxes

[b]The land premium is made up of sales by public auctions, modifications of existing leases, fees received for short term waivers and private treaty grants (see Legislative Council Secretariat Research Office, 2018, p. 5)

[c]Stamp duties are significant because they include sales or transfer of property and the lease of property; as such, the greater the land value and the more property sales, government revenue from stamp duties increase

and capture land values. The government's own report clearly admits that "land premium was the largest revenue item" (HKSAR, 2018b).

Since the Hong Kong government receives high revenues from land, it is understandable why it has been able to maintain a low-tax regime. One scholar has called the high property prices a form of "hidden tax" that the low official tax rates obscure (Choy, 2013, p. 30). If this is true, it means that the low-tax regime in Hong Kong does not truly reflect the notion of economic freedom but rather was only made possible by a lucrative government monopoly instead.

One government policy that keeps land supply low and prices high is the "Application List" system which was instituted in 2003. Rather than the government deciding the total amount of land to be supplied in a year, it would leave the onus on the developers to submit applications for specific lots to be approved by the land authority. The problem here is that this method only provides land when specific land lots are wanted by the developers, further slowing down the steady supply of land (Li, 2012, ch. 12). This should also be considered alongside the fact that as of 2009, only 23.74% of the total land has been developed, which is only a 7.69% increase since the handover in 1997 (HKSAR, 2009).

Since the government discovered an interest in maximising property value to raise higher revenues, it has carefully planned land sales. Control over the supply of land in a land-scarce city-state creates an incentive for property developers to influence the timing, execution, and process of acquiring land. There is a clear convergence of interest by the property developers and the state since both benefit from rising prices in the property sector.

Definitive "smoking-gun" types of evidence for this cannot be provided, but there have been reports of rent-seeking and collusion between political and business elites, especially in real estate. For instance, in 2010, the Secretary of the Civil Service Denise Yue was charged with committing a "grave error of judgement" after conflict-of-interest concerns arose over her handling of the appointment of Leung Chin-Man, the former Permanent Secretary for Housing, Planning and Lands as the Deputy Managing Director and Executive Director of New World China Land Ltd (Agence France-Presse, 2008). Another high-profile incident concerns Rafael Hui, a government official who occupied the second highest ranking position of Chief Secretary for Administration, who was arrested by the anti-corruption agency for suspected bribery in cahoots with property tycoons Raymond Kwok and Thomas Kwok of the Kwok family, one of Hong Kong's richest with massive property-based wealth (South China Morning Post, n.d.).

These are not merely isolated incidents of corruption. There is good reason to believe that the close connections between the real estate developers and political elites is a logical by-product of the constitutional system in Hong Kong, which institutionalises the power of organised business.

Government Business Alliance

Instead of pursuing pro-market policies that are industry neutral, the Hong Kong government, both before and after the 1997 handover, has enacted policies that favour specific business groups, including that of the property sector. It should be highlighted here that as part of the Sino-British Joint Declaration signed in 1984, there was a land supply ceiling of 50 hectares/year which artificially limited the land available for development. This had naturally caused a skyrocketing of property prices in the immediate aftermath all the way till the handover.

Another important flashpoint revealing the pro-developer bias of the government is its reaction to the 1997 financial crisis, which burst a prior property bubble. The government responded with a Nine-Point Plan to save the collapsing property market and this emphasised curbs to future supply in public housing. It also placed a one-year moratorium on land sales and abolished anti-speculation rules. This policy has been perceived as unfairly pro-business as it gave the conglomerate companies the breathing space to unload their inventories and recover from the crisis; at the same time, it blocked an increase in land supply that would have made public housing more affordable and increased competition by allowing smaller developers to enter the market (Poon, 2011).

Industrial Policy and Crowding Out

The policy choices made in the 1960s also led to another divergence between both city-states: the use of industrial policy. Since Singapore's independence in 1965, the developmental state has consistently launched industrial plans on a nationwide level to continually restructure the economy and upgrade it to higher levels of value-added. Throughout the latter part of the twentieth century, the Hong Kong government started to increase its economic intervention. Yet, it never convened any national, macro-level industrial plan, and only did so for the first time after the 1997 handover.

This section contrasts the repeated attempts of national economic planning on a macro level by the Singaporean developmental state and the fact that similar planning started to be pursued by Hong Kong only in the late-1990s onwards. Historically, there has been a resistance to government industrial support in Hong Kong for businesses. A significant episode occurred in the 1960s with the Legislative Council articulating a consensus against the provision of industrial grants based on the fear that it would engender an activist state and higher taxes (Jao, 1974).

This is not to say that state intervention in Hong Kong did not exist before 1997; it did. However, all the interventions on behalf of developmental purposes were largely sector-neutral and meant to improve the general competitiveness of the economy (Law, 2016). It was decided that rather than using a selective and interventionist industrial policy, it was better to adopt a "bottom-up" approach to remove obstacles to commercial and industrial development (Liang & Denny, 1995). Industrial policy that would identify specific sectors as worthy of focused government attention and support—common in Singapore—only started with Tung Chee Hwa, the first Chief Executive of Hong Kong after the handover.

Additionally, the practice of establishing industrial clusters was embedded into Singapore's early development strategy starting from the 1960s. This is part of the developmental state's preference for industrial clusters to generate economic growth. In contrast, Hong Kong established its first industrial cluster only in 1999 with CyberPort and the second in 2001 with Science Park.

The information presented in (Tables 3.7 and 3.8) also clearly contradicts the argument made in some quarters that Hong Kong's economy is becoming more interventionist, while Singapore's is liberalising, suggesting a reversal of roles (Lam, 2000).While both city-states have embarked on major industrial policies to boost technology and innovation, they are on vastly different scales. Significantly, after the initial $5 billion endowment into the Hong Kong Innovation and Technology Fund in 1999, only an additional $9 billion was injected 15 years after its initial establishment (see Table 3.8). The latest announcement from the Hong Kong government is for a $2 billion injection into the Innovation and Technology Venture Fund to encourage greater activity by venture capitalists (HKSAR, 2018a). This pales in comparison to the similar but more extensive S$19 billion earmarked under the single RIE2020 plan in Singapore, which is tied to the Smart Nation Initiative (Table 3.7).

Admittedly, the Hong Kong government today gives out grants and incentives to SMEs, just like the Singapore government does. In fact, there exists a similar online portal where SMEs can check out funding support in six separate categories: start-up/incubation, talent development, marketing, industry-driven grants, research and development support, and loan guarantee schemes (HKSAR, 2020b). This is similar to the Enterprise Development Grant provided by Enterprise Singapore.

However, there are important caveats. First, there are fewer grants for SMEs in Hong Kong than in Singapore. Besides the Enterprise Development Grant, there are other schemes dispensed to firms to upgrade their talents and skills, expand overseas, install green technology, or even engage in corporate social responsibility. Accordingly, a greater degree of support is given to local enterprises in Singapore which is also done in a pro-active, concerted manner, with local trade associations and government agencies actively encouraging firms to make use of them. For instance, in Hong Kong, there is only one talent development scheme called the Reindustrialisation and Technology Training Program (RTTP)

Table 3.7 National industrial plans in Singapore

Year	*Name of economic plan*	*Objectives and areas of focus*
1961	First Four-Year Development Plan	Restructure Singapore from entrepôt economy by stimulating industrialisation. The state-led industrialisation effort was meant to catalyse the development of manufacturing sectors.
1966	Second Four-Year Development Plan	Build on the First Development Plan through further capital expenditure to develop export-oriented manufacturing.
1981	Economic Development Plan for the Eighties	10-year plan to "develop Singapore into a modern industrial economy based on science, technology, skills, and knowledge" with a 4.4% productivity growth per annum target set as part of the Report of Committee on Productivity.
1986	Report of the Economic Committee titled "The Singapore Economy: New Directions"	Reviewed causes of the 1985 recession and identify "new strategies for promoting growth". Resulted in active manpower planning through adjusting university allocations, human capital upgrading in terms of productivity training, skills training, and more support and financing for entrepreneurs and SMEs.
1991	The Strategic Economic Plan	30–40-year plan to "attain the status and characteristics of a first-league developed country". Entailed efforts to increase labour productivity.
1991	National Technology Plan titled "Window of opportunities"	First of two five-year plans to develop science and technology sectors worth S$2 billion. Plan included contributions from expert committees on nine key technology programmes. The five-year plan served as the "blueprint for R&D development in nine sectors: information technology; microelectronics; electronic systems; manufacturing technology; materials technology; energy, water, environment, and resources; food and agro-technology; biotechnology; and medical sciences".
1996	National Science and Technology Plan	Continuation of the 1991 National Technology Plan with a further $4b investment. The second five-year plan saw a two-fold increase in the budget to further enhance Singapore's S&T infrastructure, identifying nine science-related sectors to be focused on.

(*continued*)

Table 3.7 (continued)

Year	*Name of economic plan*	*Objectives and areas of focus*
1998	Committee on Singapore's Competitiveness	10-year plan to transform Singapore into an advanced knowledge-based economy in the next millennium. It targeted a 3–4% increase in productivity per annum set under the Productivity 2000 initiative.
2000	Science & Technology Plan 2005	SGD 3.4 billion allocated to further promote industrial capital development and R&D capabilities for Singapore.
2000	SME 21 10-Year Masterplan titled "Positioning SMEs for the 21st Century"	Comprehensive national plan to develop the SME sector and its contributions to the economy in terms of total value-added and productivity. Resulted in a new slew of incentives and measures to develop internal capabilities.
2003	Report of Economic Review Committee titled "New challenges, fresh goals: towards a dynamic global city"	15-year plan with the goal of Singapore becoming "a leading global city and a hub of talent, enterprise, and innovation".
2005	iN2015	10-year plan to improve the national information communications infrastructure, with new initiatives to encourage the adoption of Infocomm in key economic sectors.
2006	Science & Technology Plan 2010 and the establishment of the National Research Foundation (NRF)	A total of $13 billion was put aside for the general development of R&D in Singapore. Part of the funds were assigned to the NRF for strategic projects, some to the MTI to promote investments, and some to the MOE for academic research. Two areas of rapid growth were identified: the environmental and water technologies sector and the interactive and digital media sector.
2008	National Framework for Innovation and Enterprise	The Research, Innovation and Enterprise Council (RIEC) approved the National Framework for Innovation and Enterprise to support innovation and entrepreneurship.
2010	Report of the Economic Strategies Committee titled "Highly skilled people, innovative economy, distinctive global city"	10-year plan which aimed to establish "a highly skilled workforce, an innovative economy, and a distinctive global city".

(*continued*)

Table 3.7 (continued)

Year	*Name of economic plan*	*Objectives and areas of focus*
2011	Research Innovation and Enterprise Plan 2015	Amounting to S$16.1bn, the RIE2015 plan built on the earlier 2010 plan, with six planks highlighted by Deputy Prime Minister Teo Chee Hean: "Continued emphasis on basic science and knowledge as the basis of future innovations. Focus on talent attraction and development, positioning Singapore as choice location for researchers. Greater emphasis on competitive funding as a selection means for the best ideas for optimal resource allocation. Fostering greater synergies between private and public and more funding for multi-disciplinary breakthrough science. Heavier weighting of R&D to promote positive economic outcomes. Strengthen support for commercialization to encourage development of products and services."
2017	Committee for Future Economy Report	10-year plan which aims to build on the Economic Strategies Committee's work in 2010 and transform the economy to be "future-ready". Resulted in detailed Industry Transformation Maps (ITMs) for 23 economic sectors (Committee on the Future Economy, Singapore, 2017).
2019	Research Innovation and Enterprise 2020 Plan (S$19bn) and Smart Nation Initiative	Largest R&D-related industrial plan to date, involving a S$19 billion fund "to be a knowledge-based economy which thrives on innovation and enterprise". Involves efforts to strengthen innovation ecosystem and "incentives to nudge potential entrepreneurs towards Singapore's priority sectors of tomorrow" (Ng et al., 2018).

Source: Various annual reports of relevant government departments and a publication by Ng et al. (2018).

which subsidises local companies to train their staff in the use of advanced technologies (HKSAR, 2020b). In contrast, Singapore has multiple such schemes across multiple agencies, as part of a national economic strategy to continually upgrade the local workforce.

On a related note, these schemes for SMEs are a recent policy practice in Hong Kong. As suggested by the comparison tables just displayed, the practice of sectoral industrial policy is relatively new, established since the 2017 policy address by Carrie Lam. In contrast, the strategy of providing

Table 3.8 National industrial plans in Hong Kong

Year	*Name of plan*	*Objectives and areas of focus*
1997	Innovation and Technology Commission under CE Tung Chee Hwa (first Chief Executive of post-handover HKSAR)	First introduced concept of four "pillar" industries: financial services, tourism, trading and logistics, and professional services.
1999	Announcement to develop CyberPort, an industrial facility with a private company as a joint venture.	CyberPort would focus on the IT and multimedia industries specifically. CyberPort was billed as the home to an incubator for ICT start-ups, providing office space, financial aid, training, micro funds, and network access to the investment community.
1999	Establishment of Innovation and Technology Fund (ITF)	ITF was established to finance projects with an innovation and technology element to upgrade manufacturing and service industries with the larger aim of increasing productivity and enhancing competitiveness. Established with an initial endowment of $5 billion, with subsequent injections: "$5 billion on 27 February 2015; (b) $2 billion on 10 June 2016; and (c) $2 billion for financing the Innovation and Technology Venture Fund (ITVF) on 12 July 2016" (HKSAR, 2018a).
2001	Establishment of Hong Kong Science and Technology Park Corporation (HKSTP)	Hong Kong's second industrial park and the first dedicated to catalysing science and technology for economic development purposes.
2008	Task Force on Economic Challenges under Chief Executive Donald Tsang	Identify new economic activities to enhance competitiveness in light of the 2008 financial crisis. Proposed active focus on six "new industries" in addition to four "pillars": Cultural and Creative, Medical, Education, Innovation and Technology, Testing and Certification Services, Environmental Services.
2013	Launch of "Economic Development Commission" and "Financial Services Development Council" under CE Leung Chun-Yin	Entails four working groups targeting promising and emerging industries.

(*continued*)

Table 3.8 (continued)

Year	*Name of plan*	*Objectives and areas of focus*
2014	Leung Chun-Yin's 2014 Policy Address	Policy address emphasised an appropriate proactive approach to economic development to develop strategic sectors like financial services, trade, maritime services, and logistics.
2017	Carrie Lam's 2017 Policy Address	Policy address introduced an array of policy measures to spur innovation and technological development to grow HK's creative industries, with government R&D expenditure as a percentage of GDP to grow to 1.5%.
2017	Launch of Innovation and Technology Venture Fund of HKD2bn	Aimed to encourage investment from venture capital (VC) funds in local innovation and technology start-ups.
February 2019	Announcement of the Outline Development Plan for the Guangdong-Hong Kong-Macao Greater Bay Area by Chinese Central Government	Marks the first time that HKSAR became part of larger development planning by Chinese Central government. Along with Macao, Guangzhou, and Shenzhen, Hong Kong will be "one of the core engines for development in the region".

Source: Reports and publications of the HKSAR government

incentive schemes to help local businesses is a core part of the Singaporean developmental state's strategy and has been a long-standing practice since Singapore's independence in 1965, though it was accelerated by the SME21 plan enacted in 2000.

Comparative Contributions of Small-Medium Enterprises in Hong Kong and Singapore

The large presence of GLCs and foreign MNCs have crowded out SMEs in Singapore, a problem that does not occur in Hong Kong. The contributions of SMEs to the total economy in Singapore is much lower compared to Hong Kong, despite the generous provisions of grant support to these enterprises by the developmental state.

Table 3.9 Comparison of East Asian SMEs value-add and share of exports

	No. of firms	*Workforce*	*Value-added*	*Direct exports*
Taiwan	97%	70%	55%	66%
Hong Kong	98%	62%	57%	17%
South Korea	98%	66%	38%	32%
Singapore	81%	40%	22%	15%

Source: Economic Development Board (1990)

Singapore

A general look at the industrial structure in the Singapore economy shows that SMEs do not contribute significantly to the economy. In 1990, Singapore's SME sector was weaker than its East Asian counterparts in terms of value-add and share of exports, an imbalance acknowledged by the government's own national *SME Master Plan* report (Table 3.9).

Just prior to 2000, local SMEs accounted for only 16% of total exports. This is compared to 56% in SME-intensive Taiwan, 42.4% in Korea, and 20% in Vietnam and 31.5% in India (OECD, 1997; Kim & Nugent, 1999; Badrinath, 1997). This means that local enterprises were not as globally competitive as their East Asian counterparts. Today, they only contribute 43% of the nominal value-added relative to non-SMEs (Department of Statistics, 2021). Additionally, local enterprises, most of which are SMEs, contributed to only 30% of the value-add relative to foreign enterprises in recent years (Department of Statistics, 2019, 2020a). Singapore is today a high-income country, and comparisons with other high-income economies put these numbers in perspective. Significantly, in most high-income economies in the OECD, SMEs typically contribute about 55% of national GDP, higher than in Singapore (OECD, 2004; Ayyagari et al., 2003).

SMEs in Singapore are typically locally owned, and non-SMEs are foreign owned.[4] Thus, the disparity is between local SMEs and foreign non-SMEs, which are typically MNCs. In 2018, we can observe that foreign enterprises, though they employ only 31% of the workforce, contributed 72% to the total value-added of the economy, which amounted to S$463 billion (Figs. 3.7 and 3.8).

[4] Local enterprises are those defined as having at least 30% local shareholding. SMEs are defined as those with maximum annual revenue of 100 million or having less than 200 staff.

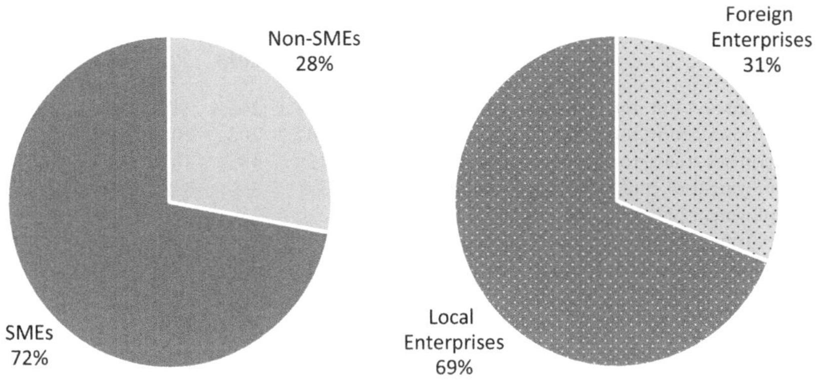

Fig. 3.7 Distribution of Singaporean workforce across SMEs vs. Non-SMEs and local vs. foreign enterprises (2018). (Source: Department of Statistics Singapore (2018))

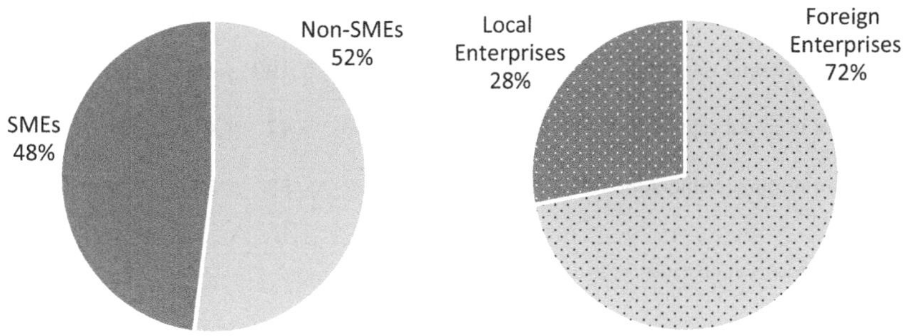

Fig. 3.8 Contribution of SMEs and local enterprises to total value-added in the Singapore economy (2018). (Source: Department of Statistics Singapore (2018))

The abovementioned snapshot data are further buttressed when a time-series perspective is incorporated. The value-add contribution of local enterprises, despite being more numerous than foreign counterparts, was a meagre 43% in 2014, declining further to 38% in 2018, suggesting that the crowding out of local enterprises does not seem to be abating (Table 3.10).

The lop-sided focus on MNC-driven growth was recognised by the government in the 1980s which led to their concerted effort to grow the SME sector. This culminated in their SME21 plan launched in 2000

Table 3.10 Comparison of value-add for local SMEs with foreign non-SMEs

Variables	*2014*	*2015*	*2016*	*2017*	*2018*
Enterprises count, total (thousand)	244.1	246.4	247.4	254.1	263.9
Enterprises count, total local (thousand)	202.2	203	203.6	209.7	217.6
Enterprises count, total foreign (thousand)	42	43.5	43.8	44.4	46.3
Employment of enterprises, total (million)	3.4	3.4	3.4	3.4	3.5
Employment of enterprises, total local (million)	2.4	2.4	2.4	2.4	2.4
Employment of enterprises, total foreign (million)	1	1	1	1	1.1
Nominal value-added of enterprises, total (billion dollars)	358	380	394	420	445
Nominal value-added of enterprises, total local (billion dollars)	155	158	160	162	169
Nominal value-added of enterprises, total foreign (billion dollars)	204	222	234	258	276
Share of enterprises count, total (%)	100	100	100	100	100
Share of enterprises count, total local (%)	83	82	82	83	82
Share of enterprises count, total foreign (%)	17	18	18	17	18
Share of employment of enterprises, total (%)	100	100	100	100	100
Share of employment of enterprises, total local (%)	72	71	70	70	69
Share of employment of enterprises, total foreign (%)	28	29	30	30	31
Share of nominal value-added of enterprises, total (%)	100	100	100	100	100
Share of nominal value-added of enterprises, total local (%)	43	42	41	39	38
Share of nominal value-added of enterprises, total foreign (%)	57	58	59	61	62

Source: Department of Statistics (2020b)

(Productivity Standards Board 2000). This was further reinforced with the Economic Review Committee Report (2003) and the Economic Strategies Committee Report (2010), both of which acknowledged the need for a stronger SME sector. Hence, the sub-par performance shown above is not due to a lack of policy effort, but despite it.

Hong Kong

The contributions of SMEs in Hong Kong are harder to discern, due to the lack of previous studies on the topic and the fact that the government does not collect these statistics directly (hence requiring statistical reconstruction). One such estimate was made by Richard Wong (1999), who showed that in 1999, "SMEs accounted for 70.2% of the total employment of 1,796,635 people in the above nine (key) industries. Further, SMEs accounted for 61.9% out of the total value-added of HK$523,025 million". When this is compared with the figures for Singapore displayed above, a stark conclusion is arrived at. If Wong's figures are correct, it means that in 1999, SMEs contributed more to the Hong Kong economy at 61.9% than Singaporean SMEs contributed to the Singapore economy in 2018 (48%).

The academic literature has also widely established the way in which Hong Kong's economy is dominated by small enterprises. Alvin Rabushka's (1979, p. 75) early study demonstrated small firm size in Hong Kong's factories. Tony Yu (1998) also ably documented how small, adaptive entrepreneurs engaged in guerrilla-capitalism, which facilitated structural change and economic development.

I also conducted my own statistical reconstruction to discern the contributions of SMEs to the Hong Kong economy. This involved a special information request from the Census and Statistics Department which provided the value-add of "four key industries" in Hong Kong, calculated separately with "other selected industries" (Table 3.11). The data synthesised from this request show that if Hong Kong SMEs' total value-added is calculated as a percentage of the total value-added of the *whole* economy, it is almost half. This might seem less than in Singapore. However, the important point here is that SMEs are defined differently in Singapore than in Hong Kong. While Singapore treats firms that are either less than 200 staff or have a revenue turnover of less than $100 million as SMEs, Hong Kong has more restrictive criteria: manufacturing firms with less than 100 staff and non-manufacturing firms with less than 50 staff.

If Hong Kong's definition were used, SMEs contribute 40.79% to the economy in 2017, less than the 48% share in Singapore. However, given the more restrictive criteria used in Hong Kong, the true comparison is very different. While there is no way to make the data commensurate across both countries, one might make a limited inference: if SMEs were considered more loosely in Hong Kong (up to 200 staff and $100 million in revenue), their percentage share contribution to the total value-added may be much higher than in Singapore.

What About the Concern of Big Firm Domination in Hong Kong?

The author is aware of the wider academic literature that condemns Hong Kong's economy for being rife with the market dominance of large

Table 3.11 Contribution of Hong Kong SMEs to the Hong Kong Economy

Year	*No. of SMEs*	*No. of persons engaged in SMEs*	*Value-added of SMEs*	*Value-added of the four key industries in the Hong Kong economy*	*Value-added of other selected industries in the Hong Kong economy*	*Total value-added*	*Percentage share of SMEs to the value-added of the economy of four key industries*	*Percentage share of SMEs to the total value-added of the economy*
2009	273,017	1,127,430	481,659	886,200	124,208	1,010,408	54.35%	47.67%
2010	281,619	1,194,553	535,028	1,014,100	143,768	1,157,868	52.76%	46.21%
2011	290,108	1,196,763	580,858	1,112,800	161,183	1,273,983	52.20%	45.59%
2012	283,168	1,250,986	639,937	1,166,800	175,899	1,342,699	54.85%	47.66%
2013	281,521	1,229,771	629,029	1,212,800	190,568	1,403,368	51.87%	44.82%
2014	282,094	1,212,496	658,657	1,269,300	202,046	1,471,346	51.89%	44.77%
2015	276,408	1,213,984	650,452	1,330,900	207,532	1,538,432	48.87%	42.28%
2016	276,261	1,173,241	667,844	1,367,300	214,641	1,581,941	48.84%	42.22%
2017	276,420	1,170,786	685,648	1,454,900	226,148	1,681,048	47.13%	40.79%

Sources: Special information request by the present author made to the Census and Statistics Department, HKSAR

corporations. It is said that business tycoons, usually family owned, dominate the market to the exclusion of smaller firms. While that may be the case in specific industries—as in real estate—the numbers here show that across the entire economy, the average firm size has actually declined in Hong Kong and remain much smaller than in Singapore.[5]

This is best seen by analysing average firm size in Hong Kong and Singapore, several results from which may be gleaned. First, the total number of enterprises in Hong Kong is more than four times that of Singapore. This is exacerbated by the fact that Hong Kong's figures (column 1) include only private businesses (both local and foreign) while that in Singapore (column 3) includes even non-profit organisations and some government agencies. Due to the much bigger number of enterprises in Hong Kong, average firm size is approximately four times lower. Notably, there are many more companies, including SMEs, in Hong Kong than in Singapore (Table 3.12).

Table 3.12 Average firm size since 2014 till the present day

	Hong Kong			*Singapore*		
	Total number of enterprises in Hong Kong (foreign + local) (1)	*Total number employed in Hong Kong (2)*	*Average Firm Size in Hong Kong (1/2)*	*Total number of enterprises in Singapore (3)*	*Total number employed in Singapore (4)*	*Average firm size in Singapore (3/4)*
2014	1,282,317	3.74 mil	2.92	244,100	3.4 mil	13.9
2015	1,298,695	3.77 mil	2.90	247,600	3.4 mil	13.7
2016	1,351,206	3.79 mil	2.80	248,700	3.4 mil	13.7
2017	1,394,380	3.82 mil	2.74	254,600	3.4 mil	13.4
2018	1,412,011	3.87 mil	2.74	265,100	3.5 mil	13.2
2019	1,392,679			273,100	3.5 mil	12.81

Source: Companies Registry of HKSAR (2020a), Labour Force Statistics of HKSAR (2020c), and Department of Statistics of Singapore (2020b).

For Singapore, "enterprises" comprise companies, businesses, non-profit organisations, ministries, statutory boards, and government / government-aided schools"

[5] This has previously been used as a proxy to measure market power, for instance, by Richard Wong (2013) and Lynne Pepall (2007).

Conclusion

This chapter has identified two major institutional differences in state-market relations in Hong Kong and Singapore. First, there are large government-linked corporations in Singapore's economy, which do not exist to the same degree in Hong Kong, though this gap is slightly closed with the entrance of Chinese state-owned enterprises in Hong Kong. Second, industrial planning has long been a staple of the Singaporean developmental state's economic policy, while sectoral-based interventions only commenced in post-1997 Hong Kong. These two factors mean that small-medium enterprises are significantly crowded out in Singapore, but which play a larger role in Hong Kong's economy. This allows us to characterise Singapore as a hybrid of big-firm and state capitalism, while Hong Kong, due to the larger role of small enterprises, notwithstanding market concentration in the real estate sectors, falls within the category of entrepreneurial capitalism.

References

Agence France-Presse. (2008, August 16). *Former HK housing chief quits developer: Report.* Retrieved August 31, 2020, from https://www.asiaone.com/News/Latest%2BNews/Business/Story/A1Story20080816-82656.html

ASEAN. (2019, March 30). *Top 30 companies from Singapore's STI.* Retrieved from ASEAN Up: https://aseanup.com/top-30-companies-singapore-sti/

Ayyagari, M., Beck, T., & Demirgüc-Kunt, A. (2003). Small and medium enterprises across the globe. *World Bank Policy Research Working Paper, 3127.*

Badrinath. (1997). *The SME and the global market place: An analysis of competitiveness constraints.* UNCTAD/ WTO International Trade Center.

Baumol, W., Litan, R., & Schramm, C. (2007). *Good capitalism, bad capitalism, and the economics of growth and prosperity.* Yale University Press.

Bellows, T. J. (1993). The Singapore polity: Community, leadership, and institutions. *Asian Journal of Political Science, 1*(1), 113–132.

Chen, E., & Lin, P. (2002). Competition Policy under Laissez-Faireism: Market power and its treatment in Hong Kong. *Review of Industrial Organisation*, 145–168.

Choy, E. (2013). *Hong Kong's economic freedom and income inequality.* .

Chung, G., & Karmali, N. (2020, February 6). *Hong Kong's Richest 2020.* Retrieved from Forbes Magazine: https://www.forbes.com/hong-kong-billionaires/#55be073d3e46

Committee on the Future Economy, Singapore. (2017). *Report of the committee on the future economy: Pioneers of the next generation.* Committee on the Future Economy, Singapore.

Consumer Council. (1996a). *Competition policy: The key to Hong Kong's future success*. Hong Kong Consumer Council.
Consumer Council. (1996b). *How competitive is the private residential property market?* Hong Kong Consumer Council.
Department of Statistics. (2018). *Enterprises*. Retrieved from Department of Statistics, Singapore: https://www.singstat.gov.sg/find-data/search-by-theme/industry/enterprises/latest-data
Department of Statistics. (2019). *Singapore economy in 2019*. Department of Statistics. Retrieved from https://www.singstat.gov.sg/modules/infographics/-/media/Files/visualising_data/infographics/Economy/singapore-economy15072020.pdf
Department of Statistics. (2020a). *Singapore economy*. Retrieved from Department of Statistics, Singapore: https://www.singstat.gov.sg/modules/infographics/economy
Department of Statistics. (2020b, July 24). *Topline estimates for all enterprises and SMEs*. Retrieved from Department of Statistics of Singapore: https://www.tablebuilder.singstat.gov.sg/publicfacing/createDataTable.action?refId=15808
Department of Statistics. (2021). *Singapore economy*. Retrieved from https://www.singstat.gov.sg/modules/infographics/-/media/Files/visualising_data/infographics/Economy/singapore-economy30042021.pdf
Economic Development Board, Singapore. (1990). *Report on enterprise development: SME Master Plan*. Economic Development Board.
Economic Review Committee, Singapore. (2003). *New challenges, fresh goals: Towards a dynamic global city*. Economic Review Committee & Ministry of Trade & Industry, Singapore.
Economic Strategies Committee, Singapore. (2010). *Report of the Economic Strategies Committee: High skilled people, innovative economy, distinctive global city*. Economic Strategies Committee, Singapore.
Goodstadt, L. (2005). *Uneasy partners: The conflict between public interest and private profit in Hong Kong*. Hong Kong University Press.
HKSAR. (2009). *Planning statistics*. Planning Department, HKSAR.
HKSAR. (2011–2015). *Government accounts, finance and insurance*. Retrieved from Census and Statistics Department, HKSAR: https://www.censtatd.gov.hk/hkstat/sub/so110.jsp
HKSAR. (2018a). *Innovation and Technology Fund*. Retrieved from HKSAR Government Budget 2018: https://www.budget.gov.hk/2018/eng/pdf/itf.pdf
HKSAR. (2018b, March 2). *Major sources of government revenue*. Retrieved March 30, 2019, from Research Office, Legislative Council Secretariat: https://www.legco.gov.hk/research-publications/english/1718issf03-major-sources-of-government-revenue-20180302-e.pdf

HKSAR. (2020a). *Number of local companies incorporated since 2014.* Retrieved from Companies Registry of Hong Kong: https://www.cr.gov.hk/en/publication/fact-stat/statistics/local-companies-incorporated/since-2014.htm
HKSAR. (2020b). *Funding schemes and support.* Retrieved from SME One: https://www.smeone.org/index.php?lang=en
HKSAR. (2020c). *Labour productivity index [dataset].* Retrieved from Census and Statistics Department, HKSAR: https://www.censtatd.gov.hk/hkstat/sub/sp70.jsp?tableID=103&ID=0&productType=8
Hong Kong Exchange. (1993–2019). *HKEX Factbook.* Retrieved from Hong Kong Exchange: https://www.hkex.com.hk/Market-Data/Statistics/Consolidated-Reports/HKEX-Fact-Book?sc_lang=en
Hong Kong Legislative Council. (2016). *Land tenure system in Hong Kong.* Retrieved from Hong Kong Legislative Council: https://www.legco.gov.hk/research-publications/english/essentials-1617ise07-land-tenure-system-in-hong-kong.htm
Huff, W. (1994). *The economic growth of Singapore.* Cambridge University Press.
Jao, Y. C. (1974). *Banking and currency in Hong Kong.* Macmillan.
Josey, A. (1980). *Lee Kuan Yew, the crucial years.* Times Books International.
Kim, L., & Nugent, J. (1999). Korean SMEs and their support mechanisms fulfilling the export potential of small and medium firms. In B. Levy, A. Berry, & J. B. Nugent (Eds.), *Fulfilling the export potential of small and medium firms.* Kluwer Academic Publishers.
Kirzner, I. (1973). *Competition and entrepreneurship.* University of Chicago Press.
Lam, N. M. (2000). Government intervention in the economy: A comparative analysis of Singapore and Hong Kong. *Public Administration and Development: The International Journal of Management Research and Practice, 20*(5), 397–421.
Law, C. K. (2016). *Industrial economics and industrial policy of Hong Kong.* Retrieved from Education Bureau of Hong Kong: https://www.edb.gov.hk/attachment/en/curriculum-development/kla/pshe/references-and-resources/economics/Industrial_Economics_Booklet_Eng_web.pdf
Lee, B. C., & Tan, W. L. (2002). Small and medium enterprises in Singapore and the new economy. *The role of SMEs in national economies in East Asia*. Retrieved from https://ink.library.smu.edu.sg/cgi/viewcontent.cgi?article=3117&context=lkcsb_research
Li, K.-W. (2012). *Economic Freedom: Lessons of Hong Kong.* Singapore: World Scientific.
Liang, W., & Denny, M. (1995). Upgrading Hong Kong's technology base. In D. F. Simon (Ed.), *The emerging technological trajectory of the Pacific Rim* (pp. 256–274). M.E. Sharpe Inc.

Lim, L. (2016). Labor, productivity and Singapore's development model. In L. Lim (Ed.), *Singapore's economic development: Retrospection and reflections* (pp. 135–168). World Scientific.

Lim, L. (2017). Singapore's success: After the miracle. In L. Lim (Ed.), *Business, government and labor: Essays on economic development in Singapore and Southeast Asia*. World Scientific.

Low, L. (1991). *The political economy of privatisation in Singapore*. McGraw-Hill Publishers.

Low, L. (2002). Rethinking Singapore Inc. And GLCs. *Southeast Asian Affairs*, 282–302. http://www.jstor.org/stable/27913213

Lyons, G. (2007). State capitalism: The rise of sovereign wealth funds. *Journal of Management Research, 7*(3), 119–146.

Ministry of Finance, Singapore. (2019a, February). *GIC manages its investment portfolio for the long term*. Retrieved from https://www.mof.gov.sg/Newsroom/Forum-Replies/GIC-manages-its-investment-portfolio-for-the-long-term

Monnery, N. (2017). *Architect of prosperity: Sir John Cowperthwaite and the making of Hong Kong*. London Publishing Partnership.

Musacchio, A., & Lazzarini, S. G. (2014). *Reinventing state capitalism*. Harvard University Press.

Nair, C. V. (1976). *Socialism that works: The Singapore way*. Federal Publications.

Newell, G. (2007). Factors influencing the performance of Hong Kong Real Estate Companies. *Journal of Real Estate Portfolio Management, 13*(1), 75–86.

Ng, R., Lim, S. Q., & Wong, P. (2018, August 8). *Singapore: 50 Years of Science and Technology*. Retrieved from Lee Kuan Yew School of Public Policy: https://lkyspp.nus.edu.sg/gia/article/singapore-50-years-of-science-and-technology

OECD. (1997). *Globalization and small and medium enterprises, V. 1: Synthesis Report*. Paris.

OECD. (2004). *Promoting SMEs for development*. OECD.

Pepall, L. (2007). *Market structure and market power*. Retrieved from https://www.blackwellpublishing.com/content/industrialorganisationlynnepepall/Pepall_4e_chpt_003.pdf

Poon, A. (2011). *Land and the ruling class in Hong Kong*. Enrich Professional Publishing.

Productivity Standards Board, Singapore. (2000). *SME 21: Positioning SMEs for the 21st century*. Productivity Standards Board, Singapore.

Rabushka, A. (1979). *Hong Kong: A study in economic freedom*. The University of Chicago.

Ramirez, C. D., & Ling, H. T. (2004). Singapore Inc. versus the private sector: Are government-linked companies different? *IMF Staff Papers, 51*(3), 510–528.

Research Office, Legislative Council Secretariat, HKSAR. (2018). *Major source of government revenue*. Retrieved from Research Office, Legislative Council

Secretariat, HKSAR: https://www.legco.gov.hk/research-publications/english/1718issf03-major-sources-of-government-revenue-20180302-e.pdf
Schumpeter, J. (2009). *Can capitalism survive?: Creative destruction and the future of the global economy*. HarperCollins.
Shome, A. (2006). *A case study of positive interventionism. Biennial conference of the Asian Studies Association* (pp. 26–29).
South China Morning Post. (n.d.). *Review: The verdicts are out in explosive graft trial of Hui, Kwoks*. Retrieved August 31, 2020, from https://www.scmp.com/news/hong-kong/article/1663193/rafael-hui-guilty-five-counts-misconduct-and-bribery-thomas-kwok
Sovereign Wealth Fund Institute. (2018). *Top 89 largest Sovereign Wealth Fund rankings by total assets*. Retrieved from Sovereign Wealth Fund Institute: https://www.swfinstitute.org/fund-rankings/sovereign-wealth-fund
Tan, H. (2019, August 15). *Economist: Hong Kong's tycoons 'are the problem' underlying recent unrest*. Retrieved from CNBC: https://www.cnbc.com/2019/08/15/hong-kong-protests-economist-says-tycoons-are-the-problem.html
Tan, T. (1985, March 8). *Singapore, Parliamentary Debates, Official Report 45, No. 7, Column 481*. Retrieved August 31, 2020, from https://www.parliament.gov.sg/parliamentary-business/official-reports-(parl-debates)
Temasek Holdings. (2018). *Temasek review*. Temasek Holdings.
Temasek Holdings. (2001–2019). *Temasek review*. Temasek Holdings.
The Straits Times. (1959, November 10). *PAP WANTS ALL CHINESE CLAN GROUPS ABOLISHED*. Retrieved August 31, 2020, from https://eresources.nlb.gov.sg/newspapers/Digitised/Article/straitstimes19591110-1.2.7
The Straits Times. (1960, March 20). *Ko proposes a liaison team to help traders and Govt*. Retrieved August 31, 2020, from https://eresources.nlb.gov.sg/newspapers/Digitised/Article/straitstimes19600320-1.2.49
Thum, P. (2012). The limitations of monolingual history. In N. Tarling (Ed.), *Studying Singapore's past: CM Turnbull and the History of Modern Singapore* (pp. 98–120). NUS Press.
Visscher, S. (2002). *Business, ethnicity and the state: The representational relationship of the Singapore Chinese chamber of commerce and the state*. Retrieved from https://www.narcis.nl/publication/RecordID/oai:research.vu.nl:publications%2F60208f34-2264-49b1-953e-7f6f9ecbed47
Williams, M. (2009). The Lion city and the fragrant harbor: The political economy of competition policy in Singapore and Hong Kong compared. *Antitrust Bulletin*, 517–577.
Wong, R. Y. (1999). *Small-medium enterprises in Hong Kong: Recent developments and policy issues*. The Hong Kong Chinese Importers' & Exporters' Association.
Wong, R. Y. (2013). *Diversity and occasional anarchy: On deep economic and social contradictions in Hong Kong*. Hong Kong University Press.

Wong, S.-L. (1984). The migration of Shanghainese entrepreneurs to Hong Kong. In D. Faure, J. H. Hayes, & A. Birch (Eds.), *From village to city, studies in the traditional roots of Hong Kong Society*. Centre of Asian Studies, University of Hong Kong.

Wong, S.-L. (1988). *Emigrant entrepreneurs: Shanghai industrialists in Hong Kong*. Oxford University Press.

Yu, T. F.-L. (1998). Adaptive entrepreneurship and the economic development of Hong Kong. *World Development, 26*(5), 897–911.

CHAPTER 4

Development Requires Freedom

Freedom and Development

Singapore's economic success has often been used as a justification to reject liberalism. Her rapid rise to economic prosperity in the late twentieth century was used by Singapore's Founding Father Lee Kuan Yew (and his numerous admirers) to claim that economic growth does not require liberal democracy. This "Lee Thesis", or "Asian Values" thesis, states that notions of freedom, individualism, and democracy are Western-centric and do not necessarily apply in other cultural contexts. According to Lee, "westerners value the freedoms and liberties of the individual. As an Asian of Chinese cultural background, my values are for a government which is honest, effective and efficient" (Lee, 1992).

This argument has proven attractive. Developing countries sang a similar tune at the Vienna Conference on Human Rights in 1993. Why care about political freedom, especially if economic needs are more pressing? And if economic growth without democracy, then perhaps democracy is not as important as Westerners frequently champion. The frequently used example is China, which supposedly maintains an open capitalist economy but an authoritarian political regime (Whyte, 2014). Developmental state theory also eschews the value of political liberty. Scholars in this tradition have argued that East Asian nations achieved prosperity by deliberately eschewing Western prescriptions of free-market capitalism and liberal democracy. Singapore, South Korea, and Taiwan all adopted some version

B. Cheang, *Economic Liberalism and the Developmental State*,
https://doi.org/10.1007/978-3-031-08100-2_4

of the developmental state model and achieved rapid growth under authoritarian regimes.

The Indian Nobel Prize winning economist Amartya Sen (1999) rightly pointed out that this line of reasoning rests on "selective information", using isolated cases to extrapolate to wider experiences. Sen, and other democratically inclined scholars, have shown that when a wide swath of cases is considered, democracy's positive contributions to economic growth become clearly established (Przeworski et al., 2000; Sen, 1999, 2000).

This book pushes back against the "Lee Thesis" and the claims of developmental state theorists. The stifling of freedom, as I show in Singapore, has had a negative impact on economic performance. When one compares the political system and political culture of Hong Kong and Singapore, one witnesses a divergence between the former's liberal system with a high degree of civil liberties (despite restrictions on electoral freedom) and Singapore's highly authoritarian electoral democracy. Hong Kong's vibrant democratic culture stands in stark contrast to the feeble political culture in Singapore. This contrast is significant because it has an impact on their respective development. Subsequent chapters will show that when economic indicators focusing on entrepreneurship, innovation, and productivity are considered, Singapore's growth experience is less impressive than Hong Kong's. Additionally, the "creative class" in Singapore is hampered by a restrictive state policy towards anti-establishment activities.

This gulf in performance echoes previous work establishing the importance of a creative entrepreneurial culture as a core ingredient for cutting-edge growth (Audretsch, 2006; Verspagen, 2006; Thierer, 2016; McCloskey, 2010). The economic historian Joel Mokyr (1992, p. 182) explained that "technological progress requires above all tolerance toward the unfamiliar and the eccentric". Another bluntly writes that "innovation flourishes in freedom" (Ridley, 2020). If such traits are stifled by a political culture that rewards compliance to authority and conformity to the status quo, then it is reasonable to expect that nation's economic competitiveness to be hampered.

Amartya Sen did not just argue that freedom was a principal means of development, but that it was also its primary objective. High incomes, material wealth, and affluence are pointless if human beings lack the capabilities to shape their lives. Political liberty is constitutive of human freedom and allows people to "lead their lives" and "take part in crucial decisions regarding public affairs" (Sen, 2000, p. 16). Freedom is a core part of what it means to achieve development. The important value of political liberty forces one to reconsider the attraction of the Singapore model. Is material wealth worth having if it comes at the cost of our political rights? I suggest not.

Additionally, political freedom works in tandem with economic freedom. There is often a "bifurcation" in the academic literature where economic freedom and political freedom are analysed separate from each other (Stroup, 2007). Some scholars also maintain that market institutions are more important than democracy itself, in promoting growth (Barro, 1996, 2013). This study integrates the political and the economic. Political and economic power are intertwined, mutually constitutive, and reinforcing. A nation with an authoritarian political system tends to also have an unfree economy, with state power in both realms reinforcing each other. Political authoritarianism in Singapore manifests itself in the economic realm through the high concentration of GLCs and industrial policy, which in turn shape economic performance. The relatively liberal Hong Kong politics on the other hand coincides with a private realm where economic action proceeds relatively undisturbed by the state.

Bringing Politics In

For good reason therefore, this chapter focuses on the political arrangements in Singapore and Hong Kong, specifically contrasting the authoritarian nature of the developmental state against the relatively liberal climate in Hong Kong. The difference between both countries became stark once politics is brought into the analysis; while both are basically capitalist economies, they operate on very different political foundations. The Singapore developmental state not only intervenes in private life but continues to practise extensive political repression and stifling civil liberties today. While Hong Kongers have never been actually able to elect their own representatives, they have enjoyed a largely liberal political climate, where political opposition and anti-establishment are not only commonplace, but very much celebrated. This divergence in political arrangements is seen not only on an institutional level, but on a deeper cultural plane as well, where a political culture of authoritarianism has been imbibed by the Singapore populace in a way not seen in Hong Kong.

Ideological power is thus worth paying attention to. Early scholarly efforts to "bring the state back in" are praiseworthy but had largely focused on the institutional and organisational characteristics that enabled the state to project power onto society (Skocpol, 1985). Other scholars have since emphasised that ideas matter in political analyses, and such studies have tended to involve qualitative methods that investigate political norms, values, and culture in a society (see Carstensen & Schmidt, 2016). Accordingly, this chapter investigates state power in the context of Hong Kong and Singapore, with an additional focus on ideological power. Indeed, state power is not merely a function of its monopoly on the use of violence and the ability of physical coercion, but also includes the capacity to shape the values, mindsets, and ideology of its people to engender mass consent.

This consideration of ideological power reveals a tremendous gulf in the role of the state in Hong Kong and Singapore. Not only is there a difference in the formal political system in Hong Kong and Singapore, with the latter's authoritarian developmental state being in contrast with the former's liberal governance, but they also differ in terms of the ideological power wielded by the state. Scholars have identified the way in which the Singapore state has intrusively shaped the very values and ideas imbibed by its people from the education system to other levels of society. Beyond simply "social engineering", this has in some quarters been called "ideological indoctrination", where the PAP government has achieved a conflation of party values with national values. The clear separation of state and society in Hong Kong for most of its history simply precludes this. It is only in the aftermath of Hong Kong's handover to China did concerns about state encroachment into civil liberties become concerning, and which elicited pushback from civil society, which is comparatively tame in Singapore.

Hong Kong's Liberal Governance Contrasted with Singapore's Authoritarian Developmental State

The obvious difference that one may observe in the political systems of both countries is that in Hong Kong, citizens do not have the right to freely elect their Chief Executive, while Singaporeans have always enjoyed free, fair, and regular elections. This has been a source of grievous resentment in Hong Kong's population, especially since entering the twenty-first century under Chinese rule, when it seems that the "one country, two systems" agreement had been violated and the Basic Law's promise for the freedom to elect the CE delayed. This has led to numerous protests on the streets, suggesting a breakdown in state-society relations in Hong Kong. In contrast, the situation in Singapore is relatively stable, with the People's Action Party enjoying electoral dominance through the ballot box.

However, it is important to assess the political environment not just in terms of the democratic right to free and fair elections. Critically, liberal democracy also encompasses the protection of civil liberties by law, which includes the freedom of assembly, speech, press, and association. It also comprises a protected sphere for individual action, unmolested from state coercion. This in turn suggests the possibility that a nation may enjoy free, regular, and fair elections, but is otherwise deprived of a wide range of civil liberties and personal freedoms under an authoritarian government.

This dichotomy between electoral freedom and civil-personal freedom is precisely what distinguishes the formal aspects of Hong Kong and Singapore's governance. While Hong Kong citizens do not enjoy the right to freely elect their representatives and are deprived of national sovereignty, being ruled by China, they have historically enjoyed a wide range of civil liberties and personal freedom under the colonial authorities and in the present situation under the Basic Law's framework. In contrast, Singapore achieved national self-determination in 1965 and holds free, fair, and regular elections, yet civil liberties and personal freedoms are stifled. As such, what we have in comparison here is Hong Kong's model of liberal governance on the one hand and Singapore's authoritarian developmental state on the other (Table 4.1).

Table 4.1 Comparison of liberal democratic institutions

	Hong Kong	*Singapore*
National self-determination	No. Hong Kong is not a sovereign nation	Yes. Singapore is a sovereign nation
Electoral freedom and democratic political representation	Not for the Chief Executive, though legislative seats and district council seats are electable	Yes, despite regular accusations of gerrymandering
Civil liberties	Wide-ranging, notwithstanding increasing and recent concerns arising from China's interference	Restricted by government authoritarianism
Personal freedom	Wide-ranging	Restricted by government paternalism

Scholars have also established the importance of state capacity for successful development, referring to its ability to raise taxes, enforce its rules, and provide public goods (Dincecco, 2017; Besley & Persson, 2011). However, it must also be remembered that state capacity can potentially descend into or entail predation, in the absence of checks on power. Hence, state capacity should also be tempered with state constraints, to facilitate successful development (Johnson & Koyama, 2017; North & Weingast, 1989). In the context of Hong Kong and Singapore, state capacity has indeed been established, resulting in a degree of development that remains absent in the poorest regions of the world today. The problem however is that power of the Singapore state is much less constrained than in Hong Kong, and for that matter, than most liberal democracies.

State-Society Relations in Singapore

Developmental State Model Entails Some Authoritarianism

Even though the relationship between authoritarianism and the developmental state is complex and contested, there is sufficient consensus amongst scholars on the affinity between both (Katzenstein, 1985; Gold, 1986; Castells, 1992). This is mainly because the "fundamental element in the ability of developmental states to fulfil their project was their political capacity to impose and internalise their logic on civil society" (Castells, 1992, p. 64). In Japan, the post-war American occupation had to aid in the destruction of entrenched class interests that would hinder the economic bureaucracy, which otherwise would not have "sufficient scope to take initiative and operate effectively" (Johnson, 1995, pp. 132–133).[1] The authoritarian Kuomintang government in Taiwan needed to subordinate the aristocratic class interests to ensure its national development plans would not be opposed (Amsden, 1985; Gold, 1986; Cheng, 1990). Significantly, the birth of South Korea's developmental state was presided by Park Chung-hee, who ruled for about two decades, during which the state had to impose its developmental logic on society (Lim, 1985; Cumings, 1987).

I do not claim that democratic institutions cannot exist in developmental states, but even if they do, an uneasy tension will exist. The strongest articulation of this is by the leading theorist of the developmental state, Stephan Haggard, who claimed that "each policy transition was

[1] Japan was not authoritarian in any meaningful sense, but party competition was limited till 1993.

accompanied by a reconsolidation of authoritarian domination in all the East Asian cases" (Chu, 2016a, p. 10). Even if this extreme is rejected, it is nonetheless true that democratic states are more exposed to popular pressures, divergent concerns, and rent-seeking. These problems frustrate the state's capacity to impose development plans, which is what occurred in the mid-1980s democratic transitions in South Korea and Taiwan (Wong, 2004; Chu, 2016b).

Granted, recent literature has explored the potential compatibility of the developmental state with liberal democracy (Robinson & White, 1998; O'Riain, 2004; Evans, 2010; Evans & Heller, 2015). Some also suggest that such a "democratic developmental state" is gaining pace in certain regions of the world (Edigheji, 2010; Rock, 2013; Chu, 2016b; Huber et al., 2017). Further research is needed to ascertain this compatibility. However, even where democratic institutions exist alongside developmental state policies, I insist that for developmentalism to be successful, the state must have the political power and capacity to suppress private economic activity that runs counter to its national economic plans.

This affinity between the developmental state and political authoritarianism was in fact reflected in the early economic history of post-war Singapore when the early developmental state embarked on a process of state-led industrialisation. This process was deliberately pursued in opposition to the predominantly trade-based, entrepôt economy that was prevalent at the time, which was inadequate in sustaining economic development in the post-war economic climate. State-led industrialisation was clearly unfavourable to the prevailing class of small and medium-sized enterprises (SMEs) that dominated the trade sector; the developmental state had actively provided industrial subsidies and favourable conditions to large firms engaged in industrial activity. To achieve industrial restructuring, the developmental state had to suppress the political power of the SME class which then dominated the economy. Predictably, the People's Action Party (PAP) took an antagonistic position towards local indigenous Chinese entrepreneurs who were both leaders of local SMEs and their ethnic communities.

Singaporean scholars have explored the clash between the English-speaking political elites in the PAP and their Chinese-educated counterparts who were framed as subversive communists. This involved the imposition of English language as the national medium of education, the political attacks on leading Chinese leaders like Tan Lark Sye, and the neglect of historically influential Chinese organisations in the community.

However, these developments cannot be understood as merely contingent contestations for political power between opposing forces. Rather, they may be understood as the logical outgrowth of a nascent developmental state in Singapore attempting to consolidate its power over society which was previously dominated by a political class antithetical to its economic vision.

Therefore, if the developmental state persists as it is, the prospects of political liberalisation remain dim. This stands in contrast to recent scholarly work announcing a supposedly new democratising climate in Singaporean politics post-2011 when opposition parties won a group-representative constituency for the first time. It is also said that a growing middle class and a more vocal citizenry has pushed the political landscape in Singapore towards a more liberal direction. Such observations, however, ignore the fundamental reality in the political landscape, which is that the Singapore state remains a developmental one. The logic of the developmental state has persisted until today, with the state continuing to be active in shaping and moulding the industrial structure of Singapore.

The Centrality of the Ideology of Technocracy

The affinity between Singapore's state-centric capitalism and its practice of political authoritarianism is recognised (Lingle, 1996; Rahim & Barr, 2019). Some scholars have provided explanations for the long-standing ability of the developmental state to maintain its legitimacy in society despite its suppression of civil society and political opposition.

It is said that the Singapore state has forged an ideology that not only guides its own governance practices but also shapes social relations and mass beliefs. Scholars have cited the presence of neoliberalism, meritocracy, and even pragmatism as an ideology.

Several social democratic scholars have argued that the Singapore state has been wedded to the ideology of neoliberalism to maintain its political hegemony. For instance, Kenneth Paul Tan (2012) has written that pragmatism was mere rhetoric meant to cover the actual principles of neoliberalism in Singapore. Teo You Yenn (2011) has also written about neoliberal morality in the context of family policy.

This position, however, is problematic. Neoliberalism pursued to its logical extent would translate into a much smaller role for the state in society, be it through the maintenance of lower taxes on profits and income and a divestment of state assets in the economy. In fact, there was an exercise of privatisation in Singapore in the late 1980s which led to a divestment of telecommunications and infrastructure assets held by the Singapore government which reduced its political influence in society. If Garry Rodan (2016) and Christopher Tremewan (1994) are right that the PAP state was in the service of foreign capital, then this would mean a devolution of state regulation on business and a much smaller role for the state. Yet, as earlier chapters have shown, this has not occurred, and the Singapore state has in fact maintained a pervasive role in the economy.

Some have insisted that meritocracy is the underlying state philosophy. While this is indeed prevalent, meritocracy is limited in accounting for the pervasive involvement of the state in Singapore society. Meritocracy has influenced public sector recruitment and the wider social expectation in Singapore of merit-based advancement, rather than by class or status. However, the practice of meritocracy itself has been shaped and defined by the state according to its national objectives. A deeper ideological layer must be identified.

Instead, I posit that the key ideology that characterises Singapore's governance is the *belief in technocracy*, which I define as a combination of (1) the conviction that governance requires not democratic participation of the masses, but rather, the leadership of a superior elite and (2) the definition of this elite not just in terms of their public-spiritedness but also in their superior wisdom necessary to achieve the public interest.

Technocracy is thus not merely a practice, but a worldview that has shaped how Singapore's political leaders structured institutions and implemented policies. It explains the aversion to democratic norms in Singapore, best expressed by Lee Kuan Yew that:

> I am often accused of interfering in the private lives of citizens. Yes, if I did not, had I not done that, we wouldn't be here today. And I say without the slightest remorse, that we wouldn't be here, we would not have made economic progress, if we had not intervened on very personal matters—who your neighbour is, how you live, the noise you make, how you spit, or what language you use. We decide what is right. (BBC, 2015)

This explains why the state is staffed with university graduates from the elite scholarship system, stemming from the belief that the best policies are formed on a rational basis by top talent rather than erroneously following the popular will. It further explains why these policies have tended to be paternalistic, shaping very personal choices of individual citizens. Such governance has roots in the Platonic suspicion of democracy as mob rule and the necessity of enlightened philosopher guardians.

What is unique in Singapore is that its political elites genuinely believe this to be true; they are not simply employing this strategically just for rhetorical purposes. This cannot be definitively proven since the author is unable to discern the inner thoughts of Singapore's leaders. However, strong evidence is available by examining the way governance institutions are structured and the leaders' words. The Center for Strategic Futures is a government-linked organisation given much latitude to conduct scenario planning for the rest of the civil service. It is believed that with big data tools and predictive technologies, national planning would be enhanced. The Civil Service College also runs courses on this topic for civil servants of all levels.

Singapore's governance is based on the belief that long-term planning in various policy areas is absolutely essential for Singapore to stay ahead of potential challenges and regional competition, and that this conviction is "deeply embedded in the culture of the public sector".[2] What is distinctive is that Singapore is the "only country in the entire world that employs scenario planning on the national level".

This belief in technocracy, which is sceptical of democratic choice, was also expressed by the interviewee, who acknowledged with the example of the foreign talent debate that government policies must often be made against popular wishes which may sometimes be irrational. This technocratic ideology is further manifested in a scepticism against a bottom-up laissez-faire approach to governance, describing it as a "nice and comfortable position to take" if one were in a big economy like the United States.[3] Echoing the entrepreneurial state theory, it is believed that considering Singapore's small size, industrial planning is necessary, without which the free market would not bring in the funds necessary to catalyse technological advancement.

Ideological Control in Singapore

Not only is the Singapore state guided by a technocratic ideology, it also engages in systematic ideological control over the population. Due to the presence of the developmental state in Singapore, people are kept

[2] Interview with a Director from the Center for Strategic Futures, November 2018.
[3] Ibid.

dependent on the state for their very survival and social advancement. The authoritarian roots of the developmental state reach into the daily lives of Singaporeans and incentivises compliance. This is in turn buttressed by the pervasive national ideology which in turn legitimises the status quo and causes citizens to actively internalise their state dependence.

The political control of the developmental state in Singapore starts with the youth, who must make educational decisions that will maximise their career prospects. Singaporean youth find themselves having to study the right course, get into the right schools, and adopt the right educational practices to get a job that provides adequate monetary compensation. The reason why this is the case is because the educational system is carefully engineered to serve the developmental state's industrial policy. The government favours certain fields of study more than others because it wishes to develop adequate labour and human capital to fill selected industries. In the early stage of state-led industrialisation, the importance of math and science was heavily emphasised to produce adequate labour resources. In the later years since the 1980s, other professions such as law, medical services, and financial services were also emphasised to meet the needs of a maturing economy.

This means that youth who find themselves having talents and career aspirations that do not fit within the national economic plan may end up marginalised. Chapters 6 and 7 will provide further details of the social costs of these policies, which include how non-technical fields of study, namely, the humanities and the creative fields, have been neglected. This way, the Singapore social system encourages youth to be compliant to the preferences of the developmental state since failure to do so would result in a relatively harder path to social advancement.

More critically, the pervasive social control of the developmental state in Singapore extends beyond the youth. In fact, it is lifelong. The two major institutions in Singapore which enable the developmental state to maintain far-reaching social control is the Central Provident Fund and housing. Because all citizens in Singapore are mandated by law to maintain the compulsory savings scheme and because public housing covers more than three quarters of the population, few residents can circumvent the influence of these two institutions.

The Central Provident Fund is a national compulsory savings scheme that was constructed with the aim to ensure Singaporeans can support themselves without being state dependents. It was based on the paternalistic belief that Singaporeans might gamble away their money and fail to save adequately for retirement (Ng, 1998). Thus, up to 20% of the monthly incomes of Singaporeans are by law automatically transferred into their CPF account, with employers contributing their share of up to 17% of the income amount. Significantly, the amount accumulated is not only available for use upon retirement but is typically used by the state for large capital expenditures.

The link between the purchase of a government flat and the use of CPF funds for financing provides the state with an ongoing ability to exert social control over Singaporeans. A most common practice in Singapore is for new members of the workforce to purchase a public home from the Housing Development Board within a few years of working, largely due to the relatively expensive prices of private accommodation and heavy subsidies for HDB flats. When individuals purchase houses from the government agency, they typically obtain a loan from the HDB or a concessionary, government-linked loan from the bank. CPF funds, which are controlled by the state, are then used to finance loan payments monthly, moving funds back to the loan providers, which is either the state or a state-linked entity.

The close interlink between all the relevant state institutions necessary for an individual to purchase, own, and maintain a home over their lifetime allows the PAP government to exercise a lifetime of social control over Singaporeans. Understandably, the political economist Christopher Tremewan expressed that the CPF "provides the government with immense control" (1994, p. 54).

This system of social control in Singapore is legitimised by the education system. Some scholars have insisted that the education system is nothing but a tool for government propaganda and ideological indoctrination (Bellows, 1970). In fact, a previous empirical study compared, through interviews and classroom observations, the perceptions of students on Singapore's national history, finding that all converged on the same discourse created by the state despite their differing backgrounds (Ho, 2010).

I will not go this far. Students and their parents do have a choice, albeit limited, to circumvent the state-dominated education system by studying overseas or by being private candidates in entrance examinations. In fact, many who do not feel accustomed to the education system in Singapore have reportedly sought preferable arrangements in neighbouring countries, most commonly Australia.

However, I affirm the underlying idea that education is a political tool to engender submission to government authorities in Singapore. I do not ascribe this to the deliberate intention of political elites because there is no way to discern what is in the minds of government officials when constructing policies. Rather, I simply show the existence of repeated attempts by the Singapore state to forge and communicate a national ideology in society through educational institutions which was absent during the colonial period of Hong Kong.

Importantly, in the late 1980s, the government published a Green Paper on National Ideology, a White Paper on Shared Values in 1991, and several government-linked academic research papers on the same topic (Quah, 1990). These papers articulated five core values which have since been a part of social studies education in Singapore, a compulsory subject taken by all high school-age students. These five principles are:

1. Nation before community and society above self
2. Family as the basic unit of society
3. Community support and respect for the individual
4. Consensus not conflict
5. Racial and religious harmony

Significantly, the state officially articulated its stance on the priority of the collective over the individual. According to the President of Singapore, Wee Kim Wee,

> putting the interests of society as a whole ahead of individual interests has been a major factor in Singapore's success...If Singaporeans had insisted on their individual rights and prerogatives, and refused to compromise these for the greater interests of the nation, they would have restricted the options available. (see Thio, 1991, p. 3)

It is clear from various sources that the PAP developmental state has sought to and very much succeeded in forging a collective ideology to legitimise their rule, an ideology that the masses are socialised in from education all the way to adulthood.

From Arm's Length to Antagonistic State-Society Relations in Hong Kong

A puzzle that needs explanation is why post-war Hong Kong enjoyed peaceful state-society relations even though the population was living under an effectively foreign government that was not democratically elected. Also, it is notable that post-1997 Hong Kong witnessed a tremendous growth in civil society activities, in marked contrast to the more docile local population before.

There were peaceful state-society relations in post-war Hong Kong because both the Chinese community and the British colonialists had settled into a mutually beneficial equilibrium which continued largely undisturbed until the 1980s when the issue of Hong Kong's future became salient. The economic growth Hong Kong experienced in the post-war period enriched the local Chinese community, and thus reduced social frictions which would otherwise have posed excessive difficulties for the British colonialists, who by the 1950s onwards began to incur more costs than benefits from maintaining overseas colonies.

Despite the low representation of the Chinese community in local governance institutions since key posts were reserved for expatriates and British individuals, the colonial government nonetheless enjoyed a semblance of political legitimacy, allowing it to sustain its existence in the colony. This legitimacy mainly stemmed from two factors. First, the rising living standards enjoyed by the population meant that they accepted the political status quo even though they did not hold political power. It should be remembered that the Chinese community since the nineteenth century were predominantly focused on wealth creation. The economic character of the local population was further entrenched by new waves of Chinese migrants entering Hong Kong in the post-war period due to upheavals in communist China. The injection of Shanghainese migrants, who brought managerial skills and industrial capital, further reinforced a positive cycle of economic growth.

The British government's legitimacy is also derived from its relatively benevolent nature compared to that in neighbouring countries. The growth of Hong Kong's economy and society has always occurred against the backdrop of China. While China was experiencing social and economic upheavals, British rule simply appeared more favourable. This also provided the British further impetus to professionalise the civil service, clean up the police, and strengthen relationships with local Chinese community leaders. In fact, multiple rounds of civil service reforms occurred under the governorship of Sir Mark Young who oversaw the appointment of Paul Tsui, the first Chinese selected to be part of the elite administrative class, and the governorship of Alexander Grantham whose administration improved public service delivery and local community relationships (Tsang, 2007, chs. 4–5).

The benign nature of Chinese society in Hong Kong during the post-war period and the sense that "it could have been worse" is very much documented in several opinion polls taken at various junctures (see Miners, 1995, ch 3). This also explains why nearing 1997, many wished for a continuation of British rule rather than being handed over to China.

The British themselves also had a vested interest in maintaining this mutually beneficial status quo. This was even though by now its past commercial advantages were gone; being a free port, the British government could not grant special privileges for itself. In fact, on a purely economic basis, the British also had to maintain the high costs of their garrison and higher costs of public service delivery. Overall, however, due to strong pressures at home for Britain to remain in Hong Kong, the desire of the local administrators to maintain their rule, and the continued moral convictions that the British had to be Hong Kong's caretaker, the ultimate decision was to remain.

Not only did the British opt to remain in Hong Kong, but they also continued practising the laissez-faire policies well into the twentieth century. This can be explained with reference to the economic constraints faced by and principles held by British leaders. On the first level, the domestic pressures at home meant that the Colonial Office had less desire to spend money on the Hong Kong colony, leaving the local administration to deal with local problems unilaterally. On a related note, Hong Kong's dependence on trade and commerce meant that Britain had to continue the laissez-fair policies that had contributed to its success in the first place. This then took on greater importance as Britain had to maintain close relationships with China to allow it to keep earning foreign exchange. Thus, the non-interventionist character of the Hong Kong state, which carried on well into the twentieth century, was not an accidental phenomenon but rather a product of calculated interests. Sir David Trench, Governor from 1964 to 1971, said, "Hong Kong's generally laissez-faire economic policies have always been based on considered decisions, not mere paralysis of mind and will".

Britain's interest in maintaining the relatively peaceful and prosperous colonial status quo of Hong Kong coincided with the interests of the Chinese communist government and the local people, what has been called a "tripod of consents" (Rabushka, 1979). Hong Kong's economic growth provided tangible economic benefits to China and acted as an outlet to the global economy. The local people, whose motivations were mainly economic, also largely benefitted from colonial rule and had little political motivation to alter the status quo.

Not only did Britain have a vested interest to maintain its laissez-faire economic policies, but its leaders also believed in the ideology of laissez-faire on a deep, ideological level. While Hong Kong governors in the nineteenth century were exposed to the philosophy in some ways, the post-war governors and financial secretaries had explicitly articulated laissez-faire principles in governance. For instance, David Trench first introduced "positive laissez-faire" as a concept, which was further extended by Phillip Haddon Cove's "positive non-interventionism" in the 1970s. Thus, the governorship of David Trench, aided by the Financial Secretaries of Arthur Clarke, John Cowperthwaite, and Phillip Haddon-Cove, etched the principle of non-interventionism into Hong Kong's governance. Cowperthwaite was especially influential, having been the Financial Secretary for over ten years. He is reported to have made repeated articulations of non-interventionism, believing that the private sector was "the best judgement of investment and the best creator of wealth", and that the government "mustn't meddle in the economy unless it had to" (Monnery, 2017). As official government statements, his pronouncements were not merely personal:

> For I still believe that, in the long run, the aggregate of the decisions of individual businessmen, exercising individual judgement in a free economy, even if often mistaken, is likely to do less harm than the centralised decisions of a government; and certainly the harm is going to be counteracted faster...it has to be recognised, and it is recognised...that the community's scarce economic resources can be efficiently allocated only by the price mechanism. (Hong Kong Hansard, 1966, pp. 216, 218)

The contributions of these few individuals are especially significant, considering that in the Hong Kong governance structure, the Governor and Financial Secretary hold the most decision-making power, with the latter having enormous latitude to approve and reject budgets (Miners, 1995, chs. 6, 9).

Due to the overall impact of these decisions made, Hongkongers enjoyed consistently rising living standards for decades under a non-interventionist government that they were largely satisfied with. However, this mutually beneficial equilibrium was unsettled from the 1980s onwards when the question of Hong Kong's future became contested. Over the next decade, as the possibility of re-integration into communist China became real, there was a distinct rise in political consciousness amongst the Hong Kong population concerned about the loss of their prosperity and civil liberties.

A critical juncture came in 1981, when the British officially started negotiations with China on Hong Kong's future, having been concerned about the fate of land leases that were to expire in 1997. This forced China to an official position. China's subsequent decisions clearly expressed their preference for Hong Kong to be reclaimed under Chinese sovereignty, albeit with internal autonomy. This clear statement of intent, which led to years of negotiation over the next decade, arguably marks the beginning of the local population's political consciousness.

From 1981 all the way to 1997, various factors contributed to the strengthening of Hong Kong's civil society and its pro-democratic, liberal orientation. Not only did people fear the consequences of being handed back to China, but they were also given more opportunities for self-governance by the British who started implementing elections such as the 1981 District Board election and the 1985 Legislative Council elections, with both receiving large turnouts. The year 1985 also marked the genesis of party competition in Hong Kong, as about 500 different candidates and parties entered the fray considering the anxiety people had about the ongoing negotiations with China. In the space of a few years, political activity increased considering domestic events within China, most significantly the Tiananmen Square incident. The year 1989 itself saw the emergence of the Hong Kong Alliance in Support of the Patriotic Democratic Movement in China and pro-democratic leader Martin Lee's rise to prominence, who remains a key civil society activist till the present day.

Such political activity, while heavily objected to by China, was encouraged by Britain and the last remaining governors, especially Chris Patten, who wished to prepare the local community for some semblance of self-government before the 1997 handover (Flowerdew, 1998). The desire of local activists, political parties, and pressure groups to secure their future autonomy, coupled with Britain's acquiesce on such political activities, against the backdrop of government oppression in China, contributed to the burgeoning of Hong Kong's strongly pro-democratic and active civil society.

Thus, Hong Kong society was politically mobilised due to factors that simply did not exist in Singapore. Hong Kong society had enjoyed an arm's length relationship vis-à-vis the colonial government which did not engage in any concerted intervention, let alone the type of social engineering pursued by the Singaporean developmental state. This arm's length separation between state and society in pre-1997 Hong Kong engendered a strengthened, activist civil society demanding greater democratic rights for Hong Kong's post-colonial future.

The Hong Kong citizenry which had been mobilised for political action since the 1980s became even more strident after 1997 under Chinese rule. While state-society relations were generally peaceful in the immediate years after 1997, the antagonistic state-society relations we witness today can be traced to the 2003 protests of China's National Security Legislation, which is estimated to have involved 60,000 citizens. Overall, the average number of annual public protests and gatherings increased from 2000 in 2006 to more than 6000 in 2015. From 2010 to 2019, as the table below shows, the total number of public meetings and processions has more than doubled (Table 4.2).

Administrative States

One important similarity between the Singaporean developmental state and the Hong Kong colonial state was the importance of the role of the civil service in governance. Both inherited and built upon the British civil service tradition of recruiting the most able men to run government agencies. This began as an internal initiative of the British Empire, starting with the 1855 introduction of a civil service commission to recruit and

Table 4.2 Public order event statistics in Hong Kong

Year	*2010*	*2011*	*2012*	*2013*	*2014*	*2015*	*2016*	*2017*	*2018*	*2019*
Public meetings	4519	5363	5599	4987	5715	4887	11,854	10,608	10,783	10,342
Public processions	1137	1515	1930	1179	1103	1142	1304	1203	1097	1094
Total	5656	6878	7529	6166	6818	6029	13,158	11,811	11,880	11,436

Source: Hong Kong Police Force (2019)

promote officials based on merit rather than patronage (Chapman, 2004). The civil service took on an important role in post-war Singapore, with the PAP government deciding to build on this institution for its own purposes. With able bureaucrats in public agencies, the developmental state could better execute its national plans for society. In Hong Kong, the civil service not only persisted into the late twentieth century, but also played a key role in governance, especially since Governors would rely heavily on elite administrative officers to meet the needs of the indigenous people, gain legitimacy in their eyes by effectively delivering public services, and liaise with officials in London. These administrative officers were also a crucial link between the colonial rulers and the mass Chinese society and thus a pillar of social stability.

The importance of the role of public administration in the governance of Singapore and Hong Kong thus warrants the label given by Anthony Cheung (2008) that both are forms of "administrative states". That is, both have a long tradition of relying on an efficient, professionally trained group of administrators to carry out policymaking who are partly shielded from political pressures. It is believed that bureaucratic autonomy would increase government efficiency and ensure the right policies to be implemented, regardless of the prevailing political winds. Ambrose King (1975) added that political groups were being co-opted in Hong Kong into administrative bodies in what he termed the "administrative absorption of politics", thus guaranteeing public acceptance of government policies and pacifying any opposition.

Contrasting Logics of the Developmental vs. Colonial State

While both countries accorded a key role to elite administrators in public governance, they differed in terms of how they saw themselves and their relationship to wider society. In Singapore, these individuals were believed to be and themselves believed they were imbued with the necessary authority and wisdom for extensive social engineering. In Hong Kong, however, there was always a strong sense of self-restraint on the part of these elite administrators which thus explains their relatively circumscribed role.

The Singaporean developmental state combined technocratic elitism with authoritarianism. Political leaders and top bureaucrats form the apex of the state apparatus, which maintains strong control over society. Importantly, there is close connection between the practice of the developmental state and political authoritarianism. The logic of the developmental state necessarily involves an expansion of state power into the private realm and thus authoritarianism. This is largely because, for a developmental state to achieve its aims of rapid economic growth, it must have the state capacity to shape the industrial structure of society according to its preconceived plans. In fact, industrial policy, which involves the use of state-owned enterprises and policy tools like subsidies to firms, is central to the identity of the developmental state. This requires the state capacity to allocate, mobilise, and redistribute resources in ways contrary to the market process.

In contrast, in the case of Hong Kong, despite colonial elites enjoying a large degree of power, they exercised considerable restraint in exercising the said power. The historian Steve Tsang (2007, ch 10) has described this as the "inhibited elitism" at the heart of colonial governance in Hong Kong whereby the colonial officers felt the "need to exert considerable restraint in the exercise of power". He explained that this was partly due to the "esprit de corps" of administrative officers which conditioned the officers to act benevolently to the best interests of the Chinese people, constituting a form of benevolent paternalism during the colonial era (Tsang, 2004, pp. 206–210).

I add a different argument. Explaining political restraint based on a sense of "esprit de corps" is problematic, because such a public sector ethos is also present in many other countries, especially in Singapore where the government has consistently inculcated public service values within government agencies. I argue that government elites in both countries faced *different political incentives*. First, Hong Kong officials relied on the support of the commercial class who were opposed to interventionist policies. Proposals for higher taxes and tariffs were hence repeatedly rejected by the political constituency of the colonial officials. However, this is also an inadequate explanation because local capitalists occasionally requested for special privileges for their own industry.

This was refused by the colonial government in Hong Kong, leading to the second issue: during the post-war period, the British Empire faced financial constraints on various fronts, reducing its ability to spend large sums on far-flung colonies. The requirement for Hong Kong to be fiscally self-sustaining imposed a strong sense of budgetary constraint on the local government. Third, and more importantly, there were external factors that incentivised colonial officers to be self-restrained. This was mainly due to the rising Chinese nationalism in the PRC and the desire of Chinese communists to retake Hong Kong. The Hong Kong government had to act in a restrained manner towards the local population, lest it experience a severe loss of legitimacy and criticism of its existence in the region. The threat of Chinese communism gave Hong Kong's colonial government a continued incentive to maintain a distinct, market-based way of life there.

Importance of Being Connected to the State, According to Social Perceptions

A clear contrast emerges. Within Singapore's state capitalism, individuals are not only dependent on the state for social and economic advancement but believe such dependence to be desirable. By contrast, the entrepreneurial capitalism in Hong Kong means that residents there have less of an incentive to rely, depend, or expect state favours to achieve similar advancement. In fact, due to the breakdown in state-society relations in Hong Kong as part of the ongoing constitutional crisis, close connections with the state are not seen by general citizens as being desirable.

This argument is important because it impacts the level of socio-economic mobility people believe they have. The economist Luigi Zingales (2012) explored how the US economy has degenerated into a "connection-based system" as opposed to a "contract-based system", such that political connections matter more than individual initiative and value creation. In such a system, rent-seeking behaviour becomes normalised, leading to significant losses of welfare in society.

Rather than relying on sweeping generalisations, this author has decided to test this empirically in Singapore and Hong Kong by asking residents directly. The independent survey conducted featured questions to test the extent to which citizens and residents in both countries perceive a need to be politically connected or to receive favours from the state to advance socially and economically (Fig. 4.1).

Looking at the results, it seems that the meritocratic orientation of Singaporean society is not fully imbibed by the population, since about 44.7% of Singaporean respondents believe that special political connections are "very important" in achieving success. Interestingly, the response in Hong Kong is more polarised, with 65.6% believing that it is either "very important" or "not important".

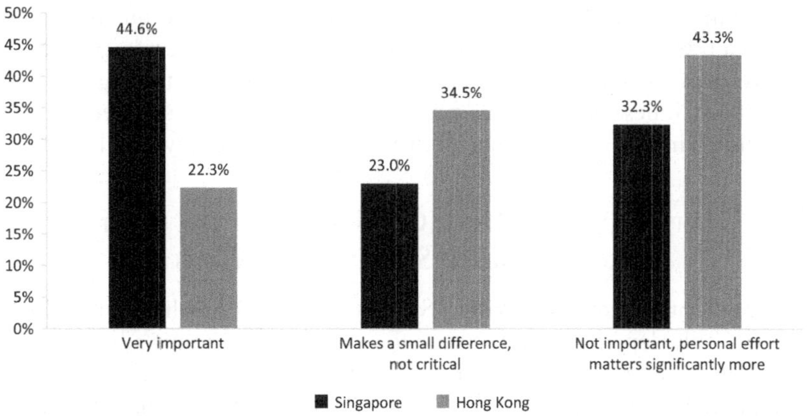

Fig. 4.1 Survey response on importance of special political connections

Comparative State of Political Culture and Civil Society

I present further empirical data to contrast the political culture and civil society in both city-states. This involves a comparison of think tanks which are important as independent sources of policy opinion in society and survey results measuring political participation in both societies.

The overall conclusion of this section is that due to the domination of the developmental state and its penetration into Singapore society, there are few independent sources of policy opinion, evinced by the very small number of think tanks that exist and the form of political contestation that is tepid at best. Survey results show that citizens of Hong Kong are more ready to participate in civil society activities, especially political initiatives that challenge the status quo. The Singaporean developmental state has achieved a degree of cultural, ideological, and intellectual hegemony in society that the Hong Kong state, in both its colonial and current versions, has never achieved. The colonial state never attempted to socially engineer society the way Singapore did, and in fact the post-1997 Hong Kong state lost legitimacy due to its inability (both perceived and actual) to deliver on the constitutional promises of the 1984 Declaration.

It is generally accepted that the strength of any democratic society lies in its civil society. An important part of civil society is its political culture which can be understood as the way individuals self-organise and participate in politics. In a society where members of the public are either apathetic about politics or restricted from participating, the rich associational life of democracy cannot thrive.

Comparison of Think Tanks

Think tanks are an important component of civil society. Not only that, being organisations that produce policy research and use the subsequent findings to champion policy reforms through advocacy, social mobilisation, public campaigns, and education, they constitute an independent locus of policy opinion aside from that produced by the state. Think tanks may champion alternative visions of governance, and thus a robust marketplace of think tanks can reasonably be said to reflect a robust civil society which discusses various pathways for social progress. Consequently, it is worthwhile to explore the prevalence of think tanks in both Hong Kong and Singapore, in terms of their origins, quantity, and reach.

The only leading study of the state of think tanks around the world is the Think Tank Index produced by McGann. Based on this study, I identify the major think tanks in both city-states and explore the background of each organisation. To supplement this list, I also rely on a generic internet search of "major think tanks" in both places. I have found that while there are numerous think tanks in both countries, all those listed in Singapore are either government linked or funded and may thus be considered extensions of the state's ideological hegemony.

According to the latest version of the Think Tank Index, there are 42 think tanks in Hong Kong, with only 18 in Singapore. While there are more identified in Hong Kong, only 5 of them are ranked, compared to 11 Singaporean think tanks ranked in the Index. On the surface this suggests that think tanks play a more influential role in public policy in Singapore despite their smaller quantity.

To obtain more information, I also conducted a generic internet search to identify major think tanks in both countries, which yielded the list in Table 4.3. An investigation into their background, nature of work, and origins reveal that all the 11 listed think tanks in Singapore are government linked. While some are also government-linked in Hong Kong, there are major organisations which toe an independent line of thinking. I define a "government-linked think tank" as either being (1) founded by an influential member of the incumbent government or (2) institutionally affiliated to organs of the state.

Table 4.3 shows that for the 11 think tanks identified in Singapore, all of them are in some way institutionally linked to the government and have

Table 4.3 Comparison of major think tanks in Hong Kong and Singapore

Major think tanks in Hong Kong[a]	*Origins and nature of work*	*Major think tanks in Singapore*[b]	*Origins and nature of work*
Civic Exchange	Independent think tank founded in 2000 by Christine Loh who joined the government *after* she left the organisation.	Singapore Institute of International Affairs	Although SIIA claims to be independent, its founding members and chair-members are all ex-government officials or government-linked individuals, such as Professor Tommy Koh, Singapore's ambassador at large, and Dr Lau Teik Soon, a previous Member of Parliament. Additionally, most of their research pertains to regional affairs and ASEAN cooperation rather than an analysis of domestic public policies and policy recommendations.
Our Hong Kong Foundation	Influential think tank founded by the first Chief Executive of post-1997 Hong Kong, Tung Chee Hwa in 2014.	Institute of Southeast Asian Studies	Its institutional affiliation to the state stems from the fact that it was established by an Act of Parliament in 1968. The current director, Mr. Choi Shing Kwok, was previously a Permanent Secretary in the Singapore government.
Lion Rock Institute	Independent think tank which adheres to a neoliberal, free-market ideology and hence critical of government policies. Founding members are Simon Lee, Andrew Work, and Andrew Shuen, who are non-government affiliated media personalities.	Centre on Asia and Globalisation	University-based think tanks affiliated with the Lee Kuan Yew School of Public Policy, a quasi-governmental educational institution.

Hong Kong Policy Research Institute	Independent think tank chaired by Prof Paul Yip, an academic and businessman. Its current director Andrew Fung was a former Executive Director of the Hong Kong University Graduates' Association Education Foundation.	Asia Competitiveness Institute	University-based think tanks affiliated with the Lee Kuan Yew School of Public Policy, a quasi-governmental educational institution.
Hong Kong Centre for Economic Research	Independent think tank founded by the political economist Prof. Richard Wong Yue Chim who subscribes to a neoliberal, free-market ideology which he uses to criticise government policies.	Institute of Policy Studies	University-based think tanks affiliated with the Lee Kuan Yew School of Public Policy, a quasi-governmental educational institution.

(*continued*)

Table 4.3 (continued)

Major think tanks in Hong Kong[a]	*Origins and nature of work*	*Major think tanks in Singapore*[b]	*Origins and nature of work*
–	–	Institute of Water Policy	
		Institute of Defence and Strategic Studies	
		East Asian Institute	
		Energy Studies Institute	
		Middle East Institute	
		National Environment Agency	The NEA wrongly listed as a think tank by the Think Tank Index since it is actually a fully government-funded statutory board.

Source: Information from Think Tank Index (McGann, 2019) and author's investigations of each organisation's public records

[a]Copied from the list of 5 ranked organisations in the Think Tank Index and confirmed by separate news article obtained from an internet search of "major think tanks in Hong Kong" (Ng, 2017)

[b]Copied from the 13 ranked organisations in the Think Tank Index (McGann, 2019)

a pro-establishment stance. Although no evidence exists that they actively coordinate with the state to produce a pro-establishment policy opinion, it should be remembered that the three major universities in Singapore, NUS, NTU, and SMU, which house eight of the listed 11 organisations, have previously been criticised for restrictions on academic freedom due to government pressure (George, 2012, 2017). The sample size for the Hong Kong list of organisations is much smaller and may not constitute a clear trend. We may observe that two out of the five ranked Hong Kong think tanks have founders or board members with links to the political establishment, such as Our Hong Kong Foundation and Hong Kong Policy Research Institute. However, what is obvious is that their institutional affiliation to the state is not apparent and not as obvious as those in Singapore. Significantly, two out of these five ranked organisations adhere to an anti-establishment small government ideology (The Lion Rock Institute[4] and the Hong Kong Centre for Economic Research), with none in Singapore following this same philosophy (Table 4.3).

Survey Results

The independent survey I conducted shows a sharp contrast in the political culture in both city-states. It is found that Hong Kong citizens, including youths, have a stronger interest in political affairs, place a higher premium on civil liberties and human rights, and engage in a wider range of political activities.

The authoritarian developmental state, as many scholars have theorised, gains its legitimacy from its economic performance, rather than any claim to democratic principles (Chu, 2016a; Haggard, 2018). Accordingly, the PAP government has on numerous occasions justified their restrictions on civil liberties based on the need for strong governance for the state to have the capacity to deliver tangible material outcomes for its citizens.

The PAP state's justification for authoritarianism has also shaped the political values of its citizens. The survey results from our independent work show that indeed, as compared to Hongkongers, Singaporeans tend to favour a strong and effective government rather than a liberal one. This effect, however, is moderated when age is considered. Singaporean youths tend to be more neutral about this trade-off compared to Singaporean

[4] One of the co-founders, Simon Lee, is also the Head of Editorials at Apple Daily, a highly read anti-establishment media platform in Hong Kong (Centre for Civil Society, India, 2020).

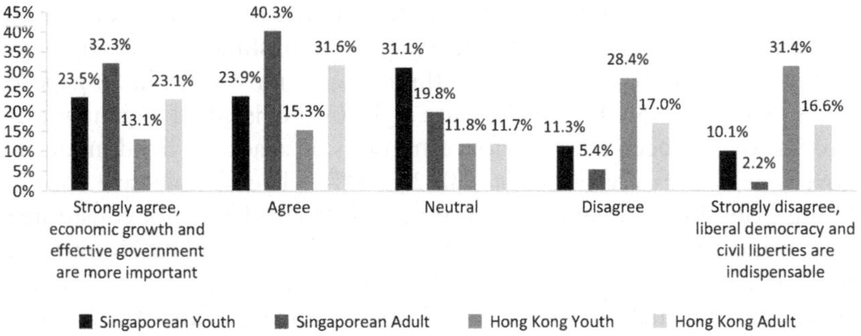

Fig. 4.2 Survey response on the importance of economics vs. liberalism, "It is far better to have an effective government that succeeds in economic growth rather than having liberal democracy and civil liberties. Do you agree?"

adults, who overwhelmingly deprioritise the importance of liberal governance. Hong Kong youths are particularly pro-liberal, which might be a product of the current political crisis over Hong Kong's constitutional future under China (Fig. 4.2).

This is a particularly important finding because it reinforces the notion that the suspension of civil liberties is unavoidable in achieving the Singaporean developmental state's goals, namely, economic performance. Such a belief is not merely elitist but seems to have pervaded the public consciousness. The general population has subscribed to the national ideology perpetuated by the authoritarian developmental state in Singapore, that civil liberties and liberalism must be sacrificed to achieve economic success. This is a counterpoint to some observations made recently that Singaporean society is fast democratising after the watershed 2011 election (Chee, 2011).

Political hegemony is not measured only in terms of electoral dominance but also in the realm of ideology. The mass socialisation of Singaporean society by elite beliefs suggests that the dominant political culture remains resistant to democratic norms.

Aside from attitudes about the trade-off between strong governance and civil liberties, the survey also investigated interest in politics more generally. The survey not only asked respondents how interested they were, but also tracked specific forms of participation in civil society activities, including those by political organisations. In terms of interest in politics, it is found that citizens of both countries are generally interested in

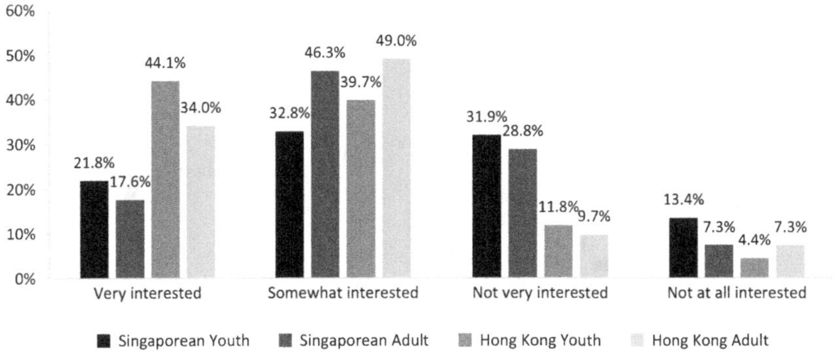

Fig. 4.3 Survey response on interest in politics, "How interested are you in politics?"

politics, since more than 50% of respondents from both countries are at least "somewhat interested". However, there is clearly higher interest in politics in Hong Kong than in Singapore, especially when Hong Kong youth are considered (Fig. 4.3).

When it comes to civil society participation, the survey found that Hongkongers were more likely to participate in a variety of civil society organisations. As for pro-democracy organisations and advocacy groups more specifically, I find that both Hong Kong youths and adults are more likely to lead such organisations and participate in their programmes. Significantly, most of the participation identified amongst Hongkongers also involve leadership activities, which means that not only do Hongkongers participate in civil society activities, but they also actively initiate, organise, and lead such organisations (Fig. 4.4).

The survey was also interested not just in interest in politics and participation in pro-democracy groups in the abstract, but the likelihood that ordinary citizens would participate in initiatives that call for socio-political change and agitate against the political status quo. Here I find a large difference in patterns of political mobilisation, including five different activities involving different levels of public disruption and legal risk, namely, "signing an online petition", "participating in a boycott", "attending a peaceful demonstration", "joining a strike", and "engaging in civil disobedience" (Figs. 4.5 and 4.6).

I notice that for the signing of petitions and participation in boycotts, both carry lower legal risks; thus, there is generally not a big difference in

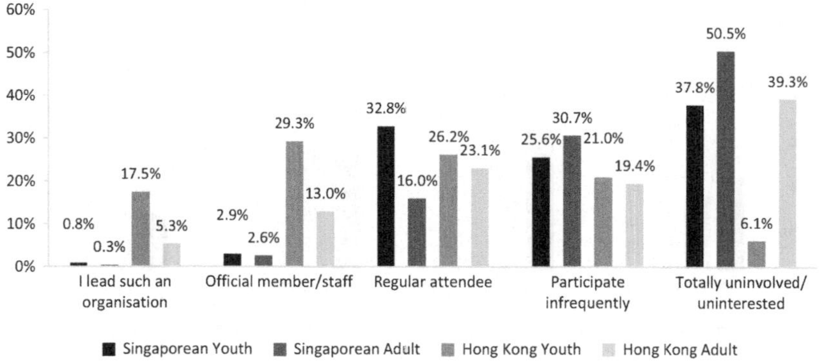

Fig. 4.4 Survey response on involvement with pro-democracy organisations & advocacy groups

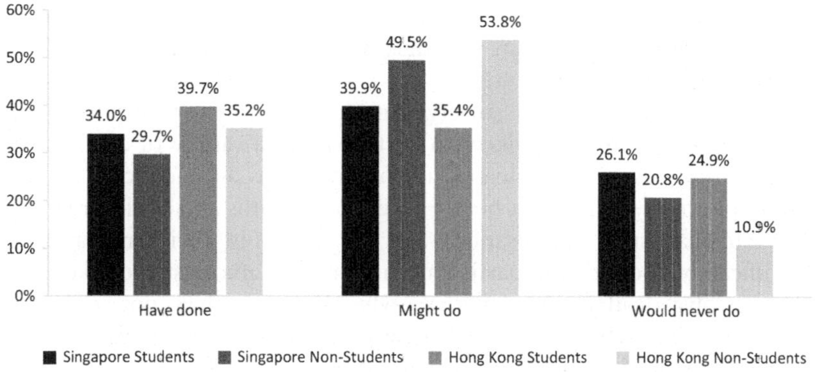

Fig. 4.5 Survey response on signing petitions

results. However, when it comes to attending demonstrations, protests, and civil disobedience, Hongkongers are more willing to engage in such actions, with the youth particularly militant on this front (Figs. 4.7, 4.8, and 4.9).

One interesting result is the generally low interest in joining a labour strike. A very small proportion of respondents reported having joined one, with large numbers saying they would not consider it at all. This is largely because labour strikes are illegal in Singapore and have been severely punished whenever they were attempted. The year 2013 saw Singapore's first

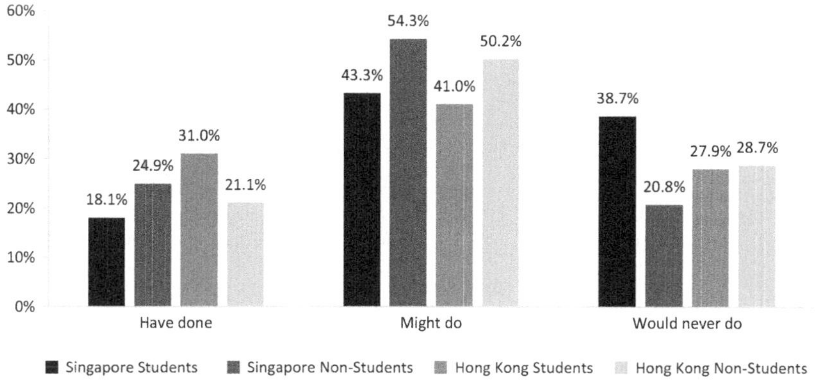

Fig. 4.6 Survey response on participating in boycotts, "Have you participated or will you participate in boycotts?"

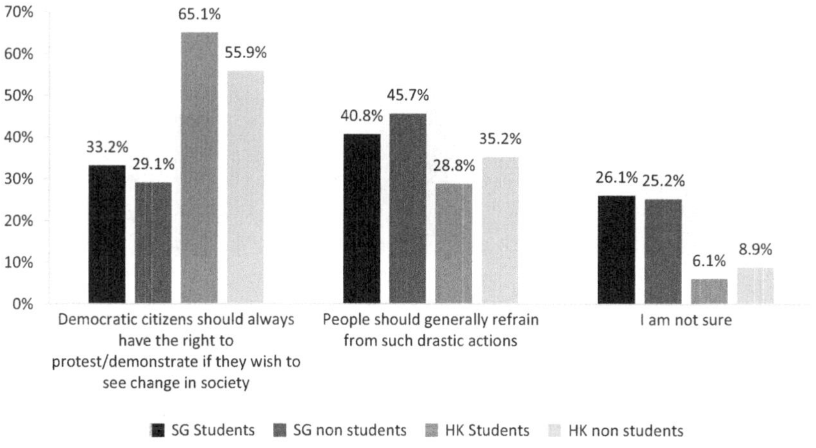

Fig. 4.7 Survey response on participating in protests, "What do you think about political protests?"

labour strike in three decades, involving only four disgruntled bus drivers; all were sentenced to imprisonment (Agence France-Presse, 2013). In Hong Kong, this is mainly because trade unionism and collective bargaining is weak (see Chap. 2), which makes it less likely that strike actions would be considered (Fig. 4.10).

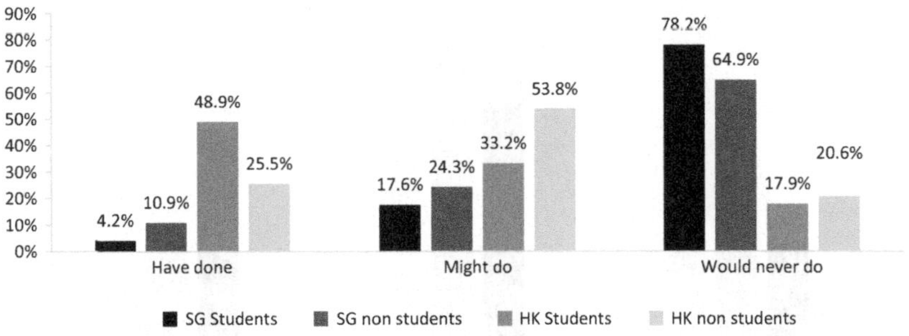

Fig. 4.8 Survey response on civil disobedience, "What you do you think about engaging in civil disobedience, i.e. breaking the law or not complying with government policies?"

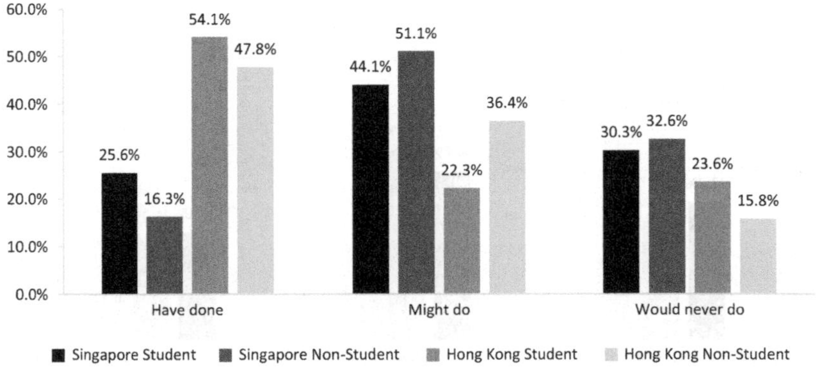

Fig. 4.9 Survey response on public demonstrations, "Would you attend or have you attended a public demonstration?"

It should be reiterated that this survey was conducted before the 2019 Hong Kong protests against the Fugitive Offenders Extradition bill which arguably reached its zenith in the June to July period with mass demonstrations organised by pro-democracy activists. As such, the potentially distorting effects of the public demonstrations, which may have inflamed public sentiments, cannot be said to have tainted the results collected.

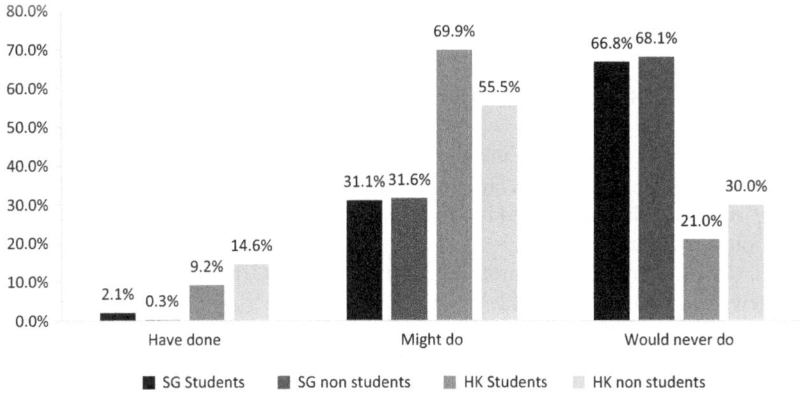

Fig. 4.10 Survey response on labour strikes, "Would you join or have you joined a labour strike?"

Conclusion

In conclusion, there is a large divergence in the political system in Hong Kong and Singapore, particularly regarding the state of political culture. In Hong Kong, citizens are more politically active and are more willing to participate in pro-democracy activities, while civil society in Singapore is comparably stunted, arguably due to the penetration of the developmental state into society. The arms-length relationship between state and society in Hong Kong means that the state has not attempted, nor managed to achieve any form of ideological control over its people, as in Singapore. I also argue that extensive state power in Singapore has not only created a pliant political society, but also contributes to a permission-based culture that has negatively affected economic performance, as will be shown in the subsequent chapters.

References

Agence France-Presse. (2013, February 26). *Singapore jails four Chinese bus drivers for going on strike*. Retrieved August 31, 2020, from https://www.scmp.com/news/asia/article/1158581/singapore-jails-four-chinese-bus-drivers-going-strike

Amartya, S. (1999). *Development as freedom*. Oxford University Press.

Amsden, A. (1985). The State and Taiwan's economic development. In T. Skocpol, P. Evans, & D. Rueschemeyer (Eds.), *Bringing the state back in* (pp. 78–106). Cambridge University Press.

Audretsch, D. B. (2006). *Entrepreneurship, innovation and economic growth*. Edward Elgar Publishing.

Barro, R. (1996). Democracy and growth. *Journal of Economic Growth, 1*(1), 1–27.

Barro, R. (2013). Democracy, law and order, and economic growth. In *2013 index of economic freedom* (pp. 41–58). Heritage Foundation and Dow Jones & Company, Inc.

BBC. (2015, March 22). In quotes: Lee Kuan Yew. *BBC*. https://www.bbc.com/news/world-asia-31582842

Bellows, T. J. (1970). *The people's action party of Singapore: Emergence of a dominant party system*. Yale University Press.

Besley, T., & Persson, T. (2011). *Pillars of prosperity: The political economics of development clusters*. Princeton University Press.

Carstensen, M., & Schmidt, V. (2016). Power through, over and in ideas: Conceptualising ideational power in discursive institutionalism. *Journal of European Public Policy, 23*(3), 318–337.

Castells, M. (1992). Four Asian tigers with a dragon head. In I. R. P. Applebaum & J. Henderson (Eds.), *States and development in the Asian Pacific Rim*. SAGE.

Centre for Civil Society, India. (2020). *Simon Lee*. Centre for Civil Society, India. https://ccs.in/people/simon-lee

Chapman, R. (2004). *The civil service commission 1855–1991*. Routledge.

Chee, S. J. (2011, May 10). Singapore is taking the first steps to true democracy. *The Guardian*. https://www.theguardian.com/commentisfree/2011/may/10/singapore-election-democracy-new-media

Cheng, T.-j. (1990). Political regimes and development strategies: South Korea and Taiwan. In G. Gereffi & D. Wyman (Eds.), *Manufacturing miracles: Patterns of development in Latin America and East Asia*. Princeton University Press.

Cheung, A. (2008). The story of two administrative states: State capacity in Hong Kong and Singapore. *Pacific Review, 21*(2), 121–145.

Chu, Y.-w. (2016a). *The Asian developmental state*. Palgrave Macmillan.

Chu, Y.-w. (2016b). Democratisation, emergence of the knowledge-based economy and the Changing developmental alliances in South Korea and Taiwan. In Y.-W. Chu (Ed.), *The Asian developmental state* (pp. 117–138). Palgrave Macmillan.

Cumings, B. (1987). The Origins and Development of the Northeast Asian Political Economy. In F. Deyo, *The Political Economy of the New Asian Industrialism* (pp. 44–83). Ithaca, NY: Cornell University Press.

Dincecco, M. (2017). *State capacity and economic development*. Cambridge University Press.

Edigheji, O. (2010). *Constructing a democratic developmental state in South Africa*. HSRC Press.

Evans, P. (2010). The challenge of 21st century development: Building capability-enhancing states. In *"Capacity is development" global event*. United Nations Development Program.

Evans, P., & Heller, P. (2015). Human development, state transformation, and the politics of the developmental state. In S. Leibfried, E. Huber, M. Lange, J. Levy, & J. Stephens (Eds.), *The Oxford handbook of transformations of the state*. Oxford University Press.

Flowerdew, J. (1998). *The final years of British Hong Kong*. Macmillan Press.

George, C. (2012). *Freedom from the press: Journalism and state power in Singapore*. NUS Press.

George, C. (2017). *Singapore, incomplete: Reflections on a first world nation's arrested political development*. Woodsville News.

Gold, T. (1986). *State and society in the Taiwan miracle*. M. E. Sharpe.

Haggard, S. (2018). *Developmental states*. Cambridge University Press.

Ho, L.-C. (2010). "Don't worry, I'm not going to report you": Education for citizenship in Singapore. *Theory and Research in Social Education, 38*(2), 217–247.

Hong Kong Hansard. (1966). Hong Kong Government.

Hong Kong Police Force. (2019). *Public order event statistics*. Hong Kong Police Force. https://www.police.gov.hk/ppp_en/09_statistics/poes.html

Huber, E., Evans, P., & Stephens, J. (2017). The political foundations of state effectiveness. In M. Centeno, A. Kohli, D. Yashar, & D. Mistree (Eds.), *States in the developing world* (pp. 380–408). Cambridge University Press.

Johnson, C. (1995). *Japan, who governs?: The rise of the developmental state*. WW Norton & Company.

Johnson, N., & Koyama, M. (2017). States and economic growth: Capacity and constraints. *Explorations in Economic History, 64*, 1–20.

Katzenstein, P. (1985). *Small states in world markets*. Cornell University Press.

King, A. (1975). Administrative absorption of politics in Hong Kong: Emphasis on the grassroot level. *Asian Survey, 15*(5), 422–439.

Lee, K. Y. (1992, November 10). Democracy, human rights and the realities. Tokyo, Japan.

Lim, H.-c. (1985). *Dependent Development in Korea, 1963–1979*. Seoul: Seoul National University Press.

Lingle, C. (1996). *Singapore's Authoritarian Capitalism: Asian Values, Free Market Illusions, and Political Dependency*. Locke Institute.

McCloskey, D. N. (2010). *Bourgeois dignity: Why economics can't explain the modern world*. University of Chicago Press.

McGann, J. (2019). *2019 Global go to think tank index report* (University of Pennsylvania) Think Tanks and Civil Societies Program. https://repository.upenn.edu/think_tanks/17/

Miners, N. (1995). *The government and politics of Hong Kong*. Oxford University Press.
Mokyr, J. (1992). *The lever of riches: Technological creativity and economic progress*. Oxford University Press.
Monnery, N. (2017). *Architect of prosperity: Sir John Cowperthwaite and the making of Hong Kong*. London Publishing Partnership.
Ng, E. (1998). *Central provident fund: Capital market boost or a drag?* Asian Development Bank.
Ng, K.-C. (2017, February 17). Five Hong Kong think tanks make it to list of region's top 90. *South China Morning Post*. https://www.scmp.com/news/hong-kong/education-community/article/2074127/five-hong-kong-think-tanks-make-it-list-regions
North, D. C., & Weingast, B. R. (1989). Constitutions and commitment: The evolution of institutions governing public choice in seventeenth-century England. *The Journal of Economic History, 49*(4), 803–832.
O'Riain, S. (2004). *The politics of high tech growth: Developmental network states in the global economy*. Cambridge University Press.
Przeworski, A., Alvarez, R. M., Alvarez, M. E., Cheibub, J. A., Limongi, F., & Neto, F. P. (2000). *Democracy and development: Political institutions and well-being in the world, 1950–1990*. Cambridge University Press.
Quah, J. (1990). *In search of Singapore's national values*. Times Academic Press.
Rabushka, A. (1979). *Hong Kong: A study in economic freedom*. The University of Chicago.
Rahim, L. Z., & Barr, M. (2019). *The limits of authoritarian governance in Singapore's developmental state*. Springer.
Ridley, M. (2020). *How innovation works: Serendipity, energy and the saving of time*. HarperCollins.
Robinson, M., & White, G. (1998). *The democratic developmental state: Political and institutional design*. Oxford University Press.
Rock, M. (2013). East Asia's democratic developmental states and economic growth. *Journal of East Asian Studies, 13*(1), 1–34.
Rodan, G. (2016). *The political economy of Singapore's industrialization: National state and international capital*. Springer.
Sen, A. (1999). Democracy as a universal value. *Journal of Democracy, 10*(3), 3–17.
Sen, A. (2000). *Development as freedom*. Random House.
Skocpol, T. (1985). Bringing the state back in: Strategies of analysis in current research. In I. P. Evans, D. Rueschemeyer, & T. Skocpol (Eds.), *Bringing the state back in*. Cambridge University Press.
Stroup, M. (2007). Economic freedom, democracy, and the quality of life. *World Development, 35*(1), 52–66.

Tan, K. P. (2012). The ideology of pragmatism: Neo-liberal globalisation and political authoritarianism in Singapore. *Journal of Contemporary Asia, 42*(1), 67–92.

Teo, Y. Y. (2011). *Neoliberal morality in Singapore: How family policies make state and society.* Routledge.

Thierer, A. (2016). *Permissionless innovation: The continuing case for comprehensive technological freedom.* Mercatus Center.

Thio, L.-A. (1991). *White paper on shared values.* Academia.edu. https://www.academia.edu/1740666/White_paper_on_shared_values_1991_

Tremewan, C. (1994). *The political economy of social control in Singapore.* St. Martin's Press.

Tsang, S. (2004). *A modern history of Hong Kong.* I.B Taurus & Co Ltd.

Tsang, S. (2007). *Governing Hong Kong—Administrative Officers from the nineteenth century to the handover to China, 1862–1997.* Hong Kong University Press.

Verspagen, B. (2006). Innovation and economic growth. In I. J. Fagerberg & D. C. Mowery (Eds.), *The Oxford handbook of innovation.* Oxford University Press.

Whyte, M. K. (2014). Sub-optimal institutions but superior growth: The puzzle of China's economic boom. In J. Li & L. Wang (Eds.), *China's economic dynamics.* Routledge.

Wong, J. (2004). The adaptive developmental state in East Asia. *Journal of East Asian Studies, 4*(3), 345–362.

Zingales, L. (2012). *A capitalism for the people: Recapturing the lost genius of American prosperity.* Basic Books.

CHAPTER 5

Hong Kong and Singapore as an Anglo-Chinese Success Story

Colonialism or Developmental State?

In order to fully understand the contributing factors of economic development in Hong Kong and Singapore, it is essential to explore their respective histories. This is especially warranted considering that both city-states were British colonies since the early nineteenth century. Founded in 1819 and 1843, respectively, by the British, Hong Kong and Singapore witnessed the introduction of British institutions, governance, and policies for more than a century before WWII. The role that British colonialism played in the development of both countries must be assessed.

State-centric interpretations of history posit that Singapore's economic growth was mainly a product of the developmental state. Revisionist historians either downplay the significance of British colonialism on Hong Kong and Singapore's growth story or evaluate it negatively. I put forth a different view, arguing that British colonialism had a significant, decisive, and positive impact on the institutional development of both city-states and thus their economic performance. Hong Kong and Singapore flourished economically for more than a century before WWII, with burgeoning trade, industry, and immigration. This success preceded the developmental state's origins in Singapore and thus diminishes its often-accepted significance.

B. Cheang, *Economic Liberalism and the Developmental State*,
https://doi.org/10.1007/978-3-031-08100-2_5

Additionally, I show that British colonialism did not run counter to any significant local opposition but in fact facilitated a collaborative and largely harmonious partnership with the local Chinese community. Hong Kong and Singapore may have started out as colonial creations, but soon evolved into Anglo-Chinese success stories.

Revisionists

On one spectrum of the debate are revisionist historians who put forth a generally negative view of the British Empire. With reference to Hong Kong's history, this perspective emphasises colonial exploitation and oppression, and how local Chinese were passive victims of alien rulers. There are several features of this approach. The first is its association with Chinese nationalism, which is why most writings here are advanced by Chinese scholars, who emphasise how "Hong Kong has been part of Chinese territory since ancient times" and highlight China's contribution to Hong Kong while downplaying the positive impact of British rule (see Yu & Liu, 1994; Liu, 1997). These scholars, from the Academy of Social Science in Beijing, emphasise how Hong Kong was born out of humiliation for the Chinese in the context of the Opium Wars and document the injustices perpetrated by the colonial masters. The clearest expression of this sentiment is that "Hong Kong was built and made prosperous on the blood, sweat and corpses of Chinese coolies" (You, 1958). Another feature of this school is its Marxist interpretation, mainly in the way colonial officials were captured by or colluded with corporate interests during the British era at the expense of the indigenous population (Hughes, 1976; Rear, 1977; Davies, 1977; Leung, 1990; Wong, 1991).

This argument is consonant with the anti-colonial sentiment that today pervades academia. Within the economic history scholarship and in the related fields of Asian history, European powers are portrayed rather negatively. Western powers in the nineteenth century are understood to have engaged in imperial domination after acquiring newfound political power following the Industrial Revolution. This apparently led to the establishment of colonial regimes, including those in East and Southeast Asia for the purposes of economic exploitation, where colonies served host cities in Europe as a source of raw materials and as markets for European produce (Hobson, 1938; Elson, 1962; Thornton, 1978, pp. 3–4; Raben, 2014).

Revisionist historians have made similar, though less trenchant, arguments regarding Singapore. Recently, these historians have insisted that

Singapore's history rightly began more than 700 years ago since its early thirteenth-century history as a maritime centre, as opposed to the more conventional perspective of it beginning in 1819 under the British (Kwa et al., 2019; Miksic, 2013). These scholars downplay the significance of 1819 as a turning point and instead focus on the *longue durée* of Singapore's pre-colonial past. There is a degree of political motivation: revisionist historians on Singapore reject what they consider as the domination of the incumbent People's Action Party government's official historical narrative which portrays it as a virtuous inheritor of Pax Britannica (Hong & Juanli, 2008).

State-Centric History

Another school of thought is presented by developmental state theorists, who have put forth a state-centric account of economic growth. This largely pertains to Singapore rather than Hong Kong, which remained under colonial rule till 1997. This group features a wide cast: the official government narrative, foreign scholars, as well as local economists.

Foreign development experts, for example, have overwhelmingly attributed Singapore's economic success to the good policies of its government planners, chief among them being the use of industrial policy. In an influential article, the economist Dani Rodrik (1999) declares that "the lesson from East Asia is clear" (p. 63), which is that those countries, including Singapore, "would not have been nearly as successful had their governments not given capital accumulation a big push[1] by subsidising, cajoling and otherwise stimulating private investors". Some local academics sing the same tune, credited Singapore's economic success to the actions of the developmental state, including its repeated use of industrial policy (Yeoh et al., 1997; Low, 2001; Pereira, 2008). For this group, the significant turning point in Singapore's history is not 1819 when the British arrived, nor even the longer 700-year frame, but the establishment of the modern state by the ruling PAP in the mid-twentieth century.

The use of the "engineering" metaphor is widespread by these voices, as well as the imagery of the economy as a machine amenable to tweaks by social engineers and architects (see Mahizhnan & Tsao, 2002; Devan, 2014, pp. 134–135). This is articulated by the well-regarded book *Singapore's Success: Engineering Economic Growth*:

[1] This "big push" argument has intellectual roots in the works of Rosenstein-Rodan and Ragnar Nurkse. See Rosenstein-Rodan (1961).

> Engineering is central to Singapore...as applied to economic strategy and even moulding society. The political elite's passionate pursuit of shared prosperity required combining together many diverse components, of policies, institutions, attitudes, and political savvy, to create an intricate and highly effective mechanism that, moreover, required constant upgrading...the strategy is an enlightened one: existing doctrines and precepts on development policies, institutions and political economy of implementation were rationally examined for their merit and pragmatically adopted, adapted, and pursued to their logical consequences. (Ghesquiere, 2007, p. 7)

For understandable reasons, the ruling party in Singapore, the PAP, has claimed this as its official history. The paradigmatic example is the book *From Third World to First: The Singapore Story* and *The Singapore Story: Memoirs of Lee Kuan Yew*, which depicts the story of the nation overcoming tremendous odds, before eventually attaining success. Written from the perspective of Singapore's first Prime Minister Lee Kuan Yew himself, the underlying theme of the transformation from a state of poverty and under-development to one of first-world prosperity casts a long shadow over historical accounts and popular representations of Singapore's past. This idea is reinforced through social studies education in schools, national holidays, books documenting the contributions of government officials, public museums, and galleries, and in much of the post-independence writings on Singapore history (Hong & Juanli, 2008).

Both Perspectives Are Incomplete

Both perspectives however ought to be rejected. The state-centric position on one hand is too ahistorical, failing to consider the factors during the colonial era that shaped contemporary economic development. By emphasising the effective state policies implemented by East Asian governments in the post-war period as the leading explanation for economic success, this school of thought assumes a larger break from history than is the case. Even before WWII, both Hong Kong and Singapore were flourishing as colonial cities under British governance. The institutional environment during the British colonial era facilitated trade and immigration which formed the basis for the modern economic growth of Singapore, a trend that was well underway before the establishment of the developmental state.

The claims of the revisionists should also be criticised. I insist that British colonialism had a significant, decisive, and largely positive impact on the institutional development of both city-states and their contemporary economic prosperity. The Marxist underpinnings of the Beijing School fail to account for the benefits of pro-capitalist institutions that Hong Kong enjoyed, which made possible decades of economic openness and prosperity. Singaporean revisionist historians, in their efforts to dismantle the official historical narrative, have "thrown the baby out with the bathwater" and wrongly downplayed the fundamental and positive influence of British colonialism. My account therefore echoes Singapore historian Constance Mary Turnbull (2009, p. xii), who argued that "modern Singapore was founded in 1819 on the initiative of one individual, Sir Stamford Raffles".

Of Course, Colonialists Pursued Their Self-Interest, But That's Not the Point

My argument, however, is not a blanket defence of colonial imperialism. Admittedly, the desire for economic profit explains much of Western powers' motivations to expand their territories in search of overseas markets in the nineteenth century, and that in many cases, exploitation occurred. However, this should be tempered by the realisation that there were also positive legacies of colonialism, and that on a comparative basis, many modern anti-colonial movements have themselves been equally harmful if not more so (Bauer, 1976; Gilley, 2017; Grier, 1999).

Nuance is necessary. Local conditions vary, and various colonial powers took different approaches to governance. Daron Acemoglu, Simon Johnson, and James Robinson (2001) clarified that "Europeans adopted very different colonisation policies in different colonies, with different associated institutions". The difference, for them, lies in the varying mortality rates due to the local conditions in settlements. In places where settlement was difficult due to disease, extractive institutions were established, to the detriment of long-run economic growth (Acemoglu et al., 2001). Colonial experience is not homogenous, and institutional differences influence whether colonies prospered (Lange et al., 2006). It is disingenuous, for instance, to conflate the oppressive conditions in the Belgian Congo, with relatively benign British rule. Indeed, British colonies particularly stand out compared to the more brutal experiences under the Dutch, French, and Belgians. Even amongst British colonies, the relatively peaceful relationship between the indigenous peoples and the British rulers in Hong Kong and Singapore differs from the social upheavals in India.

One major piece of evidence highlighting the positive legacy of British rule is the acceptance of the British shown by some of the indigenous citizens and in some cases, even a fondness. It is well documented that in the years following Hong Kong's handover to China, British rule was looked back on with nostalgia, with many fearing the negative consequences that may come with being ruled by communist China. At the time of this writing, Singapore is commemorating its 200th anniversary of the arrival of the British with a series of public festivals. Today, both city-states are ranked amongst the most prosperous in the world, with social indicators outstripping many other developed countries. It is thus not unreasonable to claim that Hong Kong and Singapore stand out as two of the most successful examples of colonialism.

My argument however does not assume any positive intentions of the colonialists. It is an institutional one. The positive impact left by the British stems from the market-based *institutions* that Hong Kong and Singapore inherited.

Academic political economists have now largely agreed that institutions are of first-order importance in economic development (Rodrik et al., 2004). Specifically, institutions that "allow and encourage participation by the great mass of people in economic activities that make the best use of their talents and skills" are the ones that bring about economic prosperity (Acemoglu & Robinson, 2012, p. 144). This is why institutions that protect private property rights, the rule of law, and a general degree of economic freedom are significant.

Hong Kong and Singapore have generally had such institutions, notwithstanding the pervasive presence of the developmental state in the latter context. But the reason for this is because they were inherited from the British. Hong Kong and Singapore flourished under more than a century of British governance, which facilitated free trade and mass immigration of Chinese peoples.

Institutional "Tabula Rasa"

The years 1819 and 1843 were what political economists call "critical junctures" for Singapore and Hong Kong, respectively, the turning point when a new set of institutions began to be imported. Critical junctures cast a long shadow in history because events in such periods have path-dependent consequences long into the future (Mahoney, 2000).

What, however, was most special about the Singapore and Hong Kong case is that unlike in other colonies, the British did not find itself in tension to a pre-existing civilisation. For example, British governance in India was always fraught with tension, since the British Empire had to essentially govern a very large population which had a pre-existing culture and a shared historical memory. This was never the case with Hong Kong and Singapore, which were sparsely populated when founded by the British.

Admittedly, some exaggerated accounts have wrongly painted the British arrival as the *genesis* of Hong Kong and Singapore histories. For instance, the British Foreign Secretary Palmerston had declared Hong Kong "a barren rock with hardly a house on it", and Governor Bowen, 40 years later, expressed how "...the Island of Hong Kong was merely a barren rock, inhabited only by a few fishermen and pirates" (Endacott, 1973, p. 18; Legislative Council of Hong Kong, 1884–1885). I accept that such claims are not true. It has been observed that in prior to 1843 in Hong Kong, farming was a "principal occupation" and that there were "several villages of some size, as well as hamlets, and a few larger coastal villages which served as market towns for the villages and as home ports for a permanent boat population ad visiting craft" (Hayes, 2015). Revisionist historians also rightly point out that Singapore was in the thirteenth to seventeenth centuries connected to regional seafaring communities and was part of a pan-Asian trade network (Miksic, 2013).

While these observations are conceded, the British arrival remains a *significant critical juncture* in the development of both city-states. It also strains credulity to believe that the pre-existing population in Hong Kong and Singapore—to the extent they existed—at the time of British arrival amounted to anything more than scattered communities. This is more pronounced in Singapore: numbering no more than a few hundred people using the best estimates, prior to 1819 Singapore had fallen into disrepair. Early immigrants no historical memory of any place called "Hong Kong" or "Singapore", since they came from far flung places like Europe, China, and India.

The fact that the arrival of the British did not fundamentally clash with any pre-existing civilisation means that the practices they imported enjoyed a higher chance of persisting into the future. Institutions that have historically been exogenously imposed or forced onto a culture typically fail, as we have seen from the failures of contemporary nation-building efforts by the West (Coyne, 2008; Boettke et al., 2015). In the unique context of Hong Kong and Singapore, not only did British rule not displace existing social structures, it also accommodated a great degree of local rule by the Chinese population. As such, a strong degree of self-governance flourished under a larger British framework.

Additionally, whatever structures of governance that these indigenous people constructed did not feed into subsequent institutional development. Notably, modern governance institutions in Hong Kong and Singapore have a *distinctly British flavour* and can trace their origins to arrival of the British. It was only after the British arrived did both territories then experience a clear, constant, and upward trend of growth, in people, trade, and wealth.

Thus, the British enjoyed an "institutional tabula rasa", a blank slate upon which their legacy came to be written. This legacy was a confluence of British trade interests, the agency of the colonial "man on the spot", and the collaborative relationship between the British and their Chinese partners. The arrival of the British set in motion a positive chain of developments that they could not ultimately predict. Thus, while the trajectory of Hong Kong and Singapore's subsequent growth was initiated by the British, it soon outgrew it.

Singapore

British Trade Interests in the Malay Peninsula

The British were primarily motivated by trade and commerce when they founded Singapore. In the larger context of Anglo-Dutch rivalry, the British were especially concerned about the Dutch harassment of their ships in Southeast Asia (Hilton & Tate, 1963, pp. 134–151; Tarling, 1962). The British thus started to search for new ports, especially after they discovered that their existing settlements, Penang and Bencoolen, were insufficient to project influence in the Straits of Malacca (Wong, 1991).

British commercial interests were also partly influenced by a liberal belief in free trade, which were in ascendance towards the end of the eighteenth century following the publication of Adam Smith's *The Wealth of Nations*. Understandably, the British opposed what they deemed as the Dutch practice of mercantilism and commercial exclusionism in Southeast Asia. This is best reflected during the Fourth Anglo-Dutch War from 1780 to 1784, where the British, together with its merchants, fought for the right of free trade in the Dutch East Indies which they were excluded from. Despite the Treaty of Paris of 1784 which guaranteed the right of British traders to access the Eastern seas unmolested by the Dutch, this was not honoured by the Dutch who tried to overturn this in the subsequent decades (see Tarling, 1962, chs. 1–2).

Even though the British had Trade Interests, the "man on the spot", Stamford Raffles, Played a Critical Role

The British interest in free trade in the region, however, had to be balanced with other political realities. The British did not want to risk another war with the Dutch over Eastern territories, and as such had to tread carefully, considering the series of high-stakes negotiations between both powers at the end of the Napoleonic War in 1815. As such, while the British authorities acknowledged a concern in the Straits of Malacca, there was no overt decision made to secure any specific site. It was within this delicate political situation that the personal initiative of Sir Stamford Raffles must be appreciated. In fact, the historian Constance Turnbull had declared that "modern Singapore was founded in 1819 on the initiative of *one individual*, Sir Stamford Raffles" (Turnbull, 2009, p. xii).

Sir Stamford Raffles exceeded the instructions given to him, highlighting the importance of the "man on the spot" in historical analysis. He initially received only instructions to explore several ports as potential options, which did not even include Singapore, but upon finding out that those options were exhausted, he proceeded onwards to the island of Singapore. Raffles also took it upon himself to negotiate with the local leaders at the time and signed a Treaty of Friendship and Alliance which gave the British the right to establish a factory in return for monetary compensation. His actions in February 1819 in Singapore led to a series of pushback from not only the Dutch, who lodged official complaints to London, but even amongst Raffles' superiors who were concerned about his overreach and his colleagues who had personal animosity against him.[2] These negative reactions are clearly documented in the many letters between Raffles himself, with his superiors Lord Hastings and Lieutenant-Colonel John Bannerman who offered stiff opposition, and are also

[2] In a letter dated 17 July 1820 to his cousin Reverend Doctor Thomas Raffles, Stamford had bemoaned that he "find them (the authorities) deserting me and giving way in every instance to the unscrupulous and enormous pretensions of the Dutch" (Boulger, 1899, p. 311).

reflected in Raffles' correspondence with top officials in London, who were sceptical of his actions (Boulger, 1899, pp. 292–340).[3]

What is the Legacy of the Institutions Implemented by Stamford Raffles?
Though it cannot be proved definitively, there is good reason to suggest that Stamford Raffles was an adherent of the philosophy of classical liberalism that prevailed in Britain at the time. Studies of his early life are unavailable, but Raffles was known to have been self-taught and to have widely consumed contemporaneous literature. His life before and up to the founding of Singapore when he was a clerk for the East India Company (EIC) coincides with the emerging ideas of free trade that were challenging the EIC's trade monopolies around the world. When he became a clerk aged 14, *The Wealth of Nations* had been published a mere 19 years earlier.

The above piece of speculation can be further supported by analysing Raffles' policy actions during his administration of the settlement of Java from 1811 to 1813 and Bencoolen in 1818. His administration of Java most clearly reveals Raffles' classical liberal tendencies which can be understood in relation to four aspects on which he reversed previous Dutch practices: slavery, trade, currency, and property in land. First, he passed policies restricting the slave trade, in line with a wider trend in British society. This was not fully successful, for slavery remained in pockets in the region, but his actions signified a policy reversal that he would replicate in other places. Raffles' abolitionist tendencies are well documented, having been a close confidante and later a neighbour of William Wilberforce.[4] More significantly, he opposed the mercantilist policy in Java which forced peasants to grow what the Dutch ordered and to sell only to the Dutch. According to Collis (2009, p. 60), Raffles "pitied the Javanese peasantry, forced to take a miserable price for their crop, taxed on that price, forced to labour on roads and public works without wages and in addition exposed to the caprices of the (Dutch) regents…who had the power to punish him and also make further exactions". In contrast, Raffles instituted British common law, allowing peasants to seek any redress from

[3] The Secret Committee of Directors, which was the inner council of the East India Company, denounced Raffles' actions; in a letter dated 14 August 1819, they said that "any difficulty with the Dutch will be created by Sir Stamford Raffles' intemperance of conduct and of language" (Boulger, 1899, pp. 326–327).

[4] Both had exchanged numerous letters and met for business and pleasure (Bastin, 2009, pp. 239–240, 298).

courts, and to either own or lease their land and sell their produce on the general market. These policies were praised by the local leaders upon his departure in 1813 and echoed by various indigenous peoples.

Raffles was a consistent advocate of economic openness. In Java, he also opposed the fiat currency system that was implemented by the Dutch, which created a currency crisis. He reformed the currency system, indexing the currency back to harder commodities to remove the volatility. Regarding free trade, he instituted the ports that he administered as free ports open to all merchants. More importantly, he opposed the remaining vestiges of monopoly held by the East India Company and insisted that it "should not seek to maintain its old restrictive habits but should make the best of the free expansion of trade it was now powerless to prevent" (Wright, 1950, p. 234). He was thus a frontline proponent of free trade at a time when larger Western society was still accepting this new doctrine. Moreover, these policies were not pursued in an ad-hoc manner, but may be said to be part of his larger belief in that free trade can humanise society and of his hope to prepare the indigenous peoples for "a liberal independence" (Raffles, 1830, pp. 76, 307–308, 463, 477, 515).

These values were clearly translated into policy in Singapore's earliest institutional framework. The 1823 Raffles' Regulations contained only six articles, but this formed the backbone of Singapore's future legal development. Singapore's law evolved in the subsequent decades but did not fundamentally deviate from its early basic structure. The six article are shown in (Table 5.1).

The institutional framework expressed in the Raffles' Regulations was significant in creating a break from the past, ushering into Singapore systems of British governance that would last for more than a century. Significantly, while local indigenous peoples existed prior to Raffles' arrival, they were scattered across communities numbering at most a few hundred, without a coherent framework of governance. In fact, most historical accounts reveal that prior to the British arrival, Singapore was either very sparsely populated or almost abandoned. This led the historian C.M. Turnbull to argue that "the modern (Singapore) nation is traced back to the imposition of free trade and British control, and to a decisive break with Malay traditions" (Tarling, 2012, p. 19).

Looking specifically at the six regulations, they largely resemble the norms and institutions that pervaded Britain at the time. Most obviously, the common law system was imported in 1823 and formed the basis of the administration of justice which endures today. The legal framework

Table 5.1 Brief description of the Six Articles of the 1823 Raffles' regulations

Regulation number	*Brief description*
Regulation No. 1 "Regulation for the Registry of Land in Singapore"	The regulation dealt with the registry of land, effectively creating a land market in Singapore, where land could be sold and leased through public auction.
Regulation No. 2 "Regulation for the Port of Singapore"	The regulation declared in the first line that "Singapore is a free port" and would be "open to ships and vessels of every nation free of duty, equally and alike to all".
Regulation No. 3 "Regulation for the Establishment of a Provisional Magistracy and the Enforcement of a due and efficient police in Singapore, with certain Provisions for the Administration of Justice in Cases of Emergency"	The regulation here provided for the administration of justice based on English law, with some allowance for local Malay customs to prevail when dealing with religious practice, marriage, and inheritance.
Regulation No. 4 "Regulation prohibiting gaming-houses and Cockpits, and for suppressing the vice of Gaming in Singapore"	The regulation here prohibited gambling and cockfighting which he deemed "disgraceful and repugnant to the British character and government" and "highly destructive to the morals and happiness of the people".
Regulation No. 5 "Regulation for the Prevention of Slave Trade at Singapore"	The regulation here prohibited the slave trade in Singapore and declared that even those who arrived before the British in January 1819 would be given free status.
Regulation No. 6 "Regulation in furtherance of the Objects of Regulation, No. III and containing additional Provisions for the Magistracy and Administration of Justice in Singapore"	The regulation here provided further specifications relevant to Regulation 3 on the administration of justice. It specifies that an active role in government and legislation would be given to the non-official European community and a measure of participation to the indigenous peoples, and not simply colonial authorities.

Source: Raffles (1830), Turnbull (2009), University of Malaya (1968)

created by Raffles has been deemed the "starting point of Singapore's modern legal system" (Bartholomew, 1976, pp. 84, 87). This common law tradition—which development experts think is superior to civil law systems—emerged from a unique British political tradition, one of the positive legacies of British colonialism in world history (Dorsett & McLaren, 2014; Ferguson, 2018; Rubin, 1977; La Porta et al., 2008).

Hong Kong

British Economic Interests in India-China Trade

Trade was also a central objective of early British policy towards Hong Kong. By the 1600s, the British were challenging the Portuguese and Dutch as trade rivals in the region. This trade was important, for China was a leading source of tea with which to serve the growing domestic demand (Rappaport, 2017). Additionally, fortune could be made in items such as silk, porcelain, and, most significantly, opium. Britain had finally secured a port in Canton in 1771, the only legal Chinese port for overseas trade. However, British merchants there had become frustrated due to the many restrictions placed on them, including the need to work exclusively with Chinese, state-appointed intermediaries. There was thus a desire for the British to establish for themselves more favourable arrangements to allow their traders to operate unimpeded. Such trade interests were a key point of explanation behind Hong Kong's acquisition; this is emphatically stated by a foremost historian on Hong Kong who declared "a healthy trade demanded settled conditions...the Chinese were thought to be unable to provide these conditions, the British had to provide them. This is fundamental to understanding any history of Hong Kong" (Endacott, 1973, pp. vii–viii) (Table 5.2).

Despite the policy orientation towards trade, the selection of Hong Kong by the British and its subsequent development was not a product of intelligent design. Just as questions surrounding the selection of Singapore and its future within the British Empire were being disputed by numerous colonial officials, Hong Kong's future in its initial years was also tenuous. This is best seen by the fact that Charles Elliot, the individual who first raised the British flag over Hong Kong in January 1841, was repudiated for his actions. He was under the instructions of the Foreign Secretary, Lord Palmerston, to conclude hostilities with the Chinese with the aim of providing security for the merchants. He was instructed to achieve this either through the opening of new treaty ports, an agreement by the Chinese to leave their ships alone, or through the acquisition of a new island. However, "the cessation of an island was not an essential demand" (Endacott, 1973, p. 15). Elliot had, in the eyes of his superiors, conceded too much by failing to acquire new treaty ports and sufficient security guarantees. His unilateral acquisition of Hong Kong did not satisfy his government's demands since it was viewed as "a barren island with hardly a house upon it". Palmerston further expressed that Hong Kong "would

Table 5.2 Primary sources of British statements announcing free trade policy orientation in Hong Kong

Context and explanation	*Archival source*
Lord Palmerston had explained to the Chinese government that Hong Kong was seized "in order that British merchants trading to China may not be subject to the arbitrary caprice either of the Government in Peking, or its local authorities at the seaports of the empire".	Morse (1910)
Elliot had proclaimed Hong Kong as a free port as soon as he took possession in January 1841. He declared that "Her Majesty's government has sought for no privilege in China exclusively for the advantage of British ships and merchants".	Slayer (1980)
Elliot's initiative to make Hong Kong a free port was officially endorsed by British policy in the subsequent years.	Colonial Office (1843a)
It was expressed that Hong Kong was not picked for colonisation by official policy, but rather it was "occupied not with a view to colonization, but for diplomatic, commercial and military purposes".	Colonial Office (1843b)
The local authority stationed in Hong Kong was instructed to maintain friendly commercial relations with the indigenous peoples. He was required from the beginning "to impress upon the officers of his squadron the necessity of cultivating as much as possible the friendly feelings which it may be hoped that the Chinese authorities and people will be disposed to entertain toward them" to enhance the colony's utility to promote trade.	Colonial Office (1843a)
The British objective was very clear from the beginning, as HK was taken "not at all because of any natural advantages which it possesses, but simply as subsidiary to the intercourse between the British and the Chinese empires" for which the most important was trade.	Colonial Office (1856)

not be a mart of trade any more than Macao" and other officials also expressed doubts that Hong Kong might become too expensive to administrate and complicate relations with other nations (Morse, 1910, p. 642, 663; Endacott, 1973, pp. 18–19; Carroll, 2007).

Thus, while the British generally had trade interests, they did not have, nor did they apply a consistent policy towards the region. It is overly simplistic to argue that the British acquisition of Hong Kong, was "the outcome of a long crusade by British free traders to promote trade with China" (Chan, 1991, p. 9). Just as in the case of Singapore, it was the colonial "man on the spot", Charles Elliot, who opposed official policy and thus bears the credit for Hong Kong's founding.

Just like Singapore, it Was the Colonial Men on the Spot who Acquired Hong Kong

Hong Kong's early governors and the values they held were thus instrumental in shaping its administrative structure and institutional framework. The actions of Sir Henry Pottinger, the first governor, and Sir John Bowring are especially important, for they presided over a period of great uncertainty spanning the conclusion of the First Opium War when the Treaty of Nanking was signed to the end of the Second Opium War when the Convention of Peking solidified British grip over Hong Kong. Pottinger had built on the initiative of Alexander Johnston, a civil servant, who had encouraged development in Hong Kong despite official instructions to the contrary (Pottinger, 1997, chs. 10–11). This is important, for he successfully overturned the official reluctance to recognise Hong Kong. Pottinger had petitioned to the home government that "this settlement has already advanced too far" not to be brought into the Crown's control (Foreign Office, 1842).

Significantly, Pottinger had declared that "the retention of Hong Kong was the only single point in which I intentionally exceeded my personal instructions" and that his experience in Hong Kong "convinced" him of the "necessity and desirability of our possessing such a settlement as an emporium for our trade" (Endacott, 2005, p. 16). This bears striking resemblance to Singapore's founding: just as Raffles unilaterally took matters into his own hands, the "man on the spot", Pottinger, also pushed for the recognition of Hong Kong based on trade against opposing forces from above.

Hong Kong's Constitutional Structure and Policy Orientation were Geared towards Commerce

The arrival of the British in Hong Kong led to the establishment of British institutions, laws, and rules, which evolved till present day. Even though the British allowed a wide scope for local customs to operate within the Chinese community, they were still subject to an overall preference for British values of property rights and the rule of law. In an important dispatch in 1843, it was declared that:

> the right of succession to immovable property and whatever regards the alienation of it should be regulated by English, and not by Chinese laws. Neither must any English subject be held amenable within the island of Hong Kong for any inflicted crime to any Chines tribunal or Chinse law.

> Again, if there by any Chinese law repugnant to those immutable principles of morality which Christians must regard as binding…the enforcement of any such law even against the Chinese must not be permitted. (Colonial Office, 1843b)

Subject to this overall baseline, British institutions were established constitutionally through the Letters Patent in 1843. This established the rule of law by setting a constitutional document for subsequent colonial governors to abide by and provided for the establishment of the judiciary, legislature, and executive branches of government. While this was amended several times, the basic structure of Hong Kong's government was largely unchanged till 1997.

Even though this constitutional framework was not democratic and did not allow for local Chinese representation, there were provisions that limited the abuse of power. The governor was directly accountable to the London government and thus ultimately subject to the supervision of the British parliament. Additionally, the independence of the judiciary was also articulated in the documents. Though the application of impartial British justice was highly imperfect, it was nonetheless comparatively better than the available alternatives and was sufficient in attracting large numbers of immigrants who voted with their feet. In 1871, the Chinese community itself had launched a petition against a racially discriminatory policy by invoking the superiority of British law (see Colonial Office, 1871). By the turn of the nineteenth century, at the Golden Jubilee of Queen Victoria, the local Chinese community made "a striking recognition of British justice" in its "splendidly embroidered address" to the Queen (Munn, 2001, p. 20).

After the Arrival of the British, Trade and Population Exploded

A major impact of the British arrival into Hong Kong and Singapore and the institutions subsequently established is that they facilitated the growth of both city-states as flourishing trading hubs and as havens for economic immigrants. Of course, this is not to deny that even before the British took control in the early nineteenth century, both city-states of Singapore and Hong Kong were in brief moments important places for trade and commerce. However, these were sporadic episodes at best. Available statistics show a clear and constant growth in trade and local population size from the arrival of the British onwards.

Available evidence points towards a rapid influx of immigrants into Hong Kong and Singapore soon after their British founding. These immigrants, largely from China, and to a lesser extent the Peninsula, were mainly motivated by economic profit and trade, and had heard about the establishment of both islands as free ports. The following table displays an estimate of population growth in the aftermath of the British arrival and is based on statistics collected by population scholars (Fig. 5.1, Table 5.3).

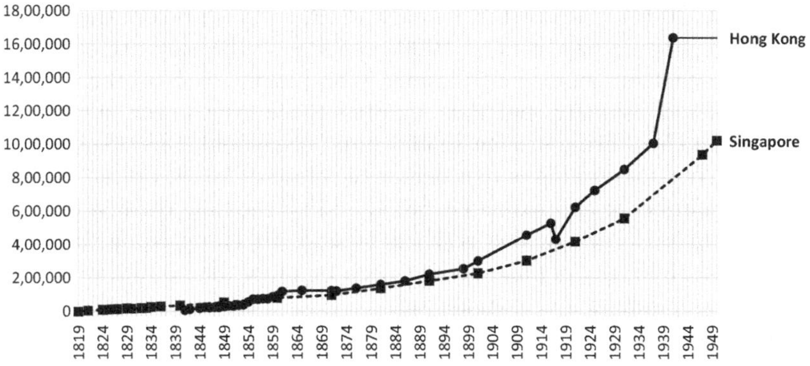

Fig. 5.1 Population in colonial Hong Kong and Singapore (1819–1950). (Official figures were obtained from the following sources. For early Hong Kong, Endacott's (1973) history is authoritative, coupled with the Hong Kong Blue Book (1844–1899). *Census of Hong Kong Chinese Population.* Hong Kong: Noronha & Co. For Singapore, Saw Swee-Hock's (2012) population records are definitive. The numbers before 1871 for Singapore are based on the available archives by T.J. Newbold and Thomas Braddell, recording the headcounts done by the colonial authorities. The 1821 count for Singapore is part of the personal records by Thomas Braddell and the first official headcount in Singapore was done only in 1824. While these statistics are subject to errors, they remain the only numbers available on population in Singapore. From 1871 onwards, however, regular population censuses were conducted and thus more reliable. The 1841 count for Hong Kong is an estimate by the Hong Kong Government Gazette of May 1841. The 1845 figures for Hong Kong are estimates found in the Report by Samuel Fearon, first Registrar-General under the Registration Ordinance)

Table 5.3 Population growth rates in Hong Kong and Singapore

	Hong Kong	*Singapore*
1819–1840	NA	23492.67% increase
1841–1870	1524% increase	162% increase
1871–1900	148% increase	133% increase

An important point is that in the immediate period prior to the British arrival, both islands were sparsely populated. The historian Constance Turnbull (2009) notes that in January 1819, a month before the British arrival, Singapore had at most 1000 inhabitants, the majority of whom were Orang Laut, nomadic tribesmen who mainly lived on their boats. Other official estimates put their number to be even lower, at nothing more than 150, "living in a few shabby huts" (Newbold, 1839; Saw, 1991, p. 219). What is striking is that before the close of 1819, official records put the number at approximately 5874, and by the time the first population count was done, it had reached 10,683. In Hong Kong, between 1841 and 1845, the population had risen by more than 300%, driven by the influx of immigrants from abroad.

Of course, population growth can be due to many factors, but migration has largely been the key one, as opposed to natural births. The most extensive study on Singapore population patterns shows that in the first phase, from 1819 to 1921, "the increase was due not to an excess of births over deaths but to a large and continuous influx of immigrants" (Saw, 1991, p. 222). This is similar in Hong Kong, where immigration has also been a result of external push factors, such as socio-political instability in China, which led to people fleeing to Hong Kong.

A similar trend can be observed in the available trade statistics. Upon the arrival of the British, the volume of trade grew rapidly, leading to both places becoming centres of trade in the surrounding regions, with entrepôt trade being the main source of economic growth. The following figures chart out the trade volume of the Straits Settlements and colonial Hong Kong from 1868 to 1914. Appendix 1 documents the data and collection method used, all of which are based on Latham's (1994) study of Hong Kong and Singapore as trade entrepots (Figs. 5.2 and 5.3).

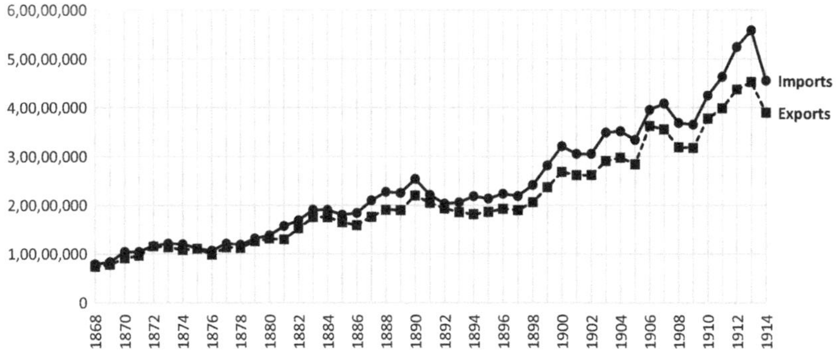

Fig. 5.2 Trade volume of Straits Settlements (in sterling pounds), 1868–1914. (Source: Latham (1994), for more details see Appendix 1)

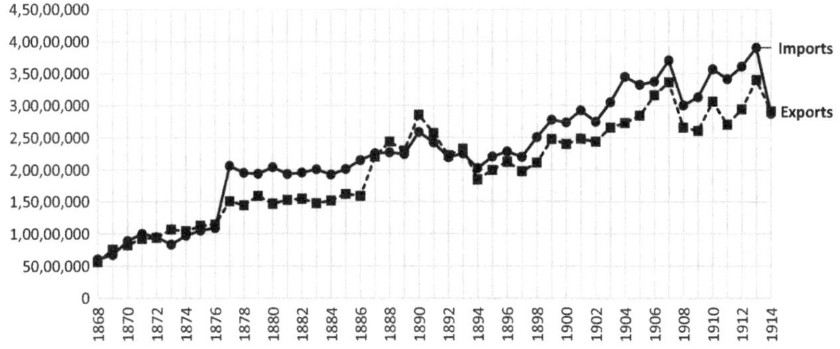

Fig. 5.3 Trade volume of Hong Kong (in sterling pounds), 1868–1914. (Source: Latham (1994), for more details see Appendix 1)

Singapore's Post-War Growth Started from a High Base

Aside from demonstrating the positive impact of British rule on the growth of trade and immigration in both city-states, my account is important for another reason: it challenges the "Singapore Story" developmental state portrayal of Singapore's economic growth which attributes its economic growth predominantly to policies undertaken by the new government of sovereign Singapore.

The new Singapore government, upon achieving independence in the 1960s, embarked on a state-led project of industrialisation which witnessed the growth of the developmental state, its organs, and policies, till the present day. The industrialisation plan, captured by the United Nations Report of 1961 (United Nations, 1961), is based on the belief that the domestic economy could not industrialise on its own without a big push by the state. Since the economy was primarily based on entrepôt trade, there were no local industrial capital, knowledge, or talent.

This premise is, however, contradicted by historical evidence. During the colonial era, the Chinese community formed extensive business organisations and networks that spanned Asia (Lim, 2013; Brown, 1995). Many of these family-owned businesses possessed industrial capital, knowledge, and skills. While many in the Chinese community were traders, their industrial activity should not be overlooked too.

In fact, in the early twentieth century, due to external events like WWI and the invention of the automobile, there was a big boom in the rubber industry. Entrepreneurial Chinese business elites moved into this sector and from 1906 to 1942, more than 60% of these top leaders became involved in this industry (Lee, 1978, pp. 101–106; Yong, 1992, pp. 64–65). There were several key effects of the rubber boom.

First, growth in the rubber sector prompted the development of modern deposit banking. Banks such as the United Overseas Bank and Overseas-Chinese Banking Corporation, which persist today, were created during this era and were involved in financing rubber industries and other related Chinese ventures. This in turn was linked to the formalisation of organisations and the modernisation of business arrangements. For Chinese merchants to do business on a global scale, they had to conform with modern business standards like accounting. During this period, many Chinese-owned business ventures became organised as limited liability companies and Western accounting methods were incorporated. The link between rubber and banking is clear: rubber and commodity production required steady capital which meant banks became increasingly important (Brown, D., 1994, p. 150). Indeed, it is not a coincidence that the biggest names in early Singapore banking also had ties to the rubber industry (Huff, 1994, pp. 233–235).

Another key impact was that the Singaporean economy had become even more globalised as the Chinese industrialists served world markets. The three largest companies in this field were the Lee Rubber, Tan Kah Kee Rubber Company, and Aik Hoe Company by Tan Lark Sye, all of whom had direct links and contacts with global cities like London and New York. In the inter-war period, Singapore had become "the biggest market in the world" for natural rubber (State of Singapore, 1963, p. 117).

While Singapore was not an industrial city compared to leading Western ones at that time, there was substantial industry, not just in rubber, but in other areas like ship building and repair. Goh Keng Swee, Singapore's economic architect in the developmental state, admitted himself that there was a reservoir of human capital, "an entrepreneur class which is both extensive in numbers and high in quality" (Goh, 1958, p. 1). The economic historian W.G. Huff (1994, p. 31) explained that "Singapore (in the 1960s) started from a high base" and that "before World War 2, Singapore had already experienced very considerable economic development".

Importantly, this picture of healthy economic growth even before the emergence of the developmental state is supported not only by statistics, but by cultural documents as well—a preferred data source of "bottom-up history" scholars. This author has consulted national archives in Singapore and advertisement materials in early Singapore from 1910 to 1960. Advertisements here are particularly important as they represent cultural documents that reflect, and even shape, the socio-economic life of ordinary people, yielding insights into their material aspirations and status (Kong & Sinha, 2015; Tarulevicz, 2013).

The advertisements reflect the emergence of the Singaporean consumer mass market within and the growing affluence and size of the middle class. Understandably, early advertising in the pre-war period focused mainly on the upper economic European and Asian classes who could afford the new products on the market. While not reflective of the entire population, the emergence of such advertising signals the entrance of consumer mass production into Singapore society. As this grew, advertising for the masses flourished in the post-war period due to the increased literacy of the local population and the improved economic situation (Kuo, 1980).

While such early advertisements are abundant, specific themes may be focused on to examine the everyday economic life of Singaporeans rather than a narrow slice of the upper classes. As such, the domains of food, household appliances, automobiles, the retail industry, and fashion market are selected here.

In the area of food, Singapore society had witnessed the entrance of supermarkets, with Cold Storage as the first founded in 1903. Supermarkets had arrived at the scene partly due to the emergence of the refrigerator and improvements in food technology like canned food, carbonated water, and preservatives. In the early twentieth century, Singaporeans began gaining access to overseas food products not available locally, mostly through supermarkets (Kong & Sinha, 2015; Tarulevicz, 2013). The following ads capture the founding of Cold Storage. The first in 1956 illustrates the varied branches of the company's activities in Singapore promoting itself as a boon to the local economy. The second in 1958 shows how middle-class Asian women were increasingly targeted, unlike the narrow European clientele of the early twentieth century (Figs. 5.4 and 5.5).

Aside from food, Singaporean society also benefitted from the advent of modern appliances like stoves, water filters, and energy equipment,

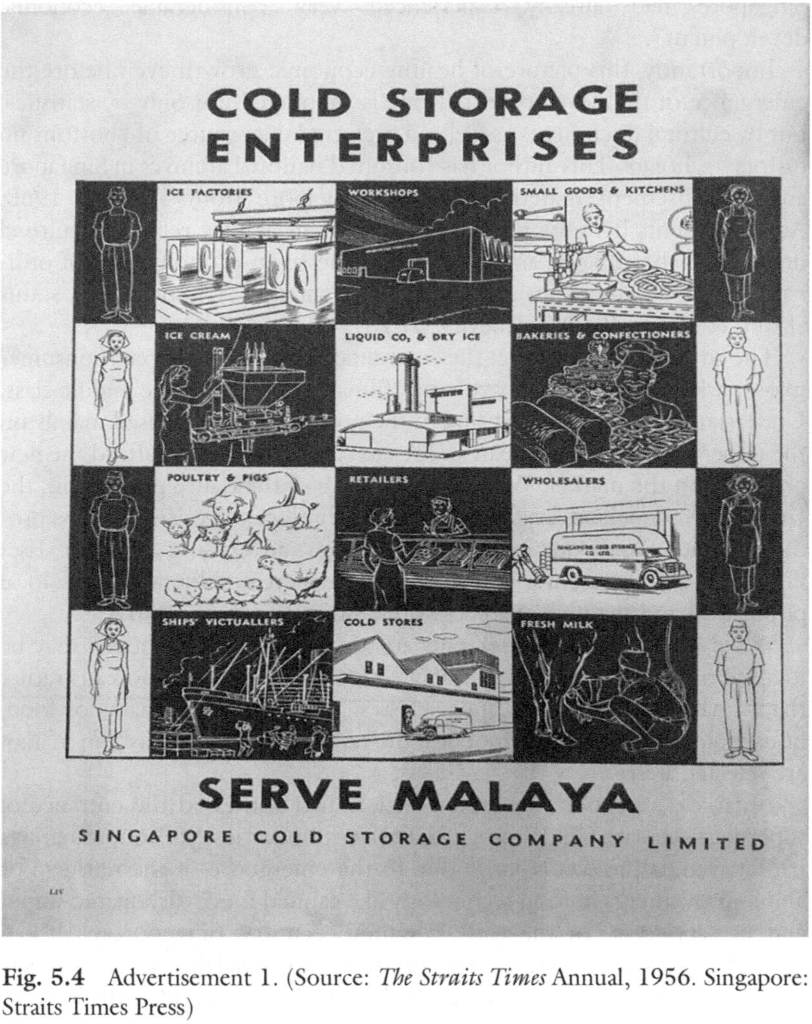

Fig. 5.4 Advertisement 1. (Source: *The Straits Times* Annual, 1956. Singapore: Straits Times Press)

Fig. 5.5 Advertisement 2. (Source: Straits Times Annual 1958. Singapore: Straits Times Press)

gradually introduced from the early twentieth century (Wong, 2018). While most household amenities were initially the luxuries of the upper class, the market for such equipment was large enough for local dealerships to import them. After the war, with greater affluence and the rise in modern housing, advertising for home appliances like washing machines and refrigerators flourished and featured in many sources in various languages (Fig. 5.6).

Fig. 5.6 Advertisement 3. (Source: *The Straits Times*, 21 September 1947. Singapore: Straits Times Press)

The following ad shows a woman in a kimono, representing Japanese brands like National—that had entered the local market—passing the "gift" of better living and economy to women dressed in a *cheongsam* and *sarong kebaya*, representing the people of Malaya (Fig. 5.7).

Another aspect of the economic life of Singaporeans is automobiles which found their way from the West in the late nineteenth century. The first car was imported in 1894 but these remained largely out of reach of

Fig. 5.7 Advertisement 4. (Source: *The Straits Times* Annual, 1961. Singapore: Straits Times Press)

ordinary Singaporeans until the 1920s when the industry took on a more mass-market flavour. Crucially, this was driven by the advent of mass production that had led to lower business costs (Archives and Oral History Department, 1981; Yap, 2007).

In 1913, Singapore had 550 cars to a population of about 333,000 people. By 1940, there were 11,000 registered cars on the island. As cars became cheaper, advertisers also began targeting the middle class. The message was that with prudent financial planning, cars are for everyone. Soon, many dealers and makers emphasised the affordability of their cars. One 1930 ad shows British manufacturer Morris emphasising the affordability of their cars through Malayan Motors. The illustration of this ad, with the Morris car set against a backdrop of boating equipment by a lake, adds a sense of adventure and leisure to the ownership of a Morris (Fig. 5.8).

Fig. 5.8 Advertisement 5. (Source: *The Straits Times*, 30 September 1930. Singapore: Straits Times Press)

Fig. 5.9 Advertisement 6. (Source: Dian Ying Yu Wen Hua, Nanyang Siang Pau Yearbook, 1951. Singapore: Nanyang Siang Pau Press)

The Vanguard Standard was a classic make of Vanguard cars, here advertised as an economical option with six seats to accommodate the whole family (Fig. 5.9).

Ford ads consistently featured their low prices and affordability as compared to other brands. The 1964 Cortina Consul ad frames the product as a "dream car" for a new generation of upwardly mobile women.

Fig. 5.10 Advertisement 7. (Source: *The Straits Times*, 23 July 1927. Singapore: Straits Times Press)

Importantly, this reflected the higher economic position of women during that time (Figs. 5.10, 5.11, and 5.12).

Early Singapore also witnessed the growth of the consumer market for retail and fashion products. Department stores—a Western phenomenon since the industrial revolution—reflected and then enhanced a growing retail culture (Whitaker, 2011). The first few were introduced in Singapore

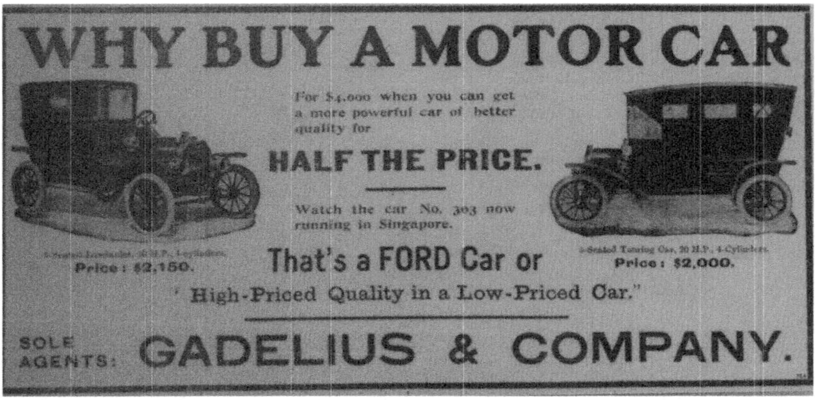

Fig. 5.11 Advertisement 8. (Source: *The Straits Times*, 24 December 1909. Singapore: Straits Times Press)

and housed the latest fashion from overseas and made them more available to the masses over time. Colonial Singapore soon acquired the reputation of a shopping haven and retail ads were commonplace, including stores from High Street and Raffles Place (MacPherson, 1998).

John Little, Singapore's oldest department store, was founded in 1845. By the 1900s, it had become one of the foremost retail outlets in Asia and by the mid-twentieth century, its narrow clientele expanded to include the growing middle class. The first image shows the glassware and crockery department. The second, from the same pictorial book, gives an interior view of the store. These photos published in *Views of Singapore* positioned it as a local attraction for locals (Figs. 5.13 and 5.14).

One retail brand that heavily served the consumer mass market was the shoe company Bata which was Europe's largest shoe manufacturer by 1905. Through competitive pricing and their own sources of cheap rubber, Bata could acquire a significant market share of ordinary Singapore consumers. The 1931 ad below published in *The Straits Times* positions the brand as one "where quality is higher than price" (Fig. 5.17). By selling its mass-produced shoes from Czechoslovakia, Bata purveyed fashion at "ridiculously low prices". Before WWII, Bata's two factories in Malaya were producing over two million pairs of shoes a year. The 1939 and 1940 ads offer style, quality, and value as Bata's main selling points (Figs. 5.15 and 5.16).

Fig. 5.12 Advertisement 9. (Source: Cortina Consul Advertisement, 1964)

The advertisements displayed and their accompanying discussions highlight that as a British colony, Singapore was long a beneficiary of the economic developments in the Western world. Many new products became available in early twentieth-century Singapore following the development of mass manufacturing in the industrial West (Wharton, 2015). Admittedly, given the cost of shipping and relative poverty of Singaporeans, these goods did not begin as mass products and were available only to the

Fig. 5.13 Publicity Photo 1 of John Little & Co. (Source: Views of Singapore. Singapore: John Little & Co., 1910s)

upper classes. After the 1920s, and especially after WWII, these products became more available to the mass consumer market, even as shopping became a leisure activity for the masses. This is also reflected through the widening range of publications and advertisements catered to the general consumer (Balasingamchow, 2018).

Even though British Colonialism had a Positive Impact, my Account is Not Purely "elite history", but Steers a Middle Course

British and Chinese as Joint Partners

The claim made so far, that the successes of Singapore and Hong Kong are a product of British colonial rule, may seem like a crude position that ignores the agency of bottom-up forces, including the role of indigenous citizens, businessmen, and social actors. Many contemporary historians insist on a "bottom-up view" which avoids the notion of the "British

Fig. 5.14 Publicity Photo 2 of John Little & Co. (Source: Views of Singapore. Singapore: John Little & Co., 1910s)

Empire bringing good to the masses". These works go beyond colonial records and rely on oral histories, private records and archives, and data sources commonly neglected by national histories.

"Bottom-up history" is burgeoning in both city-states. In the Singapore context, such scholars include James Francis Warren, Peter Rimmer and Lisa Allen, Stephen Dobbs, and Loh Kah Seng and Chua Ai Lin, all of whom share the common aim to "recapture the voice, perspective, and agency", of the "populace in general" (Hack, 2012, p. 33). In the Hong Kong context, bottom-up history transcends the pro-colonial vs. anti-colonial dichotomy and focuses on non-state institutions and their contribution to Hong Kong history. This includes the works of Henry Lethbridge, Carl T. Smith, Elizabeth Sinn, W.K. Chan, and Tsai Jung-fang.

My account integrates the importance of *both* the elite actions of the British officials and the contributions of the largely self-governing Chinese community who gradually increased in dominance and influence. Through

Fig. 5.15 Advertisement 10. (Source: The Roda. Magazine of the Rotary Clubs of Malaya and Siam, March 1939. Singapore: Roda)

Fig. 5.16 Advertisement 11. (Source: The Roda. Magazine of the Rotary Clubs of Malaya and Siam, April 1940. Singapore: Roda)

a gradual process, both became joint partners. Just like business partners in a venture, the mutual Anglo-Chinese relationship was not always cosy, but it always remained grounded in a convergence of basic interests and values.

Fig. 5.17 Advertisement 12. (Source: *The Straits Times*, 6 February 1931. Singapore: Straits Times Press)

Convergence of Interests and Values

The relationship between the British government and the local Chinese community was not always on equal or fair terms. In other words, there was a clear gap between the rhetoric of the ideal, liberal government and actual reality.

However, one must acknowledge that at the end of British rule in Hong Kong in 1997 and in Singapore in the mid-twentieth century, the Chinese population had clearly expressed a fondness and appreciation for British laws, customs, and institutions. Unlike in many other colonies, there was a peaceful transfer of power rather than a violent grab for sovereignty.

This puzzle, I argue, can be explained by looking at the convergence of interests and values of both the British and the Chinese community. On the level of interests, the British saw value in both city-states primarily as trading posts. Economic wealth always remained the principle of British governance of these two societies. This also converged with the fundamental motives of the masses of Chinese immigrants who flocked to Hong Kong and Singapore over the years. In short, both the British elites and Chinese community saw the islands as vital to their economic interests and pursued actions that aligned with this aim.

Interests are sometimes understood through one's own cultural and ideological lens. The British Empire was distinct from other Western empires at the time largely due to its pervasive classical liberal ethos that emphasised free trade and enlightened liberal government. That this was never perfectly and consistently realised in practice is beside the point; what matters here is that there was a clear consciousness in the British psyche that perceived empire through this perspective. Understandably, it was once said that China was "not a place for conquest or acquisition by any European power", but "the most hopeful place for the commerce of Britain and the world at large" (Welsh, 1993, p. 320). This was the same set of values that emphasised the importance of work ethic, thrift, and the accumulation of wealth—values that formed part of the Western story of development.

Coincidentally, these values resonated in Chinese culture which were even more pronounced in the immigrant community that coalesced in both city-states. It is widely acknowledged that these Chinese immigrants were primarily motivated by economic gain, grounded in their dream of becoming rich, and buttressed by a confidence in upward social mobility. According to Edwin Lee (1991, p. 252), "a Chinese man might have to work long years before he realised any improvement in his financial position, but the beauty is that he would go on working in pursuit of his dreams no matter how long it took". In addition, through "a powerful desire to become his own master", these immigrants believed that they could create a better future for themselves through hard work (Lee, 1991, p. 252).

These material values are based on a Confucian outlook that prizes a strong work ethic, motivating the individual to work hard, save, persevere, and acquire wealth and status. In other words, wealth and status achieved through hard work, acumen, and discipline are believed to be honourable, bringing merit to the individual, family, clan, and lineage. Sociological research has documented how "for this group of people, becoming an entrepreneur almost seemed like a mission" (see Chan & Chiang, 1994, p. 45). In other words, the Confucian emphasis on social honour was bestowed on those who pursued entrepreneurship and wealth creation.

Some clarifications are in order. This does not mean that Chinese culture is synonymous with British classical liberalism or that one implied the other. In fact, as in many Western societies, the British had a sense of cultural superiority that drove empire—the sense that Western civilisation was superior and had to be exported. This is a truism that I concede. However, what matters is that in Hong Kong and Singapore, the interests and values of the British and Chinese had a materialistic, bourgeois character that institutionally bonded both communities.

Economic Dominance of the Chinese

The Chinese immigrants who arrived in Hong Kong and Singapore in the early years were mainly poor migrants looking for better opportunities and fleeing social instability in China. There was clearly and undeniably an unequal relationship that existed in the early years of colonial rule. However, the Chinese community soon grew numerically, and more importantly, economically, with important implications.

Chinese culture forms part of the explanation for Chinese economic success. The meritocratic-bourgeois culture therefore meant that the Chinese dedicated their life mainly to commercial exploits, to great success. Although immigrants from various regions flocked to colonial Singapore, the Chinese—bringing with them their cultural norms—quickly outnumbered other ethnic groups. By the end of the nineteenth century, more than 70% of Singapore's population was Chinese, who

Table 5.4 Composition of Chinese in Singapore's population

Year	*Percentage of population comprising Chinese (%)*
1824	31
1830	39.4
1836	45.9
1849	52.9
1871	57.6
1881	63
1891	67.1
1901	72.1
1911	72.4
1921	75.3
1931	75.1
1947	77.8

Source: Saw (2012)

continued to outnumber the combined total of other migrants even by 1947 (Freedman, 1961) (Table 5.4).

These Chinese immigrants were particularly economically motivated, excelling in key sectors such as mercantile trading, banking, and finance, the growing pepper and gambier cash crops, and artisan and craft trades (Lee, 1988, 1991, pp. 246–252). Of note, the cross-country business networks developed by the Chinese community still endure today and continue to dominate the Asian economy (Mackie, 1992, 1998; Brown, R. A. 1994; Gerke & Menkhoff, 2003).

The economic dominance of the Chinese community is important because it has implications on the developmental state theory concerning Singapore's history. This is best understood through an examination of several key prominent individuals who formed the Chinese industrial class: Tan Kah Kee, Tan Lark Sye, and Tan Keng Choon.

Tan Kah Kee and his Industrial Legacy

Tan Kah Kee was a prominent Chinese rubber magnate and philanthropist and has been considered the "Henry Ford of Malaya". His life has been extensively documented as has his philanthropic contributions to the local community. For the purposes of this chapter, it should be stressed that he was a key contributor to the industrial development of Singapore in the early twentieth century.

Tan's contributions in the rubber industry were critical. He had inherited his father's early business and diversified it into rubber planting upon noticing its profit opportunity. Importantly, in 1919, he started his own company Tan Kah Kee and Co., which employed more than 30,000 by 1925. Being an early entrant into the rubber sector, he achieved economic success to the tune of almost $8 million before the end of the 1920s. His impact on industrialisation should be noted. His "Henry Ford" attribution stems from his business's deliberate involvement in all stages of the supply chain, except for those that could be outsourced more cheaply. Moreover, he had pioneered the processing of latex and the manufacturing of rubber products such as boots, tennis shoes, and tyres.

The industrialisation brought about by the rubber sector involved considerable scale and sophistication. First, the Chinese entrepreneurs operating in rubber like Tan had access to capital through banks and the substantial profits gained via other sectors they were involved in. This allowed the company to build industrial facilities and factories that involved the milling and processing of rubber and the manufacturing of rubber-based products. The industrial facilities were especially capital-intensive and certainly not primitive establishments with just a few workers. According to a study on the rubber industry, it is said that "in capital intensity, these Chinese enterprises were close to, or the equal of, European-owned industries" (Huff, 1993). Tan's factories are said to have been able to mass produce more than 20,000 pairs of shoes and 6000 bicycle tyres a day, and his factories represented a capital investment of over $8 million (Straits Settlements and Trade Commission, 1934, pp. 145, 301, 306; Singapore and Malayan directory, 1931, p. 147; Singapore and Straits Directory, 1921–1922, pp. 242–243 & 284n–284o).

The industrial facilities in rubber were also engaged in wider manufacturing. Manufactured goods catered not only to the domestic market but also for export to overseas ones. Tan himself took the lead in exporting rubber to the West and was "well known in Mincing Lane and on the New York Rubber Exchange" (Nathan, 1925, p. 24). By the 1930s, his company controlled two large rubber mills in Singapore, another 10 in Malaya, and had acquired more than 10,000 acres of rubber estates. The British leader Ormsby Gore (1928, pp. 13, 145) marvelled at Tan's manufacturing output: "one of the most remarkable enterprises in Asia, if not in the world...where rubber shoes in vast quantities, and now even motor tyres, are being manufactured under Chinese management and with Chinese labour".

Presence of a Domestic Industrial Class

Tan's economic contributions were not just limited to his own business. He had himself groomed other individuals who themselves became prominent industrialists, such as Tan Lark Sye and Lee Kong Chian. Tan Lark Sye, founder of Aik Hoe, was initially groomed by Tan. In 1933, his firm operated three mills with 90 machines. By the end of the decade, he had numerous branches and became the biggest rubber exporter in British Malaya (Straits Settlements and Trade Commission, 1934, p. 234; Sim, 1950, pp. 2–10; Yong, 1992).

The economic contributions of Chinese entrepreneurs like Tan Kah Kee, Lee Kong Chian, and Tan Lark Sye point to the larger importance of the rubber industry in the development of the early Singapore economy. Rubber is one of the oldest traded commodities in Singapore, which in the early 1900s became the world's main sorting and export centre, further increasing its attraction as a port of call (Figs. 5.18 and 5.19). Rubber was

Fig. 5.18 Image of women workers operating factory machinery in the 1950s. (Source: Ministry of Information and the Arts. Permission obtained from National Archives Singapore)

Fig. 5.19 Interior view of a local rubber factory in the 1930s. (Source: Lee Kip Lin Collection. Permission obtained from National Archives Singapore)

a catalyst for early industrialisation because it became in the Western context a versatile material for industrial use, and because of the rise of automobiles and modern transportation. Western traders and British investors were also attracted to Singapore and provided capital for rubber plantations to be developed and had also engaged in joint ventures with Chinese entrepreneurs.

In the context of Singapore, rubber catalysed industrial development because it led to the establishment of rubber smoking and milling factories, shoe manufacturing facilities, and pineapple canneries (Rubber Trade Association of Singapore, 2003; Tan, 2014, pp. 38–47, 54–75). These industrial activities involved the accumulation of foreign and local capital and provided employment for large numbers of immigrants. In 1934, despite the effects of the Great Depression, the Straits Settlements Trade Commission pointed to the "remarkable industrial progress achieved by the colony in recent years" (Straits Settlements and Trade Commission, 1934, p. 145). What was also significant is that the rubber industry led to larger positive externalities for the economy. Since Singapore mainly operated as a port of call for the processing, refinement, and re-export of rubber, supporting services also had to be developed. Rubber processing and trading activities required the services of a banking community. As such, Singapore grew as the financing centre for rubber development in the region (Tan, 2014, pp. 38–47, 54–75). These banks include the large Chinese-dominated ones. Additionally, economic infrastructure such as port facilities, roads, and railways had to be developed. The infrastructure built, especially port development, was beneficial to Singapore's further growth as a trade hub and other post-independence industrial activities (Lim, 1967, pp. 272–296).

Of course, industrial activities and manufacturing were not just limited to the rubber industry. There were other industrial enterprises such as the Ho Hong organisation, which included soap factories, sawmills, and cement works. Rubber industrialists also diversified into other areas of manufacturing. The factories of Lee Kim Soo, another industrialist, included the manufacturing of concrete works, tyre works, a nail factory, potteries, and home furniture (Singapore and Malayan directory, 1931, p. 82; Colonial Office, 1932, pp. 95, 97).

The important point to be stressed in this section is that far from having no industrial base to build upon, Singapore had a strong Chinese entrepreneurial class with industrial capital, knowledge, and experience. Huff had himself explained that "it was very largely Singapore's Chinese entrepreneurs who first demonstrated that the port could make a substantial part of its living by industrial production" (Huff, 1994, pp. 224–225). The Singapore Manufacturers' Association pointed out through a representative that "it is to the Chinese merchants of the City that Singapore is largely indebted for its industrial development" (Cresson, n.d., p. 59).

Therefore, the economic premise that motivated the developmental state's industrialisation is false. The economic advisor Albert Winsemius, a key architect of the United Nation report that drove Singapore's state industrialisation, had claimed "there was no local industrial sector to speak of, and we did not advise to build up such a sector either" (Winsemius, 1995). Many accounts of Singapore's industrial development continue to portray the government as having played a necessary role in the supposed dearth of local entrepreneurs. It is said that the "circumstances in Singapore were not wired for free-market enterprise. Singapore lacked natural resources, industrial skills and expertise, managerial abilities and structures, as well as a strong indigenous industrial capitalist class that could spearhead export-driven industrialisation" (Centre for Liveable Cities, 2013, p. 6).

How can this be true? "Free-market enterprise" had flourished under the British, and a local industrial sector, though nascent, did exist (Tables 5.5 and 5.6). The Singaporean developmental state did catalyse industrialisation in the 1960s, but in its absence, would local industries have continued to grow organically? This is anyone's guess unfortunately, since we do not enjoy the privilege of the counterfactual.

Table 5.5 Statistics estimating size of domestic manufacturing and industrial sector before 1965 in Singapore

	1921	*1923*	*1926*	*1929*	*1931*	*1934*	*1939*	*1947*	*1957*
No. of persons employed in manufacturing industry[a]	33,293 (15.6%)	NA	NA	NA	38,217 (16%)	NA	NA	60,426 (17.5%)	78,275 (16.7%)
No. of industrial establishments[b]	630	896	1024	815	747	944	729	1016	NA

[a]Sources: Sixth Census of Straits Settlements of Singapore (Nathan, 1921). Seventh Census of Straits Settlements of Singapore (Vlieland, 1931). Census of the Federation of Malaya and Colony of Singapore (Del Tufo, 1947). Population Census, 1957, Superintendent of Census (1957)

[b]Refer to Straits Settlements Blue Books in selected years, Section 22. (Department of Statistics, 1921, 1923, 1926, 1929, 1931, 1934, 1939, 1947, 1957). Industrial establishments in this source includes establishments that engage in manufactures by steam power, oil engine, by manual labour and other smaller manufacturing works such as tin smelting, rubber factories, and engineering workshops

Table 5.6 Statistics showing growth of industrial activity from 1959 to 1965[a]

	1959	*1960*	*1961*	*1962*	*1963*	*1964*	*1965*
No. of establishments	564	583	595	642	897	965	1036
No. of workers	31,855	33,799	33,885	35,533	43,184	46,284	51,959
Output (M$'000)	1,588,585	1,667,093	1,415,004	1,740,733	1,591,895	1,544,932	1,685,977
Value-added (M$'000)	159,250	189,018	293,502	241,263	291,543	310,393	368,388

Source: Report on the Census of Industrial Production (Department of Statistics, 1959–1965)

[a]1959 is the first year that the Report on the Census of Industrial Production was published and defines industrial activity in a more limited way as compared to previous Straits Settlements statistics, including only manufacturing proper, processing, servicing and repairing, and rubber processing and granite quarrying. Only establishments employing at least ten people were included. Value-added is defined as the difference between the value of gross output and the value of total input and work given out

Conclusion

For all the problems that both Hong Kong and Singapore faced throughout the years of colonial rule, they are nevertheless highly successful city-states. The late twentieth century saw living standards in both city-states surpass even those in metropolitan London and major Western cities.

At the same time, both Hong Kong and Singapore were very much a colonial paradox. The British had secured the islands primary for their own trading interests within the context of their overseas empire but set in motion developments that surpassed their intentions. Seeking better conditions for British traders was the initial concern, yet both cities became major hubs of trade and remain so today. Both societies were ruled by the British for more than a century primarily for their own self-interest yet are populated by a majority Chinese population who mostly flourished. The leaders in official government were largely British officials, yet local rules and self-governing institutions also flourished. What started out as a British economic enterprise became unintentionally, a very successful, Anglo-Chinese joint venture.

References

Acemoglu, D., Johnson, S., & Robinson, J. (2001). The colonial origins of comparative development: An empirical investigation. *American Economic Review, 91*(5), 1369–1401.

Acemoglu, D., & Robinson, J. (2012). *Why nations fail: The origins of power, prosperity and poverty.* Crown Publishers.

Archives and Oral History Department. (1981). *The land transport of Singapore: From early times to the present.* Archives. National Archives of Singapore, Singapore.

Balasingamchow, Y.-m. (2018). Introduction. In N. L. Board (Ed.), *Between the lines. Early print advertising in Singapore, 1830s–1960s* (pp. 2–19). National Library Board.

Bartholomew, G. (1976). The Singapore legal system. In R. Hassan (Ed.), *Singapore: Society in transition.* Oxford University Press.

Bastin, J. (2009). *Letters and books of Sir Stamford Raffles.* Editions Didier Millet.

Bauer, P. (1976). *Dissent on development.* Harvard University Press.

Boettke, P. J., Coyne, C. J., & Leeson, P. T. (2015). Institutional stickiness and the new development economics. In *Culture and economic action.* Edward Elgar Publishing.

Boulger, D. C. (1899). *The life of Sir Stamford Raffles.* Pepin Press.

Brown, D. (1994). *The state and ethnic politics in Southeast Asia*. Routledge.
Brown, R. A. (1994). *Capital and entrepreneurship in South-East Asia*. Macmillan Press.
Brown, R. A. (1995). *Chinese business enterprise in Asia*. Routledge.
Carroll, J. (2007). *A concise history of Hong Kong*. Rowman and Littlefield Publishers.
Centre for Liveable Cities. (2013). *Industrial infrastructure*. Cengage Learning.
Chan, K. B., & Chiang, C. (1994). *Stepping out: The making of Chinese entrepreneurs*. Prentice Hall.
Chan, W. K. (1991). *The making of Hong Kong society: Three studies of class formation in early Hong Kong*. Clarendon.
Collis, M. (2009). *Raffles: The definitive biography*. Marshall Cavendish.
Colonial Office. (1843a, January). CO129/3—Aberdeen to Pottinger, dispatch 4. *Archives of the Colonial Office*.
Colonial Office. (1843b, June). CO129/2—Stanley to Pottinger 8. *Archives of the Colonial Office*.
Colonial Office. (1856, July). CO129/55—Labouchere to Bowring 82. *Archives of the Colonial Office*.
Colonial Office. (1871, February). 129/149 Petition from the Chinese community of Hong Kong.
Colonial Office. (1932). *CO 273/582: Straits settlements original correspondence (CO 273/582/1-14)*. The National Archives (United Kingdom). Straits Settlements.
Coyne, C. J. (2008). *After war: The political economy of exporting democracy*. Stanford University Press.
Cresson, L. (n.d.). *Industrial Singapore*. Handbook, Singapore.
Davies, S. (1977). One brand of politics rekindled. *Hong Kong Law Journal, 7*(1), 44–84.
Del Tufo, M. V. (1947). *Census of the federation of Malaya and colony of Singapore*. Crown Agents for the Colonies.
Department of Statistics. (1921, 1923, 1926, 1929, 1931, 1934, 1939, 1947, 1957). *Straits settlements blue book for the year 1876*. Singapore: Government Printing Office, Singapore.
Department of Statistics. (1959–1965). *Report on the census of industrial production*. Government of Singapore, Singapore.
Devan, J. (2014). LKY: Notes towards defining His Soul-Craft. In S. Jayakumar & R. Sagar (Eds.), *The Big Ideas of Lee Kuan Yew*. Straits Times Press.
Dorsett, S., & McLaren, J. (2014). *Legal Histories of the British Empire: Laws, engagements and legacies*. Routledge.
Elson, R. (1962). International commerce, the state and society: Economic and social change. In N. Tarling & N. Tarling (Eds.), *The Cambridge history of Southeast Asia* (Vol. 2, pp. 131–196). Cambridge University Press.
Endacott, G. (1973). *A history of Hong Kong*. Oxford University Press.

Endacott, G. (2005). *A biographical sketch-book of early Hong Kong*. Hong Kong University Press.

Ferguson, N. (2018). *Empire: How Britain made the modern world*. Penguin Books Ltd.

Foreign Office. (1842, May 20). 17/60 Letter from Pottinger to Aberdeen. *Archives of the Foreign Office*.

Freedman, M. (1961). Immigrants and associations: Chinese in nineteenth-century Singapore. *Comparative Studies in Society and History, 3*(1), 25–48.

Gerke, S., & Menkhoff, T. (2003). *Chinese entrepreneurship and Asian business networks*. Routledge.

Ghesquiere, H. (2007). *Singapore's success: Engineering economic growth*. Thomson Learning.

Gilley, B. (2017). The case for colonialism. *Third World Quarterly*.

Goh, K. S. (1958). Entrepreneurship in a plural economy. *Malayan Economic Review, 3*(1), 1–7.

Grier, R. (1999). Colonial legacies and economic growth. *Public Choice, 98*, 317–335.

Hack, K. (2012). Framing Singapore's history. In N. Tarling (Ed.), *Studying Singapore's past* (pp. 17–64). NUS Press.

Hayes, J. (2015). Hong Kong Island Before 1841. In J. Carroll & C.-K. Mark (Eds.), *Critical readings on the modern history of Hong Kong* (Vol. 2, pp. 549–580). Koninklijke Brill.

Hilton, P., & Tate, D. (1963). *Southeast Asia in world history*. Oxford University Press.

Hobson, J. (1938). *Imperialism: A study*. Unwin.

Hong, L., & Juanli, H. (2008). *The scripting of a national history: Singapore and its pasts*. NUS Press.

Hong Kong Blue Book. (1844–1899). *Census of Hong Kong Chinese Population*. Hong Kong: Noronha & Co.

Huff, W. (1993). The development of the rubber market in pre-World War II Singapore. *Journal of Southeast Asian Studies, 24*(2), 285–306.

Huff, W. (1994). *The economic growth of Singapore*. Cambridge University Press.

Hughes, R. (1976). *Borrowed place borrowed time: Hong Kong and its many faces*. Andre Deutsch.

Kong, L., & Sinha, V. (2015). *Food, foodways and foodscapes: Culture, community and consumption in post-colonial Singapore*. World Scientific.

Kuo, E. (1980). The sociolinguistic situation in Singapore. In E. Afrendas & E. Kuo (Eds.), *Language and society in Singapore*. Singapore University Press.

Kwa, C. G., Heng, D., Borschberg, P., & Tan, T. Y. (2019). *Seven hundred years: A history of Singapore*. Marshall Cavendish International Asia Pte Ltd.

La Porta, R., Lopez-de-Silanes, F., & Shleifer, A. (2008). The economic consequences of legal origins. *Journal of Economic Literature, 46*(2), 285–332.

Lange, M., Mahoney, J., & von Hau, M. (2006). Colonialism and development: A comparative analysis of Spanish and British colonies. *American Journal of Sociology, 111*(5), 412–1462.

Latham, A. (1994). The great entrepots of Hong Kong and Singapore. In I. H. Kawakatsu & J. Latham (Eds.), *Japanese Industrialization and the Asian Economy* (pp. 145–183). Routledge.

Lee, E. (1991). Community, family and household. In E. Chew & E. Lim (Eds.), *A history of Singapore* (pp. 242–267). Oxford University Press.

Lee, L. T. (1988). *Early Chinese immigrant societies: Case studies from North America and British Southeast Asia*. Heinemann Asia.

Lee, P. P. (1978). *Chinese society in nineteenth-century Singapore*. Oxford University Press.

Legislative Council of Hong Kong. (1884–1885). *Sessional papers*. Papers laid before Legislative Council of Hong Kong.

Leung, B. K. (1990). Power and politics: A critical analysis. In B. K. Leung (Ed.), *Social Issues in Hong Kong*. Oxford University Press.

Lim, C. Y. (1967). *Economic development of modern malaya*. Oxford University Press.

Lim, L. (2013). Southeast Asian Chinese business and regional economic development. In C.-B. Tan (Ed.), *Routledge handbook of the Chinese diaspora* (pp. 249–260). Routledge.

Liu, S. (1997). Hong Kong: A survey of its political and economic development over the past 150 years. *China Quarterly, 151*, 10.

Low, L. (2001). The Singapore developmental state in the new economy and polity. *The Pacific Review, 14*(3), 411–441.

Mackie, J. (1992). Overseas Chinese Entrepreneurship. *Asia Pacific Economic Literature, 6*(1), 41–64.

Mackie, J. (1998). Business success among Southeast Asian Chinese: The role of culture, values, and social structures. In I. R. Hefner (Ed.), *Market cultures. Society and morality in the New Asian capitalisms* (pp. 129–146). Westview Press.

MacPherson, K. L. (1998). *Asian department stores*. University of Hawaii Press.

Mahizhnan, A., & Tsao, Y. L. (2002). *Singapore: Re-engineering success*. Institute for Policy Studies.

Mahoney, J. (2000). Path dependence in historical sociology. *Theory and society, 29*(4), 507–548.

Miksic, J. (2013). *Singapore & the Silk Road of the Sea, 1300–1800*. Singapore University Press.

Morse, H. (1910). Letter from Palmserstone to Minister of the Chinese Emperor, 20 February 1840. *The International Relations of the Chinese Empire*.

Munn, C. (2001). The rule of law and criminal justice in the nineteenth century. In S. Tsang (Ed.), *Judicial Independence and the Rule of Law in Hong Kong*. Palgrave.

Nathan, J. (1921). *Sixth census of straits settlements of Singapore.* Dunstable and Watford.

Nathan, J. (1925, February 19). Changes in the flow of trade. *Manchester Guardian Commercial, special section on British Malaya.*

Newbold, T. (1839). *Political and statistical account of the British settlements in the straits of Malacca.* John Murray.

Ormsby-Gore, W. G. A. (1928). *Report by the right honourable W. G. A. Ormsby-Gore, M. P. (Parliamentary under-secretary of state for the colonies) on his visit to Malaya, Ceylon, and Java During the Year 1928.* Colonial Office of Her Majesty's Government, London.

Pereira, A. A. (2008). Whither the developmental state? Explaining Singapore's continued developmentalism. *Third World Quarterly, 29*(6), 1189–1203.

Pottinger, G. (1997). *Sir Henry Pottinger—First governor of Hong Kong.* Pottinger.

Raben, R. (2014). The colonial intrusion: Boundaries and structures. In N. G. Owen & N. G. Owen (Eds.), *Routledge Handbook of Southeast Asian History* (pp. 25–35). Routledge.

Raffles, L. S. (1830). *Memoir of the life of Sir Thomas Stamford Raffles.*

Rappaport, E. (2017). *A thirst for empire: How tea shaped the modern world.* Princeton University Press.

Rear, J. (1977). One brand of polities. In K. Hopkins (Ed.), *Hong Kong: The industrial colony.* Oxford University Press.

Rodrik, D. (1999). *Making openness work: The new global economy and the developing countries.* Overseas Development Council.

Rodrik, D., Subramanian, A., & Trebbi, F. (2004). Institutions rule: The primacy of institutions over geography and integration in economic development. *Journal of Economic Growth, 9*(2), 131–165.

Rosenstein-Rodan, P. N. (1961). Notes on the theory of the 'big push'. In *Economic development for Latin America* (pp. 57–81). Palgrave Macmillan.

Rubber Trade Association of Singapore. (2003). *The Singapore rubber market.* Rubber Trade Association of Singapore & Singapore Commodity Exchange, Singapore.

Rubin, P. (1977). Why is the common law efficient? *Journal of Legal Studies, 6*, 51–63.

Saw, S.-H. (1991). Population growth and control. In E. Chew & E. Lee (Eds.), *A History of Singapore* (pp. 219–241). Oxford University Press.

Saw, S.-H. (2012). *The population of Singapore.* Institute of Southeast Asian Studies.

Sim, V. (1950). *Biographies of prominent Chinese in Singapore.* Singapore.

Singapore and Malayan directory. (1931). *Singapore and Malayan directory.* Singapore Printers, Singapore.

Singapore and Straits Directory. (1921–1922). *The Singapore and Straits directory.* Mission Press, Singapore.

Slayer, G. R. (1980). Additional notes 6 (Elliot's circular to British subjects, 20 January 1841). *Hong Kong 1841–1862: Birth Adolescence and Coming of Age.*

State of Singapore. (1963). *Commerce*. Annual Report 1961. State of Singapore.
Straits Settlements and Trade Commission. (1934). *Report of the commission appointed by his excellency the governor of the straits settlements to enquire into and report on the trade of the colony, 1933–1934*. University of Singapore Library.
Superintendent of Census. (1957). *Population census, 1957*. Superintendent of Census, Kuala Lumpur.
Tan, P. W. (2014). *Singapore Rubber trade—An economic heritage*. Suntree Media.
Tarling, N. (1962). *Anglo-Dutch rivalry in the Malay World 1780–1824*. Cambridge University Press.
Tarling, N. (2012). *Studying Singapore's Past: C.M. Turnbull and the history of Modern Singapore*. NUS Press.
Tarulevicz, N. (2013). *Eating her curries and Kway: A cultural history of food in Singapore*. University of Illinois Press.
Thornton, A. (1978). *Imperialism in the twentieth century*. Macmillan.
Turnbull, C. M. (2009). *A History of Singapore, 1819–2005*. NUS Press.
United Nations. (1961). *A proposed industrialization programme for the State of Singapore*. U.N. Comissioner for Technical Assistance.
University of Malaya. (1968). *Malaya law review* (Vol. 10). University of Malaya.
Vlieland, C. (1931). *Seventh census of straits settlements of Singapore*. Crown Agents for the Colonies.
Welsh, F. (1993). *A history of Hong Kong*. .
Wharton, C. (2015). *Advertising: Critical approaches*. Routledge.
Whitaker, J. (2011). *The department store: History, design, display*. Thames and Hudson.
Winsemius, A. (1995). Interview with Dr. Winsemius (T. Hague, Interviewer)
Wong, G. (2018). The Modern Malayan Home. In N. L. Board (Ed.), *Between the lines. Early print advertising in Singapore, 1830s–1960s* (pp. 118–137). National Library Board.
Wong, K. L. (1991). The strategic significance of Singapore in modern history. In E. Chew & E. Lee (Eds.), *A History of Singapore* (pp. 17–35). Oxford University Press.
Wright, H. (1950). The Anglo–Dutch dispute in the East, 1814–1824. *The Economic History Review, 3*(2), 229–239.
Yap, J. (2007). *Motoring beyond 100: Celebrating 100 years of the Automobile Association of Singapore.*. Automobile Association of Singapore.
Yeoh, B. S., Kong, L., & Perry, M. (1997). *Singapore: A developmental city state*. Wiley.
Yong, C. F. (1992). *Chinese leadership and power in colonial Singapore*. Marshall Cavendish International.
You, D. (1958). *Hong Kong's early history 1841–1907*. Joint Publishers.
Yu, S., & Liu, C. (1994). *Shijiu shiji de Xianggang (19th century Hong Kong)*. Beijing Zhonghua Shuju.

CHAPTER 6

Reassessing Relative Economic Performance

Beyond National Income

Hong Kong and Singapore are regarded as two of the most successful city-states in recent history, in terms of their high standards of living and wealth of their citizens. They represent two of the East Asian tiger economies which managed to achieve first-world living standards in one generation, a feat which took Western countries several centuries to accomplish. The image of East Asian economies as "the future" has not abated despite the 1997 Asian financial crisis. This is in part due to the alleged problems in Western liberal societies, such as the 2008 financial crisis and the European debt crisis that followed soon after. These events supposedly demonstrate the increasing inferiority of Western as compared to East Asian economics.

This perspective argues that East Asian developmental states, with their higher state capacity and communitarian culture, are superior to states bound by Western liberal democratic values. Former Dean of the Lee Kuan Yew School of Public Policy, Kishore Mahbubani, is the key

The content of this chapter is drawn from a previously published article. See Cheang, B. (2022). What Can Industrial Policy Do? Evidence from Singapore. *The Review of Austrian Economics*, 1–34.

B. Cheang, *Economic Liberalism and the Developmental State*,
https://doi.org/10.1007/978-3-031-08100-2_6

Table 6.1 Comparison of average growth rates, divided into ten-year periods

	Average GDP growth rate 1962–1970	*GDP growth rate 1971–1980*	*GDP growth rate 1981–1990*	*GDP growth rate 1991–2000*	*GDP growth rate 2001–2010*	*GDP growth rate 2011–2018*
Singapore	9.59%	8.82%	7.80%	7.14%	5.91%	4.02%
Hong Kong	8.96%	9.09%	6.80%	4.02%	4.13%	2.97%

Source: World Bank (2020b, 2020c)

proponent of this line of thinking. For him, the outbreak of COVID-19 marks the "dawn" of the East Asian century (Mahbubani, 2020). Consequently, two of the most successful East Asian countries are the city-states of Hong Kong and Singapore, both of which have been presented by others as models worth emulating.

Most scholars insist that when both are compared, Singapore has outpaced Hong Kong in terms of economic achievements, due to its proactive government intervention which has been relatively absent in Hong Kong (Fuller, 2010; Huang & Yeung, 2018, p. 142). A commonly cited piece of evidence for this is the higher rate of economic growth that Singapore has achieved relative to Hong Kong over the past several decades (Table 6.1).

On the surface, it seems like the Singaporean developmental state system is superior in delivering economic growth than laissez-faire Hong Kong. Aside from national income (Fig. 6.1), scholars have also insisted that the market-based approach has failed Hong Kong by not preparing it for global competition marked by disruptive innovation. In short, when it comes to transforming Hong Kong into a knowledge intensive economy, "laissez-faire just doesn't work" (Lo & Pang, 2007). This perspective is further echoed by a prominent civil servant whom I interviewed.[1] The civil servant, who used to spearhead the Singapore civil service, expressed that due to the proactive, forward-looking interventions of the developmental state, it has leapfrogged Hong Kong which remains "backward" on the innovation frontier.

[1] Interview with a director from the Centre for Strategic Futures, Singapore. November 2018.

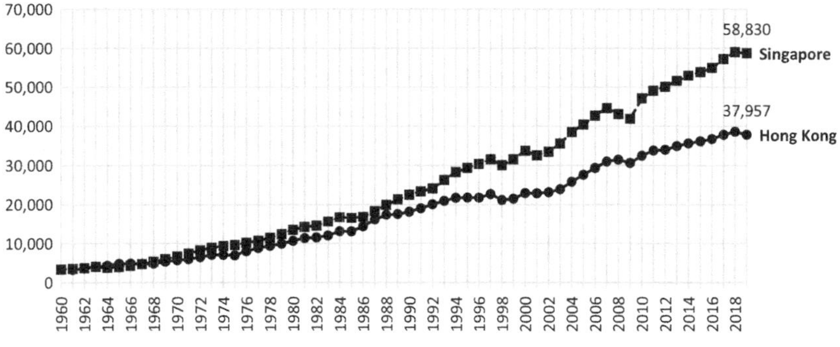

Fig. 6.1 Comparison of GDP per capita of Hong Kong and Singapore since 1960 (constant 2010 USD). (Source: World Bank Development Indicators (2020a))

Accordingly, this chapter provides a contrarian opinion on the economic performance of Hong Kong and Singapore. I argue that the predominant focus on traditional income statistics have obscured structural concerns surrounding the developmental state's ability to achieve higher-order, cutting-edge growth, that which is characterised by productivity, innovation, and entrepreneurship. A deconstruction of existing statistics also shows that Singapore's indigenous private sector innovation capacity has been stifled by state policy. The seemingly superior record of Singapore becomes less impressive, considering how Hong Kong's development was attained without the same degree of state support. These concerns on productivity, innovation, and entrepreneurship are not original to me but have been echoed by numerous Singapore scholars over the years (Tsao, 1985; Lim & Pang, 2016; Low, 2003; Tan & Tan, 2015; Bhaskaran & Chiang, 2020). This chapter builds on such earlier studies to evaluate Singapore's economic performance against Hong Kong's.

The mechanism that explains the disparity in performance is the crowding out effect in Singapore, where the state-linked entities, being so dominant in various aspects of society, have pushed out domestic enterprise. This has been echoed by Singapore scholars in the past, and also demonstrated in the earlier chapters, which estimated the large presence of the state, government-linked corporations, and big firms. As explained in Chap. 3, the domestic entrepreneurial class in Singapore was also marginalised, and even persecuted, in the post-war period. The diversion of labour into the state sector and foreign enterprise sector is particularly noteworthy, making it difficult for small local firms to compete for the best talent, a problem compounded by the high savings rate mandated by the CPF, which reduces the availability of household capital (Chia, 1989, pp. 265–266). A recent study has echoed this position: that Singapore's "entrepreneurial statism" crowded out entrepreneurship (Audretsch & Fiedler, 2022). In Hong Kong, the state simply did not bet one way or another on a particular growth trajectory or industry, and so domestic enterprises, especially small nimble entrepreneurs, were always given free rein, setting in motion decades of bottom-up development (Yu, 1997, 1998). Another related problem is the Singapore state's political authoritarianism, which fosters an economically unhospitable climate, a problem that will be further elucidated in Chap. 7. Combined, these factors have diminished the dynamism of Singapore's economy, leading to its productivity, innovation, and entrepreneurship being less than desired.

Government-Led GDP vs. Private Sector-Led GDP

Before presenting the evaluative evidence concerning productivity, innovation, and entrepreneurship, it must be further clarified that since the 1990s, the Singaporean developmental state has continued down a state-led growth path. In contrast, the post-1997 Hong Kong state has largely continued its small government tradition, even though it also started mimicking Singapore's industrial policies.

This contrast is best illustrated through a time-series econometric approach analysing the relationship between government expenditure and national income. Specifically, I conducted business cycle analysis to ascertain the cross-correlation between GDP and other macroeconomic variables. Cross-correlation is important because it establishes whether the variable of government consumption has influenced changes in national income. This approach helps to establish whether there is a pro-cyclical relationship (output following) or counter-cyclical relationship (output leading), and whether there is a lead-lag effect between GDP and other variables.

Cross-correlation is defined as:

$$\gamma_{xy}(l) = \frac{c_{xy}(l)}{\sqrt{c_{xx}(0)}.\sqrt{c_{yy}(0)}}, \tag{1}$$

where $l = 0, \pm 1, \pm 2, \ldots$ while

$$c_{xy}(l) = \left\{ \begin{array}{l} \sum_{t=1}^{T-1}\left((x_t - \underline{x})(y_{t+1} - \underline{y})\right)/T, l = 0,1,2,\ldots \\ \sum_{t=1}^{T+1}\left((y_t - \underline{y})(x_{t+1} - \underline{x})\right)/T, l = 0,-1,-2,\ldots \end{array} \right\}, \tag{2}$$

and

$$c_{xx}(0) = \sum_{t=0}^{T}(x_t - \underline{x})^2 / T, (\text{the variance of the } x \text{ series}), \tag{3}$$

and

$$c_{yy}(0) = \sum_{t=0}^{T}(y_t - \underline{y})^2 / T, (\text{the variance of the } y \text{ series}). \tag{4}$$

The time period of analysis is denoted by T. The formula demonstrates that the mean and variance do not change, because the cyclical components are fixed. Therefore, the mean of the series is 0, and the variance (of the whole series) is a constant. The cyclical component is equal to the original series, subtracting the trend series. As a result of this, we are able to derive the cyclical component after the original series is input into the Hodrick-Prescott filter.

From CEIC, I obtained the macroeconomic variables and output data of the East Asian countries for the entire sample period. The first equation is used in calculating the cross-correlation between the variables and to derive the coefficient estimates. Since we are interested in how GDP is cross correlated with the various macro variables, we use x to represent GDP and y for the different variables in the first equation.

This analysis is useful in four ways. First, we can determine, for each macroeconomic variable, their cyclical fluctuations. This is done by comparing the standard deviation of the movement of each variable and GDP in order to detect if they are more volatile than output. The second benefit of this analysis is that it ascertains whether the macroeconomic variable in question is correlated with output, for example, does GDP and government expenditure rise together? For the two variables to be correlated, the cross-correlation coefficients have to be greater than (in absolute value) $\left(2/\sqrt{T}\right)$, which is approximately 0.2425 for 68 observations. Third, we can ascertain either a pro or counter-cyclical relationship by examining the correlation coefficients. If the coefficient estimate for the cross-correlation between GDP and a specific variable is a positive number, this suggests a pro-cyclical relationship. Fourth, we can also determine the lead-lag effects, that is, whether a variable leads changes in GDP or vice versa.

An earlier study which measures these variables from 1973 to 2006 shows that in Hong Kong, there was very little correlation between GDP and government spending (Li, 2012, ch. 3). I extended the time window and input data all the way to the present day, using data from 1952 to 2019.

The following results of Table 6.2 show that the standard deviation of cyclical government consumption in Hong Kong is approximately 1.7 times higher than that of cyclical GDP. Most of the cross-correlation coefficients are not statistically significant except for lag one ($\gamma(-1)$) and lead one ($\gamma(1)$), with lag one higher in magnitude (0.377 vs. -0.331) than lead

Table 6.2 Cross-correlation of GDP cycle in the Hong Kong economy

Variables	*SD(%)*	*Cross-correlation of GDP cycle with*						
		$\gamma(-3)$	$\gamma(-2)$	$\gamma(-1)$	$\gamma(0)$	$\gamma(1)$	$\gamma(2)$	$\gamma(3)$
GDP	3.681	-0.022	-0.350	0.010	1.000	0.010	-0.350	-0.022
P-Con	6.184	-0.075	-0.089	0.468	0.512	-0.202	-0.358	0.085
G-Con	6.149	-0.005	0.167	0.377	0.099	-0.331	-0.150	0.001
Invest	14.677	-0.130	-0.164	0.301	0.726	0.031	-0.089	-0.140
Import	8.965	0.009	-0.310	0.206	0.684	-0.087	-0.245	0.105
Export	8.273	0.095	-0.340	0.046	0.720	-0.104	-0.275	0.120
Deflator	2.705	0.172	0.160	0.306	0.177	-0.326	-0.177	-0.024
CPI	2.237	0.179	0.157	0.304	-0.063	-0.389	-0.075	-0.026
M1	11.102	0.133	-0.239	-0.218	0.113	0.431	-0.022	0.060
M2	8.508	0.160	0.043	0.084	-0.037	0.133	-0.041	-0.529
HSI	25.500	0.024	-0.233	-0.062	0.594	0.330	-0.436	-0.061
Empl	1.400	-0.143	-0.026	0.249	0.321	-0.227	-0.210	0.111
Unempl	0.800	-0.042	-0.088	-0.507	-0.181	0.525	0.289	0.026
Wage	2.241	-0.221	-0.275	0.420	0.397	-0.246	-0.438	-0.165
HP	13.586	-0.221	-0.275	0.420	0.397	-0.246	-0.438	-0.165

Table 6.3 Cross-correlation of GDP cycle in Singaporean economy

Variables	*SD(%)*	*Cross-correlation of GDP cycle with*						
		$\gamma(-3)$	$\gamma(-2)$	$\gamma(-1)$	$\gamma(0)$	$\gamma(1)$	$\gamma(2)$	$\gamma(3)$
GDP	3.467	-0.040	-0.214	0.080	1.000	0.080	-0.214	-0.040
P-Con	6.884	-0.065	-0.080	0.253	0.571	-0.084	-0.199	-0.021
G-Con	7.418	0.180	0.093	0.361	0.460	-0.166	-0.121	-0.251
Invest	15.902	0.003	0.146	0.189	0.578	-0.082	-0.158	-0.012
Import	13.367	-0.100	-0.195	0.141	0.592	-0.111	-0.025	-0.021
Export	12.993	-0.109	-0.251	0.151	0.580	-0.076	-0.064	-0.017
Deflator	2.722	0.025	0.056	0.303	0.283	-0.115	-0.212	-0.098
CPI	3.487	0.002	0.112	0.285	0.013	-0.322	-0.107	-0.015
M1	8.633	0.126	0.015	-0.076	0.304	0.331	-0.172	-0.034
M2	5.661	-0.063	0.132	0.268	0.142	0.256	0.002	-0.193
STI	19.597	0.004	0.001	-0.405	0.627	0.184	-0.491	0.148
Empl	2.109	-0.013	0.046	0.437	0.350	-0.119	-0.133	-0.126
Unempl	0.436	-0.121	-0.224	-0.386	-0.129	0.509	0.251	-0.077
Wage	4.670	0.054	-0.390	0.325	0.601	-0.384	-0.187	0.094
HP	16.532	0.054	-0.390	0.325	0.601	-0.384	-0.187	0.094

one. This means that even though cyclical government consumption leads the cyclical GDP, the correlation remains minimal. This means that even in the present day, after Hong Kong has been handed over to China, its historic tradition of small government persists.

While there is low correlation between government consumption and GDP in Hong Kong, this correlation is much higher in Singapore. Tables 6.2 and 6.3 show that the standard deviation of government consumption (7.418) is higher in Singapore than that in Hong Kong (6.149), which means that government consumption in Singapore is more volatile. Crucially, the correlation estimate (0.460) is higher than that in Hong Kong (0.099), which means that government consumption in Singapore is more significant in affecting GDP changes. This supports the argument made in this study, that economic freedom is higher in Hong Kong.

The strong role of government in Singapore's economy becomes more obvious when compared to other Asian countries.

From the Tables 6.2, 6.3, 6.4, we can conclude that for Hong Kong, there is no correlation between GDP and government expenditure since the coefficient estimate is less than 0.2. For Japan, Taiwan and South Korea, the correlation is weak since the coefficients fall between a value of

Table 6.4 Cross-correlation with the output cycle: three Asian economics

Variables	*SD (%)*	*Cross-correlation of GDP cycle with*						
		$\gamma(-3)$	$\gamma(-2)$	$\gamma(-1)$	$\gamma(0)$	$\gamma(1)$	$\gamma(2)$	$\gamma(3)$
Taiwan								
GDP	2.407	-0.124	-0.313	-0.002	1.000	-0.002	-0.313	-0.124
P-Con	6.447	-0.053	-0.250	0.241	0.586	-0.317	-0.177	0.046
G-Con	6.038	0.024	-0.172	0.283	0.348	-0.339	-0.051	0.037
Invest	14.847	-0.130	-0.364	0.029	0.798	-0.251	-0.159	-0.021
Import	13.404	-0.150	-0.361	0.093	0.799	-0.343	-0.143	0.022
Export	10.515	-0.034	-0.401	-0.091	0.900	-0.287	-0.195	0.055
Stock	32.744	-0.070	0.060	0.231	0.493	-0.274	-0.342	0.124
South Korea								
GDP	2.899	-0.123	-0.216	-0.113	1.000	-0.113	-0.216	-0.123
P-Con	13.191	0.015	-0.168	0.000	0.537	-0.043	-0.223	-0.102
G-Con	13.332	0.058	-0.046	0.088	0.300	0.041	-0.132	-0.089
Invest	23.950	0.048	-0.144	-0.111	0.577	-0.062	-0.222	-0.027
Import	18.015	0.049	-0.199	0.036	0.428	-0.151	-0.159	-0.029
Export	13.664	0.108	-0.152	-0.062	0.442	-0.022	-0.147	-0.056
Stock	25.288	0.210	-0.032	-0.389	0.494	0.239	-0.100	-0.035
Japan								
GDP	1.695	-0.103	-0.196	-0.019	1.000	-0.019	-0.196	-0.103
P-Con	9.854	0.091	-0.166	-0.216	-0.246	0.107	0.351	0.132
G-Con	10.457	0.091	-0.195	-0.230	-0.306	0.119	0.354	0.140
Invest	11.730	0.011	-0.271	-0.085	0.136	0.095	0.318	0.055
Import	14.036	-0.072	-0.397	-0.057	0.566	0.074	0.111	-0.168
Export	9.659	0.126	-0.264	-0.242	0.503	-0.075	0.064	-0.007
Stock	17.914	0.085	-0.156	-0.055	0.380	0.319	0.027	-0.163

0.2 to 0.4. Singapore's correlation coefficient is the highest one of all, at a value of 0.460. While this only suggests medium correlation (coefficient must be >0.7 for strong correlation), it is the highest in East Asia.

What is especially significant is the results gleaned from comparing the growth volatility of GDP components across East Asia. Here I use a new dataset I created; the government expenditure statistics presented in Chap. 2 (which includes statutory boards). The 20.163% standard deviation demonstrates the high volatility of Singapore's government consumption (with statutory boards), suggesting its interventionist nature (Table 6.5). Notably, Singapore's government consumption (including statutory boards) is the most volatile across all five Asian economies. This implies

Table 6.5 Growth volatility of GDP components of five Asian economies: standard deviation (%)

	Whole period
Taiwan	
Private consumption	9.061
Govt. consumption	8.979
Investment	16.678
Import	14.820
Export	11.725
Singapore	
Private consumption	8.541
Govt. consumption (new)	20.163
Investment	18.454
Import	15.534
Export	15.338
South Korea	
Private consumption	15.084
Govt. consumption	15.630
Investment	26.175
Import	20.734
Export	18.004
Japan	
Private consumption	11.579
Govt. consumption	11.932
Investment	14.153
Import	16.159
Export	12.163
Hong Kong	
Private consumption	8.675
Govt. consumption	9.069
Investment	18.076
Import	11.092
Export	10.429

that Singapore's government has intervened actively in the economy comparatively more so than elsewhere. Crucially, this result is higher than a previous similar study—with a time window of 1973 to 2006 only—which reported only a 9.8198% standard deviation (Li, 2012, ch. 3).

Catch-Up vs. Cutting Edge Growth

Even though both nations have achieved rapid economic growth within several decades of the late twentieth century, the concern is that this may not be sustained, considering the distinction between catch-up growth and cutting-edge growth. The former refers to an earlier stage of growth which involves the mobilisation and accumulation of factor inputs, while the latter refers to a higher stage of growth which involves not only the quantitative increase in resource inputs, but the ability to increase the efficiency of existing resource use, represented by the concept of "productivity" and technological innovation. In simpler terms, this has been described by the economist Paul Krugman (1994) as "perspiration"-led growth vs. "inspiration"-led growth; the imagery suggesting that "inspiration" is the qualitatively superior approach not all countries can and have achieved.

An implication of this point is that the sheer accumulation of factor inputs, even if it leads to increases in GDP, does not necessarily equate to a qualitative improvement in economic welfare. The typical case that exemplifies this point is the Soviet Union, which is understood to have achieved rapid income growth, and even industrialisation, through central planning. Yet, the high growth rates of the USSR were simply a function of its massive mobilisation of resources through the force of the state, which came at the expense of the productive and efficient use of resources. Unsurprisingly, the USSR managed high rates of GDP growth, but simultaneously exhibited low productivity, resource misallocation, and inefficiency (Boettke, 1993; Roberts, 1990).

Economists have warned against the economic strategy of simply increasing factor inputs in hopes of maximising outputs. It was even speculated that the problems of the Soviet economy were due to an obsession with neoclassical growth theory's strategy of increasing output by increasing inputs into production functions (Weitzman, 1996). Unfortunately, even if output is increased, economic progress is never guaranteed (Holcombe, 2007). Additionally, merely increasing inputs and outputs also does not guarantee a conducive institutional environment needed for innovation and wealth creation.

These concerns raised are relevant to Hong Kong and Singapore. Citing a famous study by the economist Alwyn Young (1992), Paul Krugman argued in 1994 that "Singapore grew through a mobilisation of resources that would have done Stalin proud", and that "there is no sign at all of increased efficiency. In this sense, the growth of Lee Kuan Yew's

Singapore is an economic twin of the growth of Stalin's Soviet Union" (Krugman, 1994). The study by Alwyn Young (1992) was based on the insight that Singapore had simply achieved high rates of GDP growth through the sheer mobilisation of resources, namely, foreign capital, and labour, rather than by the efficient and improving use of productive resources and technological innovation.

Even Singapore's apparently superior performance on aggregate innovation statistics obscure deeper realities. Here, Lionel Robbin's (1932) distinction between technological and economic problems is helpful. The state, through its developmental interventions such as industrial policy, may be able to achieve the maximisation of given technical ends, but is unable to solve the *economic problem* of efficiently allocating resources across a multitude of ends. Accordingly, while the Singaporean developmental state has achieved higher innovation outputs, it fails to do so in an efficient manner, hence its poor performance in *innovation efficiency*. I extend this argument by showing that the state is also limited in its ability to provide a supportive cultural environment necessary for high-innovation growth. Cutting-edge development requires not only the mobilisation of economic resources into specific industries, but also intangibles such as creativity, a disruptive mindset, and a permission-less culture daring to break the status quo.

Total Factor Productivity

This damning assessment of Singapore's growth experience was contrasted with pre-1997 Hong Kong which displayed a better performance when it comes to total factor productivity (TFP), the indicator in question that motivated Young's and Krugman's analysis. TFP in turn is based on the 1956 publication of Robert Solow's growth model, which involves a simple production function with the total production being a function of capital (K_t), labour (L_t), and technical change, or total factor productivity (represented by the variable A_t). The production function is strictly increasing in all the three input factors, and so a rise in any of them leads to a rise in total production.

With a general Solow framework, Young conducted an econometric comparison of Hong Kong and Singapore specifically, and concluded that "a total factor productivity growth analysis of the two economies reveals that while TFP growth in Hong Kong accounts for over two-thirds of the increase in GDP per capita during the 1970s and 1980s, total factor productivity growth in Singapore during the same period is next to nil" (Young, 1992). This poor performance in total factor productivity was striking considering the massive mobilisation of resources by the Singaporean developmental state and the "astounding rate of structural transformation" (Young, 1992, 1995).

This argument made by Young, popularised by Krugman, led to scholarly debate in the following years on whether the measurements were truly accurate. Much ink has already been spilled over this; thus, I will not beat a dead horse here. Instead, this chapter looks at whether there has been any change in the abovementioned picture since the 1990s. Additionally, beyond reviewing the indicator of total factor productivity, I also examine the productivity improvement policies that were implemented by the Singaporean developmental state, which were in fact in response to the controversy generated by Krugman and similar critics.

Comparison of TFP between Countries

Up Until 1990

Historically, Singapore's TFP performance has been inferior to that of Hong Kong. From 1964 till 1997, the critical juncture that marked Hong Kong's handover to China, TFP in Singapore has consistently been lower than in Hong Kong (Fig. 6.2).

What is significant is that in 1964, Hong Kong's TFP was already 46.9% higher than that in Singapore. Hong Kong's TFP experienced an overall increase in this period by 39.13% to close at 0.658 in 1997. While

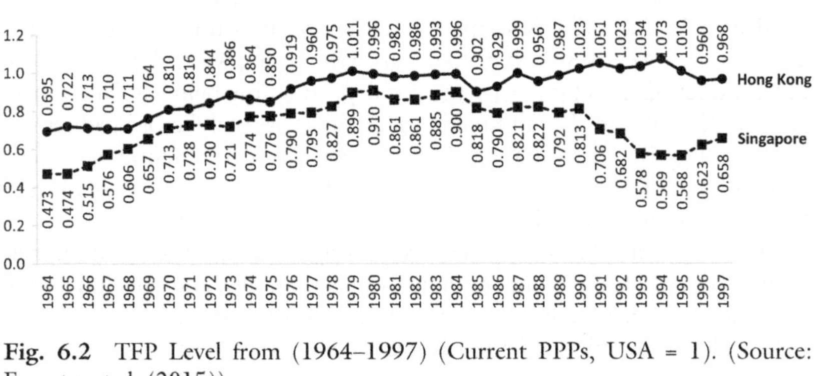

Fig. 6.2 TFP Level from (1964–1997) (Current PPPs, USA = 1). (Source: Feenstra et al. (2015))

Singapore's TFP also experienced an overall increase, there was a downward trend from a high of 0.900 in 1984 to 0.568 in 1995, which was a decline of 36.8%, before picking up again slightly. It should be repeated that during this period, from 1964 to 1997, Hong Kong remained under a colonial laissez-faire model and Singapore transitioned into a developmental state. Hence, it is not unreasonable to claim that Singapore's low TFP in this phase was not due to a lack of state support to increase economic performance. At the same time, Hong Kong's superior performance here is achieved without the same kinds of sectoral interventions into the economy.

Singapore's TFP dip in the mid-1980s also supports my argument. This was largely caused by a structural (rather than cyclical) recession, the only time in Singapore's history when its domestic economy contracted while the global economy grew. Experts acknowledge that this resulted from dissipation of earlier cost advantages and the setting in of diminishing returns to (mainly foreign) investment (Menon, 2015; Rodan, 1989). Also, the 1979 "Second Industrial Revolution" plan unintentionally lowered productivity because it artificially raised unit costs through central wage setting (Rigg, 1988). In other words, the early phase of Singapore's industrial policy "lost steam".

This disparity is also echoed by many other scholars. Despite the different methods of calculation, all leading studies show that TFP contributions played a much bigger role in Hong Kong than in Singapore which fared worse than other Asian economies until 1990 (Fig. 6.3).

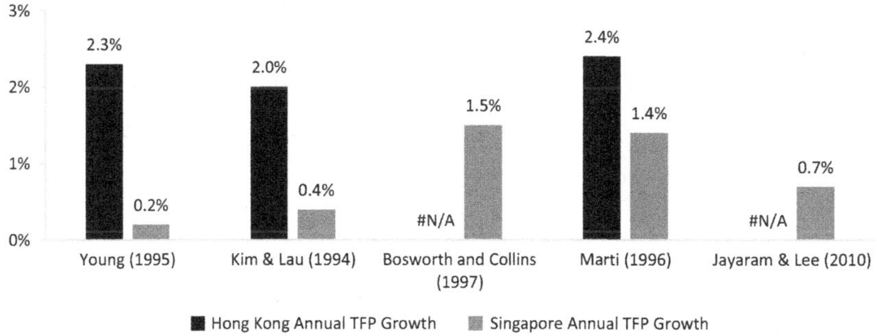

Fig. 6.3 Various scholars' historical estimates of TFP growth in Singapore vs. Hong Kong (1960–1995). (Source: Author's compilation)

Till the Present Day

While most discussions of TFP contribution to growth focused on the period leading up to the end of the twentieth century, little has been discussed since then. After the handover in 1997, Hong Kong had become part of China and had started to mimic Singapore's sectoral industrial policies, with the belief that these were needed to make up for its low level of technology. However, despite these developments, the second phase (1998–2017) saw a dramatic decline in Hong Kong's TFP performance (Fig. 6.4 and Table 6.6).

Over the last few years, Hong Kong's TFP has remained slightly higher than Singapore's, but has dropped overall during this period by 18.66%. Arguably, the current state of TFP performance in both countries is not due to Singapore's developmental state "catching up" with Hong Kong, but to the weakness in Hong Kong's system. This is arguably due to the way in which Hong Kong's economy has been changed since 1997, when it lost its colonial status and thus the market-based policies enjoyed under it. Since the turn of the century, domestic upheavals and uncertainty over its future have affected Hong Kong's economic climate, in ways not seen

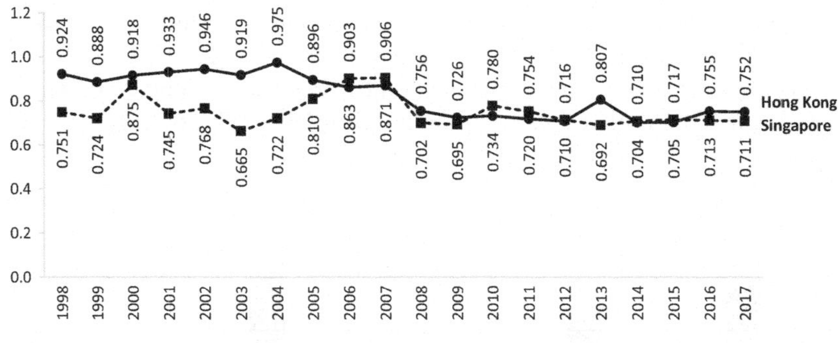

Fig. 6.4 Comparison of Hong Kong & Singapore TFP (1998–2017) (Current PPPs, USA = 1). (Source: Feenstra et al. (2015))

Table 6.6 Overall % change in TFP performance in Phase 2

	Hong Kong	*Singapore*
Overall % change in TFP Performance in Phase 2 (1998 to 2017)	-18.66%	-5.39%

Source: Author's calculations

in Singapore. Additionally, the available information shows that the overall decline in Hong Kong of 18.66% outweighs the overall 5.39% decline of TFP in Singapore in the same period.

Labour Productivity

Labour productivity is another important indicator of the quality of economic growth. Growth driven by high rates of labour productivity reflects the more efficient use of labour resources rather than the mere accumulation of more factor inputs.

A static snapshot of both economies will reveal that at this moment, the Singapore economy exhibits higher levels of labour productivity than the Hong Kong one. According to the following comparison by the International Labour Organization, Singapore ranks 5th in the world for output per worker, while Hong Kong ranks a much lower 13th (Table 6.7).

It is important however to disaggregate such statistics, which may otherwise obscure much of the economic reality. A further deconstruction of the statistics may paint a different picture.

Table 6.7 Top 15 countries in labour productivity (2019)

Rank	*Country*	*Output per worker (GDP constant 2011 international $ in PPP), 2019*
1	Luxembourg	$199,367
2	Macau, China	$178,687
3	Brunei Darussalam	$159,118
4	Ireland	$155,654
5	*Singapore*	*$151,522*
6	Qatar	$150,376
7	New Caledonia	$132,228
8	Norway	$129,989
9	Saudi Arabia	$122,167
10	Puerto Rico	$118,950
11	United States of America	$116,384
12	Kuwait	$114,903
13	*Hong Kong, China*	*$112,340*
14	Switzerland	$106,530
15	Belgium	$103,779

Source: International Labour Organization (2019)

Table 6.8 Changes in value-added per hour worked (%)

Year	*2001*	*2002*	*2003*	*2004*	*2005*	*2006*	*2007*	*2008*	*2009*	*Average*
Singapore	-4.1	6.1	4.8	6.5	2.3	2.1	-0.1	-7.5	-2.8	0.81
Hong Kong	-0.6	1.9	4.3	5.2	5.5	6.3	3.8	3.6	-0.4	3.29
Taiwan	NA	1.8	0.4	2.5	4.8	5.2	6.5	-0.6	1	2.7
Year	**2011**		**2012**	**2013**	**2014**	**2015**	**2016**	**2017**	**2018**	**Average**
Singapore	4.2		-0.4	1.3	1.5	1	2.7	5.3	3.9	2.44
Hong Kong	4.0		1.0	1.8	4.0	1.5	2.1	4.2	0.9	2.6
Taiwan	4.0		0.9	2.0	3.9	0.5	4.4	3.7	2.5	2.74

Sources: Ministry of Trade and Industry, Singapore (2011–2018); Census and Statistics Department, HKSAR (2020); and National Statistics, Republic of China (Taiwan) (n.d.)

Singapore's performance on productivity—measured by changes in value-added per hour worked—may be contrasted with Hong Kong and Taiwan on a year-on-year basis (Table 6.8). Not only has Singapore's productivity performance, fared lower on this indicator than Hong Kong's for the last two decades, also it has also been poorer than Taiwan's. The case of Taiwan is especially interesting because it has traditionally been an economy driven largely by many small-medium enterprises (Shieh, 1992; Numazaki, 1997), unlike the chaebols in S. Korea and the state-linked firms in Singapore. That both Taiwan and Hong Kong have more vibrant SME sectors than Singapore supports the notion that Singapore's low productivity is associated with its weak SME base.

A highly useful study by Manu Bhaskaran and Nigel Chiang (2020) showed that since 1990, Singapore's productivity performance actually declined over time, especially when compared against its trading partners and other "peer groups". When Singapore's performance is compared with other non-Asian developed nations, its productivity performance is not impressive. Labour productivity as a contribution to GDP growth is far lower than that of similar nations, with a difference of about at least 30%, prompting Woon Kin Chung and Loo Ya Lee, two of Singapore's leading civil servants who spearheaded productivity improvements, to conclude in a 50-year study, that "Singapore's productivity performance has not been outstanding" (Woon & Loo, 2018, p. 10).

Singapore's poor productivity performance is rooted in its two-tier economic structure. Weak labour productivity in Singapore is concentrated amongst SMEs rather than the more productive foreign corporations and government-linked corporations which dominate the economy. As Chap. 3 has shown, foreign and government-linked capital dominate the economy at the expense of local SMEs which have a much lower value-added. The Deputy Prime Minister Tharman Shanmugaratnam (2015) himself acknowledged the existence of a two-tier economy, with domestic SMEs in the lower tier: "We cannot continue with this two-track economy indefinitely. It will otherwise mean that businesses in the domestic sector get squeezed year by year as costs go up faster than productivity."

It is also important to realise that in Singapore, productivity improvements have been a deliberate strategy of the developmental state's industrial policy, which explains the slew of incentives provided. As mentioned, a unique feature of the developmental state is its proactive effort to continually upgrade firms and workers to higher levels of productivity and value-add, a drive absent in less interventionist economies like Hong Kong's, where productivity improvements arise organically. Hence, Singapore's poor productivity performance is not for a lack of deliberate policymaking. In fact, the Singapore government renewed its productivity drive in 2010 with a 10-year plan by the Economic Strategies Committee, which aimed for a 3% productivity growth per annum till 2020. However, this target was not achieved. In fact, from 2010 to 2013, it averaged at just 0.2%. This problem has been acknowledged by the Singapore government and other Singaporean scholars in recent years (Low & Auyong, 2014; Ministry of Trade and Industry, Singapore, 2014). The following table compares the expected targets of the government's productivity efforts and the actual results which have fallen short (Table 6.9).

Table 6.9 Summary of productivity targets in Singapore vs. achievements

Year	*Name of plan*	*Expected targets*	*Actual results*
1981	Economic Development Plan for the Eighties	6–8% per annum	4.4% per annum
2003	Economic Review Committee	2–3% per annum	1% per annum
2010	Economic Strategies Committee	2–3% per annum	0.4% per annum (2010 to 2015)

Source: Various national reports as displayed in Woon and Loo's study (2018)

“High-Quality” Economic Growth

Beyond productivity, I also show that indicators of innovation and entrepreneurship quality are also relevant in evaluating the degree to which high-quality, cutting-edge growth has been achieved.

In fact, innovation may be an even more important indicator of an economy’s performance than productivity since it involves the qualitative improvements of existing goods and services, the introduction of new goods and services, qualitative improvements in businesses processes, and sometimes even the creation of new markets. Even the Solow growth model acknowledges that beyond a certain point, it is technological innovation that sustains development in nations.

Innovation is also fundamentally linked to the actions of entrepreneurs who are alert to entrepreneurial opportunities and market gaps, and disrupt the status quo with new ideas, inventions, and techniques. Within the market process of competitive discovery, the rivalrous actions of entrepreneurs generate innovations that bring the entire economy greater wealth and prosperity (Holcombe, 2007).

Crucially, innovation and entrepreneurial activity do not occur in a vacuum, but rather, within a conducive institutional environment. Beyond simply the formal institutions of property rights, etc., a pro-market culture is also important in promoting entrepreneurial innovation. Such a culture should create incentives and encourage individuals to seek commercial pursuits that may disrupt the status quo. Consequently, this chapter presents both existing and new evidence to measure the degree of innovation and entrepreneurial activity in both city-states. I will show in this section, in line with the 1994 argument by Krugman that Singapore’s economic development has not, comparatively speaking, succeeded in promoting innovation and indigenous entrepreneurship.

Innovation

Conventional wisdom posits that Singapore has a more innovative economy than Hong Kong’s. Although innovation is difficult to measure, the two most used indicators are patents, which more narrowly measures innovation output, and the broader measure of expenditure on R&D as a percentage of GDP. For both indicators, it seems that Singapore’s economy outperforms Hong Kong’s. R&D expenditure as a percentage of GDP in Singapore outstrips that of Hong Kong throughout 1996 until the present day (Fig. 6.5).

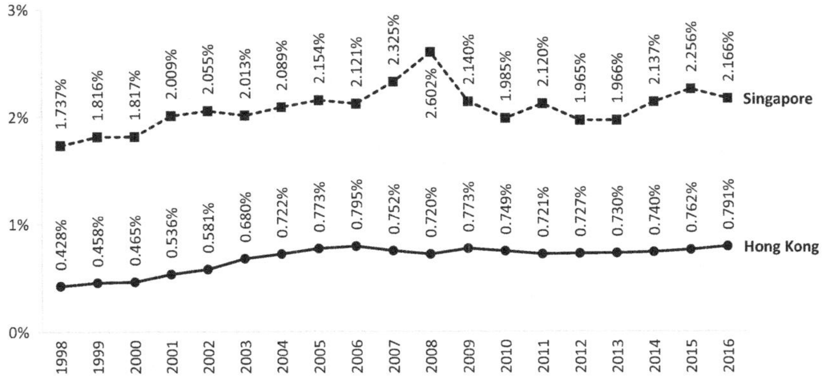

Fig. 6.5 Research and development expenditure (% of GDP) of Singapore and Hong Kong. (Source: UNESCO Institute for Statistics (2020))

Global organisations that have developed national rankings have consistently credited Singapore for its innovation performance. For instance, the latest edition of the Global Innovation Index by Cornell University, INSEAD and WIPO (2019) ranks Singapore as the 8th most innovative country in the world, with Hong Kong ranked 13th.

Importantly, this apparent superiority of the Singapore economy is said to reflect the developmental state's concerted interventions to promote technological innovation, which have been absent in laissez-faire Hong Kong. The innovation scholar Douglas Fuller (2010) has argued that Hong Kong's tradition of non-interventionism has been the key barrier to innovation and that the absence of industrial policy has caused Hong Kong to lag behind regional rivals. This is further echoed by a high-ranking former Director of the Singapore civil service, who remarked in an interview that the free market has led Hong Kong down a "dead end", focused on real estate and finance industries and lacking technology.[2]

I disagree with the conventional wisdom. The position just described is based on broad-brush aggregate statistics which obscure the finer contextual details in both economies. Once these statistics are disaggregated, the seeming gulf in performance is closed. A closer examination of the data will lend support to two claims that I make. First, while Singapore exhibits higher levels of innovation activity, most of this is concentrated in the

[2] Interview with Director of the Centre for Strategic Futures, Singapore. November 2018.

foreign sector rather than the indigenous sector. This means that foreign multinationals, rather than local citizens and local enterprises, are conducting the bulk of innovation activity and retain most assignments of patents filed. Second, I stress the importance of innovation efficiency. While Singapore scores much higher on aggregate level indicators, it is comparatively weaker in efficiently translating innovation inputs into outputs.

Government-driven vs. Private Sector-led R&D Efforts
Once again, it is important to disaggregate the statistics and examine its structural composition. A deeper look at the figures will show that while Singapore spends a larger percentage of GDP on R&D, most of the spending is by the government rather than the private sector. Tables 6.10 and 6.11 show that state spending on R&D is higher in Singapore. This is even higher when the state-linked higher education system is included. In

Table 6.10 Gross domestic expenditure on R&D by sector, in Hong Kong (HKD million)

Year	*Business*		*Government*		*Higher education*		*Total*	*Total as % of GDP*
2000	*1117.5*	*17.97%*	*111.8*	*1.80%*	*4989.2*	*80.23%*	*6218.5*	*0.47%*
2001	2082.9	29.38%	157.8	2.23%	4848.6	68.39%	7089.3	0.55%
2002	2505.8	33.22%	237.1	3.14%	4800.7	63.64%	7543.6	0.59%
2003	3545.1	41.47%	207.5	2.43%	4796.2	56.10%	8548.8	0.69%
2004	4590.3	48.29%	207.6	2.18%	4707.3	49.52%	9505.2	0.74%
2005	5621.6	51.47%	215.2	1.97%	5085	46.56%	10,921.8	0.79%
2006	6287.4	52.63%	248.6	2.08%	5410.9	45.29%	11,946.9	0.81%
2007	6054.6	48.80%	295.8	2.38%	6056.9	48.82%	12,407.3	0.77%
2008	5264.5	42.82%	378.7	3.08%	6650	54.09%	12,293.2	0.72%
2009	5473.8	42.65%	524.1	4.08%	6835.1	53.26%	12,833	0.77%
2010	5767.5	43.32%	597.1	4.49%	6948.3	52.19%	13,312.9	0.75%
2011	6193.5	44.42%	596.2	4.28%	7154.9	51.31%	13,944.6	0.72%
2012	6647.4	44.87%	592.5	4.00%	7576.3	51.14%	14,816.2	0.73%
2013	7017.4	44.95%	611.6	3.92%	7984.2	51.14%	15,613.2	0.73%
2014	7437.5	44.46%	658	3.93%	8631.8	51.60%	16,727.3	0.74%
2015	7993.7	43.75%	726.2	3.97%	9550.8	52.27%	18,270.7	0.76%
2016	8528.1	43.26%	914.1	4.64%	10,270.9	52.10%	19,713.1	0.79%
2017	9412.3	44.23%	1031	4.84%	10,837.1	50.93%	21,280.4	0.80%
2018	10,992.5	44.87%	1148	4.69%	12,356.6	50.44%	24,497.1	0.85%

Source: Reconstruction of Hong Kong Innovation Statistics, Census and Statistics Department, HKSAR (2000–2018)

Table 6.11 Gross domestic expenditure on R&D by sector in Singapore (SGD million)

Year	*Private sector*		*Institutes of higher learning*		*Government sector*		*Total*	*Total as % of GDP*
2000	*1866*	*62.00%*	*338.3*	*11.24%*	*805.2*	*26.76%*	*3009.50*	*1.82%*
2001	2045	63.26%	367	11.35%	820.7	25.39%	3232.70	2.01%
2002	2055	61.01%	430	12.77%	883.4	26.23%	3368.30	2.03%
2003	2053.60	60.46%	457.5	13.47%	885.8	26.08%	3396.90	2%
2004	2569.60	63.58%	424.7	10.51%	1047.2	25.91%	4041.50	2.08%
2005	3018.70	66.06%	478	10.46%	1072.9	23.48%	4569.50	2.15%
2006	3281.80	65.65%	575.7	11.52%	1141.1	22.83%	4998.60	2.12%
2007	4222.20	66.74%	603	9.53%	1501.1	23.73%	6326.30	2.32%
2008	5105.50	71.77%	709.8	9.98%	1298.3	18.25%	7113.60	2.60%
2009	3694.60	61.44%	854.2	14.21%	1464	24.35%	6012.90	2.13%
2010	3773.80	59.76%	968.1	15.33%	1573.3	24.91%	6315.20	1.93%
2011	4456.40	61.25%	1085.30	14.92%	1733.9	23.83%	7275.60	2.07%
2012	4249.30	60.03%	1192	16.84%	1636.9	23.13%	7078.10	1.92%
2013	4333.50	58.54%	1310.50	17.70%	1758.5	23.76%	7402.40	1.92%
2014	5006.90	60.20%	1348.20	16.21%	1961.5	23.59%	8316.60	2.08%
2015	5511.90	59.66%	1572.80	17.02%	2154.8	23.32%	9239.50	2.18%
2016	5342.40	58.45%	1648	18.03%	2149.8	23.52%	9140.20	2.08%
2017	5423.40	59.69%	1703.50	18.75%	1958.9	21.56%	9085.90	1.92%
2018	5638.40	60.75%	1651.30	17.79%	1992.1	21.46%	9281.80	1.84%

Source: National Survey on R&D, National Research Foundation, and A*Star (2000–2018) plus additional email requests (for the missing back pages for specific years. Same report)

Hong Kong, universities receive less funding from the state, and thus, it may be classified under private sector R&D spending. Approximately one-third of R&D expenditure may be traced to the state in Singapore but less than 5% for Hong Kong.

To put this into a further comparative perspective, it should be noted that Singapore is an outlier in Asia. In Singapore, according to the National Survey of R&D 2018, foreign companies were responsible for 74% of total private R&D expenditure. In contrast, foreign companies were responsible for only 2% in Korea (Korea Institute of S&T Evaluation and Planning, 2019) and 0.1% in Taiwan (Ministry of Science & Technology, Taiwan, 2018).

As the foregoing analysis will demonstrate, this has several effects. The difference in political economic structure, manifested here through R&D data, means that small medium enterprises are crowded out in the

Singapore innovation landscape and that heavy state investments have not necessarily been efficiently translated into commercial outcomes.

Indigenous Innovation Capacity

The most striking evidence for the claim that indigenous innovation capacity is stifled in Singapore is seen in the distribution of R&D expenditure across company types. What we observe is that even though R&D spending in Singapore is much higher than in Hong Kong on an aggregate level, much of this is driven by foreign multinational corporations, with local SMEs responsible for less than 15% of the total spending (Table 6.12). This is analogous to the larger institutional framework of Singapore, which is a hybrid of state and big-firm capitalism, comprising foreign multinationals.

My argument is further supported by a closer examination of the patent data. Most indicators simply track the total number of patents filed without necessarily examining where the intellectual property rights are retained. Here, I present patents filed in the United States Patent and Trademark Office (USPTO), which reflects higher commercial importance due to the tech-intensive nature of the US market. Additionally, I also track the percentage of patents that were retained by local companies, which is a proxy of a nation's indigenous innovation capacity.

Table 6.13 tracks patent registration data in both city-states over three phases: 1976 to 2000, 2001 to 2008, and 2009 to 2019. This corresponds to the critical junctures in the governance of both city-states. Phase 1 reflects the patent performance of both countries in the late twentieth century till Hong Kong's monumental handover to China. Phase 2 begins in 2001 with another key milestone in Hong Kong, which is the establishment of Hong Kong Science and Technology Park Corporation, the first time major sectoral interventions were conducted. Phase 3 reflects the period from the 2008 financial crisis onwards.

Based on the results gathered, it should be clearly noted that in Phase 1, the total patents filed by Hong Kong in the USPTO (column D) outstrips that of Singapore (column A) (Table 6.13). It should be noted that in Phase 2, performance is comparable across both countries, while in Phase 3, Singapore's patents filed have clearly eclipsed Hong Kong's. In other words, before 1997, Hong Kong fared better than Singapore, while this has reversed in recent times (see Fig. 6.6).

This reversal should be considered alongside key developments in the institutional structure and policy orientation in both city-states. In Phase

Table 6.12 Private sector R&D expenditure by enterprise ownership/size, type of R&D, and field of science and technology for the year 2018 (SGD millions)

Field of science and technology	*Local SMEs*					*Local larger enterprises*					*Foreign companies*				
	Basic research	*Applied research*	*Experi mental development*	*Total*		*Basic research*	*Applied research*	*Experimental development*	*Total*		*Basic research*	*Applied research*	*Experimental development*	*Total*	
Agricultural and food sciences	12.93	8.88	7.02	28.83	11.09%	0	2.85	1.66	4.51	1.73%	17.59	103.42	105.69	226.7	87.18%
Biomedical and related science	65.17	17.44	65.04	147.65	30.88%	0	0	0.19	0.19	0.04%	53.81	111.29	165.24	330.34	69.08%
Engineering and technology	65.99	121.82	273.73	461.54	10.99%	32.77	319.74	254.22	606.73	14.44%	524.88	878.32	1729.43	3132.63	74.57%
Natural sciences (excluding biological sciences)	13.99	17.92	31.27	63.18	10.82%	64.19	19.07	29.1	112.36	19.24%	129.68	83.94	194.73	408.35	69.94%
Energy	3.9	7.18	0.08	11.16	42.02%	0	0.14	0.82	0.96	3.61%	0.55	10.5	3.39	14.44	54.37%
Other areas	0.45	2.91	7.75	11.11	12.51%	0	9.94	0.36	10.3	11.60%	31.87	27.06	8.47	67.4	75.89%
Total	162.43	176.15	384.89	723.47	12.83%	96.96	351.74	286.35	735.05	13.04%	758.38	1214.53	2206.95	4179.86	74.13%

Source: National Research Foundation, Agency for Science, Technology and Research, Singapore (2000–2019)

Table 6.13 Comparison of patent performance (foreign vs. local share)

		Singapore				*Hong Kong*			
Time period in phases	Year	Total patents (A)	Local assignees (B)	% of total patents that were retained by local assignees (C=B/A ×100%)	Foreign assignees/ unassigned	Total patents (D)	Local assignees (E)	% of total patents that were retained by local assignees (F=E/D × 100%)	Foreign assignees/ unassigned
Phase 1 period	1976	3	0	0.00%	3	24	9	37.50%	15
	1977	5	2	40.00%	3	33	9	27.27%	24
	1978	3	0	0.00%	3	30	11	36.67%	19
	1979	0	0	NA	0	36	11	30.56%	25
	1980	6	0	0.00%	6	53	25	47.17%	28
	1981	5	0	0.00%	5	70	34	48.57%	36
	1982	6	0	0.00%	6	73	51	69.86%	22
	1983	6	3	50.00%	3	65	46	70.77%	19
	1984	4	4	100.00%	0	78	35	44.87%	43
	1985	14	3	21.43%	11	73	44	60.27%	29
	1986	5	0	0.00%	5	117	80	68.38%	37
	1987	16	3	18.75%	13	100	66	66.00%	34
	1988	12	1	8.33%	11	114	78	68.42%	36
	1989	28	9	32.14%	19	143	78	54.55%	65
	1990	21	3	14.29%	18	164	74	45.12%	90
	1991	30	9	30.00%	21	222	106	47.75%	116
	1992	41	8	19.51%	33	173	84	48.55%	89
	1993	61	14	22.95%	47	197	114	57.87%	83
	1994	79	23	29.11%	56	238	142	59.66%	96
	1995	81	24	29.63%	57	276	165	59.78%	111
	1996	124	40	32.26%	84	273	171	62.64%	102
	1997	132	47	35.61%	85	292	156	53.42%	136
	1998	181	75	41.44%	106	411	226	54.99%	185
	1999	207	94	45.41%	113	442	256	57.92%	186
	2000	299	160	53.51%	139	560	328	58.57%	232

Phase 2 period	2001	388	207	53.35%	181	593	318	53.63%	275
	2002	533	263	49.34%	270	578	285	49.31%	293
	2003	564	252	44.68%	312	620	312	50.32%	308
	2004	589	251	42.61%	338	548	271	49.45%	277
	2005	466	208	44.64%	258	489	255	52.15%	234
	2006	587	261	44.46%	326	654	304	46.48%	350
	2007	547	252	46.07%	295	720	351	48.75%	369
	2008	571	252	44.13%	319	600	301	50.17%	299
Phase 3 period	2009	622	269	43.25%	353	493	207	41.99%	286
	2010	827	373	45.10%	454	591	257	43.49%	334
	2011	891	434	48.71%	457	525	200	38.10%	325
	2012	1091	516	47.30%	575	565	255	45.13%	310
	2013	1102	557	50.54%	545	630	241	38.25%	389
	2014	1308	638	48.78%	670	624	250	40.06%	374
	2015	1368	652	47.66%	716	665	300	45.11%	365
	2016	1411	691	48.97%	720	702	336	47.86%	366
	2017	1482	615	41.50%	867	753	379	50.33%	374
	2018	1483	571	38.50%	912	804	377	46.89%	427
	2019	1668	657	39.39%	1011	893	448	50.17%	445

Source: United States Patent and Trademark Office (2020)

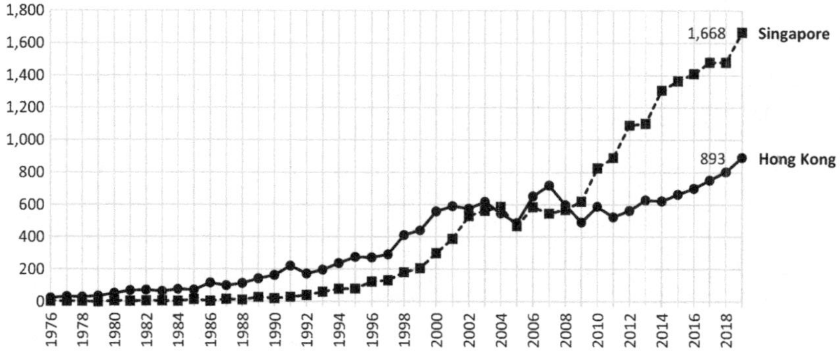

Fig. 6.6 Number of USPTO patents filed by Singapore and Hong Kong inventors. (Source: United States Patent and Trademark Office (2020))

1, the divergence between both countries is most pronounced since Hong Kong remained under the colonial laissez-faire model, while Singapore consolidated its developmental state system. It is during this phase, when Hong Kong lacked the concerted investments in R&D that Singapore enjoyed, that Hong Kong outperformed Singapore.

Critically, it should be noted that Hong Kong experienced a major transition in 1997, becoming part of China. Since then, as established in Chap. 3, it has also embarked on industrial planning for the purposes of innovation; a key marker of this phase is the establishment of the Hong Kong Science Park. In the second two phases, when Hong Kong's economic model starts to mimic Singapore's, it starts to fall behind (see Table 6.14). During this time, Hong Kong's average number of patents filed starts to be overshadowed by that of Singapore.

Aside from the reversal in performance across phases, it is also instructive to examine not just the total number of patents filed, but where the patents were eventually assigned. Total patents in column A/D refers to the total number of patents invented by at least one inventor who is a Singapore/Hong Kong citizen (see Table 6.13). Local Assignees in column B/E refers to the number of patents by a Singaporean/Hong Kong inventor whose property rights are given to a Singaporean/Hong Kong company or individual/resident. Here, it should be clarified that on average across all years, the total number of patents that were retained by a local assignee is much lower in Singapore than in Hong Kong (Fig. 6.7).

Table 6.14 Comparison of growth rate of patents filed and local vs. foreign composition of patent assignees

	Phase 1 (1976 to 2000)	*Phase 2 (2001 to 2008)*	*Phase 3 (2009 to 2019)*
Average number of patents filed in Hong Kong	Average number of patents each year is 170, much higher than that of Singapore	Average number of patents each year is 600, higher than that of Singapore, but the difference is much lesser	Average number of patents each year is 659, much lower than that of Singapore
Average number of patents filed in Singapore	Average number of patents each year is 55, much lower than Hong Kong	Average number of patents each year is 531, lower than Hong Kong, but the difference is much lesser	Average number of patents each year is 1205, much higher than Hong Kong
Average rate of patents being retained by local Singapore assignees	24.97%. It is much lower than in Hong Kong	46.16%. Still lower than Hong Kong, but the difference is much lesser	45.43%. Slightly higher than Hong Kong's 44.3%
Average rate of patents being retained by local HK assignees	53.48%. It is much higher than that of Singapore	50.03%. Still higher than Singapore, but the difference is much lesser	44.31%. Slightly lower than Singapore

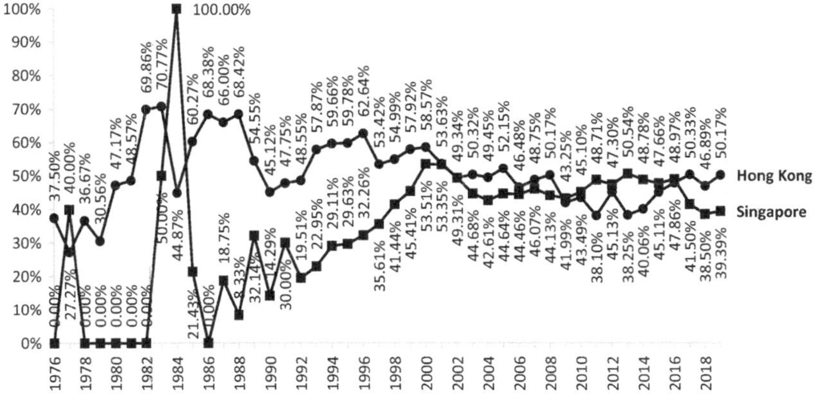

Fig. 6.7 Ratio of total patents that were retained by local assignees. (Source: United States Patent and Trademark Office (2020))

This suggests that for most of the entire period, even when there was a higher number of patents filed by Singapore in the USPTO, much of it was driven by foreign multinationals and foreign companies rather than local enterprises. In simpler words, most patents filed in Singapore were by foreign entities and were unretained within the domestic economy nor enjoyed by domestic firms.

The disparity in patent performance between foreign and local enterprises is even starker when the most recent year, 2018, is isolated. A total of 79.79% of all private sector patents in Singapore applied for were by foreign entities, and not domestic ones (Table 6.15).

Aggregate statistics that compare Singapore and Hong Kong on a broad level thus obscure much of the reality. They do not say anything about the relative balance of public and private sector innovation activity. An important point to note here is that much innovation activity in

Table 6.15 Private sector patents applied by enterprise ownership and industrial classification for the year 2018, Singapore

Industrial classification	*Local SMEs*		*Local LEs*		*Foreign companies*		*Total*
Primary industries and construction	*12*	*85.71%*	*2*	*14.29%*	*0*	*0.00%*	*14*
Biomedical manufacturing	13	44.83%	0	0.00%	16	55.17%	29
Chemicals	0	0.00%	0	0.00%	4	100.00%	4
Electronics	9	4.00%	34	15.11%	182	80.89%	225
Precision engineering	39	49.37%	0	0.00%	40	50.63%	79
Transport engineering	9	14.75%	8	13.11%	44	72.13%	61
General manufacturing	5	20.83%	0	0.00%	19	79.17%	24
(Total manufacturing)	75	17.77%	42	9.95%	305	72.27%	422
R&D	220	73.83%	0	0.00%	78	26.17%	298
Financial intermediation and other business activities	37	35.92%	5	4.85%	61	59.22%	103
Education, health, social services	5	100.00%	0	0.00%	0	0.00%	5
Information and communications	26	55.32%	0	0.00%	21	44.68%	47
Logistics	0	0.00%	1	100.00%	0	0.00%	1
Wholesale and retail trade	15	1.11%	11	0.82%	1323	98.07%	1349
Other services	2	100.00%	0	0.00%	0	0.00%	2
(Total services)	305	16.90%	17	0.94%	1483	82.16%	1805
Total	392	17.49%	61	2.72%	1788	79.79%	2241

Source: National Research Foundation, Agency for Science, Technology and Research, Singapore (2000–2019)

Singapore is driven by the state-linked and foreign MNC sector rather than indigenous private enterprise. This is echoed by Wang (2018, p. 407) who recently expressed that the "number of local innovation players is quite limited in Singapore, with GLCs largely dominating the local innovation system". This imbalance stems from the developmental state's growth strategy of partnering foreign multinationals to create jobs and catalyse innovation. It is thus important to examine the nature of patents registered to investigate the country of origin, rather than simply looking at the top-line aggregate of the number of patents.

The lop-sided nature of the foreign-local divide provides further explanation as to why despite large sums of government investment into key industries, the results have not been forthcoming. The knowledge transfers and positive spill-overs to local firms that foreign MNCs were supposed to bring Singapore did not materialise, as confirmed by Joseph Wong (2011) in his critique of Asia's industrial policies.

The analysis so far shows that indigenous, Singaporean-assigned patents pale in comparison to their foreign counterparts and that Singapore's local patents take up a smaller percentage of overall patents than is the case in Hong Kong. This provides empirical support to claims made by academic scholars that Singapore's economic accomplishments "have been achieved without developing the inherent production and indigenous innovation capacity" (Tan & Bhaskaran, 2015, p. 51; Carney & Loh, 2009).

Innovation Efficiency

Not only is it important to ascertain the indigenous innovation capacity, and the actual quality of patents, but it is also essential to determine if innovation inputs are efficiently translated into commercialisable products.

It is unsurprising that Singapore's R&D expenditures have outstripped Hong Kong's. This is simply explained by the large sums of state investment channelled in Singapore, which have been absent in Hong Kong due to its laissez-faire tradition. However, simply spending money does not necessarily guarantee results, especially if the inputs directed are not maximising outcomes. While Singapore's state spends more on R&D than Hong Kong, the results do not correspond: there were six times more R&D-oriented firms in Hong Kong than in Singapore in 2013 (HKSAR, 2000–2018; National Research Foundation & Agency for Science, Technology and Research, Singapore, 2000–2019).

Innovation is not a technical problem involving the maximisation of a given end, that is, it does not occur simply by investing large sums of resources to develop a specific technology or tool, whether artificial intelligence, or driverless cars. For innovation to be a significant driver of the entire economy's development over the long run, innovation inputs (which include private and public R&D expenditures) must *efficiently utilise* resources across a variety of different (and often conflicting) avenues of potentially innovative activities. There is some evidence that this has not occurred in Singapore, despite the large amounts of resources channelled towards R&D.

This is best seen when the concept of "innovation efficiency" is examined, which is a discrete indicator, rather than the Global Innovation Index, an aggregate indicator. This is a crucial indicator because a nation's performance on aggregate innovation indices may be artificially inflated due to government spending on R&D. Even though Singapore ranks highly on global innovation indices, closer scrutiny reveals that it scores poorly on the sub-component of innovation efficiency. Throughout 2013 to 2015, it scored outside of the top 100 in innovation efficiency, even though it was within the top 10 "most innovative economies". A recent edition of the Global Innovation Index declares that "Singapore produces less innovation outputs relative to its level of innovation investments" (World Intellectual Property Office, 2019, p. 3). This suggests that the top-down approach to innovation in Singapore has not fetched the corresponding results in terms of commercialisable outputs. This is further triangulated with the only edition of the Creative Productivity Index in which Singapore is the poorest ranked Asian country. Even though Singapore scores the highest in inputs—a logical result of heavy government investment—these investments have not translated efficiently into the corresponding outputs (Table 6.16).

The report concludes the following about Singapore's poor performance:

> Singapore provides the starkest example of the importance of efficiency in turning creative inputs into creative outputs. The city-state is far from an innovation laggard: it is ranked first in the level of creative inputs and sixth in the level of creative outputs. However, given its level of creative inputs, Singapore could be achieving even more creative outputs. Japan; Hong Kong, China; and New Zealand all have a lower level of creative inputs than Singapore, yet achieve a higher level of creative output. This is because Singapore is less effective at turning creative inputs into outputs, as evidenced by its ranking of 10th in the CPI (Asian Development Bank and Economist Intelligence Unit, 2014).

Table 6.16 Comparison of Asian countries ranked in Top 10 of Creative Productivity Index in 2014

Country	*Overall*	*Input*	*Output*
Japan	1	8	4
Korea	3	9	8
Taiwan	5	7	9
Hong Kong	7	2	2
Laos	9	23	17
Singapore	10	1	6

Source: Asian Development Bank and Economist Intelligence Unit, 2014

Cultural Disposition Towards Disruptive Innovation

Whether an economy achieves innovation is not just a function of R&D spending, patents filed, or even the legal framework established by the state, but it is also associated with cultural values that promote innovation. Indeed, the essence of entrepreneurship is to discover unrealised possibilities and to break from the current market trends. Government policy promoting entrepreneurship and innovation will therefore fall short if it is unable to foster these intangible, cultural ingredients, which may even be more important than its more formal ingredients.

I argue that while Singapore's government has been more proactive than Hong Kong's in providing the formal ingredients to promote entrepreneurship and innovation, it falls short in the intangible aspect. Hong Kong's entrepreneurs and citizens may not enjoy the same amount of funding or attention by the state as Singapore's do, but they are embedded within a stronger cultural predisposition towards innovation. I make this claim by drawing on a pre-existing body of research linking culture to entrepreneurship and innovation.

Sociologists, cultural scholars, and economists have provided numerous studies exploring the cultural values necessary for economic development and innovation. Out of all the existing studies, the most acknowledged cultural ingredient associated with radical and disruptive innovation is that of individualism—the emphasis on the self as an independent, autonomous agent—as opposed to collectivism, the emphasis on a group and the willingness to sacrifice for it (Hofstede 1980; Triandis 1995; Kirkman, Lowe and Gibson 2006). Meta-analyses of various studies acknowledge this as a key differentiator of innovative societies (see Leung and Wang 2015).

I propose a simpler approach, which retains the essence of the above-mentioned idea, but is far less sweeping. Rather than classifying a national culture as individualist or collectivist in broad strokes, I inquire merely into how ready and willing individuals will disrupt the status quo, seek novelty, and break from existing customs and regulations. I administered a survey asking several hundred respondents from Hong Kong and Singapore the extent to which they agree with the following statements (Figs. 6.8, 6.9, 6.10, 6.11, 6.12 and 6.13):

- "It is important to this person to think up new ideas and be creative; to do things one's own way".
- "Living in secure surroundings is important to this person; to avoid anything that might be dangerous".
- "It is important to abide by the customs, regulations and norms of society, rather than trying to be different from others".
- "Adventure and taking risks are important to this person; to have an exciting life".
- "It is important to this person to always behave properly; to avoid doing anything people would say is wrong".
- "Better to stick with the tried and tested, rather than opt for what's new and uncertain".

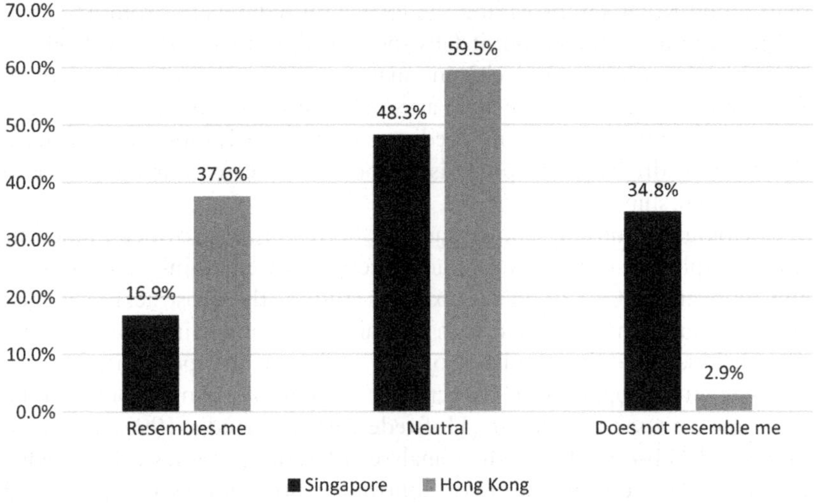

Fig. 6.8 Survey response: "It is important to this person to think up new ideas and be creative; to do things one's own way"

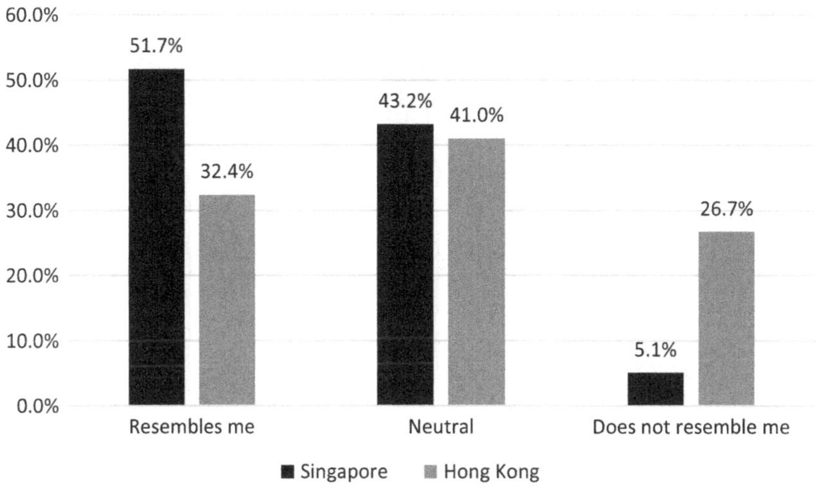

Fig. 6.9 Survey response: "Living in secure surroundings is important to this person; to avoid anything that might be dangerous"

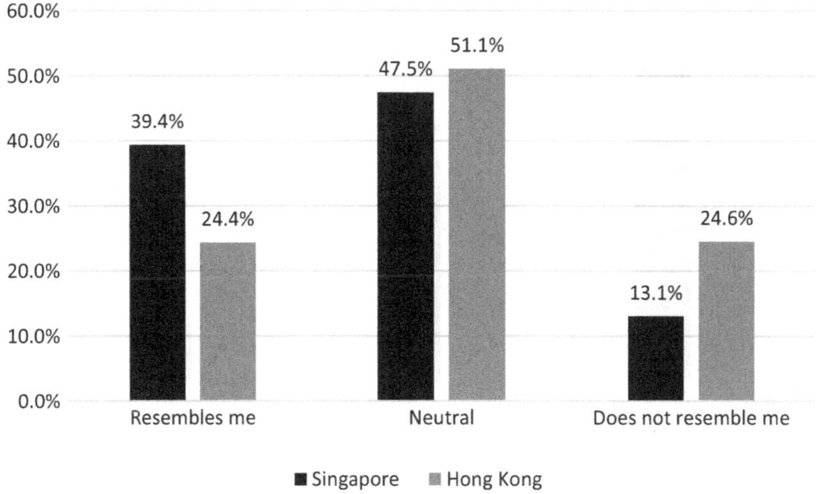

Fig. 6.10 Survey response: "It is important to abide by the customs, regulations and norms of society; rather than trying to be different from others"

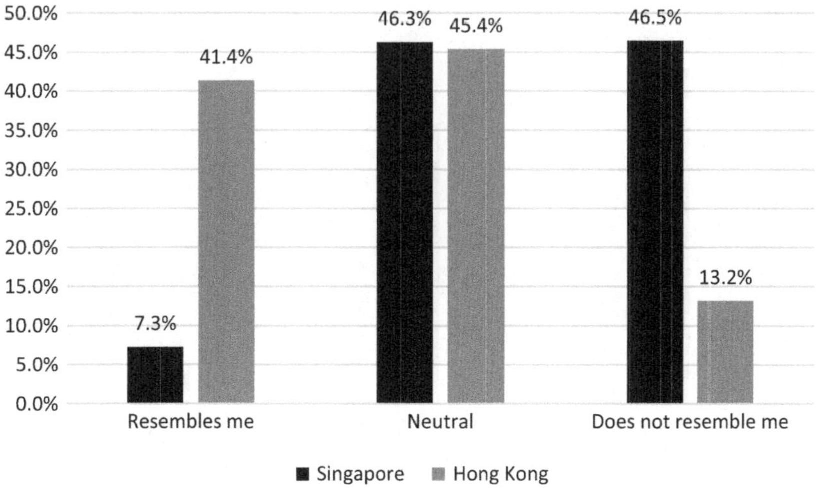

Fig. 6.11 Survey response: "Adventure and taking risks are important to this person; to have an exciting life"

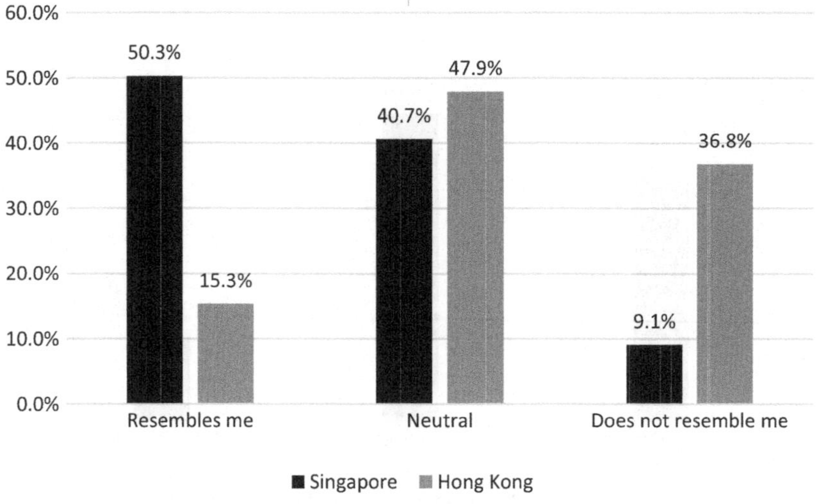

Fig. 6.12 Survey response: "It is important to this person to always behave properly; to avoid doing anything people would say is wrong"

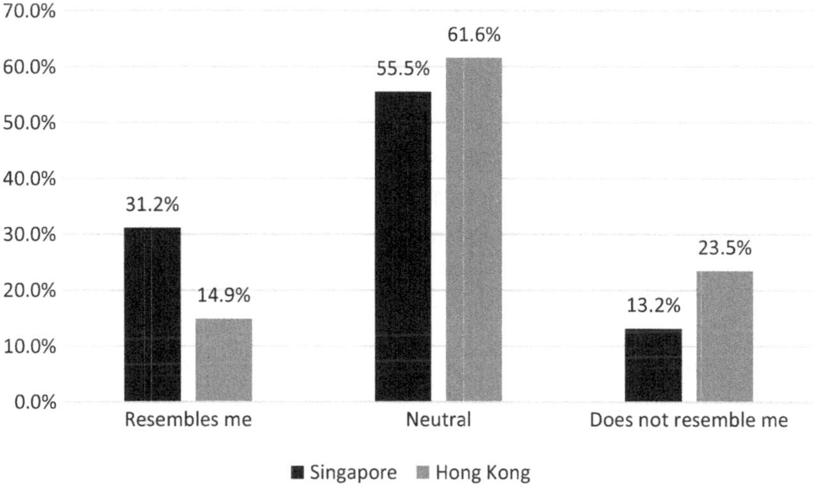

Fig. 6.13 Survey response: "Better to stick with the tried and tested, rather than opt for what's new and uncertain"

These results here show a clear contrast between Singaporeans and Hongkongers. The latter group has a greater inclination to take risks and question rather than accept the status quo. This comparative survey done is also more fine-grained than previous studies, since it focuses only on these two countries, rather than lumping them together under the category of "East Asia", which previous studies have tended to do in order to contrast them with "Western countries" (see Cline, 1982).

I hypothesise that the result obtained relates to the political culture—described in Chap. 4. Hongkongers, given their strong sense of individual sovereignty vis-à-vis the state, are used to questioning the status quo, while Singaporeans tend to colour within the lines. These are strong statements which cannot be definitively proven. Aside from the survey results displayed here, the subsequent chapter will strengthen the evidentiary case being made by examining the creative industries. I show that despite the concerted efforts by the Singaporean developmental state, its creative industries has lagged in performance relative to Hong Kong's, which has flourished free from government regulation. The choice of examining the creative industries is important for two reasons. First, creative industries, which include aspects such as media, entertainment, books and publishing, and arts and culture, are part of a nation's ongoing strategies to achieve a knowledge-based economy. Second, the creative industries, perhaps more than other industries, reflect a nation's cultural attitudes towards innovation.

Entrepreneurial Culture

A culture of entrepreneurship is also important in any economy. Previous research has shown a difference in the inclination amongst young people to become entrepreneurs in East Asian countries. A recent comparative survey conducted by the World Economic Forum, titled "ASEAN Youth: Skills, Technology and the Future of Work", involved 56,000 people across Singapore, Indonesia, Thailand, Malaysia, Vietnam, and the Philippines (Seow, 2019). The scale of this makes it one of the most comprehensive surveys in recent history, and it focuses particularly on whether youths have any desire to seek overseas learning opportunities or become entrepreneurs. The results clearly show that out of the six countries surveyed, Singapore ranked last, with only 16.9% expressing this aspiration (Table 6.17).

In a separate survey done by the Randstad Workmonitor in 2017, 73% of respondents in Singapore preferred to work for an MNC compared to just 63% and 57% of respondents who prefer to work for an SME and start-up, respectively. The results bucked the global trend where employees tend to favour working for a SME or start-up compared to an MNC (Randstad, 2017). These results show how traditional employment remains preferable to starting a business.

Another important piece of data is the Global Entrepreneurship Monitor (GEM), arguably the prime study on entrepreneurship, which shows that entrepreneurial desire in Singapore is lacking, as compared to

Table 6.17 Youth entrepreneurial aspirations across Asia

Rank	*Country*	*% of youths expressing a desire to become an entrepreneur*
1	Indonesia	35.5%
2	Thailand	31.9%
3	Viet Nam	25.7%
4	Malaysia	22.9%
5	Philippines	18.7%
6	Singapore	16.9%

Source: World Economic Forum (2019)

its Asia Pacific and OECD counterparts.[3] From 2011 to 2014, where Singapore was included in the GEM Global Study, the percentage of Singaporean employees who believed "entrepreneurship is a good career choice" or that "successful entrepreneurs enjoy high status" have consistently lagged behind that of the Asia Pacific and OECD average (Fig. 6.14).

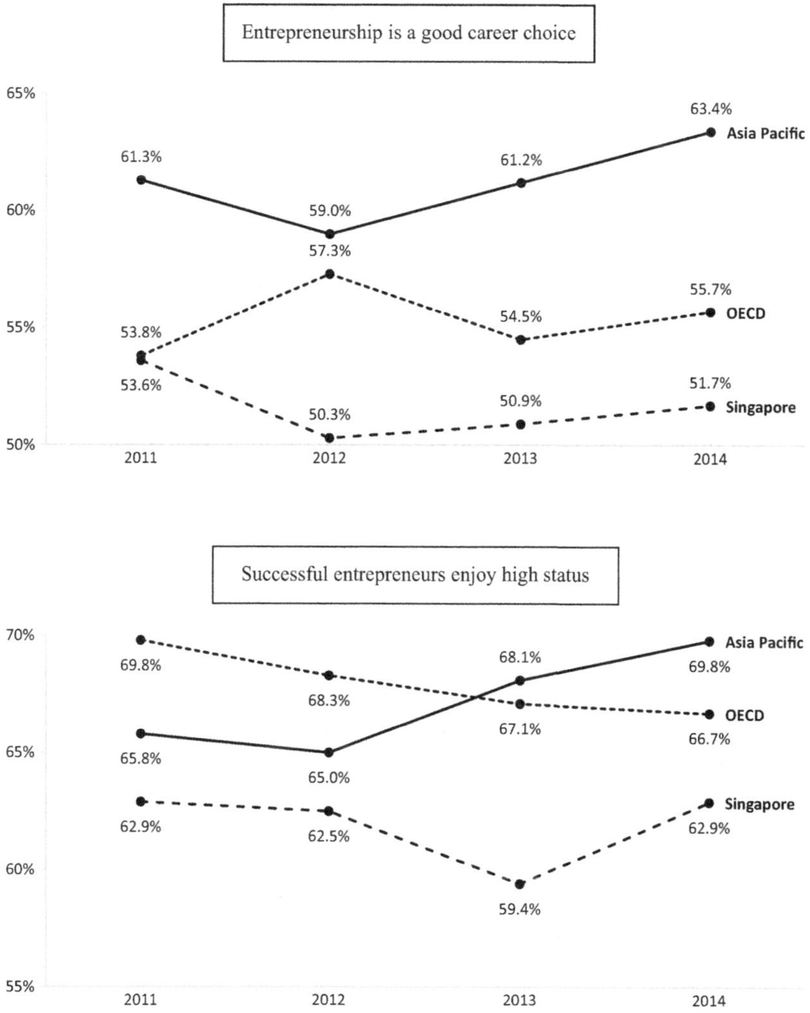

Fig. 6.14 GEM responses in Singapore, the Asia Pacific, and the OECD

[3] Singapore was no longer included in the GEM after 2014.

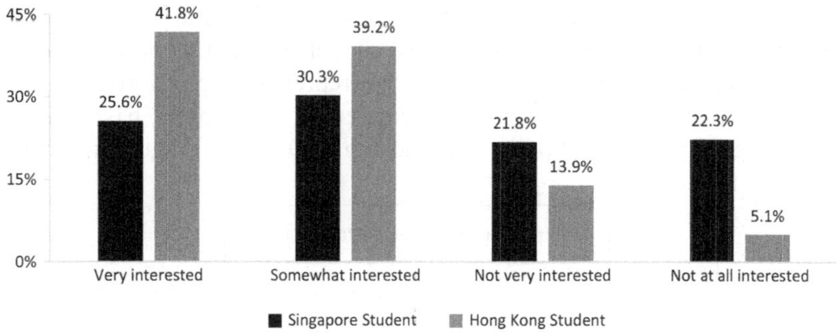

Fig. 6.15 Survey response: "How interested are you in becoming an entrepreneur?"

This result is triangulated. An independent survey involving 229 Hong Kong and 238 Singaporean students affirms the finding above. The results are displayed in the following bar chart, showing that there are more Hong Kong students who are "very interested" and "somewhat interested" in being an entrepreneur upon graduation (Fig. 6.15).

Not only are few Singaporean youths keen on an entrepreneurial career, they also perceive government careers as more attractive, in terms of the status, monetary benefits, and learning opportunities available. Hence, it can be said that the Singaporean developmental state's national talent policy has systematically channeled young students towards the public sector away from the private sector.

The above results do not just apply to the youth specifically but also to the general population in both city-states. The survey conducted also asked "I prefer being a salaried employee with a stable and comfortable income rather than being my own boss: how much do you agree with this statement?", to which a greater percentage of Hongkongers disagreed, expressing a preference for entrepreneurship rather than a stable salary (Fig. 6.16). This sense of self-reliance arguably explains why despite Hong Kong spending a smaller overall amount on R&D than in Singapore, most of its local firms "have performed self-financed spontaneous innovation that is not backed by the government, which forms a good base for Hong Kong to draw on for the development of innovation economy" (Wang, 2018, p. 407).

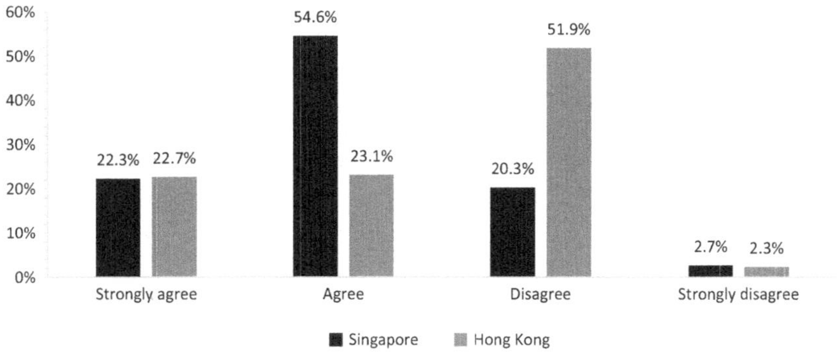

Fig. 6.16 Survey response: "I prefer being a salaried employee with a stable and comfortable income rather than being my own boss: how much do you agree with this statement?"

Looking Beyond Conventional Income Statistics

A holistic assessment of economic performance must go beyond conventional indicators of national income, which is a purely quantitative measurement of the amount of goods and services produced by various sectors of the economy. Such an indicator, while useful for the purpose of calculating overall production and making cross-national comparisons, nonetheless obscures deeper underlying factors within a nation's economic structure which affect its performance in the long run. Such factors may include the economic strategy undertaken, which may garner high GDP for a time, but which may be unsustainable in the long run, as evident in the economic history of the Soviet Union. In the twenty-first century, cutting-edge economic growth requires productivity, innovation, and entrepreneurship, which as the chapter has shown have not been achieved in equal measure in both nations.

Another qualitative factor to be taken seriously is the share of economic activity driven by indigenous factors of production rather than foreign ones (Fig. 6.17). Accordingly, a closer examination reveals that while aggregate statistics point to higher research activity in Singapore, much of it is driven by foreign firms who reap the investment returns. This in turn suggests that the innovation capability of the indigenous economy is comparably weak.

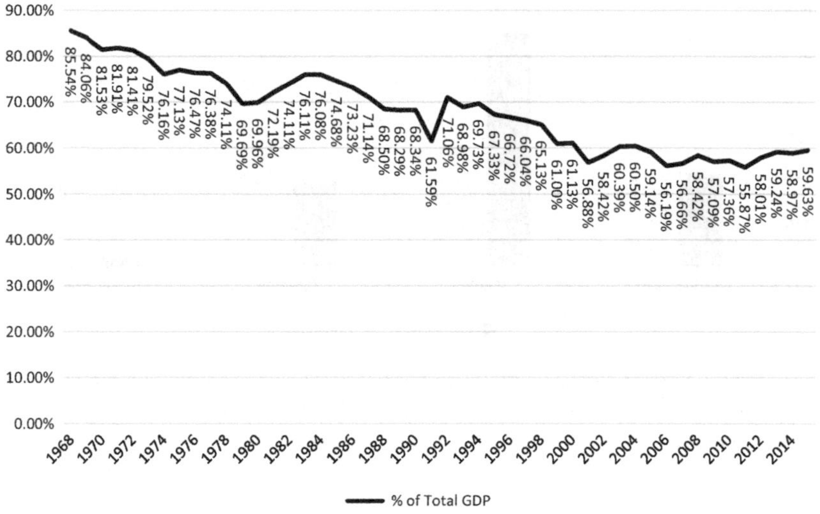

Fig. 6.17 Singapore's indigenous GDP as a share of total GDP. (Source: Department of Statistics (1969–2011) and Ministry of Trade and Industry (2016))

Whether economic growth translates into benefits for domestic residents in an economy is also an important indicator of standard of living. Does higher GDP translate into greater well-being for Hong Kong and Singapore residents? The only evidence available so far is for Singapore, based on the indigenous share of the GDP in Singapore, which was discontinued—amid some cynicism by academics—in 2014. The available evidence from 1985 to 2015 shows a consistent decline in the share of Singapore's indigenous GDP as a share of total GDP from 74.68% to 59.63%. Resident citizens, permanent residents, and local companies have received an increasingly smaller share of the economic pie since 1985.

In conclusion, this chapter has shown that despite the impressive performance in national income, Singapore's economic performance is not without its structural flaws, particularly when it relates to productivity, innovation, and entrepreneurship, three aspects that are typically associated with dynamic, higher-order development. Hong Kong's economy is by no means perfect, and especially since its domestic struggles over the past decade. But what is impressive is its ability to achieve structural change and development up till the turn of the twenty-first century despite minimal state support.

References

Asian Development Bank & Economist Intelligence Unit. (2014, August). *Creative productivity index: Analysing creativity and innovation in Asia*. Retrieved from Asian Development Bank: https://www.adb.org/publications/creative-productivity-index-analysing-creativity-and-innovation-asia

Audretsch, D. B., & Fiedler, A. (2022). Does the entrepreneurial state crowd out entrepreneurship? *Small Business Economics*, 1–17.

Bhaskaran, M., & Chiang, N. (2020). *Singapore's poor productivity performance*. Retrieved from Academia.sg: https://www.academia.sg/academic-views/singapores-poor-productivity-performance/

Boettke, P. (1993). *Why Perestroika failed*. Routledge.

Carney, R. W., & Loh, Y. Z. (2009). Institutional (dis) incentives to innovate: An explanation for Singapore's innovation gap. *Journal of East Asian Studies, 9*(2), 291–319.

Cheang, B. (2022). What Can Industrial Policy Do? Evidence from Singapore. *The Review of Austrian Economics*, 1–34.

Chia, S. Y. (1989). The character and progress of industrialisation. In K. S. Sandhu & P. Wheatley (Eds.), *Management of success: The moulding of modern Singapore* (pp. 250–279). Institute of Southeast Asian Studies.

Cline, W. R. (1982). Can the East Asian model of development be generalized? *World development, 10*(2), 81–90.

Collins, S., & Bosworth, B. P. (1997). Economic growth in East Asia: Accumulation versus Assimilation. In W. C. Brainard, & G. L. Perry (Eds.), *Brookings papers in economic activity* (Vol. 2, pp. 135–203). Brookings Institution.

Cornell University, INSEAD & World Intellectual Property Organisation Global Initiative. (2019). *Global Innovation Index 2019*. Retrieved from World Intellectual Property Office: https://www.wipo.int/edocs/pubdocs/en/wipo_pub_gii_2019.pdf

Department of Statistics. (1969–2011). *Yearbook of statistics*. Department of Statistics.

Feenstra, R., Inklaar, R., & Timmer, M. (2015). The next generation of the Penn World Table. *American Economic Review, 105*(10), 3150–3182.

Fuller, D. (2010). *Innovation policy and the limits of laissez-faire: Hong Kong's policy in comparative perspective*. Springer.

HKSAR. (2000–2018). *Hong Kong Innovation Statistics*. Retrieved from Census and Statistics Department, HKSAR: https://www.censtatd.gov.hk/hkstat/sub/sp120.jsp?productCode=B1110010

HKSAR. (2020c). *Labour productivity index [dataset]*. Retrieved from Census and Statistics Department, HKSAR: https://www.censtatd.gov.hk/hkstat/sub/sp70.jsp?tableID=103&ID=0&productType=8

Hofstede, G. (1980). *Culture's consequences: International differences in work-related values*. Sage Publications.

Holcombe, R. (2007). *Entrepreneurship and Economic Progress*. Routledge.

Huang, F., & Yeung, H. (2018). *Institutions and economic growth in Asia: The case of Mainland China, Hong Kong, Singapore and Malaysia*. Routledge.

International Labour Organization. (2019). *Labour productivity rankings*. Retrieved from International Labour Organization: https://ilostat.ilo.org/topics/labour-productivity/

Jayaram, S., & Lee, T. (2010). Singapore's productivity puzzle: Estimating Singapore's total factor productivity growth using the dual method. *Economic Survey of Singapore, Third Quarter 2010*, 15–26.

Kim, J., & Lau, L. (1994). The sources of economic growth of the East Asian newly industrialized countries. *Journal of the Japanese and international Economies, 8*(3), 235–271.

Kirkman, B. L., Lowe, K. B., & Gibson, C. B. (2006). A quarter century of Culture's Conse quences: A review of empirical research incorporating Hofstede's cultural values frame work. *Journal of International Business Studies, 37*(3), 285–320.

Korea Institute of S&T Evaluation and Planning. (2019). *Main Science & Technology Indicators of Korea 2019–2*. Retrieved from Korea Institute of S&T Evaluation and Planning: https://www.kistep.re.kr/en/c3/sub2.jsp?

Krugman, P. (1994). The myth of Asia's miracle. *Foreign Affairs*, pp. 62–78.

Leung, K., & Wang, J. (2015). A cross-cultural analysis of creativity. In C. E. Shalley, M. A. Hitt, & J. Zhou (Eds.), *The Oxford handbook of creativity, entrepreneurship and innovation*. Oxford University Press.

Li, K.-W. (2012). *Economic freedom: Lessons of Hong Kong*. World Scientific.

Lim, L., & Pang, E. F. (2016). Labor, productivity and Singapore's development model. In L. Lim (Ed.), *Singapore's economic development: Retrospection and reflections* (pp. 135–168). World Scientific.

Lo, K.-C., & Pang, L. (2007). Hong Kong: Ten years after colonialism. *Postcolonial Studies, 10*(4), 349–356.

Low, D., & Auyong, H. (2014). *Singapore's productivity challenge Part IV*. Lee Kuan Yew School of Public Policy.

Low, L. (2003). Singapore Inc: A success story. *South African Journal of International Affairs, 10*(1), 49–63.

Mahbubani, K. (2020, April 23). *Kishore Mahbubani on the dawn of the Asian century*. Retrieved from The Economist: https://www.economist.com/by-invitation/2020/04/20/kishore-mahbubani-on-the-dawn-of-the-asian-century

Marti, C. (1996, 10). Is there an East Asian miracle? *Union Bank of Switzerland Economic Research Working Paper*.

Menon, R. (2015). *Ravi Menon: An economic history of Singapore—1965–2065*. Retrieved from Bank for International Settlements: https://www.bis.org/review/r150807b.htm

Ministry of Science & Technology, Taiwan. (2018). *Indicators of science and technology*. Retrieved from Ministry of Science & Technology, Taiwan: https://wsts.most.gov.tw/stsweb/technology/TechnologyDataIndex.aspx?language=E
Ministry of Trade & Industry, Singapore. (2011–2018). *Economic survey of Singapore (various editions)*. Retrieved from Ministry of Trade & Industry, Singapore: https://www.mti.gov.sg/Resources/Economic-Survey-of-Singapore
Ministry of Trade & Industry, Singapore. (2014). *The Singapore economy in economic survey of Singapore: Second quarter 2014*. Retrieved from Ministry of Trade & Industry, Singapore: https://www.mti.gov.sg/-/media/MTI/Resources/Economic-Survey-of-Singapore/2014/Economic-Survey-of-Singapore-Second-Quarter-2014/fullreport_2q14.pdf
Ministry of Trade & Industry, Singapore. (2016, October 10). *Written reply to PQ on Singapore's indigenous GDP*. Retrieved from Ministry of Trade & Industry, Singapore: https://www.mti.gov.sg/Newsroom/Parliamentary-Replies/2016/10/Written-reply-to-PQ-on-Singapore-indigenous-GDP
National Research Foundation & Agency for Science, Technology and Research, Singapore. (2000–2019). *National survey of research and development in Singapore*. Retrieved from National Research Foundation: https://www.a-star.edu.sg/News-and-Events/publications
National Statistics, Republic of China (Taiwan). (n.d.). *Indicators in labour productivity [dataset]*. Retrieved from https://www.stat.gov.tw/ct.asp?mp=4&xItem=45809&ctNode=526
Numazaki, I. (1997). The Laoban-led development of business enterprises in Taiwan: An analysis of the Chinese entrepreneurship. *The Developing Economies, XXXV*(4), 440–457.
Randstad. (2017, March 17). *MNCs still employers of choice in Singapore, Hong Kong SAR and Malaysia*. Retrieved from Randstad: https://www.randstad.com.sg/about-us/press-releases/mncs-still-employers-of-choice-in-singapore-hong-kong-and-malaysia/#:~:text=The%20Randstad%20Workmonitor%20research%20report,large%20multinational%20corporations%20(MNCs).
Rigg, J. (1988). Singapore and the recession of 1985. *Asian Survey, 28*(3), 340–352.
Robbins, L. (1932). *An essay on the nature and significance of economic science*. Macmillan and Co. Limited.
Roberts, P. C. (1990). *Meltdown: Inside the soviet economy*. Cato Institute.
Rodan, G. (1989). Singapore's future as a NIC. In *The political economy of Singapore's industrialization: National state and international capital* (pp. 189–206). Palgrave Macmillan.
Seow, J. (2019, August 17). *Poll: Singapore youth less keen on being entrepreneurs than ASEAN peers*. Retrieved from https://www.straitstimes.com/business/poll-spore-youth-less-keen-on-being-entrepreneurs-than-asean-peers
Shanmugaratnam, T. (2015, April 29). *Speech by Mr Tharman Shanmugaratnam, Deputy Prime Minister and Minister for Finance, at the May Day Dinner*.

Retrieved from Ministry of Finance, Singapore: https://www.mof.gov.sg/newsroom/speeches/Speech-by-Mr-Tharman-Shanmugaratnam-Deputy-Prime-Minister-and-Minister-for-Finance-at-the-May-Day-Dinner

Shieh, G. (1992). *'Boss' Island: The subcontracting network and micro-entrepreneurship in Taiwan's development*. Peter Lang Publishing.

Tan, K. G., & Tan, Y. Y. (2015). Promoting SMEs and enhancing labor productivity in Singapore: A policy analysis. In K. G. Tan & Y. Y. Tan (Eds.), *Foreign direct investment and small and medium enterprises: Productivity and access to finance* (pp. 133–144). World Scientific.

Tan, K. S., & Bhaskaran, M. (2015). The role of the state in Singapore: Pragmatism in pursuit of growth. In L. Lim (Ed.), *Singapore's economic development—Retrospection and reflections* (pp. 51–82). World Scientific.

Triandis, H. C. (1995). *Individualism & collectivism*. Westview Press.

Tsao, Y. (1985). Growth without productivity: Singapore manufacturing in the 1970s. *Journal of Development Economics, 19*(1–2), 25–38.

UNESCO Institute for Statistics. (2020). *Research and development expenditure (% of GDP) [data file]*. Retrieved from https://data.worldbank.org/indicator/GB.XPD.RSDV.GD.ZS

United States Patent and Trademark Office. (2020). *USPTO Patent full-text and image database [online dataset]*. Retrieved from http://patft.uspto.gov/netahtml/PTO/search-adv.htm

Wang, J. (2018). Innovation and government intervention: A comparison of Singapore and Hong Kong. *Research Policy, 47*(2), 399–412.

Weitzman, M. L. (1996). Hybridizing Growth Theory. *American Economic Review, 86*(2), 207–212.

Wong, J. (2011). *Betting on biotech: Innovation and the limits of Asia's developmental state*. Cornell University Press.

Woon, K. C., & Loo, Y. L. (2018). *50 Years of Singapore's productivity drive*. World Scientific.

World Bank. (2020a). *GDP (constant 2010 US$)*. Retrieved from World Bank Development Indicators: https://data.worldbank.org/indicator/NY.GDP.MKTP.KD

World Bank. (2020b). *GDP growth (annual %)—Singapore [dataset]*. Retrieved from World Bank Development Indicators: https://databank.worldbank.org/

World Bank. (2020c). *GDP growth (annual %)—Hong Kong SAR China [dataset]*. Retrieved from World Bank Development Indicators: https://databank.worldbank.org/

World Economic Forum. (2019). *ASEAN Youth: Technology, skills and the future of work*. Retrieved from World Economic Forum: http://www3.weforum.org/docs/WEF_ASEAN_Youth_Survey_2019_Report.pdf

World Intellectual Property Office. (2019). *Singapore*. Retrieved from Global Innovation Index: https://www.wipo.int/edocs/pubdocs/en/wipo_pub_gii_2020/sg.pdf

Young, A. (1992). A tale of two cities: Factor accumulation and technical change in Hong Kong and Singapore. *NBER Macroeconomics Annual, 7*, 13–54.

Young, A. (1995). The tyranny of numbers: Confronting the statistical realities of the East Asian growth experience. *The Quarterly Journal of Economics, 110*(3), 641–680.

Yu, T. F.-L. (1997). *Entrepreneurship and economic development in Hong Kong*. Routledge.

Yu, T. F.-L. (1998). Adaptive entrepreneurship and the economic development of Hong Kong. *World Development, 26*(5), 897–911.

CHAPTER 7

State and the Creative Class

High-Quality Economic Growth and the Creative Class

Economic growth, as scholars have clarified, may proceed on the path of "perspiration", or "inspiration", the latter of which is characterised by qualitative improvements in productivity, innovation, and entrepreneurship. The strength of a nation's creative class reflects the extent to which cutting-edge development has been achieved, and its ability to thrive in the knowledge-based economic landscape of the future. Accordingly, I conduct a comparative analysis into the creative sectors in both city-states and highlight a gap in relative performance: despite higher levels of state support by the Singapore government, its arts and creative sectors perform worse than that in Hong Kong.

Significant to this argument is the premise that a strong economy is not just one that enjoys rapid growth rates of national income. It is also one that achieves "high-quality economic growth". This insight is based on the distinction between economic growth that proceeds based on the mere accumulation of factor inputs and that which involves an improvement in the quality of factors of production and the creative synthesis of these resources by innovative entrepreneurs. Today, such high-quality economic growth goes by many names, "innovation-led growth", "cutting-edge growth", or "inspiration-based growth".

B. Cheang, *Economic Liberalism and the Developmental State*,
https://doi.org/10.1007/978-3-031-08100-2_7

This distinction was first popularised by Paul Krugman (1994) who coined the terms "perspiration-led" and "inspiration-led" growth. Why does this matter? First, innovation-driven growth ('inspiration') is more sustainable. There is a limit to how much a nation can quantitatively accumulate factor inputs. Innovation transcends physical constraints and taps on a potentially limitless resource: human creativity. Where capital may reach a point of diminishing returns, and labour and land may be constrained by natural limitations, ideas are potentially limitless, and may be creatively harnessed to meet a variety of human desires. Second, the mere accumulation of resources may not translate into a substantive improvement in material well-being, even if it increases gross domestic product. People are better off not simply because random stuff is produced by the economy, but because their individual material needs are satisfied by goods and services that are themselves improving over time (Holcombe, 2007). The case of the Soviet Union amply exemplifies the basic insight that a mere increase in national income, however rapid, does not equate to a substantive or sustainable improvement in the actual welfare of people.

Numerous countries today precisely aim for this higher-order form of growth. The global community has mobilised its economic policies around the belief that the Fourth Industrial Revolution is underway, one where technological innovation will proliferate across the global economy at an unprecedented fashion (World Economic Forum, 2019a). This conviction has meant that governments have started to invest more in human capital, R&D, and innovation-based industries more than ever before in order to climb the value chain.

The desire to reach this "higher" phase of economic development has been at the heart of the developmental state's policy initiatives, and which explains the Singapore government's perpetual aim to upgrade the quality of local firms and workers. Even the Hong Kong government has of late embarked on industrial policies to achieve innovation-driven growth.

This chapter provides further evidence that unfortunately, the Singapore economy has fallen short of this ideal, as compared to its Hong Kong counterpart. Even though the Singapore state has provided state support on a far more generous basis to firms than laissez-faire Hong Kong, the results of such support have not kept pace. While the previous chapter made this argument through a macro-level analysis of productivity, innovation, and entrepreneurship, this chapter extends the same line of reasoning by focusing more specifically on the state of the creative industries.

An Innovative Economy Is One with Strong Creative Industries

The health of a nation's creative industries is a good reflection of how well its economy is performing from an "inspiration" perspective. The very nature of the creative industries requires the innovative synthesis of various factors of production, rather than its mere accumulation.

Accordingly, the creative industries may be further broken down into two categories: arts and media (Table 7.1).

The close linkage between the health of a nation's creative industries and innovation-based development has been explored through academic scholarship as well as in practical economic policy. The leading scholar on this matter is Richard Florida (2002), who argued that "places that succeed in attracting and retaining creative class people prosper; those that fail don't." Public policy has the power to shape whether there are creative individuals with the ability to generate new ideas and commercialise products and services that enhance welfare. Innovation-based growth may fail if the creative capacity of the population is suppressed.

Scholars have also admitted that this ability to compete based on creativity is especially pronounced in the twenty-first century, since the world economy has fundamentally transitioned into a knowledge-based structure. This explains why various experts have become consultants for governments interested in pushing the frontiers of growth (see Porter, 1998; Florida, 2012), and why creative industries have been part of governmental agendas to promote cutting-edge development (UNESCO, 2013;

Table 7.1 Definition of the arts and media

Arts	
Performing arts	*Classical arts*
Theatre (musical and drama)	Exhibitions and festivals
Concerts and recitals	Museums
Stand-up comedy	Graffiti
Media	
Traditional media	*Digital media*
Books	Internet
Magazines	Films and shows (online platforms)
Newspapers	YouTube
Radio	News websites
Films (cinemas and DVDs)	Social media
Shows (television)	Blogs
	Video games

OECD, 2014). Significantly, the World Economic Forum's Global Competitiveness Index (2019b) includes innovation capability as one of the 12 pillars of growth in the twenty-first century. The WEF also emphasised that "creativity must be encouraged" (World Economic Forum, 2019b, p. 7). This weight on the need to embrace and engage in "creative destruction" and creativity, particularly against the backdrop of a shift towards a knowledge-based economy, is also made by a leading Hong Kong scholar Grace Leung (2018, p. 2), who acknowledges that "creativity is the most prominent characteristic of the 21st century economy, just as manufacturing dominated the 19th and 20th centuries".

It is unsurprising that both Hong Kong and Singapore have developed a concerted policy to enhance the profile of their creative industries. Owing to the nature of the developmental state, the Singapore government embarked on a national arts policy as early as in the 1990s in anticipation of the new millennium. Even though Hong Kong has been late to the game—a national policy towards the creative sector was "virtually non-existent" before 1997 (Leung, 2018, p. 164)—various CEs have since identified the creative industries as a major pillar of Hong Kong's economy.

Freedom, Public Policy and Creative Industries

This book contends that the developmental state model, with its penetration of the state into the very culture of society, has an adverse, though unintentional impact on the development of the creative sector, in contrast to the relatively liberal society in Hong Kong.

The very nature of the creative industries, as the term suggests, involves a high degree of individual self-expression. This in turn necessitates a specific institutional environment to ensure its continued flourishing. On an abstract plane, many concede that a degree of individual freedom is necessary. Richard Florida (2012) has written extensively on the association between civil liberties and creative cities. Historically, John Stuart Mill defended a regime of individualism as necessary to sustain the generation of new ideas. By granting people the freedom to express themselves, it not only facilitates the emergence of new ideas but also for society to test, debate, and refine those ideas, ultimately facilitating progress (Mill, 1859/2015).

Accordingly, this book argues that the hegemonic control wielded by the developmental state in Singapore—demonstrated in Chap. 4—has had a negative impact on the development of the creative industries as opposed to Hong Kong's situation. While it is an open secret that the political regime in Singapore is relatively authoritarian vs. that of Hong Kong, what I particularly emphasise here is not merely the formal levers of censorship common to state policy but also the subtle, informal influences that a state has on creative activities. Therein lies a deeper, less visible distinction between Hong Kong and Singapore society: the former relies on overt forms of censorship common to most states, while various layers of restrictions are used by the developmental state in the latter.

A brief look at the cultural landscape provides preliminary evidence. Japan's global status is long recognised. It became a cultural power soon after its economic success and is regarded as the forerunner to the creation of a distinct East Asian pop culture (McGray, 2009; Otmazgin, 2014). South Korea is today a global cultural power in its own right: K-Pop, Squid Game, and BTS are household names (Choe, 2021).

Even Hong Kong, with its much smaller population, has also enjoyed much fame in the global entertainment industry, specifically with its prowess in Cantopop music and renown film industry (Wang, 2020; Wong & McDonogh, 2013). There are recent concerns that Hong Kong's cultural prowess has waned,[1] but this is beside the point. The fact that it achieved great cultural pre-eminence in the first place is the focus of this chapter. At its height, Hong Kong was the second largest film exporter in the world, with the entertainment powerhouse Shaw Brothers playing a leading role to present day (Leung, 1993). What is striking is that even in 1956, Hong Kong's annual film production was fifth in the world, closely following the United States, India, and Japan (Yu, 1997, p. 84).

Why is it that Singapore, part of the same family of East Asian nations with comparable levels of economic growth, has not achieved the same level of cultural power? Its creative industries and cultural exports do not rise to the same level of prominence and popular attention. I argue that this is a by-product of public policy, specifically, the unfree environment in Singapore has hampered the development of the creative industries. It is

[1] SCMP Editorial. (2021, July 27). *Hong Kong creative industries in need of a boost.* South China Morning Post. https://www.scmp.com/comment/opinion/article/3142781/hong-kong-creative-industries-need-boost

no coincidence that these other East Asian nations, with a freer political atmosphere, enjoy a more free-wheeling cultural landscape.[2]

If my position is accepted, then this constitutes a further reason for rejecting state-led economic growth. Some scholars have argued that economic growth can occur in the absence of political freedom or may even be enhanced in its absence. It has been said that China and Singapore's economic successes (the former has often sought to emulate the latter) is proof that rapid growth is possible without needing to follow the neoliberal prescriptions to "get the institutions" right (Ramo, 2004; French, 2007; Ash, 2008; Halper, 2010). Critics press: the neoliberal "Washington Consensus", which pushes for free market capitalism and liberal democracy, is wrong; democracy and liberalism are not required for economic success.

This book insists that while such rapid growth may be possible, the quality of the growth will be hampered. High-quality economic growth requires an environment of freedom in the fullest sense.

Restrictive Stance Towards Arts and Media in Singapore

The Singaporean developmental state's approach to the creative industries is arguably self-contradictory. On the one hand, it has invested heavily into support schemes to develop the creative industries; however, this is arguably undermined by its unfree political environment as elucidated in Chap. 4. This negative effect stems from both overt censorship, indirect censorship, and the cultural environment it has forged which encourages arts practitioners to censor themselves. The multiple layers of control reinforce the fact that state power is not defined simply by overt physical coercion but also the covert ideological influences on its subjects' behaviour.

These restrictions stem fundamentally from the socially conservative character of the incumbent People's Action Party (PAP). Conservatism as a philosophy is one that prizes stability, virtue, and order, and which unsurprisingly conditions clampdowns on creative content which are deemed to be subversive in this regard. The government's restrictions on free expression extend beyond the political realm and touch on areas such as race, religion, and homosexuality.

[2] It is granted that Taiwan and S. Korea used to be authoritarian regimes too, but they have since liberalised and democratised.

Political Censorship

The PAP government has a long history of suppressing political expression. Its rule has been characterised by observers and scholars as authoritarian (Ortmann, 2011). This "iron-fist" and authoritarian-like rule has its origins in the bitter fight PAP had against the threat of communism from the Barisan Sosialis (BS). The most famous example of this is Operation Coldstore, whereby political opponents were arrested and detained without trial (Singh, 2017). Authoritarian tendencies, which continued after Singapore obtained independence, were extended to censorship and the overregulation of the arts and media.

The substantial degree of influence that the government wields over the mass media is common knowledge. For instance, Singapore occupies a low position of 160 (of 180 countries) on the 2021 Press Freedom Index (Reporters Without Borders, 2022). The late Lee Kuan Yew (LKY) was unequivocal about the role of the mass media in Singapore: which is simply to reinforce and propagate government values and policies (Singh, 2017).

However, Singapore is by no means a Stalinist regime. Clearly, political speech is not explicitly banned by the IMDA. Opposition parties are free to have their own social media platforms. They are also free to produce and disseminate any form of media if it is deemed by the state to be factually accurate,[3] However, given the wide latitude the state enjoys in interpreting and crafting the rules of the game, political censorship nonetheless occurs, though under the justifications of protecting national interests and security.[4]

Testament to the informal power that the state elites enjoy, private litigations are also used against civil society activities deemed to have defamed

[3] This, however, was not always the case. The Films act previously prohibited the making, reproducing, importing, distributing, and exhibiting "party political films" (Tan, 2016). This was amended in 2009, with the exemption of any documentary film that was "without any animation and composed wholly of an accurate account depicting actual events, persons (deceased or otherwise) or situations, but not a film (i) wholly or substantially based on unscripted or 'reality' type programmes; or (ii) that depicts those events, persons or situations in a dramatic way" (Tan, 2016).

[4] IMDA internet guidelines state that "prohibited material is material that is objectionable on the grounds of public interest, public morality, public order, public security, national harmony, or is otherwise prohibited by applicable Singapore laws", while arts entertainment guidelines mention that "content should not undermine public order, national security and/or stability" (IMDA, 2020).

government officials. Of note in this regard, in 2020, a blogger Leong Sze Hian was accused of defamation for resharing a Facebook post accusing the Prime Minister of being complicit in the IMDB scandal in Malaysia.

Such restrictions have a chilling effect on the expression of creative individuals, and hence the health of the creative industries. Interestingly, this effect is achieved not merely through strict official guidelines but also through the social ostracism that arts and media practitioners experience when they violate "OB markers", which are informal norms regarding taboo topics in Singapore.

Clampdowns on Socially Sensitive Content

What illustrates the far-reaching power of the Singapore state is its desire to regulate speech that it deems socially sensitive, and hence, potentially disruptive to the social order.

IMDA has explicit guidelines over race and religion that extend to most, if not all, forms of the arts and media.[5] Race and religion are perhaps the two most important OB markers in Singapore. Scholars attribute this to racial tensions that resulted in riots during the pre-independence years of Singapore (Singh, 2017). Religion was also a cause for riots, with a prominent example being the Maria Hertogh riots of 1964.

Due to the historical scars from the riots, the People's Action Party (PAP) government made racial and religious harmony a priority post-independence. Strict policies were enacted and one of those measures was the circumscribing of free speech to prevent seditious acts being committed with regard to race and religion. A secondary aspect of censorship with societal stability in mind is the prohibition of content that is potentially offensive to various religions.

In addition to race and religion, homosexuality is also taboo in socially conservative Singapore. Accordingly, there are explicit guidelines in place restricting homosexual content.[6] As with political censorship, censorship

[5] Film guidelines, for instance, state that "[films that] are likely to denigrate any racial or religious group or promote feelings of ill-will or hostility between different racial or religious groups will be refused classification" (IMDA, 2020).

[6] For example, free-to-air radio has the following guideline: "Information, themes, or sub-plots on lifestyles such as homosexuality, lesbianism, bisexualism, transsexualism, transvestism, paedophilia and incest should be treated with utmost caution. Their treatment should not in any way promote, justify, or glamorise such lifestyles. Explicit dialogue or information concerning the above topics should not be broadcast" (IMDA, 2020).

over homosexuality occurs directly and indirectly. But unlike political censorship, most censorship over homosexual content these days tends to result in the upgrade of the classification rating to R21 rather than an outright ban, though there are instances of banning especially before the turn of the new millennium.

What is noteworthy about the restriction on homosexual content is its arguably chilling effect on creative potential. The scholar Richard Florida (2012) has argued that a creative class is one which embraces tolerance and a diversity of lifestyles, including alternative gender and sexual norms. Some evidence exists, including that gathered by this author, suggesting that individuals in Singapore who do not confirm to these enforced social norms have chosen to migrate elsewhere, including to Hong Kong.

Direct Censorship

The Singapore state employs a range of overt censorship methods, including the use of classification ratings, as punitive measures to punish those who flout regulations regarding the explicit prohibitions of certain content and events.

Censoring the Arts

Censorship in the performing arts on racial and religious grounds tends to apply to concerts. The last-minute cancellation of a concert by Swedish metal band Watain in March 2019 substantiates my point. According to the Minister of Home Affairs, many Christians complained that Watain songs contain offensive lyrics from a religious standpoint and their songs may attract people of a fanatical nature (CNA, 2019d). As a result, the Ministry of Home Affairs was asked to advise IMDA to cancel the Watain concert for fear of the "lawlessness, violence, crime, madness that can follow" (CNA, 2019d).

Other artistes in the past have been banned from performing in Singapore as well. Madonna is a prominent example. She was banned from performing in 1993 as her Girlie Show tour "border[ed] on the obscene" and is "known to be objectionable to many on moral and religious grounds" (Chow, 2015). Even when Madonna could perform in 2016, she had to remove the song "Holy Water" from her repertoire as it contains religiously sensitive lyrics (Hadi, 2016).

Censoring the Media

Books have been banned in Singapore on religious grounds. As recently as 2018, three books were banned for promoting divisive views towards non-Islam religions as well as extremist views (Choo, 2018). This ban is in line with a 2017 ban of four books which promoted extremist views, with the Ministry of Communications and Information (MCI) citing the potential of the books to "cause social distancing, distrust, hatred and even violence among people of different faiths and religions" (Tham, 2017b). There are other reasons behind book banning. The National Library Board recently moved eight books containing homosexual content from the children's section to sections for older readers. Minister Iswaran justified the move as follows: "The NLB seeks to balance the need for a wide-ranging library collection with sensitivity towards our community norms" (Seow, 2018).

Other publications have been subjected to bans as well. Magazines of a hardcore pornographic nature such as *Playboy* are banned in Singapore as their explicit content may be offensive to certain religions and Singapore society at large (Chong, 2015). A newspaper, *Al Fathihin*, produced by a media group linked to ISIS was gazetted as a prohibited publication by MCI in 2016 (Lim, 2016). IMDA reasoned that material that promotes terrorism is detrimental to society as it influences people to act in divisive ways which can destabilise the harmony that Singapore currently enjoys (Lim, 2016).

Magazines by Watch Tower Bible and Tract Society and International Bible Students Association are also on the prohibited list of publications in Singapore (Chong, 2015). The two groups are part of Jehovah's Witness, an extreme Christian denomination which forbids the bearing of arms and serving in the military. This undermines the Singapore government's requirement for all males above the age of 18 to serve National Service.

Insensitive racial remarks have resulted in a radio station in Singapore being fined $7000 in 2017. DJs from Kiss 92FM's morning shows remarked that Malays and Indians got less sleep than the Chinese in Singapore as the former work less and "go[es] out and party", while the latter go to bed early as they had to send their children to school early and head to work after (Yuen, 2017). By making racial stereotypes, the DJs' remarks contravened the free-to-air programme code and the radio station was penalised as a result.

There have been films banned on religious grounds too. One such example is *A Jihad for Love*. The film is a documentary on gay and lesbian Muslims, and their struggle to reconcile their faith and sexuality (Helfand,

2008). Given the controversial and sensitive nature of the film across two fronts (religion and homosexuality), it is banned by Singapore (Helfand, 2008).

Examples from digital media platforms are drawn from YouTube and social media. For the former, there exist two prominent cases in recent years: Amos Yee and Preetipls. Amos Yee was charged and convicted of hate speech against Christians in 2015 and was found guilty of the same offence against Christians and Muslims in 2016 (Today Online, 2017). After Lee Kuan Yew passed away in 2015, Amos Yee compared him to Jesus Christ, describing both as "power-hungry and malicious but deceive others into thinking they are both compassionate and kind" (Han, 2015). In 2016, Yee remarked that Muslims follow a "sky wizard and paedophile prophet" amongst other seditious comments (Tham, 2017a).

In 2019, YouTuber Preeti Nair and her brother Subhas Nair were given conditional warnings for producing and uploading an offensive video. In response to a brownface ad by the electronic payment service provider NETS, the siblings produced a rap video which contained expletive-laden lyrics about Chinese people (CNA, 2019c). Citing that Singapore has taken an unequivocal approach with regard to racially and religiously offensive speech, they were ordered to take the video down from YouTube.

Regulation of racially insensitive remarks also extends to social media. In 2019, a Singaporean man was sentenced to four weeks in jail and was given a $1000 fine for making racist remarks towards an Indian construction worker (Lam, 2019).

In addition, several movies are banned in Singapore and a common theme ties them together—they are centred around the recounts of past political detainees and their dissatisfaction towards the Singapore government. *To Singapore With Love* (2014), *Zahari's 17 years* (2007) and *Dr Lim Hock Siew* (2010) are prominent examples. They document the narratives of historical events by various political detainees, most of which undermine the government's own recount of history (Tan, 2016).

There are examples of political censorship on the internet, social media, as well as blogs. The infamous Prevention of Online Falsehoods and Manipulation Act (POFMA) was used on a Malaysian NGO's website to request for them to correct misinformation reported on the execution method employed by Singapore and when they failed to do so, IMDA asked local internet service providers to block the site (The Straits Times, 2020). POFMA was used on Facebook to disable Singaporean users' access to 'States Times Review', an anti-establishment news platform

(Kurohi, 2020). Meanwhile, POFMA was also applied on several other occasions against opposition parties such as the Singapore Democratic Party (CNA, 2019b) and individuals from opposition parties such as Brad Bowyer, a member of the Progress Singapore Party (CNA, 2019a).

Homosexual scenes in movies are typically cut off or censored before low classification levels are issued. A recent example is *Star Wars: The Rise of Skywalker* where producers had to remove a scene depicting a kiss between two female actors before it could be classified PG-13 (Today Online, 2019). In addition, free-to-air television shows have portions removed if they contravene regulations vis-à-vis homosexuality. For example, a section where former US President Barack Obama advocated for gay rights on the Ellen DeGeneres Show was removed when the episode aired in Singapore (Yip, 2016). Songs and music videos (MV) containing homosexual content have also been banned from the radio and television. An example is "I Kissed a Girl" by Katy Perry and an MV example is Jolin Tsai's "We're All Different, Yet the Same" (Words by Bandwagon, 2015).

Crucially, the explicit prohibition of digital media is hard to find, and as the subsequent section will show, covert censorship is more common. The most explicit forms of censorship on films would be the use of ratings, applied on socially taboo topics such as LGBT, racial, and religious sensitivities.

Indirect Censorship

What is unique about the Singaporean developmental state's policy on the creative sector is not its overt censorship, which exists in numerous countries, and even in those more liberal ones, but rather the indirect control that it has over practitioners in the creative industries. Due to the extensive state support the developmental state offers to creative practitioners, it has forged a relationship of dependency whereby those receiving state aid feel compelled to obey the rules for fear of having their funding withdrawn.

Withholding State Aid

Numerous parties operating in the arts and media sectors have had their funding either denied or withdrawn after being approved. In 2010, Wild Rice had $20,000 cut from its NAC grants. Its artistic director Ivan Heng explained that these cuts were due to the company staging "productions which ran contrary to mainstream societal values and which were critical of the Government" (Teo, 2010). The NAC subsequently made it unequivocal that it "will not fund projects which are incompatible with the core values promoted by the Government and society or disparage the Government" (Teo, 2010).

An example of the withdrawal of grants concerns the renown comic artist Sonny Liew's graphic novel, *The Art of Charlie Chan Hock Chye*, which challenges the dominant historical narrative and portrays Barisan Sosialis member and alleged communist Lim Chin Siong in a more favourable light. The National Arts Council (NAC) withdrew its initial publishing grant for the book citing that it contained content that "potentially undermines the authority and legitimacy of the government and its public institutions" (Harmon, 2017). While this may seem like the classic case of state withdrawal of funds, it is intriguing to note that the book did not change from the draft that won the funding. This has led Liew to suspect that someone of a higher authority vetoed the funding (Harmon, 2017).

A noteworthy example where the withdrawal of funding has had a chilling effect on creative expression involves the 1988 case in which the Ministry of Community Development withdrew funding for two TheatreWorks productions on HIV/AIDS, *Ten Little Indians*, and *Jackson on a Jaunt*. Funding was withdrawn on the grounds that homosexuality was possibly portrayed as a "natural and acceptable form of sexuality" as the productions were sympathetic towards gay men (Ng, 2006). The result was that the production and its participants had to migrate elsewhere, taking with them their human capital.

That creative individuals who identify as LGBT feel compelled to leave is not merely anecdotal but a repeated pattern. For instance, in 2014, another similar case occurred. As part of the 2014 revival of the Singapore International Festival of Arts (SIFA), Singapore cultural medallion recipient Ong Keng Sen was tasked to run it and was given full autonomy to do so. He organised an exhibition discussing LGBTQ issues amongst others and screened films that were exempted from licencing regulations. However, in 2015, the IMDA reinstated licencing regulations and asked for "finalised scripts and content checklists to be sent in at least two months before [the] opening night" (Harmon, 2017). Eventually, key members of this initiative, several whom were LGBT individuals, resigned and decided to ply their craft elsewhere.

Self-censorship

Chapter 4 elucidated the power exercised by the Singapore state which extends into the ideological, cultural, and intellectual realm. This is best exemplified by the way in which the phenomenon of self-censorship adds to the developmental state's overt censorship of creative content and its withholding of arts funding to recipients. In other words, not only is the Singapore government able to directly restrict creative expression, it has also influenced individuals into restricting their own forms of expression.

This applies to media organisations, arts practitioners, and others in the creative sector. The scholar Lee (1998) defines this as "a set of editorial actions ranging from omission, dilution, distortion, and change of emphasis to choice of rhetorical devices by journalists, their organisations, and even the entire media community in anticipation of currying reward and avoiding punishments from the power structure".

This practice of self-censorship is most prevalent in the realm of performing arts. The academic Kenneth Paul Tan (2016) briefly traced the history of direct state censorship on theatre productions and performing art. He found that while there has been a history of direct censorship when forum theatres were banned, there have been no actual bans on performing art and productions since 2004 (Tan, 2016). Despite this, practitioners are encouraged to engage in self-classification. However, many fear that this promotes self-censorship rather than true autonomy (Tan, 2016). This fear arose because as playwright Alfian Sa'at points out "the fine print is that [practitioner] have to follow the guidelines that the MDA has already devised" rather than having the "freedom to come up with [their] own classification scheme" (Wild Rice, 2014).

In Singapore, self-censorship is the by-product of certain social and structural phenomena. First, the education system discourages anti-establishment narratives, especially through social studies and national education initiatives. These curricula provide a mainstream interpretation of controversial events in history, such as Operation Coldstore, which is often framed by the state as a necessary arrest of subversive Marxist revolutionaries.[7] Unsurprisingly, the education system in Singapore is acknowledged by many to have been a tool used by the state for nation-building purposes.

Second, the state-dominated media also encourages self-censorship. Individuals, sometimes prominent opposition politicians, can be arrested for acts of political protest which are featured in the news. Barring small-scale political party media platforms and anti-establishment blogs, there

[7] Operation Coldstore was an internal security operation which resulted in the arrest and detaining of over a hundred alleged communists and political dissidents.

are no anti-establishment media companies in Singapore of any sizable scale. State-owned companies dominate the print media scene as well as visual media platforms, propagating state narratives and pro-establishment content. This further contributes to the perception that criticism is not tolerated. Third, challenges to state narratives are often publicly rebuked. Attempts to challenge state narratives, especially that of historical events, are actively discredited by the government. An example of this would be the concerted effort by the Minister for Home Affairs to question PJ Thum's academic credentials when Thum challenged the state narrative with regard to the exigency of Operation Coldstore (Yahya, 2018).

These factors strengthen the state's ideological hegemony over its citizens, who are discouraged from criticising it, with many even believing that such restrictions are desirable for the preservation of law and order. Scholars have accordingly admitted how the political culture fostered by the PAP in Singapore is characterised by docility and submissiveness to the state (see Rahim & Barr, 2019), a perception that is not without merit, as evidenced by the results gleaned from surveys conducted in this book.

Light Touch Approach in Hong Kong

Lack of Industrial Policy Targeting the Creative Industries

Unlike Singapore, Hong Kong did not have a national strategy to develop the creative sectors for most of its history. This is consonant with its minimal state approach that accorded large leeway for private arts groups, creative practitioners, and media companies. It was only after the 1997 handover when successive administrations mimicked the developmental state approach of identifying the creative sectors as crucial in catalysing innovation-driven economic growth. The year 2003, articulated in CE Tung's Policy Address, was in fact the first time that the creative sector was the target of industrial policy (HKSAR, 2003). This is unlike Singapore, which targeted the creative sector as early as in the 1990s as part of its efforts to spearhead a new phase of economic development.

Clear evidence of the limited involvement of the state in developing the arts sector can be gleaned from an analysis of the pre-1997 arts-related state bodies that were formed. The earliest government initiative to promote the creative industry came only in 1982 with the establishment of the Council of Performing Art, but this was merely an advisory body that had no executive power or policymaking capacity. Significantly, the HK

Arts Development Council was formed in 1994 to support the broad development of arts in Hong Kong, with responsibilities that included giving out grants and promoting the sector. However, due to the relatively overlapping and polycentric nature of the Hong Kong state bureaucracy before 1997, this body failed to exercise overarching leadership in relation to lower-level municipal arts bodies and private firms (see Ooi, 1995, p. 278 for an account of the intra-governmental rivalry of arts bodies), which led to it being abolished in 1999.

Even after the 1997 handover, despite the new focus of the Hong Kong government on the creative industries, state support for the arts remains piecemeal, in keeping with its historical laissez-faire tradition. Scholars have identified the piecemeal fashion in which state support was provided and the lack of expertise of the government officials involved (Chu, 2002; Woo, 2009), and how creative sector practitioners still do not receive direct funding from the government but can only do so through third-party intermediaries. An influential comparative study showed that out of various Asian countries, Hong Kong's direct state support for creative firms lags that of Singapore, Taiwan, Korea, and other Chinese cities, even though said funding has increased quantitatively (Commission on Strategic Development, 2016).

An additional point demonstrating the limited state support of the creative sector in Hong Kong lies in the seeming dependence of its arts policy on China's initiatives. Even though successive administrations after 1997 have announced industrial policy initiatives in the creative sector, some have doubted whether they are simply a replication of China's own efforts in this regard or a genuine policy initiative developed within Hong Kong. An analysis into the timing of such policy announcements shows that many initiatives were announced and timed just after China's national policy announcements. For example, the term "creative industries" was first included in Hong Kong's policy agenda in 2002, only after China inscribed this industry as part of its national strategy in the 16th National Congress in the same year (Hong Kong Legislative Council, 2006). After Xi Jinping became China's leader in 2012, one observes a succession of creative and arts related industrial policy initiatives announced in Hong Kong: the setting up of the Innovation and Technology Bureau in 2015, the build-up of a Chinese "Silicon-Valley" in the Big Bay Area, and the 2017 launch of the Smart City Initiative (Commission on Strategic Development, 2016). These coincidences prompted Leung (2018, p. 170) to articulate that the HK administrations under C.Y. Leung and

Carrie Lam "might be faithful executors to the national policy but they did not have their own visions...in the development of local creative and cultural industries".

Therefore, this book reiterates the following: the economic performance of the creative industries in Hong Kong, which is tracked in this chapter, cannot reasonably be attributed directly to active industrial policy support. The development of the creative industries has been largely a bottom-up process that has occurred outside of the state sector, unlike the case in Singapore.

Creative Freedoms Tolerated in Hong Kong

Even as direct state support for the creative industries has lagged in Hong Kong, the larger political environment towards the related sub-industries is relatively liberal and open. Even though Hong Kong's Chinese community is on the whole conservative, its experience under British colonial rule has largely familiarised it with the norms of liberal democracy. Thus, restrictions on sensitive speech and taboo subjects are not present to the same degree as in Singapore. There exists a modicum of control over creative expression in the political realm, especially since China has begun to exert further control, but even so it is less extensive as in Singapore and remains on the level of overt censorship only.

Constitutionally speaking, despite recent concerns over China's intrusion, civil liberties are recognised. This can be attributed to Hong Kong's constitution, specifically Article 27, which states that "Hong Kong residents shall have freedom of speech, of the press and of publication; freedom of association, of assembly, of procession and of demonstration; and the right and freedom to form and join trade unions, and to strike" (HKSAR, 1997, p. 67). This promotes and safeguards a relatively high amount of political freedom, especially when one considers the Singaporean equivalent. Singapore also has a similar provision in the form of its constitution's Article 14. Clause 1 of Article 14 states that "(a) every citizen of Singapore has the right to freedom of speech and expression" and "(b) all citizens of Singapore have the right to assemble peaceably and without arms". However, Clause 2 goes on to state that Parliament may by law impose "on the rights conferred by clause (1)(a), such restrictions as it considers necessary or expedient in the interest of the security of Singapore or any part thereof, friendly relations with other countries, public order or morality and restrictions designed to protect the privileges of Parliament or to provide against contempt of court, defamation or incitement to any offence" and "on the right conferred by clause (1)(b), such restrictions as it considers necessary or expedient in the interest of the security of Singapore or any part thereof or public order" (Republic of Singapore, 2020).

The more liberal and formal institutional framework in Hong Kong is also further complemented by a political culture that embraces free expression, even to the point of outright anti-government hostility. Many Hong Kong journalists believe in press freedom while a large part of the population is pro-democratic (Lee & Lin, 2006). An anchor-woman from Hong Kong cable TV that I spoke to shared her experiences of investigative journalism, which often involved hard-hitting commentary on government policies. This is consonant with the nature of state-society relations in Hong Kong outlined in Chap. 4, whereby societal actors have often taken the liberty to assert their autonomy from what is deemed as an encroaching state. In recent months however, various activists, including the anchor woman I spoke with, have had to curb their own activities out of fear. As an example, the said anchor-woman recently had to change her LinkedIn profile to increase her anonymity considering political developments in 2019.[8]

External Pressure from Mainland China

Despite the generally liberal environment that affords a wide latitude for the creative industries, there is nonetheless increasing political pressure from Mainland China, both in the form of direct censorship and indirect co-optation of media outlets in Hong Kong. It must however be strongly emphasised here that the degree of state penetration into the creative space in Hong Kong is not as deep as in Singapore, since there also exists a high degree of self-censorship in the latter context. This difference reinforces the point made in Chap. 4, which is that while the developmental state in Singapore has managed to elicit a strong ideological allegiance from its people, the Hong Kong state remains at arm's length from society. Thus, the control that the Hong Kong state has (and by extension the Chinese Communist Party) over the creative sector is not as far-reaching as that in Singapore.

[8] Interview with Hong Kong Cable TV Anchor-woman.

That said, there are several methods of control enjoyed by the Hong Kong state, one of which is the co-optation of media owners. As Lee and Chan (2009) note, "most media organisations in Hong Kong are owned by businesspeople who either have formal political appointments in China or have extensive business interests in the Mainland". The corollary of this is that China can adversely affect the ability of business owners to do business and make money. Prominent examples include the purchase of *South China Morning Post* (SCMP) by Robert Kuok and the Chinese daily *Ming Pao* by Tiong Hiew King (Lee, 2018). There are two presumed consequences of these vested interests. First, business owners could directly intervene in the newsroom to appease the Mainland, and second, journalists could be induced to practise self-censorship. One such intervention was *Ming Pao*'s change of chief editorship in 2014. Malaysian journalist Chong Tien Siong was "parachuted" into the position of chief editor when the former chief editor was assigned to another role (Lee, 2018). Chong was inexperienced when it came to Hong Kong affairs and this aroused suspicion that the ownership was intervening to appease China. Lee (2018) observes that "many *Ming Pao* journalists [were] worried that his arrival signified Tiong Hiew King's attempt to tighten his control of the newspaper" against the backdrop of the 2014 Occupy Central Movement.

However, direct intervention has rarely transpired. As Lee (2018) observes, "ownership does not entail direct intervention into newsrooms by the owners, but [rather] it entails the possibility of intervention when needed". Owners may also not have the time to excessively intervene. Furthermore, some owners have already been confronted by the fact that a significant percentage of the population value press freedom (Lee, 2018). In sum, excessive control will lead to content that is overly censored which in turn produces an adverse effect on profits.

On an indirect level, media outlets in Hong Kong may themselves regulate the expression of their journalists. One such strategy is the strategic distribution of journalists. There exist multiple aspects of current affairs that journalists can cover, and each aspect would require journalists to make different types of decisions. As Lee and Chan (2009) argue, "putting the "right" type of journalists into the "right" locations can minimise conflicts and frictions in the news-making process". Assigning a pro-democratisation journalist to write non-democratisation-related articles is one such example of strategically distributing journalists. This attempt to blunt any potentially thorny articles implicitly sends a message that being too liberal may work against you, resulting in self-censorship.

The co-optation of key personnel in media organisations, mainly news editors, has also been practised. Meanwhile, journalists are given autonomy to research and express their thoughts in articles, but these may not be published by the editor. In addition, some media companies have informal "blacklists" that contain matters, persons, or organisations that they do not report on (Lee & Chan, 2009). Journalists below a certain rank may not be privy to the "blacklist", and again, the editors can simply choose not to publish their articles.

Another indirect strategy undertaken in Hong Kong is the vague commands and instructions used in the newsroom on journalistic practice. One journalist that this author interviewed recalled a moment when his superior merely told him to "be smart" when it comes to reporting about the Tiananmen incident.[9] Other ambiguous instructions have also included "be cautious" and "be objective" (Lee & Chan, 2009). This results in journalists having to undertake a practice of "trial and error" to see what is allowed and what is not. This also creates a sense of self-censorship when one constantly doubts if reporting from a certain angle or mentioning certain content is "smart" or "being cautious". Having said this however, it should be stressed that while such incidents have been reported in academic scholarship and the popular media, the overwhelming sentiment gathered from a review of these sources, coupled with the personal interviews conducted, is that these are the exception rather than the rule.

It should be reiterated that the state in Singapore is pervasive and permeates the formal and informal realm with regard to censorship of the arts and media. There exists a wide range of measures to control discourse as well as to condition arts practitioners to adhere to state-sanctioned narratives and priorities as much as possible. Hong Kong, on the other hand, possesses some state presence in the formal realm—especially in the last few years when China's intrusions have become a concern—but not so much in the informal realm. Individuals tend to hold independent mindsets and actively challenge narratives and directives from the central government as much as possible.

[9] Interview with journalist from Headline Daily, March 2019.

What Is the Overall Impact on the Performance of the Arts in Both City-States?

Two trends are clear at this stage: first, the creative industries have been a target of the Singapore government's effort to catalyse innovation-based growth, owing to the very motivations of the developmental state framework, while similar levels of state support in Hong Kong have lagged; second, the larger social environment in Hong Kong has accorded a greater tolerance to free creative expression than in Singapore, stemming from the latter's political authoritarianism. These two distinctions matter in influencing the subsequent development of the creative industries. Through quantitative and qualitative evidence, this book shows that the restrictive controls in Singapore have severely impaired the arts, culture, and creative industries in a way not seen in Hong Kong.

Comparative Quantitative Analysis

Using the available statistics, this quantitative analysis shows that the performance of the creative industries in Hong Kong outperforms that in Singapore, despite the much smaller degree of state support.

Merging the Definitions

While both countries define arts and culture differently, this book has disentangled the differences and harmonised the relevant classifications pertaining to the performing arts, cultural heritage and publishing sectors, as well as the sectors of visual arts, and film and video.

The performing arts sector in Singapore comprises of live performing arts and associated professions such as venue operators, light and sound system technicians, and agents. Live performing art forms comprise operas, wayang shows, puppet shows, orchestras, musical bands, choirs, dance groups, stage plays, musicals, and theatre productions (Ministry of Culture, Community and Youth, 2019). It has to be said that MCCY does consider recorded music and associated industries under the performing arts, but I subsumed the data for recorded music under film and video so that it matches with Hong Kong's definitions. In Hong Kong, a similar range of jobs is covered under performing arts based on the Hong Kong Census and Statistics Department June 2019 report.[10]

Cultural heritage consists of "associations for hobbies, recreational, cultural, extra- curricular activities, museums, art galleries, preservation of historical sites, buildings, artefacts and paintings, cultural villages and other related activities" (Ministry of Culture, Community and Youth, 2019, p. 16). Hong Kong labels this sector as "cultural education and library, archive and museum services". It includes "instruction in arts, drama, music, dance, painting, photography in the private sector [as well as] general fine arts and performing arts schools (except academic) [in addition to] the operation and management of libraries and archives, museums and historical sites in the private sector" (HKSAR, 2019).

Publishing comprises of "printing, publishing, and wholesale and retail of books, newspapers and periodicals. It also covers news agency and other information service activities" (HKSAR, 2019) in the case of Hong Kong. Its Singapore equivalent, literary arts, covers "wholesale of books and magazines, Retail sale of books, newspapers and stationery (including news vendors), publishing of books, brochures, musical books and other publications" (Ministry of Culture, Community and Youth, 2019, p. 16).

Visual arts in Singapore consists of two categories: "fine art, crafts & collectibles" and "photography". The former consists of "wholesale of antiques and works of art, wholesale of handicrafts and gifts, retail sale of antiques and works of art [as well as the] retail sale of handicrafts, collectibles and gifts" (Ministry of Culture, Community and Youth, 2019, p. 17). The latter includes "wholesale of optical equipment and supplies (excluding binoculars), wholesale of photographic equipment and supplies (including binoculars), retail sale of cameras and other photographic goods, photo taking services (e.g. portrait or studio photography) photo processing and finishing services, and photographic activities" (Ministry of Culture, Community and Youth, 2019, p. 17). The Hong Kong equivalent, "art, antiques and crafts", scopes it as the "manufacture of jewellery and related articles (including cutting and setting of precious stones; engraving on precious metals; goldsmithing and silversmithing), the

[10] The report outlines that "performing arts domain covers creative and performing arts activities (e.g., orchestras, ballet and concert show groups, stage designers, theatrical producers, etc.); creative artists; musicians and writers; as well as performing arts venue operation (e.g., theatres for live performance) in the private sector. It also includes agents for artistes and models" (HKSAR, 2019).

wholesale and retail of jewellery and precious metal accessories, antiques, and works of art and crafts" (HKSAR, 2019). The main difference observed here is that Singapore includes photography and its associated industries in its definition of visual arts which Hong Kong does not. Instead, Hong Kong includes jewellery and associated industries which Singapore does not.

In Singapore, film consists of "motion picture/movie production, animation production, motion picture/movie distribution, production of advertisements, corporate videos and event videos, motion picture, video and television programme production activities, motion picture, video, television and other programme distribution activities, motion picture, video, television and other programme post- production activities (including remastering), motion picture projection activities (including cinemas), renting of VCDs and DVDs" (Ministry of Culture, Community and Youth, 2019, p. 17). In Hong Kong, film and video are combined with music under the category "film, video and music". The category includes "motion picture, video and television programme production activities, sound recording and music publishing activities, photographic activities; reproduction of recorded media, manufacture of musical instruments; as well as wholesale, retail and renting of music and video recordings" (HKSAR, 2019).

Comparative Employment Statistics of Creative Sectors

From Table 7.2, it can be seen that with regard to the proportion of employment in the creative industries, Hong Kong outstrips Singapore by nearly four times. Heavy censorship creates a stifling atmosphere which in turn manifests itself in a lower proportion of people wanting to work in the creative industries as well as there being less jobs created in those industries. These data are supported by the employment statistics of several creative sectors in the two societies.

From Tables 7.3, 7.4, 7.5, and 7.6, it can be seen that Hong Kong has a higher proportion of its workforce working in various creative subsectors compared to Singapore. At the very least, Hong Kong has double the proportion of workers that Singapore has in the same sector (visual arts; film, video, and music); at the most extreme, it has seven to eight times that of Singapore (cultural heritage).

Some of the dissonance can be attributed to the differences in definition and scope of each sector by Singapore and Hong Kong, particularly for visual arts, which could in turn mean that the gap between the two

Table 7.2 Percentage of workforce employed in creative industries

Country	*% of workforce employed in creative industries*
Singapore	1.5 (2017)
Hong Kong	5.7 (2015)

Source: Cultural Statistics from MCCY Singapore (2019) and HKSAR (2019)

Table 7.3 Number of people employed in the cultural heritage industry and percentage of the labour force that it comprises

Year	*Total employment in cultural heritage in Singapore (rounded off to nearest hundred)*	*% of Singapore's Labour force (up to 3 s.f)*	*Total employment in cultural Heritage in Hong Kong (rounded off to nearest ten)*	*% of Hong Kong's Labour force (up to 3 s.f)*	*Ratio of % (Singapore) and % (Hong Kong)*
2012	1000	0.0298	–	–	–
2013	1000	0.029	9420	0.244	1: 8.4
2014	1300	0.0368	10430	0.269	1: 7.31
2015	1300	0.036	10800	0.277	1: 7.69
2016	1400	0.0381	11870	0.303	1: 7.95
2017	1500	0.041	12270	0.311	1: 7.59

Source: Author's reconstruction from MCCY Singapore and HK Census and Statistics Department

Table 7.4 Number of people employed in the publishing industry and percentage of the labour force that it comprises

Year	*Total employment in publishing in Singapore (rounded off to nearest hundred)*	*% of Singapore's labour force (up to 3 s.f)*	*Total employment in publishing in Hong Kong (rounded off to nearest ten)*	*% of Hong Kong's labour force (up to 3 s.f)*	*Ratio of % (Singapore) and % (Hong Kong)*
2012	7200	0.214	–	–	–
2013	7000	0.203	43900	1.14	1: 5.62
2014	7400	0.21	42660	1.1	1: 5.24
2015	7300	0.202	40810	1.05	1: 5.2
2016	7300	0.199	39090	0.997	1: 5
2017	6800	0.186	37730	0.956	1: 5.14

Source: Author's reconstruction from MCCY Singapore and HK Census and Statistics Department

Table 7.5 Number of people employed in the visual arts industry and percentage of the labour force that it comprises

Year	*Total employment in visual arts in Singapore (rounded off to nearest hundred)*	*% of Singapore's labour force (up to 3 s.f)*	*Total employment in visual arts in Hong Kong (rounded off to nearest ten)*	*% of Hong Kong's labour force (up to 3 s.f)*	*Ratio of % (Singapore) and % (Hong Kong)*
2012	6800	0.202	–	–	–
2013	7300	0.212	18430	0.478	1: 2.26
2014	8500	0.241	19240	0.497	1: 2.06
2015	7700	0.213	18810	0.482	1: 2.26
2016	7600	0.207	18120	0.462	1: 2.23
2017	7200	0.197	17760	0.450	1: 2.28

Source: Author's reconstruction from MCCY Singapore and HK Census and Statistics Department

Table 7.6 Number of people employed in the film, video, and music industry and percentage of the labour force that it comprises

Year	*Total employment in film, video, and music in Singapore (rounded off to nearest hundred)*	*% of Singapore's labour force (up to 3 s.f)*	*Total employment in film, video, and music in Hong Kong (rounded off to nearest ten)*	*% of Hong Kong's labour force (up to 3 s.f)*	*Ratio of % (Singapore) and % (Hong Kong)*
2012	5600	0.167	–	–	–
2013	5400	0.157	14990	0.389	1: 2.48
2014	6200	0.176	14960	0.387	1: 2.2
2015	5900	0.163	15050	0.386	1: 2.37
2016	5400	0.147	14840	0.379	1: 2.58
2017	5600	0.153	14970	0.379	1: 2.48

Source: Author's reconstruction from MCCY Singapore and HK Census and Statistics Department

societies are closer than the data indicate. That said, the categories that are similarly defined and scoped like publishing demonstrate a high level of dissonance between Singapore and Hong Kong, in favour of the latter. This strongly suggests that the heavier and more comprehensive censorship policies that Singapore have in place has led to a more diminished job market in creative sectors compared to Hong Kong.

Economic Contribution of Creative Sectors
A similar pattern of Hong Kong's creative industries being more vibrant when compared to Singapore emerges with respect to the economic contribution.

Tables 7.7, 7.8, 7.9, 7.10, and 7.11 indicate that Hong Kong's creative sectors contribute more to its economy, both in terms of absolute value and proportion of GDP. At the most extreme, the contribution is 20 times (cultural heritage) that of Singapore in the equivalent sector. This stark difference also plays itself out in the United Nations Conference on Trade and Development creative economy profile of each society (Tables 7.12 and 7.13).

Creative Industries Trade Performance
The values of Singapore's creative industry exports and imports pale in comparison to Hong Kong's (Tables 7.12 and 7.13). This is therefore consistent with the notion that Hong Kong has a much more vibrant creative economy, in terms of both exporting and importing creative goods and services, compared to Singapore. In addition, UNCTAD's profile on Hong Kong identified that the country "has developed a leading edge in key areas of creative industries like film, television, music, design, architecture, advertising, digital entertainment, and publishing and printing" (UNCTAD, 2018, p. 132).

Table 7.7 Total value-added of the performing arts industry and the percentage of GDP that it comprises

Year	*Total value-added of the performing arts in Singapore from 2010 to 2017 (in million Singapore dollars)*	*% of Singapore's GDP (up to 3 s.f)*	*Total value-added of the performing arts in Hong Kong from 2010 to 2017 (in million Hong Kong dollars)*	*% of Hong Kong's GDP (up to 3 s.f)*	*Ratio of % (Singapore) and % (Hong Kong)*
2012	164.7	0.0447	–	–	–
2013	160.2	0.0416	9420	0.441	1: 10.6
2014	181.3	0.0454	10430	0.462	1: 10.2
2015	198.5	0.0469	10800	0.45	1: 9.6
2016	185.7	0.0422	11870	0.477	1: 11.3
2017	174.5	0.037	12270	0.461	1: 12.5

Source: Author's reconstruction from MCCY Singapore and HK Census and Statistics Department

Table 7.8 Total value-added of the cultural heritage industry and the percentage of GDP that it comprises

Year	*Total value-added of cultural heritage in Singapore from 2010 to 2017 (in million Singapore dollars)*	*% of Singapore's GDP (up to 3 s.f)*	*Total value-added of cultural heritage in Hong Kong from 2010 to 2017 (in million Hong Kong dollars)*	*% of Hong Kong's GDP (up to 3 s.f)*	*Ratio of % (Singapore) and % (Hong Kong)*
2012	93.4	0.0253	–	–	–
2013	86.6	0.0225	9420	0.441	1: 19.6
2014	91.8	0.023	10430	0.462	1: 20.1
2015	115.5	0.0273	10800	0.45	1: 16.5
2016	110.6	0.0251	11870	0.477	1: 19
2017	120.1	0.0254	12270	0.461	1: 18.2

Source: Author's reconstruction from MCCY Singapore and HK Census and Statistics Department

Table 7.9 Total value-added of the publishing industry and the percentage of GDP that it comprises

Year	*Total value-added of publishing in Singapore from 2010 to 2017 (in million Singapore dollars)*	*% of Singapore's GDP (up to 3 s.f)*	*Total value-added of the publishing in Hong Kong from 2010 to 2017 (in million Hong Kong dollars)*	*% of Hong Kong's GDP (up to 3 s.f)*	*Ratio of % (Singapore) and % (Hong Kong)*
2012	473.1	0.128	–	–	–
2013	432.2	0.112	43900	2.05	1: 18
2014	466.2	0.117	42660	1.89	1: 16.2
2015	455.9	0.108	40810	1.7	1: 15.7
2016	475.3	0.108	39090	1.57	1: 14.5
2017	455.2	0.0964	37730	1.42	1: 14.7

Source: Author's reconstruction from MCCY Singapore and HK Census and Statistics Department

The contrast is stark. The World Intellectual Property Office confirms that while Singapore exhibits low levels of creative outputs, Hong Kong is praised for being "1st in the world" in this aspect (World Intellectual Property Office, 2019, p. 6).

Table 7.10 Total value-added of the visual arts industry and the percentage of GDP that it comprises

Year	*Total value-added of visual arts in Singapore from 2010 to 2017 (in million Singapore dollars)*	*% of Singapore's GDP (up to 3 s.f)*	*Total value-added of visual arts in Hong Kong from 2010 to 2017 (in million Hong Kong dollars)*	*% of Hong Kong's GDP (up to 3 s.f)*	*Ratio of % (Singapore) and % (Hong Kong)*
2012	546.4	0.148	–	–	–
2013	552.7	0.144	13633	0.638	1: 4.43
2014	639.4	0.160	12199	0.540	1: 3.38
2015	608.9	0.144	10157	0.424	1: 2.94
2016	617.3	0.140	8020	0.322	1: 2.3
2017	630.3	0.134	8871	0.334	1: 2.49

Source: Author's reconstruction from MCCY Singapore and HK Census and Statistics Department

Table 7.11 Total value-added of the film, video, and music industry and the percentage of GDP that it comprises

Year	*Total value-added of film, video, and music in Singapore from 2010 to 2017 (in million Singapore dollars)*	*% of Singapore's GDP (up to 3 s.f)*	*Total value-added of film, video, and music in Hong Kong from 2010 to 2017 (in million Hong Kong dollars)*	*% of Hong Kong's GDP (up to 3 s.f)*	*Ratio of % (Singapore) and % (Hong Kong)*
2012	284.4	0.0771	–	–	–
2013	322	0.0837	3524	0.165	1: 1.97
2014	340.3	0.0853	3106	0.137	1: 1.61
2015	344.3	0.0813	3469	0.145	1: 1.78
2016	374.7	0.0851	3713	0.149	1: 1.75
2017	416.9	0.0883	3930	0.148	1: 1.68

Source: Author's reconstruction from MCCY Singapore and HK Census and Statistics Department

This gulf in the creative economy is also found in a 2016 McKinsey study, which found that Hong Kong's digital music market is also estimated to be twice as valuable as Singapore's as seen in Fig. 7.1. Furthermore, Singapore's position is also low-ranked for an Asian

Table 7.12 Value of exports of creative industries

Creative industries trade performance (in millions USD)			
Year	*Singapore*	*Hong Kong*	*Ratio between Singapore and Hong Kong*
2005	2,188.51	26,446.10	1: 12.1
2006	2,516.01	26,959.20	1: 10.7
2007	7,612.43	32,889.80	1: 4.32
2008	8,687.81	34,789.70	1: 4
2009	7,555.28	29,806.40	1: 3.95
2010	9,666.27	29,829.60	1: 3.09
2011	10,585.08	33,843.40	1: 3.2
2012	11,214.67	34,144.90	1: 3.05
2013	11,157.33	31,684.50	1: 2.84
2014	10,900.36	29,824.30	1: 2.74

Source: UNCTAD country profiles (2018)

Table 7.13 Value of imports of creative industries

Creative industries trade performance (in millions USD)			
Year	*Singapore*	*Hong Kong*	*Ratio between Singapore and Hong Kong*
2005	3,079.13	19,857.00	1: 6.45
2006	3,267.90	21,832.30	1: 6.68
2007	5,391.15	28,362.30	1: 5.26
2008	6,207.33	31,345.50	1: 5.05
2009	5,127.69	27,758.50	1: 5.41
2010	6,731.00	29,511.80	1: 4.38
2011	7,631.42	36,563.60	1: 4.79
2012	9,080.68	37,659.60	1: 4.15
2013	9,301.82	36,550.20	1: 3.93
2014	8,667.75	37,284.10	1: 4.3

Source: UNCTAD country profiles (2018)

economic powerhouse, with countries like Malaysia, Thailand, and Indonesia all ahead of it in the same study.

Quantity and Quality of Creative Goods

Another way to 'estimate' the effects of censorship policies (or the lack thereof) is through the quantity and quality of creative goods produced by members of that society. I have chosen to examine the quantity and quality of local films in the individual societies (Tables 7.14 and 7.15), as well as

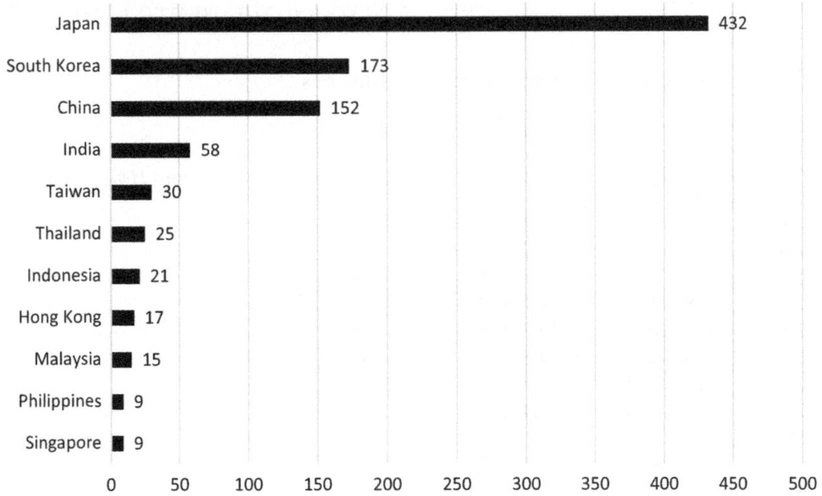

Fig. 7.1 Estimated size of the digital music market in 2015, by country (in million USD). (Source: Estimated digital music market size in 2015 (McKinsey, 2016))

Table 7.14 Number of local films produced annually

	Number of local films	
Year	*Singapore*	*Hong Kong*
2000	1	95
2001	3	126
2002	2	92
2003	3	79
2004	2	64
2005	8	55
2006	11	51
2007	13	60
2008	17	67
2009	9	51
2010	13	54
2011	14	59
2012	12	52
2013	14	43
2014	26	52
2015	17	59
2016	13	61
2017	13	53
2018	12	53
2019	12	46

Source: Social Indicators of Hong Kong, Hong Kong Council of Social Service (2021), and Hong Kong Trade and Development Council (2020). Film Director, IMDA Database (2021)

Table 7.15 Number of local films that make it to the yearly top 10 grossing

	Number of local films in top 10 grossing films	
Year	*Singapore*	*Hong Kong*
2003	0	6
2004	0	2
2005	0	2
2006	1	1
2007	0	3
2008	1	2
2009	0	1
2010	0	2
2011	0	2
2012	0	1
2013	0	2
2014	0	1
2015	1	1
2016	0	2
2017	0	0
2018	0	1
2019	0	0

Source: List of top 10 grossing films (Box Office Mojo, 2020) by Box Office Mojo

Table 7.16 Number of new albums released by top five artistes

	Number of albums (excluding singles, eps, and compilations)			
	Artiste	*Hong Kong*	*Artiste*	*Singapore*
1.	Roman Tam	32	JJ Lin	10
2.	Anita Mui	31	Stefanie Sun	14
3.	Eason Chan	38	Kit Chan	18
4.	Faye Wong	25	A-Do	8
5.	Andy Lau	54	Tanya Chua	18

Source: Selection of artistes based on lists (The World of Chinese, 2014; Ong, 2017). Data provided by Discogs (2021), online music database, correct as of 14 Nov 2021

the number of original albums by the top singers of each society (Table 7.16). Films and music were chosen as they are among the most ubiquitous creative goods produced and consumed. Note that local films refer to film that directed or co-directed by a local and not simply films that are filmed on the territory.

It can be seen from Table 7.14 that Hong Kong has produced more films than Singapore every year between 2000 and 2019. At its peak in 2005, Hong Kong produced 57 more films than Singapore. In addition, Table 7.15 depicts Hong Kong consistently having more local films in their top 10 grossing films for the year compared to Singapore, highlighting that Hong Kong films tend to appeal to the local population more than Singaporean films which in turn suggests the gulf in quality between films produced by both societies. Both sets of statistics support the argument that Hong Kong's less heavy-handed approach to censorship has resulted in a more vibrant and competitive creative economy.

A similar trend bears out with regard to the music industry. Table 7.16 identifies the top five musicians from each country based on publicly available lists. The total number of albums of each musician is then counted from the same music database. The results show that Hong Kong outperforms Singapore. It is also worth mentioning that few, if any, of the Singaporean singers are actually based in Singapore; JJ Lin for instance is based in Taiwan.

These results are significant especially if one considers that Hong Kong has not had much governmental support to develop its film industry in the past three decades. Leung (2018) highlights that the Hong Kong government has not been as willing to contribute more monetary resources to support the local arts scene. On the other hand, Singapore enjoys fairly strong state support. This should in theory provide Singapore with a better chance of success at developing its film industry. However, that does not seem to be the case given the data.

The level of support (or lack thereof) provided by both societies is supported by the Economist Intelligence Unit 2014 report on the "creativity productivity" of various societies. The report also supports the idea that Hong Kong produces more creative goods. Table 7.17 depicts the level of input and output that Singapore and Hong Kong has. For inputs, Singapore is ranked first, while Hong Kong is ranked second. However, when it comes to outputs, the former is ranked sixth, while the latter is ranked second. This indicates that the quality and quantity of Singapore's creative outputs, films included, pales in comparison to Hong Kong. In addition, the report highlights that film outputs are one of Singapore's main areas of lack (Asian Development Bank & Economist Intelligence Unit, 2014).

Table 7.17 Creativity Productivity Index comparing level of input vs. level of output

Creativity productivity index		
	Singapore	*Hong Kong*
Input Ranking (out of 24)	1	2
Output Ranking (out of 24)	6	2
Overall Ranking (out of 24)	10	7

Source: Creative Productivity Index (2014) by Asian Development Bank and Economist Intelligence Unit

Beyond ranking inputs and outputs, the report also provides an overall ranking which factors in how effectively and efficiently a society converts its inputs into outputs. Hong Kong is ranked seventh and Singapore tenth which indicates that Hong Kong is creatively more productive compared to Singapore. The ranking of tenth puts Singapore below Laos (ranked ninth) even though the latter has a GDP per capita of $2,542.5 (Singapore has a GDP per capita of US$64,581.9, World Bank, 2020).

In sum, the Economist Intelligence Unit 2014 report supports the argument that Singapore's comprehensive approach to censorship has negative ramifications on the creative economy. The lack of funding is demonstrably not the main reason for Singapore's relatively poor performance with regard to creative goods output. Given that one can eliminate funding as a reason, censorship thus emerges as a key explanation.

Comparative Qualitative Analysis

Consonant with the overall approach of this study, it is insisted here that quantitative statistics should never be taken at face value. The quantitative analysis in the previous section is triangulated here with original qualitative data which have been obtained in the form of interviews and a cross-national survey.

Survey Results

Generally, most youths across both nations are more heavily involved in the arts than their adult counterparts. However, there is a slightly higher interest in the arts in Hong Kong than in Singapore, especially amongst adults (Figs. 7.2 and 7.3).

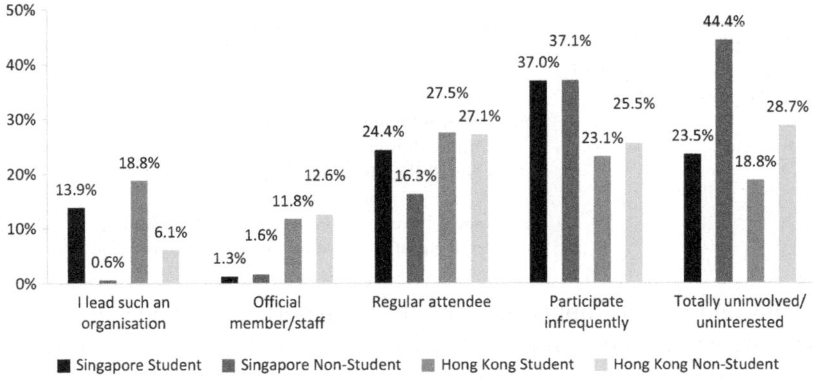

Fig. 7.2 Survey response: "How involved are you with arts and culture groups?"

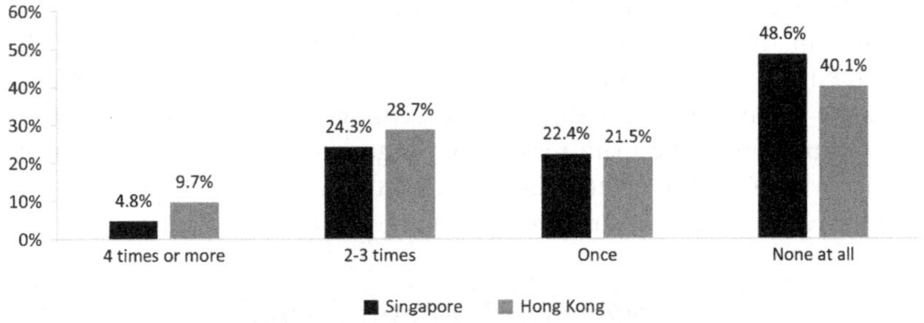

Fig. 7.3 Survey response: "Over the past month, how many times have you attended a concert or event by a local home-grown artiste"?

I also paid particular attention to students, to gauge their interest in pursuing arts-related careers. Consonant with my overall findings, Singaporean youths had a lower interest in such careers than their Hong Kong counterparts, based on Fig. 7.4, which registers the degree of interest in each career, with a higher integer reflecting a stronger desire.

Additionally, most youths are also unsure about the prospects of an arts-based career, which is not unusual. However, there is a slightly higher proportion of Hong Kong youths who would more readily consider it (Fig. 7.5).

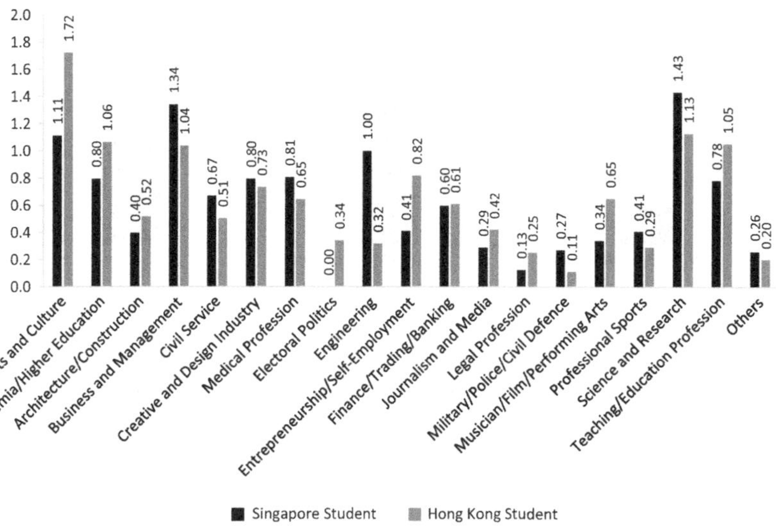

Fig. 7.4 Survey response: "What is your ideal career path?"

Aside from testing students' views, I also wanted to gauge adults' perceptions towards the arts, by asking if they would encourage their child to enter the industry. This is a relevant question, considering the long-standing perception of Asian parents discouraging the humanities in favour of STEM fields instead. I found that most parents would not discourage their child from pursuing arts-based careers in general, but they do display clear preferences for some over others, with STEM fields being more favoured while politics in Singapore and gaming in Hong Kong are the most discouraged (Figs. 7.6, 7.7 and 7.8).

Interviews Conducted

I also conducted a total of 10 interviews with Singaporean arts practitioners and 11 interviews with Hong Kong arts practitioners, some of whom decided to remain anonymous. The findings are consonant with my larger argument, that is, in Singapore, the pervasive role of the state, especially its censorship activities, has adversely affected the arts scene. Surely, arts practitioners in Hong Kong face challenges too; they have in fact reported a high degree of uncertainty given the political climate and resentment with the high costs of living.

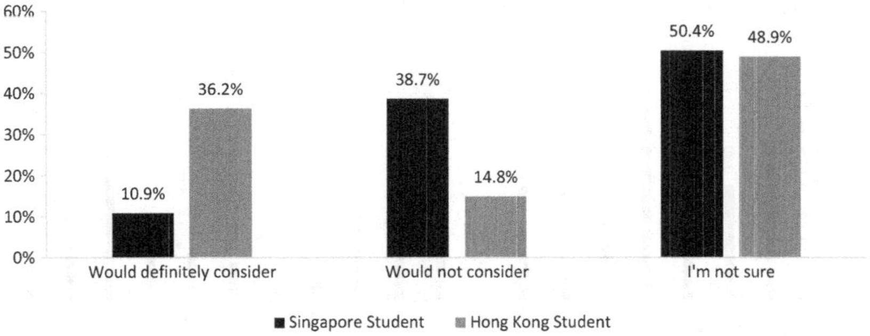

Fig. 7.5 Survey response: "How much do you agree with the following statement: 'I would consider pursuing a career in the arts, music, and entertainment industry in my country.'"

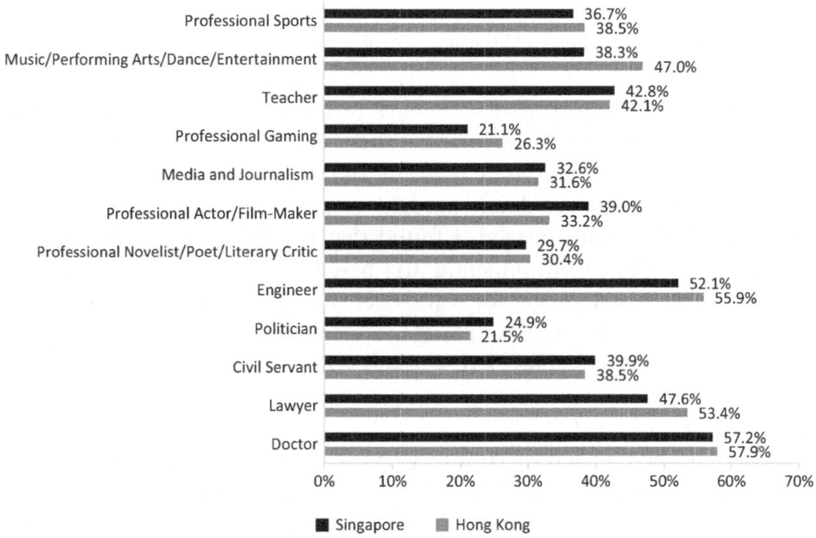

Fig. 7.6 Response "Will encourage my child" to "Would you encourage your child to take up the following occupations?"

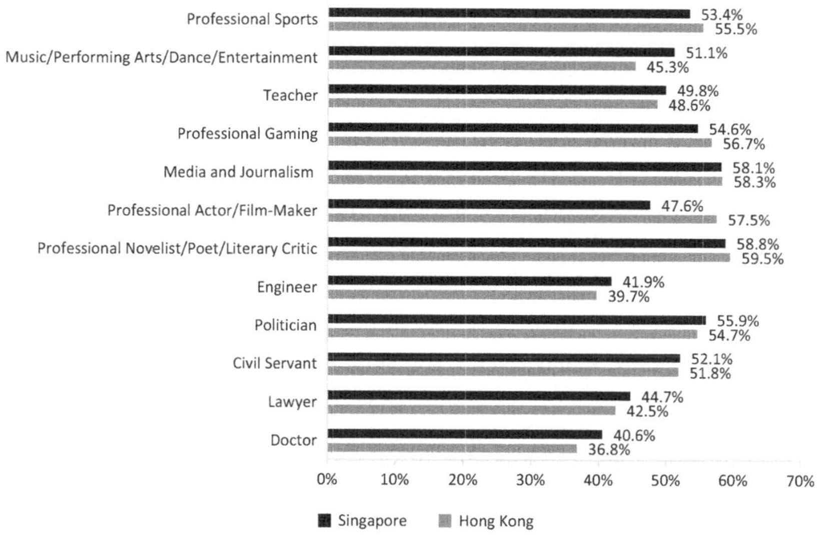

Fig. 7.7 Response "Neutral" to "Would you encourage your child to take up the following occupations?"

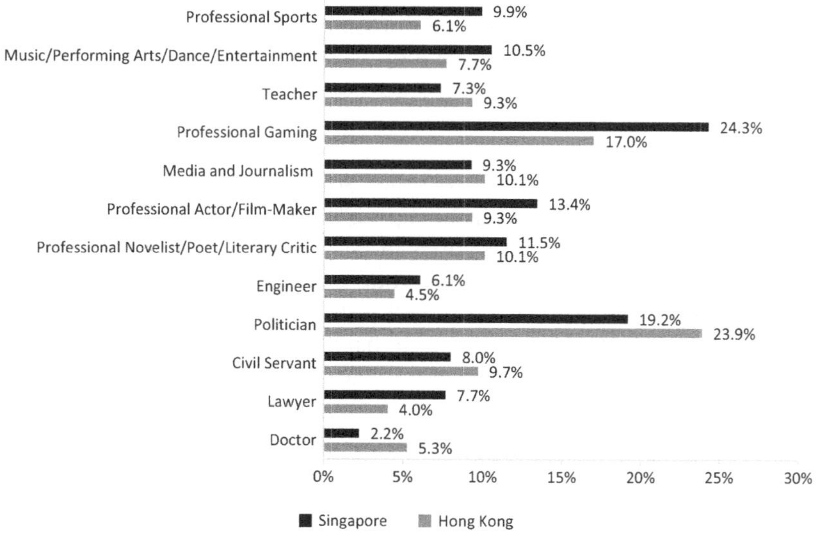

Fig. 7.8 Response "Will discourage my child" to: "Would you encourage your child to take up the following occupations?"

Censorship is a Problem in Singapore

Ng Yi-Sheng (2011), a prominent Singapore gay writer, reported on a case of censorship during the Singapore Biennale 2011. Award-winning Japanese-British artist Simon Fujiwara's artwork was to be displayed but it was censored two weeks into the event after foreign press reviews. Ng (2011) argues that such an attempt to paint a more liberal image of Singapore is nothing but a veneer and censorship will ultimately deter other international artists from wanting to display their works in Singapore, citing that there will be no artist who "is going to be fool enough to show his work here".

Interviews with Singaporean arts practitioners allude to the phenomenon of censorship. When asked if the Singapore government has provided an adequate amount of support (financial or otherwise), Melissa Lim, the general manager of The Necessary Stage (TNS),[11] a dramaturge for a few TNS's productions and the executive producer of the M1 Singapore Fringe Festival, echoes the statistics provided by the EIU report, citing that "it's only fair to say that we are getting a good amount of support". She also credited the government for having "initiatives to promote community art and participation". However, she highlighted that there needs to be other forms of non-financial support such as the reform of censorship laws, though she did not elaborate.

In addition, it is interesting that practitioners that belong to an organisation such as Melissa tend to be more reticent about the heavy-handed censorship compared to individual practitioners. For instance, when Sonny Liew, author of the (in)famous comic book *The Art of Charlie Chan Hock Chye*, was asked the same question, he acknowledged the relatively high amount of funding compared to other South East Asian countries but focused on the presence of censorship via the mechanism of gatekeepers. He highlighted how the authorities in charge of approving funding and grants "tend not to support what they see as anti-establishment viewpoints", further adding that authorities justify their actions by arguing that "you cannot expect the government to hand out public funds to folks who express anti-government sentiments". He also described the culture of anxiety amongst arts practitioners as "real". Kenneth Chia, a Singaporean playwright, seconded the role of gatekeepers, citing how the "most well-funded works are of course, those which promote and support

[11] TNS is a Singaporean non-profit theatre company established in 1987.

state-sanctioned narratives and the policy of the day".[12] The framework is described as "obsessive, restrictive and bogged down by red-tape" which strongly hints at heavy censorship.

Beyond laying out the presence of censorship, the interviews with Singaporean art practitioners reveal the effects that the censorship has on the vibrancy of the local arts scene, which are twofold.

One aspect is the reluctance of young Singaporeans to join the arts scene as professionals, even if they have a profound interest in the arts. When asked how to make Singapore's art scene more vibrant, the playwright Kenneth Chia answered that it is a matter of "letting go and letting loose". He expressed that "we have all the pieces in place, but are held back by the state's paranoia, outdated belief systems and lack of nuanced understanding of our own arts scene". In addition, he pointed out that the state's heavy interference is exerted in a "fickle and unpredictable" manner which causes "artists [to] continue to get the short end of the stick". This generates a tremendous level of stress which in turn hold potential artists back from pursuing a full-time career in the arts.

An interesting pattern that emerged in the interview process concerns multiple individuals who identify as LGBT, all of whom felt compelled to migrate from Singapore to Hong Kong in search for a freer environment for creative expression.[13] A 26-year-old youth in the fashion industry who confided in this author shared that he "did not feel welcome in his community (in Singapore)", which led him to apply for emigration at the earliest opportunity; he now operates in the similar field at a leading retail boutique in central Hong Kong. Another similar experience involves a 28-year-old aspiring writer with an interest in feminist literature and who identities as lesbian. She shared that "there's simply no market in Singapore for such things", and thus emigrated to Hong Kong recently and now works for a rights-advocacy organisation there.

Additionally, individuals are also held back due to the stress over the financial viability of a creative career. In part due to the conservative preference of parents for the hard sciences, business, and technology-related disciplines, some youth perceive a creative career to be low-paying. Even when artists do not mind drawing a less stable and lower sum of money, the amount is often not worth the level of stress that the job comes with.

[12] Interview with Kenneth Chia, Singaporean filmmaker, February 2019.

[13] There were four such individuals interviewed in November 2019, all who refused to be named.

Specifically, concerns over finances tend to come from those whose works challenge government narratives. After all, most of the money put aside for arts is granted to pro-establishment views and projects. A theatre specialist this author interviewed shared about the stress he faced when submitting a grant application to the government, and the many rounds of reviews he had to undergo. The chilling effect such practices may cause inadvertently compels practitioners to make a choice between a sustainable livelihood and artistic creativity. If the former is chosen over the latter, artistic creativity is compromised.

Another aspect is the reduced quality of "artistic goods". Sonny Liew commented that "an environment where some choices are not punished would allow for a much richer and more diverse arts scene".[14] He added that "Aside from the right to criticise, I'd also argue that the voices of the lower-income public would tend to be more critical of the establishment, so cutting off funding from such views means perpetuating an arts scene dominated by the middle-income and up". This implies that the content produced is compromised as it only represents a narrow and singular viewpoint. To this end, he also cited an interview with a foreign arts practitioner who quipped that "culture will die if obedience to power becomes a requisite for receiving public funding".

Political Uncertainty and High Costs are a Problem in Hong Kong

I do not assume that Hong Kong's arts scene has faced no challenges. The two major problems are the political uncertainty that the city has increasingly experienced over the past decade and also the high costs of living.

Arts practitioners I spoke to explained that while they are generally not the target of censorship during most of Hong Kong's history, the constitutional crisis over the city's future has indeed affected the economy. A bookstore owner and publisher explained that her sales have gone down gradually over the past five years, and that she has experienced a deficit in recent years due to multiple rounds of political street protests.[15] Business planning and financial and manpower management have become difficult with volatility. She expressed her concern about the economy-wide disruption to the city-state as a whole, and the prospects of her trade.

[14] Interview with Sonny Liew, bestselling Singaporean author, December 2019.

[15] Interview with business owner in Hong Kong's publishing industry, December 2018.

Her sentiments are echoed by an international trade lawyer who resides in Hong Kong, having moved there from Singapore.[16] Having the benefit of living in both cities, he admits that "Hongkongers definitely have a higher risk appetite" and that they are "more daring in what they say, and push the limits further". This was highlighted in the context of press freedom and how "Hong Kong has traditionally been a bastion of freedom of the press". This same risk-taking attitude could just as easily be found in the arts and creative industry, whereby arts practitioners push the social and political boundaries in their respective fields. Of course the opposite applies to Singapore, whereby "heavy handedness [has] influence(d) how people view civil liberties" and resulted in a society where "Singaporeans themselves are very quick to self-police and criticise anyone who steps outside of the traditional mold". This results in a society that is "generally quite 'cookie cutter', (which) reinforces the existing structures".

The criticism of Singapore as a "cookie-cutter" society echoes public comments made by a local Singaporean entrepreneur who was responsible for organising Singapore's first and largest night market, Artbox Asia. Lee Haoming (2018), co-founder of Invade and the lead organiser, faced what he deemed as overly precautionary government restrictions when he pitched his project to officials. Personal feedback provided to the present author revealed that his contacts in other East Asian nations faced less bureaucratic experiences.[17]

Hong Kongers face uncertainty about the financial viability of an arts career. The concern by both the bookstore owner and trade lawyer is that "being an artist in Hong Kong is difficult because of the high rent. Artists need space to practice, perform, paint, gather, debate, discuss, and because real estate in Hong Kong is expensive, that just gets baked into everyone's profit margins. In such an environment, people generally push towards banking, finance, logistics for career choices". Sarah Dyson from Faust International Youth Theatre confirms this, sharing that "space is expensive to rent a lot of theatre gets unseen because people cannot travel so far."[18] This is consonant with my finding in Chap. 3 about the market dominance in real estate as a potential contributing factor to the high land and property prices in Hong Kong.

[16] Interview with international trade lawyer from Hong Kong, December 2018.

[17] Interview with Lee Haoming, co-founder of Invade, February 2019.

[18] Interview with Sarah Dyson, Education Outreach Manager from Faust International Youth Theatre, January 2019.

A PR and marketing associate who works in a leading fashion brand in Hong Kong shares similar thoughts. He explained that pursuing an arts-based career requires one to pursue a sense of "self-actualisation", but that this is unfortunately made difficult because "most youths are worried about the bread-and-butter issues of rising unemployment, high rents and rising authoritarianism". This brings to mind a separate interview conducted four months before with a group of three undergraduates from HKU, Alice, Lorenz, and Joe, who collectively shared their worry about future prospects in Hong Kong. Alice candidly shared the following: "many of my friends are just looking to find a job, whether in arts or not is not the matter (roughly translated from Cantonese)". Her expression of concern is in part associated with a larger chorus of similar sentiments reported in the media in the past few years (see Lo, 2016; Ng & Woo, 2018). Lorenz and Joe both also echoed these sentiments and have formulated active plans to pursue overseas educational opportunities with the possibility of full emigration.

In conclusion, the arts are an important metric of a nation's economic competitiveness, especially in its creative and innovation capabilities. Both Singapore and Hong Kong face challenges in this scene, albeit for different reasons. While both have seen challenges, the data provided here *on net* show that the creative industries in Singapore have not performed proportionately to the level of state support provided. This constitutes a strong reason to reject the developmental state growth model.

References

Ash, T. G. (2008, September 11). China, Russia and the new world disorder. *The Los Angeles Times*. http://www.latimes.com/news/opinion/la-oe-ash11-2008sep11,0,5312908.story

Asian Development Bank & Economist Intelligence Unit. (2014, August). *Creative productivity index: Analysing creativity and innovation in Asia*. Asian Development Bank: https://www.adb.org/publications/creative-productivity-index-analysing-creativity-and-innovation-asia

Box Office Mojo. (2020). *List of top 10 grossing films*. Box Office Mojo. https://www.boxofficemojo.com/chart

Choe, S.-H. (2021, November 3). From BTS to squid game: How South Korea became a cultural juggernaut. *New York Times*. https://www.nytimes.com/2021/11/03/world/asia/squid-game-korea-bts.html

Chong, Z. L. (2015, November 25). MDA lifts ban on 240 publications ranging from communist material to adult interest. *The Straits Times*. https://www.

straitstimes.com/singapore/mda-lifts-ban-on-240-publications-ranging-from-communist-material-to-adult-interest
Choo, Y. T. (2018, November 21). 3 books banned for advocating extremist religious views. *The Straits Times*. https://www.straitstimes.com/singapore/3-books-banned-for-advocating-extremist-religious-views
Chow, J. (2015, November 29). Madonna could perform in Singapore for first time. *The Straits Times*. https://www.straitstimes.com/singapore/madonna-could-perform-in-singapore-for-first-time
Chu, Y. (2002). *Local myth: Narrative production at a global age*. Student Books.
CNA. (2019a, November 25). *POFMA office directs Brad Bowyer to correct Facebook post in first use of 'fake news' law*. CNA. https://www.channelnewsasia.com/news/singapore/brad-bowyer-facebook-post-falsehood-pofma-fake-news-12122952?cid=h3_referral_inarticlelinks_24082018_cna
CNA. (2019b, December 14). *SDP directed to correct Facebook posts and article under online falsehoods law*. CNA. https://www.channelnewsasia.com/news/singapore/sdp-singapore-democratic-party-fake-news-pofma-facebook-12184352?cid=h3_referral_inarticlelinks_24082018_cna
CNA. (2019c, August 14). *Preetipls and Subhas Nair given conditional warning for 'offensive' rap video: Police*. CNA. https://www.channelnewsasia.com/news/singapore/preetipls-subhas-nair-conditional-warning-rap-video-police-11807422
CNA. (2019d, April 01). *Watain concert cancelled based on Christian community's reaction after initial approval*. CNA. https://www.channelnewsasia.com/news/singapore/watain-concert-cancelled-christian-community-reaction-shanmugam-11399434
Commission on Strategic Development. (2016). *Promotion of cultural and creative industries in Hong Kong*. HKSAR.
Discogs. (2021). *Music database*. Discogs. https://www.discogs.com/about
Florida, R. (2002, May). The rise of the creative class. *Washington Monthly*. https://washingtonmonthly.com/magazine/may-2002/the-rise-of-the-creative-class/
Florida, R. (2012). *The rise of the creative class-revisited*. Basic Books.
French, H. W. (2007, November 2). A China model, what if Beijing is right? *International Herald Tribune*.
Hadi, E. A. (2016, February 23). Madonna not allowed to perform religiously sensitive songs such as Holy Water at her concert here. *The Straits Times*. straitstimes.com/lifestyle/entertainment/madonna-not-allowed-to-perform-religiously-sensitive-songs-such-as-holy
Halper, S. (2010). *The Beijing consensus: How China's authoritarian model will dominate the twenty-first century*. Basic Books.
Han, K. (2015, March 30). Singapore police arrest 17-year-old over critical Lee Kuan Yew video. *The Guardian*. https://www.theguardian.com/world/2015/

mar/30/singapore-police-arrest-17-year-old-amos-yee-critical-lee-kuan-yew-video

Harmon, S. (2017, September 09). Art v government in Singapore: 'I fear once I leave, they will punish me'. *The Guardian*. https://www.theguardian.com/world/2017/sep/09/art-v-government-at-singapore-festival-i-fear-once-i-leave-they-will-punish-me

Helfand, D. (2008, July 26). Filmmaker uncovers the struggle of gay Muslims in 'A Jihad for Love'. *Los Angeles Times*. https://www.latimes.com/world/middleeast/la-me-beliefs26-2008jul26-story.html

HKSAR. (1997). *The basic law of the Hong Kong special administrative region of the People's Republic of China*. Hong Kong Special Administrative Region. https://www.basiclaw.gov.hk/en/basiclawtext/images/basiclaw_full_text_en.pdf

HKSAR. (2003). *2003 Policy address by chief executive*. HKSAR. https://www.info.gov.hk/gia/general/200301/08/0108141.htm

HKSAR. (2019). *The cultural and creative industries in Hong Kong*. Hong Kong Census and Statistics Department, HKSAR. https://www.statistics.gov.hk/pub/B71906FB2019XXXXB0100.pdf

Holcombe, R. (2007). *Entrepreneurship and economic progress*. Routledge.

Hong Kong Council of Social Service. (2021). *Number of films locally produced*. Social Indicators of Hong Kong. https://www.socialindicators.org.hk/en/indicators/arts_and_entertainment/21.10

Hong Kong Legislative Council. (2006). *Art and culture development in Hong Kong*. Hong Kong: Hong Kong Legislative Council.

IMDA. (2020, February 24). *Codes of practice—media*. Infocomm Media Development Authority. https://www.imda.gov.sg/regulations-and-licensing/Regulations/Codes-of-Practice/Codes-of-Practice-and-Guidelines%2D%2D-Media

Infocomm and Media Development Authority, Singapore (IMDA). (2021). *Film directory*. Infocomm and Media Development Authority, Singapore. https://www.imda.gov.sg/for-industry/sectors/Media/film/directory?search=

Krugman, P. (1994). The myth of Asia's miracle. *Foreign Affairs, 73*, 62–78.

Kurohi, R. (2020). *States Times Review's application to cancel Pofma order rejected; SDP files separate application*. [online] Straits Times. Available at: https://www.straitstimes.com/singapore/states-times-reviews-application-to-cancel-pofma-order-rejected-sdp-files-separate

Lam, L. (2019, July 26). *Man who called lift passenger 'smelly' in racist remarks gets jail, fine*. CNA: https://www.channelnewsasia.com/news/singapore/man-called-lift-passenger-smelly-racist-remarks-gets-jail-11756066

Lee, C.-C. (1998). Press self-censorship and political transition in Hong Kong. *Harvard International Journal of Press/Politics, 3*, 55–73.

Lee, F. L. (2018). Changing political economy of the Hong Kong media. *China Perspectives*, 2018(2018/3), 9–18.

Lee, H. (2018). *Artbox Asia & Invade - Mr Lee Haoming*. [online] YouTube. Available at: https://www.youtube.com/watch?v=gJ5eKfiz_Ug [Accessed 19 Sep. 2022].

Lee, F., & Chan, J. (2009). Organisational production of self-censorship in the Hong Kong Media. *International Journal of Press/Politics, 14*, 112–133.

Lee, F., & Lin, A. (2006). Newspaper editorial discourse and the politics of self-censorship in Hong Kong. *Discourse & Society, 17*, 331–358.

Leung, G. L. (2018). *Innovative and creative industries in Hong Kong*. Routledge.

Leung, L. K. (1993). *The evolution of Hong Kong as regional movie production and export centre*. Chinese University of Hong Kong.

Lim, Y. L. (2016, July 23). ISIS linked newspaper banned in Singapore. *The Straits Times*. https://www.straitstimes.com/singapore/isis-linked-newspaper-banned-in-singapore

Lo, A. (2016, October 16). So half of our youth want to leave Hong Kong? We need to make sure they have reasons to stay. *South China Morning Post*. https://www.scmp.com/comment/insight-opinion/article/2027560/so-half-our-youth-want-leave-hong-kong-we-need-make-sure

Man, C. (2020, October 23). *Film entertainment industry in Hong Kong*. Hong Kong Trade and Development Council. https://research.hktdc.com/en/article/MzExMjc4NDIz

McGray, D. (2009, November 11). *Japan's gross national cool*. Foreign Policy. https://foreignpolicy.com/2009/11/11/japans-gross-national-cool/

McKinsey. (2016). *Global media report*. McKinsey. https://www.mckinsey.com/industries/technology-media-and-telecommunications/our-insights/global-media-report-2016

Mill, J. S. (2015 (1859)). *On liberty, utilitarianism, and other essays*. Oxford University Press.

Ministry of Culture, Community and Youth, Singapore. (2019). *Singapore cultural statistics*. Ministry of Culture, Community and Youth, Singapore. https://www.mccy.gov.sg/about-us/news-and-resources/statistics/2019/jan/-/media/5526A857C8E84CD1A506C040369BC186.ashx

Ng, D., & Woo, G. (2018, May 17). Hong Kong's brain drain: Why its young are losing hope and leaving. *Channel Newsasia*. https://www.channelnewsasia.com/news/cnainsider/hong-kong-brain-drain-young-emigration-housing-prices-china-10240236

Ng, Y.-S. (2006, August 1). A look back at gay theatre in Singapore. *Fridae*. https://www.fridae.asia/gay-news/2006/08/01/1680.a-look-back-on-gay-theatre-in-singapore?n=sec

Ng, Y.-S. (2011, March). Simon Fujiwara: Censored at the Singapore Biennale 2011. *Fridae*. https://www.fridae.asia/gay-news/2011/03/25/10744.simon-fujiwara-censored-at-the-singapore-biennale-2011

OECD. (2014). *Programme for the forum on resilient economies for inclusive societies, 5–6 May.* www.oecd.org/media/oecdorg/satellitesites/oecdforum/OECD-Forum-2014-Programme.pdf
Ong, R. (2017, January 18). Rich and famous, but these 5 local artistes show that success is much more than that. *DiscoverSG.* https://discoversg.com/2017/01/18/local-artistes-made-it-big-music-scene/
Ooi, V. (1995). The best cultural policy is no cultural policy: cultural policy in Hong Kong. *International Journal of Cultural Policy, 1*(2), 273–287.
Ortmann, S. (2011). Singapore: Authoritarian but newly competitive. *Journal of Democracy, 22*, 153–164.
Otmazgin, N. (2014). A regional gateway: Japanese popular culture in Hong Kong, 1990–2005. *Inter-Asia Cultural Studies, 15*(2), 323–335.
Porter, M. (1998). *The competitive advantage of nations.* Free Press.
Rahim, L. Z., & Barr, M. (2019). *The limits of authoritarian governance in Singapore's developmental state.* Springer.
Ramo, J. C. (2004). *Beijing consensus: Notes on the new physics of Chinese power.* Foreign Policy Center.
Reporters Without Borders (2022). Singapore. [online] Reporters Without Borders. Available at: https://rsf.org/en/country/singapore
Republic of Singapore. (2020). *Constitution of the republic of Singapore.* Singapore Statutes Online. https://sso.agc.gov.sg/Act/CONS1963#pr14-
Seow, B. Y. (2018, September 10). Parliament: 11 complaints made about library books with homosexual content since 2014. *The Straits Time.* https://www.straitstimes.com/singapore/parliament-11-complaints-made-about-library-books-with-homosexual-content-since-2014
Singh, B. (2017). *Understanding Singapore politics.* World Scientific Publishing.
Tan, K. P. (2016). Choosing what to remember in neoliberal Singapore: The Singapore story, state censorship and state-sponsored Nostalgia. *Asian Studies Review, 40*, 231–249.
Teo, X. (2010, May 6). NAC cuts funding for Wild Rice. *Today.* https://www.wildrice.com.sg/images/doc/news/2010/20100506TODAY.pdf
Tham, Y.-C. (2017a, April 13). Amos Yee prosecuted for hate speech; not political dissent: Singapore to the Economist. *The Straits Times.* https://www.straitstimes.com/singapore/amos-yee-prosecuted-for-hate-speech-not-political-dissent-singapore-high-commissioner-for
Tham, Y.-C. (2017b, October 30). Four books banned for extremist content. *The Straits Times.* https://www.straitstimes.com/politics/four-books-banned-for-extremist-content
The Straits Times. (2020, January 22). MHA refutes Malaysia NGO's claims against S'pore's execution method, issues Pofma correction orders against parties. *The Straits Times.* https://www.straitstimes.com/singapore/courts-crime/mha-refutes-malaysia-ngos-allegations-against-spores-execution-method-to

The World of Chinese. (2014, April). *Top 10 Cantopop artistes*. The World of Chinese. https://web.archive.org/web/20200804003101/https://www.theworldofchinese.com/2014/04/top-ten-cantopop-countdown/

Today Online. (2019, December 26). Disney removes same-sex kiss from 'Star Wars' film in Singapore. *Today*. https://www.todayonline.com/world/disney-removes-same-sex-kiss-star-wars-film-singapore

Today Online. (2017, April 13). Amos Yee prosecuted 'for vicious statements, not political dissent'. *Today Online*. https://www.todayonline.com/singapore/amos-yee-prosecuted-vicious-statements-not-political-dissent

UNESCO. (2013). *Creative economy report 2013: Widening local development pathways*. United Nations Development Programme. www.unesco.org/culture/pdf/creative-economy-report-2013.pdf

United Nations. (2018). *Creative economy country profiles*. United Nations Conference on Trade and Development (UNCTAD). https://unctad.org/en/PublicationsLibrary/ditcted2018d3_en.pdf

Wang, K. (2020). *Hong Kong popular culture*. Palgrave Macmillan.

Wild Rice. (2014, June). Censorship and the arts: In conversation with Alfian Sa'at and Ivan Heng. *Wild Times*. https://www.wildrice.com.sg/newsletter/NL15/article01.html

Wong, C., & McDonogh, G. (2013). *Global Hong Kong*. Routledge.

Woo, M. (2009). *Cultural opportunities in economic crisis?* Zuni Organization.

Words by Bandwagon. (2015, May 27). *5 songs previously banned in Singapore*. Bandwagon Asia. https://www.bandwagon.asia/articles/5-songs-previously-banned-in-singapore

World Bank (2020). *GDP (constant 2015 US$) - Singapore, Lao PDR*. [online] World Bank. Available at: https://data.worldbank.org/indicator/NY.GDP.MKTP.KD?locations=SG-LA

World Economic Forum. (2019a). *Policy pathways for the new economy: Shaping economic policy in the fourth industrial revolution*. https://www3.weforum.org/docs/WEF_Policy_Pathways_for_the_New_Economy.pdf

World Economic Forum. (2019b). *The global competitiveness report 2019*. World Economic Forum. http://www3.weforum.org/docs/WEF_TheGlobalCompetitivenessReport2019.pdf

World Intellectual Property Office. (2019). *Hong Kong*. Global Innovation Index. https://www.wipo.int/edocs/pubdocs/en/wipo_pub_gii_2019/hk.pdf

Yahya, Y. (2018, September 21). No weight given to historian's views as he was found lacking in credibility. *Straits Times*. https://www.straitstimes.com/singapore/no-weight-given-to-historians-views-as-he-was-found-lacking-in-credibility

Yip, W. Y. (2016, February 26). Singapore cuts Obama's LGBT comments on Ellen. *The Straits Times*. https://www.straitstimes.com/lifestyle/entertainment/singapore-cuts-obamas-lgbt-comments-on-ellen-0

Yu, M. W. (1997). *History of Hong Kong Film (vol. four II)—The ninety-fifties (香港 電影史話-卷五—五十年代下)*. Sub-culture Publisher.

Yuen, S. (2017, March 21). SPH radio fined 7000 for racially insenstive remarks. *The Straits Times*. https://www.straitstimes.com/singapore/sph-radio-fined-7000-for-racially-insensitive-remarks

CHAPTER 8

Conclusion: Reconsidering Developmental State Exceptionalism

Within the political economy of development, the role the state has been subject to much debate. The economic success of East Asian countries in the late twentieth century provided vindication for some scholars who were critical of the "neoliberal consensus" of trade liberalisation, privatisation, and the rapid transition to market economies (Chang, 2006). Despite deliberately deviating from neoliberal prescriptions, East Asian countries—which consciously pursued interventionist industrial policies, infant industry protection, and state-owned enterprises—have performed well, shifting the debate in favour of those advocating an activist government.

What was unique about the East Asian model was not simply its blind use of government intervention, which is common throughout history but its claim to synthesise both state and market mechanisms in policymaking. Where market mechanisms are more efficient, the state would give way, and similarly, in critical areas of policy, the state would retain its influence. Additionally, the developmental state model is said to simultaneously enjoy state capacity and autonomy at the same time (Evans, 1994). Its embeddedness in society meant it could shape social and market forces according to its plans, and its autonomy meant that it could remain free from being captured by narrow interests. This promised to be a "third way" approach that transcended what was supposedly a crude state-market dichotomy.

B. Cheang, *Economic Liberalism and the Developmental State*,
https://doi.org/10.1007/978-3-031-08100-2_8

The political economy of Singapore, far more than any other East Asian nation, stands out as the archetype of this special synthesis. Motivated by a sense of pragmatism, Singapore's leaders embraced a policy of free trade and capital flows but, at the same time, subverted market forces by its heavy presence of government-linked corporations, industrial policy, and political paternalism. The relatively open economy existed beside a relatively closed political system which has seen the same ruling party in power since independence.

Compared with the other East Asian developmental states of Japan, South Korea, and Taiwan, Singapore has taken the developmental state model to the furthest extent. While the other three states have all transitioned to liberal democracy, Singapore remains a semi-authoritarian political system. Its state involvement in the economy has not waned but has persisted till today.

The case of Singapore lends seem to lend strong credence to the claims of developmental state theorists of the superiority of their model. The fact that Singapore ranks amongst the top few countries in various measures of living standards suggests that other nations might emulate this approach, with great benefits to follow. While no scholar would recommend any nation imitates the Singapore experience wholesale, some nonetheless commend the communitarian, state-capitalist model as a possibility worth considering. This is exactly the argument made by the Singapore-based sociologist Chua Beng Huat: "Singapore's apparent success in building an electoral parliamentary system without liberalism might suggest another path to political development, showing why social and collective responsibility is preferable to the atomising tendency of liberal capitalism" (2017, p. 184).

The East Asian model remains a worthy subject of study since Western nations today have been experiencing various challenges. These include the 2008 financial crisis, the Eurozone crisis and the debt concerns that followed soon after, and more recently, the problems in the West concerning the coronavirus outbreak. A leading champion of the East Asian model, Kishore Mahbubani (2020), argues that 2020 marks the "dawn" of an Asian century, specifically with reference to East Asia's governance. Singapore's seemingly successful use of industrial policy and developmental statism more specifically has led heterodox economist Chang Ha-Joon (2011) to consider its growth model to be an "effrontery" to various schools of economic thought, but mostly free-market economics.

The developmental state model since stepped out of the narrow context of East Asia. Today, the leading pro-interventionist paradigm is Mariana Mazzucato's (2013) "entrepreneurial state". While the developmental state's chief objective is economic growth, the entrepreneurial state's ambitions are far grander and include various social challenges of our time (Kattel & Mazzucato, 2018). It is in this context that this study recommends caution in adopting a top-down model like Singapore did.

At the same time, the case of Hong Kong is a peculiar exception. This is because the city-state continued its small government principle, a colonial vestige, up until the late twentieth century. To a lesser extent, the tradition of non-intervention remains a policy preference today. This is despite the conscious strategy of post-1997 Hong Kong administrations to resort to industrial policy more actively, mimicking Singapore. Even in recent years, the tradition of positive non-interventionism remains strong in Hong Kong governance.

This fact has meant Hong Kong constitutes an uneasy challenge to developmental state theory. Developmental state theorists, when pointing to how East Asian nations have successfully used state capitalism to great effect, understandably have left out Hong Kong from their analysis. In fact, its leading advocate, Ha-Joon Chang, rationalised that Hong Kong is merely an "exception that proves the rule" (2003, p. 108), with the rule being that policies deviating from neoliberalism can be successfully adopted.

Of course, it must be acknowledged that Hong Kong today is a very different place than it was two decades ago before its handover to China, which diminished its free-market past. Ironically, Hong Kong today has moved towards the industrial policy of Singapore and pursued more concerted government interventions, all under the shadow of authoritarian China. As some have presciently warned at the turn of the century, the handover to China would begin a process of diminishing Hong Kong's exceptional achievements under more than a century of economic liberalism (Rabushka, 1997). Thus, by no means should this book be seen as a naive defence of Hong Kong's institutions. The point being emphasised in this study is that *pre-2000*, when the institutional arrangements between developmental state Singapore and liberal Hong Kong are considered, the developmental strategies they adopted were in stark contrast.

That Singapore and (pre-2000) Hong Kong practised vastly different models of political economy in their pathway to development invites a comparative study. This is further justified by the fact that both are city-states with a roughly similar Chinese-majority demographic, a common colonial heritage, and geopolitical history as a trade-based entrepôt. The critical juncture which saw two nations diverge was the mid-twentieth century which saw Singapore develop its developmental state apparatus, while Hong Kong persisted with its colonial-type free-market model. This divergence provides an opportunity for this study to answer two research questions: first, what is the nature and role of the state in the political-economic structure of Hong Kong and Singapore in the late twentieth century? Second, how has this variation affected their development performance and prospects?

This comparative study found it necessary to begin by ascertaining the facts about the precise role of the state in the governance of both city-states, given competing portrayals of Singapore as a "neoliberal state" (Teo, 2011), an "authoritarian state" (Rodan, 2006) a "free-market beacon" (Hannan, 2019) and Hong Kong as a "neo-colonial state" (Lo & Pang, 2007), "laissez-faire state", and as a "weak state". Chapters 2, 3, and 4 juxtaposed state-market and state-society relations in Hong Kong and Singapore. We find that Singapore exemplifies the developmental state model, with Hong Kong (till 1997) remaining as a non-interventionist colonial state (Table 8.1). While both had a strong emphasis on merit-based civil service and an emphasis on being open to trade and investment, they diverged significantly in terms of the state's role in shaping industrial outcomes. Significant government intrusion exists in the Singapore case, due to its previously underestimated statutory boards and extensive government-linked corporations. The data collected for this study aimed to capture their true extent, through scrutiny of their annual reports and a recalculation of their expenditures as a percentage of the annual budget.

This institutional analysis has been necessary to avoid the weaknesses of aggregate statistics which tend to create superficial impressions of state-market dynamics. The approach of this study is influenced by the importance of comparative historical political economy in generating useful insights into the wealth of nations. This field acknowledges that (1) economic behaviour exist within a larger institutional context, that (2) historical path dependence matters, and that (3) a comparative approach is needful in analyses (Boettke et al., 2013). Qualitative data is also useful in such comparative works since "aggregate macroeconomic data is not the only data we can analyse" (Boettke et al., 2005, p. 295).

Table 8.1 Final summary of state-market relations of Singapore vs. Hong Kong

	Singapore	*Hong Kong*
Industrial policy tools	Yes, since independence	Minimal before 1997, but increasingly so since then
Strong state capacity to shape society	Yes	No, due to non-interventionist sentiment of colonial officials and loss of legitimacy since 1997
Performance legitimacy/ ideological control	Yes	No, due to weak state capacity and loss of legitimacy since 1997
Developmental state model?	Yes. Authoritarian, developmental state capitalist model with "big firm" elements (Baumol et al., 2007)	No, does not fulfil conditions of developmental state. Laissez-faire free-market model/"Entrepreneurial capitalism" of Baumol et al. (2007)

The finer contextual details of how the state is structured in relation to other institutions are necessarily obscured in large-N studies, but which may be uncovered through an in-depth, thick description that this study has employed. The distinction between product and factor markets, which had previously been neglected, is emphasised in this study, showing that while product markets in East Asia are relatively free, the state retains a commanding influence over factor markets of labour, capital, and land. Land is subject to state monopolisation, even in Hong Kong, to detrimental outcomes. The Singapore state however has gone even further by interfering also in the capital and labour market. With the use of qualitative data, I also uncover the fact that the Singapore has exercised a high degree of ideological hegemony over its citizens in a way not possible in Hong Kong, where state-society relations are far more antagonistic. Thus, the difference between Hong Kong and Singapore, as this study reveals, in terms of the true extent of state power, is more pronounced than previously conceived.

The larger implications of this study are multiple. Not only is it a corrective of dominant accounts of Singapore and Hong Kong's development as free-market success stories, it also suggests a methodological approach of understanding capitalist diversity grounded on a comparative approach with rich empirical facts. Scholars may investigate the role of myriad institutions, be they history, culture, the state on state-market relations, and economic performance.

Economic Performance Reassessed

This study also evaluates the economic performance of both Hong Kong and Singapore, particularly since 1960. Previous studies, and popular observation, have adequately established both economies to have experienced rapid economic growth in the late twentieth century, rising living standards and prosperity. Economic development, however, entails more than an increase in national income. This is based on the distinction previously articulated between catch-up growth and cutting-edge growth, of which the latter involves not just the mere accumulation of factor inputs, but also the efficient use of resources, as evident through productivity, innovation, entrepreneurship, and technological progress.

This study builds on past studies on East Asian economic performance by investigating the extent to which Hong Kong and Singapore have achieved high-quality, cutting-edge economic growth. The conventional wisdom has provided the view that Hong Kong's lack of concerted state action has caused it to fall behind in the areas of productivity, innovation, entrepreneurship, and technological progress, even though it had achieved rapid growth in national incomes the late twentieth century. This is a view supported by aggregate statistics displaying Singapore's superior ranking in innovation indices, patent statistics and productivity tables, as well as various qualitative sources.

I have provided a more nuanced argument. This book acknowledges that the developmental state approach, exemplified by Singapore, is indeed superior in terms of being able to mobilise resources and influence non-state actors to conform to its national objectives and, as a result, can achieve growth that is premised on the quantitative accumulation of factor inputs. However, when it comes to higher-quality growth, involving the need to use resources efficiently and productively, promote disruptive innovation, and encourage a culture of entrepreneurship, the developmental state approach is limited. Chapter 6 demonstrated the poor labour and total factor productivity performance in Singapore as compared to Hong Kong. A disaggregation of patent data also shows that while Singapore outspends Hong Kong in R&D, and has registered more patents per capita, innovation efficiency is comparably low, suggesting that the innovation outcomes have not reflected the scale and degree of direct government stimulation. Most of the innovation activity in Singapore is driven by large multinational corporations, which are not indicative of the underlying indigenous innovation capacity of the nation. This is despite innovation being the very target of government policy.

These insights are important because it demystifies a puzzle that had previously been present. Despite Singapore's high scores on innovation indices and patent statistics, there have been reports, albeit anecdotal, of Singaporeans being deemed as uncreative. Most famously, Steve Wozniack, the co-founder of Apple Inc., had commented that Singaporeans are too "strait-laced", and uncreative as compared to other staff he had encountered (Mahtani, 2012; Lim, 2011). How do we reconcile the high rankings with these anecdotal comments? Why has the Singapore government sought to reform its education system to foster creativity (Kuah, 2018)? This study suggests that state policy succeeds in channelling and accumulating resources to achieve specific outcomes—hence the many patents filed and high spending on R&D—but may not necessarily be effective in harnessing the latent potential of creative thinking and innovation. A more organic approach may be required for creativity and innovation to flourish.

The cultural emphasis in this study also strengthens the argument that an entrepreneurial culture remains constrained in the developmental state of Singapore. The comparative strength of creative industries in both city-states is instructive. The creative industries is a good benchmark of whether a nation has achieved high-quality, cutting-edge development characterised not by "mere perspiration" but also "inspiration", that is, one based on creative thinking, disruptive innovation, and entrepreneurship. Despite the lack of a national blueprint for developing the creative industries, Hong Kong had developed into a cultural hub in the past few decades, with a thriving film, media, and arts scene. Various sources indeed show that Hong Kong is a key exporter of cultural goods and services in Asia and beyond.

Assessing the comparative economic performance of both Singapore and Hong Kong will ultimately depend on how "economic development" is understood. If it is understood as the rapid growth in national incomes, then both have fared very well as compared to other nations, with Singapore having higher growth rates than Hong Kong since the 1970s. If it is understood as involving the ability of an economy to foster high-technology industries, then the developmental state system in Singapore has outpaced Hong Kong.

Economic development may however be understood in a more holistic fashion. It should consider aspects of cutting-edge development (inspiration), namely, how productive labour and factor inputs are used, and how innovative and creative the economy is. If one believes that a *culture* of entrepreneurial innovation is a key ingredient for a nation's economic potential, then one would bet on Hong Kong rather than Singapore.

Second, I propose that economic development should also work for *all residents* within a national community. National income may increase but often this benefits only narrow segments in society. This has often been measured by inequality statistics. Instead, I touched on whether indigenous residents enjoy a majority share of economic growth. The government's own indigenous GDP statistics suggests that the developmental state's growth strategy in Singapore, unlike Hong Kong, has led to a severe foreign-local distortion, with the fruits of economic growth largely reaped by foreign nationals rather than locals.

Theorising the Limits of the Developmental State

I conclude by providing a theoretical explanation on the importance of entrepreneurship and innovation in achieving sustainable economic development, and on why the developmental state approach in Singapore has struggled comparatively vis-à-vis Hong Kong to attain it.

The Solow growth model posited that economic growth may happen through the quantitative increase in capital and labour inputs, as well as through new ideas and technology. Growth that proceeds simply through the first approach, the accumulation of factor inputs, is called catch-up growth and is unsustainable. If economic growth is to be sustained, economies must operate along the cutting edge, that is, by generating new ideas and technology that expand a nation's productive capacity. This distinction has also been labelled by Paul Krugman as "perspiration" as opposed to "inspiration".

This study takes the above formulation as given. Various studies, both theoretical and empirical, have highlighted the importance of research and innovation in generating continued economic growth, especially in the twenty-first-century knowledge-based economic landscape (Verspagen, 2006; Porter, 2011). Previous scholars had alluded to the late twentieth-century growth performance of Hong Kong proceeded on a path of "inspiration", while Singapore had used "perspiration" instead. This study inquires whether since the early debates of the 1990s, there has been any substantial change in the growth strategy undertaken by both city-states and whether performance has changed.

Singapore achieved catch-up growth in the post-war period through the method of perspiration. The developmental state had operated on the belief that given the lack of domestic industrial capital, foreign capital, and state-linked capital had to be injected, giving the economy a "big push". This is reminiscent of the growth theories of the 1960s, which saw developing countries as lacking capital investment, and hence the need for exogenous injections of it to stimulate industrial activity. By contrast, the political environment in Hong Kong precluded this option. The British colonial government had resumed control after the war and decided to maintain its old approach of non-interventionism, partly since it had worked well previously and because it had to prioritise domestic problems at home. This meant that for the large part of the twentieth century, Hong Kong did not witness any large-scale industrialisation effort by the state, or industrial policy plans to fundamentally restructure the economy.

The Singaporean developmental state was faced, in the 1990s, with criticism about the sustainability of its growth strategy. It then started to emphasise productivity, innovation, and entrepreneurship (PIE) to achieve cutting-edge, rather than catch-up, growth. However, I argue that this new objective was pursued without any fundamental change in the underlying policy approach. The state, now moving away from the mere accumulation of capital and labour, started to encourage PIE improvements, but did so through the same method of simply directing more economic resources to this end, an approach characteristic of the developmental state. The state had wanted to achieve qualitative improvements in economic development through the same philosophy of quantitatively increasing investments in PIE.

The poor performance of Singapore is this regard can be understood through the lens of economic theory. This is best understood through the famous distinction by Lionel Robbins (1932) between technological problems and economic problems: the former being concerned with finding the most effective means to accomplish a given end, with the latter focused on allocating scarce resources across multiple competing ends. This distinction was made to explain that the study of economics was not one of mere technical maximisation, but about efficient resource allocation. This concept was further developed by James Buchanan, who in turn suggested that the economic problem was in turn broken down into three components: (1) economics was also an *exchange problem* whereby there are many conflicting and diverse ends of individuals that cannot be harmonised into some overall utility function, (2) economics was also a *coordination problem* whereby these diverse ends are satisfied in ways that require decentralised coordination between multiple actors and that (3) economics was in turn a *governance problem* whereby exchange relationships are influenced by a larger set of rules that influence behaviour.[1] These concepts explain the limits of the developmental state approach to development.

The Singapore government had channelled large amounts of resources to promote PIE improvements, through various industrial policy levers, such as subsidies, incentives, and government-linked corporations. This in turn is said to have helped Singapore become a highly prosperous and developed economy, pointing to the numerous successful industries that have been created and to high-performing SOEs and GLCs as evidence of economic success. It is said that by the 1980s, industrial policy had led to the creation of a world-class petrochemicals hub (Pillai, 2006), a successful national airline (Bowen, 1994, ch. 4), a first-rate financial services industry, and to Singapore being the "leading communications hub and largest container port" in the region (Turnbull, 2009, p. 307, 310).

The problem with this line of reasoning is that it collapses economic development into a technical problem of merely increasing the quantity of a given end, be it the construction of an airline, a seaport, or a biomedical research faciality. Industrial policy, by selectively diverting resources into a given industry, is understandably able to bring about piecemeal achievements in specific industries. This explains why Singapore has registered more patents than Hong Kong in the USPTO and has a housing system deemed superior to Hong Kong (Wong, 2015) and higher R&D spending (Fuller, 2010). These were specific ends that were maximised by the concentrated investments made by the developmental state, which were not similarly copied in Hong Kong. The comment made in an interview by Peter Ho, ex-head of Singapore civil service, that Hong Kong's economy "lacks technology" and is overly concentrated in finance and real estate, is also unsurprising, because the state had not actively restructured the economy to move into high-tech industries like Singapore did.

However, economic development is not just a technical problem of achieving specific ends as these but involves the allocation of scarce resources amongst competing ends. David Skarbek and Peter Leeson (2009) had used this insight to show how foreign aid may have made clear achievements in specific areas but has failed to generate society-wide

[1] Martin and Petersen (2019) expounded on Buchanan's concept.

development. Adam Martin and Matias Petersen (2019) also showed how poverty alleviation is multi-dimensional, and not simply a matter of increasing the wealth of the poor. Similar, I argue here that development—especially the cutting-edge kind—is also similarly an economic problem that involves allocating resources efficiently across a variety of ends. Developmental states face these trade-offs: should resources be channelled towards industry or other needs, which industries warrant assistance, and which various modes of assistance should be chosen from when providing aid to firms.

While there is good reason to be sceptical about the efficacy of industrial policy (Wong, 2011), this book willingly concedes that it has created many successful industries in Singapore.[2] However, the creation of a successful sector through industrial policy alone does not equate to or constitute development, just as successful instances of aid to build hospitals in the third world does not on its own constitute economic progress. The fundamental problem concerning the use of industrial policy is that it operates outside of the context of market rivalry, and thus it is impossible to discern whether the gain in the favoured industry outweighs the opportunity cost of other industries that may have developed in the absence of industrial policy (Powell, 2005; Lavoie, 2016). Consequently, the concept of innovation efficiency is important; Singapore has ranked outside the top 100 in this specific indicator, despite having more patents than Hong Kong and outspending it in R&D.

Additionally, the active use of industrial policy in Singapore has also led to the *inefficient use of resources*, due to the unproductive entrepreneurship encouraged by the generous flow of grants. As of the time of this writing, any local SME in Singapore is eligible for $30k worth of grants (renewed annually) at a subsidy rate of 98% on a range of digital solutions, including buying a new laptop, installing a new e-commerce site, and even installing temperature screening systems outside shopfronts. By way of illustration, any SME can engage a vendor to install a Customer Relations System costing $10k and pay only $200.[3] A different scheme allows an SME to hire a university intern at $1000/month and claim back 70% from the state. It is

[2] Some Singaporean scholars have pointed out specific industrial policy failures, such as the Suzhou industrial complex, from which the government eventually disengaged (Pereira, 2008). The point made here is different: *even if* industrial policy leads to "successes", development cannot be so easily and causally inferred to have resulted from central planning.

[3] This author made an official enquiry though the official channels to verify this.

not unreasonable to argue that such generous grants skew the incentives of business leaders towards rent-seeking activities.

Economic development, being an economic problem, also has a governance dimension to it. Economic activity occurs within a larger institutional framework, and whether specific PIE improvements can be achieved also depend on how firms and people are affected by the rules at large. The developmental state's focus on making investments into favoured industries and its employment of state-owned enterprises omit the fact that the political system that it generates will affect economic performance, however well run these enterprises are. Political repression in Singapore has stunted civil society and led to a compliant political culture, and conversely, that the arms-length approach in colonial society has led to the flourishing of grassroots political organisations in Hong Kong, especially accelerated after 1997. This has an impact on economic performance because it affects the industrial structure and people's employment choices. In lieu of this, it is unsurprising, that the creative industries in Singapore have been stunted, standing in stark contrast with the fact that Hong Kong has been a leading cultural exporter since the early success of its Cantonese film industry and Cantopop music.

Is Economic Growth Sustainable?

In this final segment, I conclude by making the argument that while Singapore has achieved higher economic growth in its recent history than Hong Kong, many of its government policies, and the institutions created, may have adversely affected its economic competitiveness. This higher economic growth in Singapore is evident by the higher rates of growth there, which started to outstrip Hong Kong from 1960 onwards. This is obvious and has been well established in the existing literature. Where this study adds value is its reflection on the economic competitiveness of both city-states.

A distinction between growth and competitiveness must be made (Table 8.2). Economic growth measures the achievement of higher output and national incomes. For economic competitiveness, I follow John Cantwell (2005), who defines it as "the possession of the capabilities needed for sustained economic growth in an internationally competitive selection environment, in which environment there are others than have an equivalent but differentiated set of capabilities of their own".

Table 8.2 Economic growth vs. economic competitiveness

	Economic growth	*Economic competitiveness*
Nature of concept	Retrospective	Forward-looking
What it measures	The growth in national output and incomes over time	The potential of a nation to sustain its growth in future
Contributing factors	Catch-up: accumulation of factor inputs Cutting-edge: improvements in productivity, innovation, entrepreneurship, and technology	A variety of institutional, political, and cultural ingredients depending on approach used

Looking at it this way, competitiveness is a forward-looking concept; it seeks to understand *how much past economic growth can be sustained in the future*, which is necessary for continually higher living standards for citizens. Thus, even if economic growth has been achieved in the past, continually rising living standards for citizens is not guaranteed if economic competitiveness is lacking.

This definition encapsulates the various competitiveness initiatives and reports pursued on a regional, national, and even firm level. The World Economic Forum, for instance, publishes the Global Competitiveness Report (GCR), which tracks the "institutions, policies and factors that determine the level of productivity in a country" and recommends actions that nations can take. A prominent intellectual influence on these competitiveness indices is the research by Michael Porter (2011), who foresaw various stages of competition between nations: factor-driven, efficiency-driven, and innovation-led competition, a rubric that neatly maps with the catch-up vs. cutting-edge distinction this study has relied upon.

Accordingly, this study has shown that even though national incomes have risen faster in Singapore since 1960, the developmental state has not achieved a comparable level of productivity, innovation, and entrepreneurship, which are key aspects of innovation-driven, cutting-edge development. The deep dive into the arts sector in this study resulted in findings consonant with the overall argument here. This suggests that the national competitiveness of the Singapore economy has been negatively hampered. The Singapore economy's ability to "sustain growth in an internationally competitive selection environment"—which is the very definition of competitiveness—may be compromised.

The top-down model of Singapore, as compared to Hong Kong's bottom-up approach, has implications on its economic future. In an uncertain economic landscape, adaptability is a crucial ingredient for success. Additionally, it has been explained that the market, if allowed to operate unhampered, is a complex adaptive system (see Lewis, 2017). Singapore's centrally planned industrial policy and absence of a strong domestic entrepreneurial class pose a problem for its ability to adapt to shifting circumstances. The Singapore economy may be analogous to a single steamliner, whereas the Hong Kong one, a network of small tugboats. Notably, Hong Kong's structural transformation from an agriculture-based economy to one based on manufacturing, and then on finance and other services, was achieved through a bottom-up adaptive process (Yu, 1998). By contrast, some scholars have pointed out how the Singapore economy seems "stuck" on a reliance on manufacturing, limiting its ability to reap the benefits of being a regional provider of services (Choy, 2010; Lim, 2018, pp. 124–135; Chia, 1989, p. 274). Problematically, successive national plans have persisted to bet on manufacturing despite ongoing de-industrialisation trends globally and increasing market opportunity in the region to provide high-quality services. Adaptation to changing circumstances requires a dynamic and unhampered market process.

The economic competitiveness of Hong Kong and Singapore, which affects whether they will be growth leaders in future, is also affected by economic culture[4] (Moon & Choi, 2001; Nukic & Braje, 2017; Sum & Jessop, 2013). Accordingly, this study argues that an important trait to consider is the extent to which citizens feel compelled to ask for permission before acting. This creates a contrast between permission-less societies, where individuals tend to colour outside the lines without necessarily seeking permission from higher authorities (act first before asking), and permission-based societies, where individuals feel a stronger need to follow hierarchical authority before taking a risk (play safe first). This particular trait of how much individuals feel compelled to seek permission before acting speaks to the very essence of entrepreneurial innovation, which most scholars, including the competitiveness advocate Michael Porter, have acknowledged to be contributing to Schumpeterian creative destruction. Permission-based societies, according to this perspective being developed, will be less competitive, that is, less able to sustain economic growth

[4] This is based on extensive previous research emphasising the importance of culture in affecting development outcomes; see, for example, Harrison (2002).

into the future through higher order improvements such as in productivity, innovation, and entrepreneurship.

Accordingly, I have interacted with numerous research subjects from both city-states in the past three years. I hosted two focus groups involving business leaders (9 participants in Hong Kong and 12 in Singapore), conducted 79 individual interviews, and ran an online survey via Pollfish[5] (551 respondents from Singapore and 476 from Hong Kong)[6] to gauge the cultural values in both places. A case can be made that Hong Kong culture is relatively more permission-less, which in part accounts for its stronger civil society, pro-democratic political culture, and higher performance in the arts. Singapore society is relatively more permission-based where economic agents have greater conformity to authority and are more reliant on state support for business expansion and where it has a weaker creative sector.

Getting the Story Right

As clarification, this study makes no projection about whether these nations will succeed or fail in the future, which will involve economic forecasts beyond the scope of this study.

Rather, a core argument in this study is that when a diverse range of data is accumulated in rich empirical detail, one benefits from deeper understanding of state-market relations and the resulting economic effects than is otherwise possible within the typical positivist paradigm. The case study approach provides a close-up analysis of institutions and micro-processes that purely quantitative, statistical studies alone cannot reveal. I emulate Huang's case study on China (2008), which showed that the earlier economic successes of the 1980s were undermined in the 1990s when a "technocratic industrial policy blueprint" (p. xv) was imposed. Similarly, I show that the post-1965 developmental state phase of Singapore's development has fostered high GDP growth rates, but also simultaneously stifled the indigenous development of a productive, innovative entrepreneurial class. Hong Kong, even though performing less impressively on raw GDP figures, has performed better on higher-order metrics of productivity, innovation, and entrepreneurship which scholars

[5] Refer to Methodological Appendix for more details.

[6] Further broken down to 238 and 229 students in Singapore and Hong Kong, respectively, and 313 and 247 non-students (21 years and above) in Singapore and Hong Kong, respectively.

today believe are crucial for the twenty-first-century landscape, even though the gap has closed somewhat after Hong Kong started mimicking the Singapore approach since 2000. Additionally, Hong Kong SMEs have not experienced the same crowding-out effect as in Singapore did due to the pervasive role of GLEs and foreign MNCs and hence contribute more to total value-add.

This is not to say that Singapore's achievements are to be dismissed, or that it will "fail", rather, it is to say that its economic performance has been far less impressive, especially when placed against pre-1997 Hong Kong, which grew in the absence of industrial policy support. Just as the Soviet Union's impressive growth was overstated, and just as China's performance has also been overstated (Huang, 2008), Singapore's performance, typically viewed as a function of rapid GDP growth, has also been overstated. The pervasive developmental state in Singapore has exhibited diminishing returns over time, while Hong Kong is currently beset by state-society upheavals which threaten to undo the positive achievements under the earlier colonial era.

References

Baumol, W., Litan, R., & Schramm, C. (2007). *Good capitalism, bad capitalism, and the economics of growth and prosperity*. Yale University Press.

Boettke, P. J., Coyne, C. J., & Leeson, P. T. (2013). Comparative historical political economy. *Journal of Institutional Economics, 9*(3), 285–301.

Boettke, P. J., Coyne, C. J., Peter, T. L., & Sautet, F. (2005). The new comparative political economy. *The Review of Austrian Economics, 18*(3–4), 295.

Bowen, J. T. (1994). *The global airline industry and economic development in Singapore*.

Cantwell, J. (2005). Innovation and competitiveness. In *The Oxford handbook of innovation* (pp. 543–567). Oxford University Press.

Chang, H. J. (2011). Reply to the comments on 'Institutions and economic development: theory, policy and history'. *Journal of Institutional Economics, 7*(4), 595–613.

Chang, H.-J. (2003). *Rethinking development economics*. Anthem Press.

Chang, H.-J. (2006). *The East Asian development experience: The miracle, the crisis and the future*. Zed Books.

Chia, S. Y. (1989). The character and progress of industrialization. In K. S. Sandhu & P. Wheatley (Eds.), *Management of success: The Moulding of modern Singapore* (pp. 250–279). Institute for Southeast Asian Studies.

Choy, K. M. (2010). Singapore's changing economic model. In T. Chong (Ed.), *Management of success: Singapore revisted* (pp. 124–138). Institute for Southeast Asian Studies.

Chua, B. H. (2017). *Liberalism disavowed: Communitarianism and state capitalism in Singapore*. Cornell University Press.

Evans, P. (1994). The state as problem and solution: Predation, embedded autonomy, and structural change. In *The state: Critical concepts* (pp. 386–425). Routledge.

Fuller, D. (2010). *Innovation policy and the limits of laissez-faire: Hong Kong's policy in comparative perspective*. Springer.

Hannan, D. (2019, January 27). Singapore shows us how we might make a success of Brexit—even if it's by accident. *The Telegraph*. Retrieved May 15, 2020, from https://www.telegraph.co.uk/politics/2019/01/27/singapore-shows-us-might-make-success-brexit-even-get-accident/

Harrison, L. (2002). *Culture matters: How values shape human progress*. Basic Books.

Huang, Y. (2008). *Capitalism with Chinese Characteristics—Entrepreneurship and the State*. Cambridge University Press.

Kattel, R., & Mazzucato, M. (2018). Mission-oriented innovation policy and dynamic capabilities in the public sector. *Industrial and Corporate Change, 27*(5), 787–801.

Kuah, A. (2018, January 18). Can we really make Singapore students imaginative and inquisitive? *Today Online*. https://www.todayonline.com/daily-focus/education/can-we-really-make-singapore-students-imaginative-and-inquisitive

Lavoie, D. (2016). *National economic planning*. Mercatus Center.

Lewis, P. (2017). The Ostroms and Hayek as theorists of complex adaptive systems: commonality and complementarity. In P. D. Aligica, P. Lewis, & V. Storr (Eds.), *The Austrian and Bloomington schools of political economy* (pp. 35–66). Emerald Publishing Limited.

Lim, K. (2011, December 15). 'Singapore far too straight-laced': Apple co-founder. *Asia One*. https://www.asiaone.com/News/AsiaOne%2BNews/Singapore/Story/A1Story20111215-316424.html

Lim, L. (2018). Beyond the "Global City" Paradigm. In L. Lim (Ed.), *Business, government and labor* (pp. 105–136). World Scientific.

Lo, K.-C., & Pang, L. (2007). Hong Kong: ten years after colonialism. *Postcolonial Studies, 10*(4), 349–356.

Mahbubani, K. (2020, April 23). Kishore Mahbubani on the dawn of the Asian century. *The Economist*. https://www.economist.com/by-invitation/2020/04/20/kishore-mahbubani-on-the-dawn-of-the-asian-century

Mahtani, S. (2012, January 6). Wozniak: Apple couldn't emerge in Singapore. *Wall Street Journal*. https://blogs.wsj.com/indonesiarealtime/2011/12/15/wozniak-apple-couldnt-emerge-in-singapore/

Martin, A., & Petersen, M. (2019). Poverty alleviation as an economic problem. *Cambridge Journal of Economics, 43*(1), 205–221.
Mazzucato, M. (2013). *The entrepreneurial state: Debunking public vs. private sector myths*. Anthem Press.
Moon, H.-C., & Choi, E.-K. (2001). Cultural impact on national competitiveness. *Journal of International and Area Studies, 8*(2), 21–36.
Nukic, I., & Braje, I. (2017). Considerations of National culture's role in explaining competitiveness. *Ekonomski Vjesnik, 30*(2), 383–397.
Pereira, A. A. (2008). The Suzhou industrial park project (1994–2001): The failure of a development strategy. *Asian Journal of Political Science, 10*(2), 122–142.
Pillai, J. (2006). Importance of clusters in industry development: A case of Singapore's petrochemical industry. *Asian Journal of Technology Innovation, 14*(2), 1–27.
Porter, M. (2011). *Competitive advantage of nations: Creating and sustaining superior performance*. Simon and Schuster.
Powell, B. (2005). State development planning: did it create an east Asian miracle? *The Review of Austrian Economics, 18*(3–4), 305–323.
Rabushka, A. (1997). *Freedom's fall in Hong Kong*. Hoover Press.
Robbins, L. (1932). *An essay on the nature and significance of economic science*. Macmillan and Co. Limited.
Rodan, G. (2006). *Singapore 'Exceptionalism'? Authoritarian rule and state transformation*. Asia Research Centre.
Skarbek, D., & Leeson, P. (2009). What can aid do? *Cato Journal, 29*, 391–397.
Sum, N.-L., & Jessop, B. (2013). A cultural political economy of competitiveness and its implications for higher education. *Journal of the Knowledge Economy, 4*(1), 24–44.
Teo, Y. Y. (2011). *Neoliberal morality in Singapore: How family policies make state and society*. Routledge.
Turnbull, C. M. (2009). *A history of Singapore, 1819–2005*. NUS Press.
Verspagen, B. (2006). Innovation and economic growth. In I. J. Fagerberg & D. C. Mowery (Eds.), *The Oxford handbook of innovation*. Oxford University Press.
Wong, J. (2011). *Betting on Biotech: Innovation and the limits of Asia's developmental State*. Cornell University Press.
Wong, R. Y. (2015). *Hong Kong land for Hong Kong People—Fixing the failures of our housing policy*. Hong Kong University Press.
Yu, T. F.-L. (1998). Adaptive entrepreneurship and the economic development of Hong Kong. *World Development, 26*(5), 897–911.

Methodological Appendix

This book is a comparative case study into the role of the state in the recent development history of the city-states of Hong Kong and Singapore. This study believes that there exist unique contextual factors in Hong Kong and Singapore which, if understood, reveal interesting insights about the dynamics of development more broadly, and thus, the case study's benefit of "holistic analysis and thick description"—in the words of John Gerring[1]—is especially welcome in this case. Since Singapore and Hong Kong both exhibited rapid development in the twentieth century, many have looked to them for lessons to be drawn, and as such, the case study design allows the researcher to ascertain "what is special", if anything, about both nations.

This study accepts that the selection of only two cases ($N = 2$) means that external validity is limited. Yet, what this study emphasises is that it is crucial to know more about less rather than less about more. Additionally, the use of comparison between Hong Kong and Singapore helps the researcher focus on their difference in state-market relations (independent variable) and the impact it has had on economic performance (dependent variable).

[1] Gerring, J. (2009). The Case Study—What it is an What it Does. In C. Boix, & S. Stokes, *The Oxford Handbook of Comparative Politics*. Oxford University Press.

B. Cheang, *Economic Liberalism and the Developmental State*,
https://doi.org/10.1007/978-3-031-08100-2

In line with the spirit of this study to generate a depth of understanding, a mixed methods approach to data collection is employed, involving both quantitative and qualitative evidence. Both types of data are triangulated one with the other in order to compensate for the inadequacies of using each in isolation. A core argument of this study is that aggregate statistics, common in development studies, may sometimes be misleading, and as such, other forms of less quantifiable data are also necessary. Thus, economic statistics are analysed in this study, but also complemented with interviews, surveys, focus groups, archival material and documentary evidence.

Of course, economic statistics have not been totally neglected however, and multiple points of this study extends and refines available statistical evidence. For instance, Chap. 2 builds on existing budget data about the size of the Singapore government and creates a new dataset by including statutory boards which were previously excluded. This dataset was in turn fed into a cross-correlation analysis in Chap. 6 to examine the relationships between GDP variables, with the aim of finding out how much government expenditure in East Asian nations drive changes in national income.

On the quantitative front, I show that measurements of economic performance must extend beyond conventional comparisons of gross domestic product, especially if one is concerned with economic competitiveness in the twenty-first century. I present available economic statistics to show that while Singapore has performed better on the pure rate of GDP growth, it lags in measurements of productivity, innovation, and entrepreneurship, especially when its local indigenous sector is concerned. By shifting the focus of economic statistics on these higher-order indicators, the "growth miracle" of Singapore becomes less impressive.

This study has particularly emphasised the use of qualitative data as well, in order to capture norms, cultural perceptions, and attitudes of various stakeholders, which are difficult to capture quantitatively. This is important because much of the "facts of the social sciences are what people think and believe",[2] and in the area of economic development specifically, cultural factors may hinder growth and government policies also

[2] Storr, Virgil Henry, The Facts of Social Sciences are What People Believe and Think (October 1, 2010). Handbook of Austrian Economics, Peter Boettke, ed., Edward Elgar Publishing, 2010. Retrieved from SSRN: https://ssrn.com/abstract=2203029

have an impact on such cultural factors. I have claimed that the major difference of both nations is in their political culture. Singapore's political authoritarianism has meant that citizens are less averse to risk-taking, creative expression and challenging the status-quo. Hong Kong has a tradition of liberalism, which has seen its civil society grow, and in recent years, acting as a bulwark against tyranny. These cultural differences have economic implications, as shown for instance by the stark gap in their creative industries. Domestic entrepreneurship, which in its essence entails some degree of 'breaking away', is also relatively tame in Singapore.

Survey and Sampling Methodology

In order to ascertain the values and attitudes of residents, an original online survey was conducted which garnered a total of 476 and 551 responses from Hong Kong and Singapore respectively. All 1027 respondents are unique individuals and who answered all questions on the survey, no incomplete surveys were accepted. Thus, every question displayed throughout the chapters of this book were answered by everyone.

The online survey ran for a period of 26 months and targeted anyone and everyone within the geographical territories of Hong Kong and Singapore. Anyone had an equally random chance of receiving the survey *as long as* they own a mobile device. Respondents were asked their age group and to identify whether they are from Hong Kong or Singapore, allowing easy differentiation as shown in the diagrams in this book.

Significantly, in all respondents received incentives, albeit non-monetary. The criticism may be: "why did you do so?" I respond by saying that not providing any incentives would have made it very difficult to garner responses, especially considering the media-rich environment which compete for the limited attention spans of individuals. Additionally, my online survey overcomes the common problem of paid surveys which typically attract professional survey takers. First, this is because no pre-packaged panel data was purchased. Every response garnered was unique to the questions asked. Second, the concern is mitigated because of Pollfish's unique albeit expensive delivery mechanism: "Random Device Engagement" (RDE). According to Pollfish, "by delivering your survey inside popular mobile apps, RDE utilises the same neutral environment as Random Digit Dialling (RDD), and an audience who are not taking premeditated surveys, by reaching them inside mobile apps they were using anyway".[3]

Traditionally, most paid survey platforms garner responses from survey respondents who purposely and deliberately register simply to earn rewards. Because these incentives are fixed and predictable, the surveys attract professional survey takers, since they "understand how, and are motivated to, bypass screening questions to ensure they can take as many surveys as possible".[4] Pollfish operates differently. While incentives are offered, they are non-monetary and are native to the app that users are already on. For example, those reading the news might earn premium articles, or those on restaurant apps may receive a free dish at their next visit. Such an arrangement lessens the likelihood of attracting professional survey takers.[5]

In sum, the value proposition of Pollfish is as follows. First, it randomly engages mobile app users (RDE) just like traditional pollsters typically call random phone numbers (RDD) and so retains the *randomness* desired in good surveys. Second, it is similarly *organic*: it reaches out to individuals in the digital environment they are already inhabiting, whether it's a Facebook App, News App or game app, rather than soliciting responses *in an artificial environment that the respondents would otherwise not be on* if not for the incentive offered. According to experts of organic sampling, this is important because traditional online surveys removes respondents "from their regular routine" and opens up "the opportunity for panel fatigue and conditioning responses to move through the process. This does not produce organic responses and the panellists are often incentivized with a gift card or a cash reward, further encouraging them to submit more surveys rather than quality ones".[6] Third, it is an improvement to

[3] Pollfish. (2019, September 16). *How the Pollfish Methodology Works*. Pollfish. https://resources.pollfish.com/pollfish-school/how-the-pollfish-methodology-works/

[4] Pollfish. (2019). *Target Audience*. Retrieved from https://www.pollfish.com/survey-target-audience/

[5] Rothschild, D., & Konitzer, T. (2018, August). *Random Device Engagement (RDE) with Organic Samples*. Pollfish. Retrieved from https://www.pollfish.com/lp/files/organic-sampling-survey-method.pdf

[6] Papadakis, J., Rothschild, D., & Konitzer, T. (2018, October 11). *The Methodology That is Overcoming Some of Market Research's Biggest Obstacles*. Greenbook. Retrieved from https://www.greenbook.org/mr/market-research-methodology/organic-sampling-methodology/

typical polling that uses RDD, such as that by Pew Research,[7] because it taps on a growing network of mobile users rather than be limited by the dwindling number of users on fixed telephone lines.

The chief limitation of the Pollfish methodology, however, remains that it is a form of non-probability sampling. Not everyone in the population (Hong Kong and Singapore population) has an equal chance of being represented, since only those on online mobile apps are targeted. This is however an unavoidable limitation if an online survey platform is to be used; other online survey platforms like SurveyMonkey and Qualtrics also suffer from a similar defect. To achieve a truly random sample would require logistical resources beyond the means of present author. That would require regular international travel into and out of both countries and physical movements from random household to random household, which is also impossible given the public health circumstances of 2020. Last and most importantly, Singapore and Hong Kong are highly global cities with two of the highest broadband penetration rates (ranked 29th and 20th, respectively), suggesting that a broad swath of their population is reachable online.[8]

Interviews and Focus Groups

Supplementing the use of the online survey, the study also conducted 79 direct interviews either physically, on email or via videoconference. Two in-person focus group sessions were also conducted in Singapore (12 people) and Hong Kong (9 people), respectively.

The interviews included a mix of individuals from different backgrounds, namely, business owners, managers, students, journalists, government officials, and even random citizens on the street. As much as possible, they were approached in a variety of ways: randomly on the street, through cold emails made to publicly available email addresses, and through personal contacts. Each interviewee was also asked to introduce the author to other willing participants.

[7] Pew Research. (2015, January 29). *Sampling*. Pew Research Center, United States. Retrieved from https://www.pewresearch.org/methods/u-s-survey-research/sampling/

[8] Soo, Z. (2018, August 13). *Singapore beats Hong Kong to retain No 1 spot globally for fixed broadband speed*. South China Morning Post. Retrieved from https://www.scmp.com/tech/article/2159403/singapore-retains-no-1-spot-globally-fixed-broadband-speeds-lags-mobile

This study acknowledges that a degree of selection bias is unavoidable. In order to mitigate this, the interview process was repeated over a course of two years so as to avoid over-featuring and relying on a certain group of subjects. Additionally, interview evidence is as far as possible triangulated by other publicly available secondary sources such as media articles and academic works. For instance, the interviews done with practitioners in the creative industries (Chap. 7) is cross-referred to academic works that have explored the state of the creative industries in both cities as well as the quantitative evidence comparing the size and health of those industries.

However, when it comes to government officials, attaining access is a problem. In this study, only officials that agreed to participate are included, and even so, not all were willing to be named. The elite interviews that were conducted are however heavily triangulated with other sources so as to minimise the possibility of bias. This is buttressed by numerous other independent sources either on popular media, academic works, and even government announcements identifying the same problem.

Special attention was also paid to the conduct of the two focus groups. First, the participants were identified with the help of influential gatekeepers in the business community, namely, those from the Singapore Business Federation, EPIC Entrepreneurs Network Singapore, Hong Kong Management Association, and Hong Kong Trade and Development Council, who helped to make introductions. This is to avoid relying on the personal preferences of the author, which might introduce selection bias.

Second, I acknowledge that focus groups are sometimes tainted by the biased leading questions asked by the moderator and also the possibility that vocal individuals dominate the discussion.[9] In order to avoid this, the author expended money to hire two independent moderators for each focus group. The participants were split into three groups to encourage individual participation, and each group was moderated separately. The responses were transcribed and recorded by the four moderators and sent to the author. By removing myself from the execution of the process, personal bias was limited, as far as possible.

[9] Kitzinger, J., & Barbour, R. (Eds.). (1999). *Developing focus group research: politics, theory and practice.* Sage.

Messiness and Data Collection Limitations

The process of data collection has faced challenges. First, it was difficult to garner survey responses from business leaders and professionals, which most probably stems from their tight schedules. Thus, the author directly approached individuals from this target audience to compensate for the shortfall and supplement the responses already received organically online. All 1–1 interviewees and focus group participants were also asked to fill in the survey, as well as additional contacts recommended by specific gatekeepers. On a related note, soliciting interviews from members of the government was also challenging. This was fortunately mitigated due to the author's personal contacts from both governments, and these contacts' willingness to recommend other individuals. Reputable gatekeepers included the Association of Small Medium Enterprises in Singapore and Hong Kong Management Association.

Naturally, the anti-government protests which began in March 2019 posed a problem for survey responses, raising the chance of the results being "distorted" by excessively anti-government sentiments. This possibility was minimised because the survey collection began in early 2018, months before protests broke out, and lasted till throughout 2020, which moderated the possibility of any spike in anti-government views. Additionally, numerous direct responses were also solicited in 2020, when the focus of attention veered away to the coronavirus.

On a larger level, survey responses and interviews were conducted throughout the entire period of the last three years, without being concentrated into one specific period. This long time window ensures that responses are not overly distorted by the events in any specific time period and which hopefully evens out any distortions that may have arisen.

This Book Is an Exercise in Triangulation

Data triangulation, which is the use of multiple methods of data collection and cross-referencing them, is understandably used and emphasised in this study.[10] This is especially important for mixed methods research designs where depth of understanding is aimed for, and also where qualitative data is used, which may otherwise suffer from subjectivity and personal bias.

[10] Triangulation, D. S. (2014, September). The use of triangulation in qualitative research. In *Oncology nursing forum* (Vol. 41, No. 5, p. 545).

In this study, the quantitative data and qualitative data are triangulated against each other. For example, Chap. 5 presented Hong Kong and Singapore's trade and immigration statistics, to highlight the impact of the arrival of the British and the resulting growth trajectory created. Complementing these statistics are qualitative data in the form of pictures, advertisements, and magazine clippings in Singapore which are meant to show that growth in Singapore had already started from a high base even before the developmental state was established. Chapter 7 does something similar, with statistics and qualitative evidence showing the superior performance of Hong Kong's creative industries.

Quantitative data is also triangulated against other quantitative data and qualitative data was also triangulated against other qualitative data. Innovation statistics are numerous as seen in Chap. 6, and various types of such statistics were analysed, including patent data and aggregate innovation indices. Productivity, innovation, and entrepreneurship statistics, which are all connected, are analysed together, and used to build the argument. Triangulating data within the qualitative realm is especially important since it is more prone to subjectivity and personal bias. Chapter 4 especially necessitated this since direct interviews by some individuals may paint a one-sided critical perspective against the government. Hence, such interviews are cross-referenced against public available information and other secondary sources.

All data collected, be it quantitative and qualitative, are also checked against an extensive amount of published government data, including websites, legislative records, budget reports, and archives. Documentary analysis provides an additional source of triangulation and is especially useful in social science research to ascertain the formal policies and arrangements in a society.[11] This study's documentary analysis includes but is not exclusive to the 739 annual reports in Singapore that were drawn from the archives and reviewed in order to generate a new dataset of government consumption that is more reliable.

In conclusion, it is acknowledged that the use of so many different modes of data collection in this study may cause the results to lack an empirical focus. A similar study that purely uses interviews or which purely uses historical documents may yield greater validity and accuracy in *one*

[11] Harrison, L., & Startin, N. (2013). *Political research: An introduction*. Routledge.

given area. However, in the spirit of "holistic analysis and thick description", an eclectic method is used here instead. By using a whole range of data, we can know more about less (the two cases). The strategy undertaken here is by no means perfect and may be further enhanced with research.

Appendix 1: Statistics on Export and Import Volume in Straits Settlements and Hong Kong from 1868 Onwards[12]

	Straits Settlements[13]		Hong Kong[14]	
	Exports	*Imports*	*Exports*	*Imports*
1868	7,450,225	7,949,080	5,706,374	6,101,209
1869	7,878,823	8,400,927	7,607,008	6,793,424

(*continued*)

[12] Data and calculations are taken from Latham's (1994) study of Hong Kong and Singapore as trade entrepots. All prices are converted to Sterling pounds and follows conversion method by statistician Findlay Shirras (1919). The raw figures are from the value of silver/ounce, which is then adjusted to the weight of the dollar; see Straits Settlements Bluebook 1876 Department of Statistics, 1876 (Department of Statistics, 1876).

[13] The trade statistics of Singapore are counted as part of the larger Straits Settlements, which also includes Penang and Malacca. Figures for Straits Settlements are from *Statistical abstract for British Colonies.*

[14] Trade statistics were never collected by the British officials in Hong Kong at all. These figures are reconstructions based on statistics from other major trade partners of Hong Kong with the assumption that the exports of Hong Kong's trade partners constitute her imports and vice versa. For instance, the import volume of Hong Kong in 1868 comprises the export volume from the United Kingdom, China, Straits Settlements, Australia, and French Indochina. Sources include databases compiled by Hsiao (1974, pp. 148–151, 190–191), Coquerel (1911), Ishibashi (1935), Department of Finance, Government of Japan (1902) and Department of Customs, Statistical Office, Government of Siam (1910–1912. Additional sources include the Annual Statements of the Trade of the United Kingdom, *British Parliamentary Papers*, Diplomatic and Consular reports on the Trade and Commerce of Bangkok, *Bulletin economique de l'Indochine*, 4(1902)–17(1915) and lastly, *Statistical Bulletin of the Philippine Islands*, Manila. For more details, see Latham (1994).

B. Cheang, *Economic Liberalism and the Developmental State*,
https://doi.org/10.1007/978-3-031-08100-2

(continued)

	Straits Settlements[13]		*Hong Kong*[14]	
	Exports	*Imports*	*Exports*	*Imports*
1870	9,165,767	10,498,110	8,293,844[15]	8,938,223
1871	9,706,145	10,473,522	9,273,004	10,041,311
1872	11,601,306	11,770,257	9,401,499	9,530,713
1873	11,407,432	12,232,960	10,704,651	8,374,605
1874	10,869,360	12,111,739	10,436,886	9,745,575
1875	11,146,103	11,178,486	11,286,443	10,550,562
1876	9,905,284	10,714,130	11,483,214	10,926,991
1877	11,395,052	12,249,118	15,096,134[16]	20,675,162[17]
1878	11,292,426	12,016,704	14,490,961	19,572,454
1879	12,645,484	13,274,608	15,942,542	19,405,446
1880	13,207,431	13,904,489	14,716,070	20,451,106
1881	13,046,502	15,829,074	15,301,343	19,371,368
1882	15,347,003	16,994,206	15,482,727	19,615,060
1883	17,592,067	19,153,425	14,803,905	20,122,303
1884	17,657,121	19,106,331	15,199,470	19,305,624
1885	16,625,897	18,134,306	16,235,353	20,158,269
1886	16,008,910	18,477,689	15,935,165	21,546,020
1887	17,716,626	21,051,410	22,064,747	22,588,915
1888	19,152,831	22,797,654	24,406,509	22,737,663
1889	19,073,904	22,582,816	23,024,502[18]	22,474,638[19]
1890	22,088,156	25,433,336	28,603,658	25,932,489
1891	20,521,476	22,165,802	25,730,450	24,276,373
1892	19,403,649	20,382,243	22,294,001	21,992,110
1893	18,674,447	20,660,038	23,345,650	22,577,120
1894	18,216,057	21,919,855	18,549,845	20,301,892
1895	18,709,403	21,439,678	20,026,361	22,108,236
1896	19,345,388	22,421,336	21,286,720	22,887,915
1897	19,088,407	21,944,483	19,810,633	22,045,618
1898	20,708,348	24,200,496	21,143,152	25,108,194
1899	23,748,095	28,207,017	24,816,662	27,819,572
1900	26,852,624	32,115,688	24,043,117	27,403,945
1901	26,231,840	30,544,991	24,870,706	29,292,098
1902	26,253,031	30,607,989	24,436,200	27,569,736
1903	29,100,619	34,951,557	26,643,715[20]	30,587,390[21]
1904	29,842,517	35,220,736	27,352,957	34,519,676

(*continued*)

[15] The import figures for Bangkok are included from 1870 onwards.
[16] The import figures for India are included from 1877 onwards.
[17] The export figures for India are included from 1877 onwards.
[18] The import figures for Japan are included from 1889 onwards.
[19] The export figures for Japan are included from 1889 onwards.
[20] The import figures for Philippines are included from 1903 onwards.
[21] The export figures for Philippines are included from 1903 onwards.

(continued)

	Straits Settlements[13]		*Hong Kong*[14]	
	Exports	*Imports*	*Exports*	*Imports*
1905	28,482,823	33,443,656	28,476,540	33,282,419
1906	36,284,011	39,585,967	31,638,392	33,781,433
1907	35,618,556	40,899,857	33,651,259	37,059,390
1908	31,945,448	36,912,860	26,626,541	30,092,053
1909	31,804,686	36,558,483	26,119,687	31,343,703
1910	37,822,142	42,521,576	30,656,863	35,704,525
1911	39,887,146	46,437,349	27,092,059	34,161,859
1912	43,765,022	52,504,552	29,485,652	36,127,422
1913	45,375,132	55,936,471	34,032,063	39,054,906
1914	38,981,369	45,660,198	29,174,926	28,783,613

Appendix 2: Measurement of Economic Freedom by Fraser Institute

Categories	*Details*	*Data sources used*
Size of government	General government consumption spending as a percentage of total consumption, transfer, and subsidies as a percentage of GDP, government enterprises and investment, and top marginal income tax rate, and income and payroll tax rates	World Development Indicators by World Bank, International Financial Statistics & Government Finance Statistics by International Monetary Fund, United Nations National Accounts, Worldwide Tax Summaries Online by PricewaterhouseCoopers
Legal structure and security of property rights	Judicial independence, impartial courts, protection of property rights, military interference in rule of law and political process, integrity of the legal system, legal enforcement of contracts, and regulatory restrictions on sale of real property	World Economic Forum, Global Competitiveness Report, World Bank's Governance Indicators, PRS Group, International Country Risk Guide, World Bank, Doing Business
Access to sound money	Money growth, standard deviation of inflation, inflation of most recent years, and freedom to own foreign currency bank accounts	World Bank, World Development Indicators; International Monetary Fund, International Financial Statistics; United Nations National Accounts International Monetary Fund, Annual Report on Exchange Arrangements and Exchange Restrictions

(*continued*)

B. Cheang, *Economic Liberalism and the Developmental State*,
https://doi.org/10.1007/978-3-031-08100-2

(continued)

Categories	*Details*	*Data sources used*
Freedom to trade internationally	Taxes on international trade that include revenue from taxes on international trade as a percentage of exports and imports, mean tariff rate and standard deviation of tariff rates, regulatory trade barriers that include non-tariff trade barriers and compliance cost of importing and exporting, size of trade sector, black market exchange rates, international capital market controls that include foreign ownership, or investment restrictions and capital control	International Monetary Fund, Government Finance Statistics Yearbook; International Monetary Fund, International Financial Statistics World Trade Organisation, World Tariff Profiles MRI Bankers' Guide to Foreign Currency International Monetary Fund, Annual Report on Exchange Arrangements and Exchange Restrictions
Regulation of credit, labour, and business	Credit market regulations that include ownership of banks, foreign bank competition, private sector credit and interest rate controls, labour market regulations that include minimum wage, hiring and firing regulations, centralized collective bargaining, mandated cost of hiring, mandated cost of worker dismissal and conscription, business regulations that include price controls, administrative requirements, bureaucracy costs, starting a business, extra payment and bribes, licencing restrictions, and cost of tax compliance	World Bank, Bank Regulation and Supervision Survey; James R. Barth, Gerard Caprio, and Ross Levine (2006). Rethinking Bank Regulation: Till Angels Govern. Cambridge University Press World Bank, World Development Indicators; World Economic Forum, Global Competitiveness Report; International Monetary Fund, International Financial Statistics World Bank, World Development Indicators; International Monetary Fund, International Financial Statistics; CIA, The World Factbook World Bank, Doing Business International Institute for Strategic Studies, The Military Balance; War Resisters International, World Survey of Conscription and Conscientious Objection to Military Service; additional online sources used as necessary

Source: Economic Freedom of the World Annual Reports, Fraser Institute, Vancouver

Appendix 3: Compilation of New Dataset for Revenue and Expenditures of Singapore Statutory Boards Since 1994

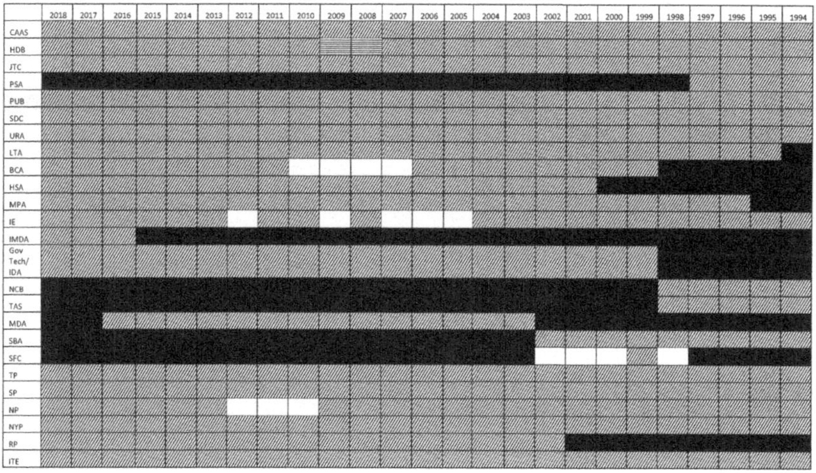

B. Cheang, *Economic Liberalism and the Developmental State*,
https://doi.org/10.1007/978-3-031-08100-2

Notes:

- 449 Annual Reports and Financial Statements of 25 Statutory Boards analysed over a 25-year period.
- Annual reports and Financial Statements were obtained from the National Archives of Singapore, or hard copies were requested from the National Library of Singapore or the National University of Singapore Central Library.
- For 2008 and 2009, due to the missing data for the capital expenditures for Housing Development Board, the true government expenditure will be even more understated, since capital expenditures are typically in the sum of SGD1billion/year/statutory board.

Legend:

Data Entered	
Data Not Found	
Data Incomplete (Capital Expenditure Missing)	
Statutory Board Does Not Exist for the Year	

Appendix 4: New Dataset on Singapore's Government Expenditure/Consumption (Including Statutory Boards Previously Omitted)

B. Cheang, *Economic Liberalism and the Developmental State*,
https://doi.org/10.1007/978-3-031-08100-2

	Govt. revenue (1)	Govt expenditure (2)	Statutory boards' revenue (3)	Statutory boards' expenditure (4)	Total govt revenue (5) = (1) + (3)	Total govt expenditure (6) = (2) + (4)	New rev as % of old rev	New exp. as % of old exp	Rev adjust ment in % (7)	Exp adjust ment in % (8)	Old rev as % of GDP	Old exp. as % of GDP	New rev as % of GDP	New exp. as % of GDP	Rev adjust ment as % of GDP (9)	Exp adjust ment as % of GDP (10)
1994	28,095	14,273	7785.853022	14023.51816	35880.85302	28296.51816	127.7	198.3	27.7	98.3	25.0	12.7	31.9	25.1	6.9	12.5
1995	29,248	12,289	6816.164372	15304.1478	36064.16437	27593.1478	123.3	224.5	23.3	124.5	23.5	9.9	29.0	22.2	5.5	12.3
1996	31,869	14,844	7993.035909	17435.1947	39862.03591	32279.1947	125.1	217.5	25.1	117.5	23.5	10.9	29.4	23.8	5.9	12.8
1997	37,936	21,948	8984.70583	19112.00272	46920.70583	41060.00272	123.7	187.1	23.7	87.1	25.5	14.8	31.6	27.6	6.0	12.9
1998	39,883	20,265	6653.217823	16610.31111	46536.21782	36875.31111	116.7	182.0	16.7	82.0	27.8	14.1	32.4	25.7	4.6	11.6
1999	38,612	22,557	7860.653471	14098.67371	46472.65347	36655.67371	120.4	162.5	20.4	62.5	26.4	15.4	31.8	25.1	5.4	9.6
2000	40,330	21,605	7716.063957	11561.48133	48046.06396	33166.48133	119.1	153.5	19.1	53.5	24.3	13.0	29.0	20.0	4.7	7.0
2001	42,537	26,032	7990.217002	11558.34901	50527.217	37590.34901	118.8	144.4	18.8	44.4	26.4	16.2	31.4	23.4	5.0	7.2
2002	39,173	29,232	7711.378597	8945.489061	46884.3786	38177.48906	119.7	130.6	19.7	30.6	23.6	17.6	28.3	23.0	4.7	5.4
2003	35,100	26,753	7577.303265	7546.706118	42677.30327	34299.70612	121.6	128.2	21.6	28.2	20.6	15.7	25.1	20.2	4.5	4.4
2004	33,046	27,112	8088.873316	8672.355597	41134.87332	35784.3556	124.5	132.0	24.5	32.0	17.0	13.9	21.2	18.4	4.2	4.5
2005	36,518	27,983	9293.437925	9918.927947	45811.43793	37901.92795	125.4	135.4	25.4	35.4	17.2	13.2	21.5	17.8	4.4	4.7
2006	38,663	26,790	10071.44147	9735.208995	48734.44147	36525.209	126.0	136.3	26.0	36.3	16.4	11.3	20.6	15.5	4.3	4.1
2007	42,266	30,835	10948.28101	11701.42893	53214.28101	42536.42893	125.9	137.9	25.9	37.9	15.5	11.3	19.5	15.6	4.0	4.3
2008	52,495	33,130	8064.328557	9319.025406	60559.32856	42449.02541	115.4	128.1	15.4	28.1	19.2	12.1	22.1	15.5	2.9	3.4
2009	55,925	39,735	7623.781883	8440.604894	63548.78188	48175.60489	113.6	121.2	13.6	21.2	19.8	14.1	22.5	17.1	2.7	3.0
2010	48,161	40393.678	9025.791363	14748.48683	57186.79136	55142.16483	118.7	136.5	18.7	36.5	14.7	12.4	17.5	16.9	2.8	4.5
2011	54864.2	40587.4	9225.504557	15371.28627	64089.70456	55958.68627	116.8	137.9	16.8	37.9	15.6	11.6	18.2	15.9	2.6	4.4
2012	59806.2	44,879	9144.870646	17875.75761	68951.07065	62754.75761	115.3	139.8	15.3	39.8	16.2	12.2	18.7	17.0	2.5	4.8
2013	64449.3	45668.4	8473.131965	20053.53422	72922.43197	65721.93422	113.1	143.9	13.1	43.9	16.7	11.9	18.9	17.1	2.2	5.2
2014	66350.3	47,629	8231.460597	19424.05185	74581.7606	67053.05185	112.4	140.8	12.4	40.8	16.6	11.9	18.7	16.8	2.1	4.9
2015	71,894	52465.9	9094.139602	19613.3984	80988.1396	72079.2984	112.6	137.4	12.6	37.4	17.0	12.4	19.1	17.0	2.1	4.6
2016	76207.7	67435.7	10573.39044	19557.64882	86781.09044	86993.34882	113.9	129.0	13.9	29.0	17.3	15.3	19.7	19.8	2.4	4.4
2017	81396.4932	63661.38804	10917.90217	19726.34774	92314.39536	83387.73578	113.4	131.0	13.4	31.0	17.2	13.5	19.6	17.7	2.3	4.2
2018	95696.1366	67,809	11656.06725	18672.79636	107352.2038	86481.79636	112.2	127.5	12.2	27.5	19.0	13.5	21.3	17.2	2.3	3.7
	SGD mn (nominal)						%									

Notes:

- Revenue and expenditures of statutory boards (3) and (4) are newly collated by the present author, allowing (5) and (6) to be tabulated.
- The significance of the previous omission of statutory boards is demonstrated in columns (7), (8), (9), and (10). For example, in 2018, the total government expenditure is 27.5% higher when statutory boards are included, and total government expenditure as a % of GDP is 3.7% higher when statutory boards are included.

Appendix 5: List of Tier 1 and Tier 2 Government-Linked Corporations, as of August 2020

Tier 1 government-linked corporation in Singapore	*Tier 2 government-linked corporation in Singapore under the management of tier 1 entity*
DBS Group Holdings Ltd	DBS Bank Ltd
Singapore Technologies Telemedia Pte Ltd	ST Telemedia Connect
	LEAP (G) Pte Ltd
	STT Communications Pte Ltd
	ST Telemedia Global Data Centres
	TeleChoice International Limited
	Starhub

(*continued*)

B. Cheang, *Economic Liberalism and the Developmental State*, https://doi.org/10.1007/978-3-031-08100-2

(continued)

Tier 1 government-linked corporation in Singapore	*Tier 2 government-linked corporation in Singapore under the management of tier 1 entity*
Singapore Telecommunications Limited	Amobee Asia Pte. Ltd.
	Computer Systems Holdings Pte Ltd
	CVSI Pte Ltd
	DataSpark Pte. Ltd.
	Group Enterprise Pte. Ltd.
	Hawk Digital Holding Co Pte. Ltd.
	Hawk Digital Pte. Ltd.
	HOOQ Digital Holdings Pte. Ltd.
	HOOQ Digital Pte. Ltd
	HOOQ Digital SG1 Pte. Ltd.
	HOOQ Digital SG2 Pte. Ltd.
	HOOQ Holdings Pte. Ltd.
	NCS Communications Engineering Pte. Ltd.
	NCS Pte. Ltd.
	NCSI Holdings Pte. Ltd.
	NCSI Solutions Pte. Ltd.
	SCS Computer Systems Pte. Ltd.
	Singapore Telecom Mobile Pte Ltd
	Singapore Telecom Paging Pte Ltd
	Singapore Telecom International Pte Ltd
	SingNet Pte Ltd
	Singtel Asia Pacific Investments Pte. Ltd.
	Singtel Asian Investments Pte Ltd
	Singtel Digital Life Pte. Ltd.
	Singtel Group Treasury Pte. Ltd.
	Singtel Idea Factory Pte. Ltd
	Singtel Singapore Pte Ltd
	Singtel Strategic Investments Pte Ltd
	Singtel Cyber Security (Singapore) Pte. Ltd.
	Singtel Innov8 Ventures Pte. Ltd.
	SingTel Investments Private Limited
	Singtel Mobile Singapore Pte. Ltd.
	Singtel International Investments Private Limited
	SingTel Ventures (Singapore) Private Limited
	Subsea Network Services Pte Ltd
	ST-2 Satellite Ventures Private Limited
	Sembawang Cable Depot Pte Ltd
	Singtel Digital Media Pte Ltd
	SingtelSat Pte Ltd
	Telecom Equipment Pte Ltd
	Trustwave Pte. Ltd.
	2359 Media Pte. Ltd.

(*continued*)

(continued)

Tier 1 government-linked corporation in Singapore	*Tier 2 government-linked corporation in Singapore under the management of tier 1 entity*
	HOPE Technik Pte Ltd
	Kai Square
	NetLink Trust
	NetLink NBN Trust
	OpenNet Pte. Ltd
	Singapore Post Limited
	SESTO Robotics Pte Ltd
	Viewers Choice Pte Ltd
	ACPL Marine Pte Ltd
	Abacus Travel Systems Pte Ltd
	ASEAN Cableship Pte Ltd
	Bridge Mobile Pte. Ltd
	Grid Communications Pte. Ltd
	Indian Ocean Cableship Pte. Ltd.
	International Cableship Pte Ltd
	Radiance Communications Pte Ltd
	Telescience Singapore Pte Ltd
	Integrated Payment Ventures Pte Ltd
	TeleTech Park Pte Ltd
	SSBI Pte Ltd
CapitaLand Limited	Areca Investment Pte Ltd
	CapitaLand VN Limited
	CapitaLand China Investments Limited
	CapitaLand GCC Holdings Pte Ltd
	CapitaLand ILEC Pte Ltd
	CapitaLand Singapore (R&R) Limited
	CapitaLand Treasury Limited
	CapitaLand Mall Asia Limited
	CapitaLand Business Services Pte Ltd
	Pidemco Land Singapore Pte Ltd
	Somerset Capital Pte Ltd
	Somerset Land Pte Ltd
	The Ascott Limited
	CapitaLand Financial Limited
	CapitaLand International Pte Ltd
	Ascendas Pte Ltd
Olam International Limited	Caraway Pte Ltd
	Olam Cocoa Pte Limited
	Olam Treasury Pte Limited
	Far East Agri Pte Ltd
	Invenio Holdings Pte. Ltd.
	Olea Investment Holdings Pte. Ltd.
	Carmel Investment Holdings Pte Ltd

(continued)

(continued)

Tier 1 government-linked corporation in Singapore	*Tier 2 government-linked corporation in Singapore under the management of tier 1 entity*
Ascendas-Singbridge Pte Ltd	Bougainvillea Realty Pte Ltd
Mapletree Investments Pte Ltd	Heliconia Realty Pte Ltd
	Lock + Store Self Storage Pte Ltd
	Mapletree Dextra Pte. Ltd
	Mapletree Capital Management Pte Ltd
	Mapletree Logistics Properties Pte Ltd
	Mapletree Trustee Pte. Ltd.
	Meranti Investments Pte Ltd
	Mapletree Treasury Services Limited
	Mapletree Property Management Pte. Ltd.
	Mulberry Pte Ltd
	Mangrove Pte Ltd
	Gemstone Asset Holdings Pte Ltd
	Mapletree DC Ventures Pte Ltd
	CoQoons Coworking Pte Ltd
	Mapletree US Office Assets Pte Ltd
	Amberstone Asset Holdings Pte Ltd
	Mapletree US Logistic Assets Pte Ltd
	Sienna Pte Ltd
	Mapletree Developments Pte Ltd
	Mapletree Waterfront Holdings Pte Ltd
	The HarbourFront Pte Ltd
	Mapletree Real Estate Mezzanine Fund I Limited
	Mapletree Management Consultancy Pte Ltd
	Mapletree Property Services Pte Ltd
	Kent Assets Pte Ltd
	Suffolk Assets Pte Ltd
	Mapletree PE Pte Ltd
	Mapletree Oakwood Holdings Pte Ltd
	Moonstone Assets Pte Ltd
	Mapletree Trustee Pte Ltd

(*continued*)

(continued)

Tier 1 government-linked corporation in Singapore	*Tier 2 government-linked corporation in Singapore under the management of tier 1 entity*
Keppel Corporation Limited	Keppel Offshore and Marine Ltd
	Keppel Land Ltd
	Keppel Infrastructure Holdings Pte Ltd
	Keppel Tianjin Eco-City Investments Pte Ltd
	Keppel Telecommunications & Transportations Ltd
	Keppel Capital Holdings Pte Ltd
	Kephinance Investment Pte Ltd
	Kepmount Shipping (Pte) Ltd
	Keppel Oil & Gas Services Pte Ltd
	Kepinvest Holdings Pte Ltd
	Keppel Group Eco-City Investments Pte Ltd
	Keppel Hi-Tech InnovationPark Holdings Pte Ltd
	Keppel Konnect Pte Ltd
	Keppel Point Pte Ltd
	Keppel GMTN Pte Ltd
	Kepventure Pte Ltd
	Travelmore Pte Ltd
	KV Management Pte Ltd
	Keppel Bay Pte Ltd
	Atlantic Marina Services (Asia Pacific) Pte Ltd
	FELS Property Holdings Pte Ltd
	FELS SES International Pte Ltd
	Esqin Pte Ltd
	Keppel Real Estate Investment Pte Ltd
	Keppel Energy Pte Ltd
	Keppel Integrated Engineering Ltd
	k1 eBiz Holdings Pte Ltd
PSA International Pte Ltd	PSA Corporation Limited
	PSA Marine (Pte) Ltd

(*continued*)

(continued)

Tier 1 government-linked corporation in Singapore	*Tier 2 government-linked corporation in Singapore under the management of tier 1 entity*
Sembcorp Industries Ltd	Sembcorp Utilities Pte Ltd
	Sembcorp Cogen Pte Ltd
	Sembcorp Gas Pte Ltd
	Sembcorp Air Products (Hyco) Pte Ltd
	Sembcorp Environment Pte. Ltd
	SembWaste Pte Ltd
	Sembcorp Marine Ltd
	Jurong Shipyard Pte Ltd
	PPL Shipyard Pte Ltd
	Sembcorp Marine Repairs & Upgrades Pte. Ltd.
	Sembcorp Marine Offshore Platforms Pte Ltd
	Sembcorp Development Ltd
	Vietnam Singapore Industrial Park Pte Ltd
	Singapore Technologies Industrial Corp Ltd
	Sembcorp Design and Construction Pte Ltd
	Singapore Precision Industries Pte Ltd
	SembSITA Pacific Pte Ltd
	Gallant Venture Ltd
Singapore Technologies Engineering Ltd	ST Engineering Aerospace Ltd
	ST Engineering Electronics Ltd
	ST Engineering Land Systems Ltd
	ST Engineering Marine Ltd
	ST Engineering Treasury Pte. Ltd.
	ST Engineering Financial II Pte. Ltd.
	ST Engineering Financial I Ltd.
	ST Engineering Management Services Pte. Ltd.
	FusionTech Pte. Ltd.
	ST Synthesis Pte Ltd
	Singapore Technologies Dynamics Pte Ltd
Singapore Power Limited	SP PowerAssets Limited
	PowerGas Limited
	SP PowerGrid Limited
	SP Services Limited
	SP Cross Island Tunnel Trust
	Singapore Power International Pte Ltd
	Singapore District Cooling Pte Ltd
Mandai Park Holdings Pte Ltd	Mandai Park Development
	Corporate Services, Mandai Park Holdings
Wildlife Reserves Singapore	Singapore Zoo
	Night Safari
	Jurong Bird Park
	RIver Safari

(*continued*)

(continued)

Tier 1 government-linked corporation in Singapore	*Tier 2 government-linked corporation in Singapore under the management of tier 1 entity*
SMRT Corporation Ltd	SMRT Trains
	SMRT Road Holdings
	SMRT Institute Pte Ltd
	SMRT Capital Pte Ltd
	SMRT Commercial
	SMRT Far East Pte Ltd
	Singapore Rail Engineering
	SMRT International
	SMRT Services
	Bus Plus Services Pte Ltd
	RFP Investments Pte Ltd
	Transit Link Pte Ltd
Mediacorp Pte Ltd	Singapore Media Academy
	1-Net Singapore Pte Ltd.
	TV12
	Mediacorp Press Limited
	Mediacorp TV Holdings Pte. Ltd
	Mediacorp TV Singapore Pte. Ltd
	Mediacorp News Pte Ltd
	Raintree Pictures
Surbana Jurong Private Limited	KTP Consultants Pte Ltd
	SAA Architects Pte Ltd
	Aetos Security Management
M+S Pte Ltd	Ophir-Rochor Residential Pte. Ltd.
	Ophir-Rochor Hotel Pte Ltd
STATS ChipPAC Ltd	NA
Neptune Orient Lines Limited	American President Lines
Chartered Semiconductor Manufacturing Ltd	Chartered Silicon Partners Pte Ltd
	Chartered Semiconductor Manufacturing (Tampines) Pte. Ltd.
Fraser and Neave, Limited	Fraser & Neave (Singapore) Pte. Limited
	F&N Investments Pte Ltd
	F&N Foods Pte Ltd
	Asia Dairies (S) Pte Ltd
	F&N Dairy Investments Pte Ltd
	F&N Interflavine Pte Ltd
	Times Publishing Limited
	F&N Treasury Pte Ltd
	InterF&B Pte. Ltd.
Power Seraya	Seraya Energy
	PetroSeraya
	Seraya Energy and Investment Pte. Ltd.

(continued)

(continued)

Tier 1 government-linked corporation in Singapore	*Tier 2 government-linked corporation in Singapore under the management of tier 1 entity*
Senoko Power	Senoko Energy Supply Pte Ltd (SES)
	Senoko Services Pte Ltd (SSPL)
	Senoko Power Limited
	Senoko Gas Supply Pte Ltd (SGS)
Tuas Power	Tuas Power Supply Pte Ltd
	TP Utilities Pte Ltd
	NewEarth Pte Ltd
	Tuas Power Generation Pte Ltd
	TP Utilities Pte Ltd
	Tuas Power Asset Management Pte Ltd
	TPGS Green Energy Pte Ltd
Singapore Airlines Limited	SilkAir
	Scoot
	SIA Engineering Company
	Singapore Airlines Cargo
	Singapore Flying College
SATS Ltd	SATS Airport Services Pte Ltd
	SATS Catering Pte Ltd
	SATS Security Services Pte Ltd
	SATS Aero Laundry Pte Ltd
	SATS Aerolog Express Pte Ltd
	Country Foods Pte Ltd
	SATS Asia-Pacific Star Pte Ltd
	SATS Investments Pte Ltd
	SATS Investments (II) Pte Ltd
	Cemerlang Pte Ltd
	Ready to Travel Pte Ltd
	SATS Ground Services Singapore Pte Ltd
SATS Food Services Pte Ltd	NA

Notes:

- The list of Tier 1 GLCs are derived from respective annual reports of Temasek Holdings, and the list of Tier 2 GLCS are derived from the respective annual reports, websites, and public statements of each of the individual Tier 1 GLCs.
- Tier 1 GLCs are those which are directly owned and managed by Temasek Holdings.
- Tier 2 GLCs are those which are directly owned and managed by Tier 1 GLCs, and so on for those in lower tiers.
- GLREITs are usually owned and managed by Tier 3 GLCs, and thus indirectly owned and managed by Temasek Holdings.
- A total of 290 Annual Reports and Public Statements of Tier 1 and Tier 2 GLCs were analysed, not including GLREITs mentioned in Appendix 6.

Appendix 6: List of Government-Linked Real Estate Investment Trusts (GLREITs), as of 2019

Name of GLREITs	*Stock market value*	*% of total Singapore stock market capitalisation*
ASCENDAS REAL ESTATE INV TRT	10729700352.00	
CAPITALAND MALL TRUST	9074457600.00	
MAPLETREE COMMERCIAL TRUST	7902502912.00	
CAPITALAND COMMERCIAL TRUST	7676794880.00	
MAPLETREE LOGISTICS TRUST	6606842368.00	
MAPLETREE INDUSTRIAL TRUST	5721946624.00	
KEPPEL REIT	4174832128.00	62.33%
MAPLETREE NORTH ASIA COMMERC	3705437952.00	
KEPPEL DC REIT	3395382272.00	
ASCOTT RESIDENCE TRUST	2897819136.00	
CAPITALAND RETAIL CHINA TRUS	1946598144.00	
ASCENDAS HOSPITALITY TRUST	1275240064.00	
KEPPEL PACIFIC OAK US REIT	728636224.00	

Source: Bloomberg Stock Market Capitalisation Data

B. Cheang, *Economic Liberalism and the Developmental State*,
https://doi.org/10.1007/978-3-031-08100-2

Index[1]

[1] Note: Page numbers followed by 'n' refer to notes.

B. Cheang, *Economic Liberalism and the Developmental State*, https://doi.org/10.1007/978-3-031-08100-2

The manufacturer's authorised representative in the EU is Springer
Nature Customer Service Centre GmbH, Europaplatz 3, 69115 Heidelberg,
Germany. If you have any concerns regarding our products, please
contact ProductSafety@springernature.com

Printed and bound by CPI Group (UK) Ltd, Croydon, CR0 4YY
30/09/2026
02225490-0013